CW00820115

Intellectual Origins of the Republic

Studies in the History of Political Thought

Edited by

Terence Ball (*Arizona State University*)
Jörn Leonhard (*Albert-Ludwigs-Universität Freiburg*)
Wyger Velema (*University of Amsterdam*)

Advisory Board

Janet Coleman (*London School of Economics and Political Science, UK*)
Vittor Ivo Comparato (*University of Perugia, Italy*)
Jacques Guilhaumou (*CNRS, France*)
John Marshall (*Johns Hopkins University, Baltimore, USA*)
Markku Peltonen (*University of Helsinki, Finland*)

VOLUME 10

The titles published in this series are listed at *brill.com/ship*

Ahmet Ağaoğlu's Portrait (photographer and date unknown).

Intellectual Origins
of the Republic

*Ahmet Ağaoğlu and the Genealogy of
Liberalism in Turkey*

By

H. Ozan Özavcı

BRILL

LEIDEN | BOSTON

Cover illustration: *Puteshestviye idey* / *The Journey of Ideas* (2015), by Tatiana N. Kondruchina; created specially for the cover of this book.

Library of Congress Cataloging-in-Publication Data

Özavci, Hilmi Ozan.
  Intellectual origins of the republic : Ahmet Ağaoğlu and the genealogy of liberalism in Turkey / by Hilmi Ozan Özavci.
      pages cm. -- (Studies in the history of political thought ; v. 10)
  Includes bibliographical references and index.
  ISBN 978-90-04-29737-1 (hardback : alk. paper) -- ISBN 978-90-04-29736-4 (e-book : alk. paper) 1. Agaoglu, Ahmet, 1869-1939. 2. Liberalism--Turkey. 3. Turkey--Politics and government. 4. Intellectuals--Turkey--Biography. I. Title.

  DR592.A47O93 2015
  320.5109561--dc23

                            2015021127

This publication has been typeset in the multilingual "Brill" typeface. With over 5,100 characters covering Latin, IPA, Greek, and Cyrillic, this typeface is especially suitable for use in the humanities.
For more information, please see www.brill.com/brill-typeface.

ISSN 1873-6548
ISBN 978-90-04-29737-1 (hardback)
ISBN 978-90-04-29736-4 (e-book)

Copyright 2015 by Koninklijke Brill NV, Leiden, The Netherlands.
Koninklijke Brill NV incorporates the imprints Brill, Brill Hes & De Graaf, Brill Nijhoff, Brill Rodopi and Hotei Publishing.
All rights reserved. No part of this publication may be reproduced, translated, stored in a retrieval system, or transmitted in any form or by any means, electronic, mechanical, photocopying, recording or otherwise, without prior written permission from the publisher.
Authorization to photocopy items for internal or personal use is granted by Koninklijke Brill NV provided that the appropriate fees are paid directly to The Copyright Clearance Center, 222 Rosewood Drive, Suite 910, Danvers, MA 01923, USA.
Fees are subject to change.

This book is printed on acid-free paper.

Contents

Preface

This book is the result of several years of research and writing. As the Republic of Turkey is nearing its centenary and, as things stand today, the country is still suffering from a version of authoritarianism under the Justice and Development Party, the very roots of authoritarian governance and the idea of liberty in Turkey, I believe, need to be revisited. My study is one of these attempts. It aims to trace the intellectual origins of Republican Turkey and its founding mentality with a focus on the ideas, life and times of on one of the most prominent writers of his time, Ahmet Ağaoğlu. I seek to show here the features, merits and limits of his ideas, and their making, as an important representative of late Ottoman and early republican political, social and economic thought.

If the book will be of any use for the readers of intellectual and political history, this is thanks to the support of many. I was fortunate that Dr Feroze Yasamee, Professor Stefan Berger, Dr David Laven, Professor François Georgeon, Professor Alex Samely and the anonymous referees of Brill have read earlier drafts of the book and made extremely helpful comments to improve its quality. I have also found the opportunity to receive generous support from the British Institute at Ankara (BIAA), which provided me with funding for research. One of the greatest pleasures of my work was to visit libraries and archives in Europe and the Near East. Of all I would especially like to thank Dr Lala Hajiyeva, the Director of AR Prezidentinin İşlər İdarəsinin Siyasi Sənədlər Arxivi in Baku for providing me with materials on the work of Ağaoğlu in the Caucasus. Kadın Eserleri Kütüphanesi in Istanbul allowed me to see Süreyya Ağaoğlu papers while they were still being catalogued. Now there is a rich amount of material about the Ağaoğlu family in this library, waiting to be examined by researchers. The staff at Rossijskaja Nacional'naja Biblioteka in St Petersburg were most helpful in locating primary and secondary materials. Rahmi Koç Müzesi in Istanbul was generous in sharing photos of Ağaoğlu's house in Istanbul for the use of this book.

Mrs Nilufer Gürsoy, the daughter of Celal Bayar, and Mr Tektaş Ağaoğlu, grandson of Ahmet Ağaoğlu, were very kind to accept my visits and share their stories about early republican life. I received enormous support from my colleagues at Manchester, Southampton, Izmir and Utrecht during the preparation of this book; namely, Mrs Mutlu Bosson, Osen Kılıç-Yıldırım, Professor Stuart Jones, Dr Jonathan Conlin, Dr Tuba İnal and Professor Beatrice de Graaf. I must also thank my three teachers back in Istanbul, Dr Şahin Alpay and Professors İlkay Sunar and Ahmet Sözen for being an inspiration to me in my scholarly work and for drawing my attention to the history of liberalism.

And many thanks to Mr Enver Yucel for his financial and moral support to my academic work and for his trust in me.

Since there is more to life than work, I must thank my friends for being with me at different stages of the preparation of this book, for accepting me at their houses in my research trips or discussing the content of my work. Special thanks to Tatiana Kondruchina for the illustration on the cover page, 'the Journey of Ideas', and for her great support during the preparation of the book. Esther Meininghaus, Ferhat Koksal, Hercai Yüksel, Yasemin Akyol, Alp Okan Kaya, Juliette Laquila, Benjamin Paynter, Drs Ben and Sevinç Garner, thank you. And Julia Kozak, for bearing with me and encouraging me enormously, when I was making the final touches on the manuscript in the little time we had together in London.

Last but by no means the least, my family, to whom my biggest thanks go: My parents, Nilgün and Nuri Özavcı, have given me their unequivocal support throughout, as always, for which my mere expression of thanks does not suffice. My super cute niece, Şiir, has been my source of happiness and motivation; my elder brother, Şadi, has wholeheartedly supported and encouraged my scholarly studies; and my sister, Işıl, who taught me to read and write well before I should have learned, has become a great supporter and a best friend to me; this book I dedicate to them.

Needless to say, if there is any mistake or flaw in this book, grammatical, stylistic or other, the responsibility is solely mine.

H. Ozan Özavcı

Paris, 2015

CHAPTER 1

Introduction

This book is about one of those 'other liberalisms', that which was formed in the mind of Ahmet Ağaoğlu (1868–1939). Perhaps little known to the English-speaking world, Ağaoğlu was one of the most prominent writers of his time in the Russian Caucasus, the late Ottoman Empire and in the Azerbaijani and Turkish republics. He was a man who situated at the forefront as a political figure only in 1905 and 1930; first, in the immediate aftermath of the Russian Revolution as an advocate of the rights of Russian Muslims, and then as a founding member of the Free Party (FP) which was established as a loyal opposition to Mustafa Kemal Atatürk's Republican People's Party (RPP). Yet his writings exerted great influences during the Russian Muslim struggle for communal rights and on the development of Turkish nationalism (c. 1892–1919) and on the formulation of a liberal thought which flirted with Kemalism (c. 1921–1939).

Together with Ziya Gökalp (1876–1924) and Yusuf Akçura (1876–1935), two pioneers of Turkish nationalism, Ağaoğlu sat at the committees that penned the first party program of the RPP and that drafted the first constitution of the Turkish Republic. As a professor of law in the late Ottoman Empire and early Republican Turkey, he taught generations of young students who filled the posts of bureaucracy in twentieth century Turkey. As a columnist who wrote prolifically in popular journals and newspapers, he disseminated ideas beyond the doors of classrooms he taught and was involved in public discussions.

It would not be false to say that Ağaoğlu stood between 'classic' Western and Eastern intellectuals, on the one hand, and the masses, on the other. He was a 'secondary' or 'reproductive' intellectual, acting as a channel of institutionalisation and contributing to the creation of new types of symbols of "cultural orientation, of traditions, and of collective and cultural identity."[1] He not only introduced new ideas into his political and social environments by either popularising them or working to get them embodied by political, administrative and bureaucratic decision-makers. He also contributed to the formation of new institutions and creation of new symbols of Turkish identity, and a tradition of liberal mentality in the Caucasus and in modern Turkey.

The liberal mentality in question carried various elements of Enlightenment thought and nineteenth-century liberalism: opposition to absolute power,

---

1 Kosaku Yoshino, *Cultural Nationalism in Contemporary Japan: A Social Enquiry*, London, N.Y.: Routledge, 1992, p. 167.

© KONINKLIJKE BRILL NV, LEIDEN, 2015 | DOI 10.1163/9789004297364_002

constitutional government, freedom of thought, liberty of the press and equality of opportunity. Yet Ağaoğlu was in many ways a modern liberal, perhaps the first in Turkey, with his emphasis on mutual interdependence and his praises of the New Deal policies in the United States and the Turkish liberal étatism, as he calls it. He sought to reconcile government intervention in the economy and the liberal ideal of individual rights and self-determination. In his interpretation, the duties and rights of the individual (labour), the capital and the state were complementary.

To these beliefs Ağaoğlu arrived after a long intellectual evolution. He went through a conscience crisis in his early teens soon after he received an intense religious education. In his entire work, he argued that the fundamental problem of Eastern societies in general, and of the Turkish society, in particular, was the triumph of egoism in individual and societal morality. People in the East, he maintained, were ready to easily sacrifice their societies' long-term interests for their immediate private interests, whereas in the West the complete opposite was the case. This was the main cause of many political, economic and social ills of Eastern societies, and yet the main reason for Western superiority. He did not, however, make an essentialist distinction between what he called Eastern and Western civilisations. He sought to explain through historical explanation the differences between the two worlds, one which he was originally from and where he pursued most of his political and intellectual career, and the other where he received his high school and higher education. His account of the history of freedom in the West is important not only because it allows us to see how he conceived of the Western civilisation in the fin de siècle. It also enables us to see the intellectual origins of the Turkish idea of Westernisation, and the genealogy of liberalism and nationalism in Turkey. His evolving idea of how the individual in the East could be freed from his or her shackles, on the other hand, provides us with a unique account of non-Western (other) liberalisms, which does not sit perfectly well with the mainstream understanding of liberal thought.

In using the phrase 'other liberalisms', I depart from the idea that, since the linguistic turn in the 1970s, it has become customary to highlight the fact that liberalism has many competing definitions on which there is little agreement. Rather than one, it has been argued, there are different liberalisms influenced by historical circumstances and national trajectories.[2] Even in the narrower ideological sense, each of these has carried different 'symbolic meanings'[3] in different periods, countries and languages, and at times among different groups

---

2   Lucien Jaume, *L'individu effacé ou le paradoxe du libéralisme français*, Paris: Fayard, 1997, p. 19.

3   Arthur Sanders, "The Meaning of Liberalism and Conservatism," *Polity*, Vol. 19, No. 1 (Aug., 1986), p. 124.

speaking the same language.[4] And if we want to place liberalism as a political, economic or moral philosophy into a broader framework, as Mills wrote, we find ourselves obliged to take into account also its differing value commitments, social onthology (e.g. atomic individualism), and in certain cases, its various theories of history.[5] Proceeding in this direction, we can find "as many distinct kinds of liberalism as there are original writers, if not distinct periods in their writings," and see that their core values are not always compatible.[6]

This argument does not, however, refute the view that there actually exists a broader political and intellectual tradition of liberalism which has encompassed irreconcilable principles or even opposed sub-traditions.[7] As Manning puts it,

> a tradition of ideological writing does not possess, and is not in need of, the kind of coherence which an academic explanation requires. It may readily embrace incompatible principles and programmes... It is an ongoing evaluation of changing circumstances.[8]

Acknowledging the internal diversity of liberalism helps intellectual historians to defy the orthodox liberal discourse that is often found in standard textbooks and which locates the origins of liberalism in seventeenth-century theories of the state of nature and the social contract. This discourse depicts the direct succession of ideas from Thomas Hobbes and John Locke to their successors Adam Smith, the utilitarians and J.S. Mill, and explains the rise of 'Anglo-American liberalism'. The main principles of liberalism are identified as the central values of the liberalism of the English-speaking world, such as individualism, rationalism and utilitarianism, whose main actors are "autonomous rational individuals seeking to maximise the satisfaction of their personal wants."[9] According to this account, those who have not readily embraced the central values of this particular strand are generally marginalised and regarded as 'strange' or unconventional members of the tradition.[10]

---

4   Massimo Salvadori, *The Liberal Heresy: Origins and Historical Development*, New York: St. Martin's Press, 1977, p. 17.

5   Charles W. Mills, "Race and the Social Contract Tradition," in *Ethics: The Big Questions*, ed. James P. Sterba, London: Wiley-Blackwell, 2009, p. 324.

6   D.J. Manning, *Liberalism*, N.Y.: St. Martin's Press, 1976, p. 140.

7   John Gray, *Liberalism*, Buckingham: Open University Press, 1995, p. 22.

8   Manning, *Liberalism*, p. 140.

9   Aurelian Craiutu, *Liberalism under Siege: The Political Thought of the French Doctrinaires*, Oxford: Lexington Books, 2003, p. 287.

10   Ibid., p. 288.

Craiutu rightly argues that this interpretation deserves to be revised, because of its unidimensional and misleading account of the nature and evolution of liberalism, and that it should be replaced by an interpretation heightening the awareness of liberalism as a multivocal system of ideas, discourses, practices and institutions in which it is difficult to discern a hegemonic voice. There is need for "extensive historical comparative investigations of the various types of liberal ideas and practices that would also shed light on unorthodox forms of liberalism, such as that of [the French] Doctrinaires."[11] He brings this up when discussing the existence of various different grand liberal traditions on both sides of the Channel and the Atlantic. The liberalisms in the French, German and Italian contexts afford many dramatic contrasts to the Anglo-American tradition, which has had its own peculiar variances.[12] Therefore, it has been the task of intellectual historians, historians of ideas and political theorists to define and examine the prominent features of these different accounts of liberalism and the differences and interplays between them, in their attempts to outline the characteristics of 'Western liberalism' through either a historical or a purely conceptual type of analysis.

However, in the study of the history of liberalism, less attention has been paid to its genealogy in European periphery or non-Western contexts or the export of liberal ideas into these societies. Few studies tracing the history of liberalism or trying to discern its 'guiding spirit' have taken into account that its reception outside or at the periphery of the West, in the form of the denial or acceptance of its core values and institutions, is an important aspect of the liberal tradition. Such a lacuna in existing literature is in large measure a consequence of the fact that liberalism has long been regarded as the fruit of 'capitalist development, commercial spirit and a strong third estate' and the belief that no liberalism was possible unless all of these three 'outer conditions' were present.[13] However, even in those countries where liberal political and economic institutions did not exist or function as successfully, or otherwise put, where the requirements of capitalist free enterprise at an institutional level were hardly met, there has been a history of liberalism as observed in the political, economic and intellectual struggles of certain groups or individuals, and in their 'inner convictions'.[14] Having encountered and embraced the values of one

11   Craiutu, *Liberalism under Siege*, p. 289.
12   Richard Bellamy, *Liberalism and Modern Society: A historical argument*, Oxford: Polity Press, 1992.
13   Maciej Janowski, *Polish Liberal Thought before 1918*, Budapest: Central European Press, 2004, p. vii.
14   Salvadori, *The Liberal Heresy*, p. 10.

or perhaps more than one account of liberalism, these groups or individuals have served as transmitters of liberal ideas and projected them onto the particular social, political and economic conditions of their regions. Through the works of these groups, the journey of liberal ideas as a set, in Krzywicki's words, of 'migrant ideas' from a certain region (where they were born) into regions with different social structures and traditions has resulted in liberalism's taking new forms and thus adding new features to the intellectual tradition. These migrant liberal ideas gradually transform the local conditions in their new settings, 'at the same time being subject to transformation themselves.'[15]

A strand of liberalism transformed Turkey at the end of World War I and it was subject to transformation itself in early Republican Turkish context. It was one of the major channels of ideas that bred the generation of republican mentality, which has long reigned in Turkish political culture. A British observer wrote in 1924 that "the ideas of the advanced members of [the Turkish intelligentsia] have crystallised about such expressions as 'national sovereignty', 'republic', 'liberal' and a notable addition to the vocabulary of the Turkish revolution—'laic'."[16] He was not mistaken. The new intelligentsia of the young republic, aspiring to be doctrinaires of some kind for the reconstitution of Turkish society, indeed dwelled much on these concepts and wrote prolifically about them. Among this intelligentsia Ağaoğlu occupied a significant place.

As a matter of fact, he was once described by Recep Peker, the Minister of Public Works at the time, as the most arduous and liberal of liberals (*liberalin liberali*) within the entourage of Kemal Atatürk.[17] As I shall discuss in this book, the Kemalist intelligentsia and political elites who controlled political power indeed regarded themselves as liberals in the first years of the republic. Ağaoğlu's position as a 'doubly liberal' writer within this group, his critiques to the regime and his ideas of new Turkey display the limits of the prevailing political thought at the time. This prevailing thought sought to marry a version of liberalism with republicanism, to exclude non-Muslims and non-Turks (or those who did not consciously call themselves Turk) from the political mechanism and it was rooted, at one and the same time, on the rule of people, on national sovereignty and on a distrust for the uneducated masses.

What I would like to do in this book is to place under scrutiny, through the prism of the life and ideas of Ağaoğlu, the merits and limits of liberalism in early republican Turkey in reference to a set of questions. Born in the Caucasus

---

15   Janowski, *Polish Liberal Thought*, p. vii.
16   Letter from Neville Henderson to the Marquess Curzon of Kedleston, January 9, 1924, TNA FO 424/260/7.
17   Ağaoğlu, *Serbest Fırka Hatıraları*, p. 16.

to a rather traditional family, Ağaoğlu was educated in Russian schools and later in Paris, embracing republican, nationalist and what he regarded as liberal ideas in his youth. What were the ideas which he was introduced to at the time? To what extend did they contribute to, and influence, his evolving system of thought? He subsequently became a famous political Pan-Islamist/nationalist agitator in the Russian and Ottoman empires. How were his Pan-Islamism and nationalism linked to his later liberal and republican views? Were there continuities between them? And he finally became one of the most respected intellectuals in early Republican Turkey.[18] How did he perceive the Kemalist Revolution and its cultural reforms? How did he view the increasing authoritarianism of the RPP? Why was it only in this period that he emerged as a self-defined liberal writer but not before?

With the emerging scholarly interest in liberalism in Turkey since the late 1980s, Ağaoğlu's liberal thought, which had remained terra incognita until then, has become the subject of a number of studies.[19] The budding literature on Ağaoğlu's liberalism has approached his work as if he had cut all his intellectual ties with his earlier nationalist and Pan-Islamist ideas, but with no indication of when or how such a break occurred. Focusing overwhelmingly on his 1930s writings, a large part of this literature has paid scant attention to his intellectual evolution, hardly considered what happened to his nationalism in this decade and devoted little space to analyse the moral thought he propounded from a liberal viewpoint. Instead, Ağaoğlu's liberal work has often been examined as a critique of the Kemalist rule.

My argument is that it was true that Ağaoğlu's ideas were shaped in large measure within the parameters of those of the political groups with which he worked and that he was able only after 1930 to lay out an unequivocal defence of liberalism. But this was only part of the story. As a prolific writer who contributed articles to numerous journals and newspapers on social, political, economic and moral issues, Ağaoğlu had already created for himself a relatively

---

18   Saffet Örfi Betin, *Atatürk İnkılâbı ve Ziya Gökalp, Yahya Kemal, Halide Edip Adıvar*, Istanbul: Güven Basımevi, 1951, p. 10.

19   Simten Coşar, "Ahmet Ağaoğlu: Türk Liberalizminin Açmazlarına Giriş," *Toplum ve Bilim*, 74, (Fall 1997), pp. 155–175; "Liberal Thought and Democracy in Turkey," *Journal of Political Ideologies* (February 2004), vol. 9, 1, pp. 71–98; Ayşe Kadıoğlu, "Citizenship and Individuation in Turkey: The Triumph of Will over Reason," in *Civil Society, Religion and Nation: Modernization in Intercultural Context: Russia, Japan, Turkey,* ed. Gerrit Steunebrink, Evert van der Zweerde, Amsterdam: Editions Rodopi, 2004, pp. 191–212; Murat Yılmaz, "Ahmet Ağaoğlu ve Liberalizm Anlayışı," *Türkiye Günlüğü,* (Summer 1993), pp. 56–71; Ufuk Özcan, *Ahmet Ağaoğlu ve Rol Değişikliği: Yüzyıl Dönümünde Batıcı Bir Aydın,* Istanbul: Don Kişot Yayınları, 2002; Bülent Aras, "Ahmet Ağaoğlu ve Ekonomik Alternatifi," *Birikim,* vol. 90, pp. 69–76.

independent intellectual space, within which he developed certain ideas which he had often associated with liberalism, even before 1930. His liberal thought essentially stretched back to his early writings in *La Nouvelle Revue* and *La revue bleue* in the early 1890s. Since his first writings, regardless of the immediate political, social or intellectual contexts of which he was a part, his ideas contained an element of continuity, especially where his permanent emphasis on the elevation and emancipation of the Eastern individual was concerned.

I will also argue that Ağaoğlu's ideas contained an element of originality because, fusing a variety of Western and Islamic sources, he sought to bring novel solutions to contemporary domestic and international problems. A clear understanding of his writings therefore requires an intellectual excavation, tracing the origins of his thought.

The early French influences on Ağaoğlu's thought, exerted by James Darmesteter and Ernest Renan, and the interplay with his Pan-Islamist and nationalist ideas with his later liberalisms have been partly acknowledged in Shissler's study.[20] The deep Durkheimian and Kropotkinian effects on his thought, on the other hand, have been examined in no scholarly work, with the exception of Bakırezer's article, which refers to the impact of Durkheim's sociology on Ağaoğlu as 'a weak point' of his liberal individualism.[21]

Since all these formative factors in Ağaoğlu's liberalism have long received little attention, some of the existing arguments about it have tended to be misleading, if not plainly false. On his death in May 1939, he was lauded as a champion of individualism.[22] The emphasis in his writings on the predicament of the individual in the East, his role as co-founder and ideologue of the Free Party and his criticisms directed against the corruption and the étatism of the Republican People's Party have remained the defining aspects of his intellectual work in Turkey.[23] Since then, Ağaoğlu has been well known as one of the first representatives of liberal individualism. It has been widely claimed, as far as the economy is concerned, that he remained a lifelong opponent of étatism.[24] In some studies, his ideas have been viewed as derivative of those of classical

---

20   Shissler, *Between Two Empires*.
21   Güven Bakırezer, "Batı Medeniyeti Hayranı Bir Liberal Aydının Çelişki ve Sınırları: Ahmet Ağaoğlu," *Toplumsal Tarih*, vol. 41, (May 1997), pp. 39–43.
22   Peyami Safa, "Ahmet Ağaoğlu," *Cumhuriyet*, May 24, 1939. Hilmi Ziya Ülken, "Ağaoğlu Ahmet ve Fikir Hayatı ve Mücadeleleri," *Ses*, May 25, 1939.
23   Holly Shissler, *Between Two Empires: Ahmet Ağaoğlu and the New Turkey*, London; New York: I.B. Tauris, 2003, p. 199.
24   Shissler, *Between Two Empires*, p. 80; Coşar, "Türk Liberalizminin Açmazlarına Giriş"; "Liberal Thought and Democracy in Turkey"; Kadıoğlu, "Citizenship and Individuation in Turkey"; Yılmaz, "Ahmet Ağaoğlu ve Liberalizm Anlayışı".

economic liberals and his notion of individualism has been embedded within this perspective.[25] Moreover, since no deep examination of the separate political, economic and moral layers of his thought has been made, his anti-individualist moral thought has been mistakenly depicted as a proof of his individualism.[26] Briefly, Ağaoğlu has usually been introduced as a controversial thinker who prematurely incorporated liberal, individualist and nationalist teachings into his thought without absorbing the main teachings of these ideas and ideologies. As yet, no dissenting voice has noted his defence of communitarianism, which seems to contradict, at least in part, the individualist view.

This is why I will attempt here to offer an alternative to these interpretations arguing that Ağaoğlu was one of the early representatives of communitarian liberalism in Turkey. The question thus arises of how Ağaoğlu has come to be known both as a pioneer of Turkish nationalism and a liberal individualist. How could he be for and against individualism at one and the same time? And what were the characteristics of his liberal thought?

The answering of these questions entails an analysis of Ahmet Ağaoğlu's entire intellectual evolution, life and activities also, as together they comprise a remarkable process of political learning which furnished his liberal thought with a number of characteristics peculiar to the Turkish or Near Eastern context. Ağaoğlu was a writer who lived and wrote in five different countries—the Russian Empire (1869–1888/1894–1908), France (1888–1894), the Ottoman Empire (1908–1918), the Democratic Republic of Azerbaijan (1918–1919) and the Republic of Turkey (1923–1939)[27]—and in five different languages: French, Azerbaijani, Turkish, Russian and Persian. During his lifetime, he saw the outbreak of five revolutions in Russia, Iran and Turkey, the fall of the Tsarist Russian and Ottoman empires and the persistent threat of Western encroachments in the Near East. Against the arrogant attitudes of Western statesmen and thinkers towards Muslim populations, even though it was uncertain whether he remained a believer of Islam all his life, he needed to defend Islam not as a set of beliefs *per se*, but as a communal identity from a liberal, Pan-Islamist and nationalist perspective. This gave his liberalism a defensive and communitarian character. As noted above, the intellectual sources he exploited, with the exception of the works of his acquaintance Ernest Renan, were also mainly nurtured by communitarian leanings.

---

25   Aras, "Ahmet Ağaoğlu ve Ekonomik Alternatifi".

26   Kadıoğlu, "Citizenship and Individuation in Turkey".

27   Between 1919 and 1921, Ağaoğlu was interned in Malta by the British forces on charges of war crimes, due to his pro-German writings.

I shall note at the outset that by communitarianism, I refer not only to the rejection of atomism or contractualism where individuals are conceived to predate society as isolated units. I also consider that the fundamental relationship between individuals and between the individual and society is not Hobbessian antagonism, but Kropotkinian mutual aid.[28] According to this view, the individual gains meaning only within society; he or she has no happiness beyond the happiness of society. What differs communitarianism from collectivism is its respect for persons. As I shall discuss in reference to Ağaoğlu's work, the former is argued to encourage individuality, tolerance, pluralism and the politics of difference, and to mitigate against conformism, homogeneity and repression.[29] The prevailing political mentality in early republican Turkey fell, in this scheme of things, closer to the collectivist mentality.

1.1   The Making of a Liberal in Turkey

In response to his frequent travels and the oft-changing political conditions and intellectual contexts in which he found himself, Ağaoğlu's ideas and identity went through remarkable changes, mostly for pragmatic reasons. For example, he was born in the Tsarist Russian Empire with the Azerbaijani family name of Aghayef, but after receiving a reader's letter, he decided to change it to Ağaoğlu in 1915, in the belief that this would sound more Turkish. During his studentship in France (1888–1894), he regarded and introduced himself as a Persian, but upon his return to the Caucasus, he advocated Turkish nationalism.

Moreover, like most Near Eastern intellectuals of his time, he pursued a versatile career. In distinct periods of his life, he appeared as a language teacher, political agitator, bureaucrat, Member of Parliament, leader of clandestine organisations, ideologue of political parties, university professor and military consultant. However, all his life, Ağaoğlu's main occupation was journalism: while pursuing one or more of the above-listed occupations, he wrote for numerous journals and newspapers and published his most important books, initially as instalments (*tefrika*) in these journals. In fact, this was the case for almost all Turkish intellectuals at the time: the works of various novelists and poets, as well as books on political and social issues, were published first in popular journals or newspapers, for financial and social reasons. Most Turkish writers at the time

---

28   Thomas Moody, "Some Comparisons between Liberalism and an Eccentric Communitarianism," in C.F. Delaney (ed.), *The Liberalism-Communitarianism Debate*, Maryland: Rowman & Littlefield Publishers, 1994, p. 92.

29   Ibid., pp. 92–93.

could make a living only from journalism. In a region where there was only a small book readership, due to a very low literacy rate, and where the publication of books was expensive and required much effort, it was wiser to publish through journals and newspapers. In addition, taking their activities as a 'public duty', Turkish intellectuals were anxious to reach as many people in as little time as possible. It is perhaps because they preferred to contribute to journals and news-papers on a regular basis, rather than working on 'grand works' which embodied well-structured ideas of great originality and required much time and patience, that there were often inconsistencies or contradictions in their writings.

This was frequently the case for Ağaoğlu. There are obvious inconsistencies in a number of his writings which at times make it difficult for later commenta-tors to capture the meaning of his ideas. These inconsistencies such as his call for decentralised governance in the Russian context and his denouncing decentralisation in the Ottoman Empire were at the same time a consequence of the fact that his inner convictions were at times informed by his social and political surroundings. Under the authoritarian rules of the Tsarist Russian government and the Republican People's Party, he knew that any writings going against the grain of the government could lead to the closing of his jour-nals and his imprisonment; indeed, he actually experienced such conse-quences during his long intellectual life: he was imprisoned by the Kâmil Paşa government in 1912 and he had journals closed by both the Tsarist Russian and the Republican People's Party governments.

None of the questions of the present study raised above, however, were the outcome of the inconsistencies in Ağaoğlu's writings. Tracing his uses of certain concepts such as individualism, communitarianism and étatism, and mapping out the main elements of his thinking, such as the role he accorded to the indi-vidual in social progress, his notion of history and his subsequent sociologism reveal that there was a remarkable cohesion and continuity of liberal ideas with strong communitarian tendencies in his evolving system of thought.

The focus of the study will be on his writings about the emancipation of the individual, individual and social rights in the Russian and Ottoman imperial and Republican Turkish contexts and his idea of nationalism. His liberal views were presented most unequivocally in early Republican Turkey, when the republic was founded, and he emerged as one of the spokesman of the 'liberal revolutionaries'. As the meaning of the term liberal became subject to change in the 1920s and '30s, he had a temporary breakup with the entourage of Kemal Atatürk. He came to defend in this period the importance of absorbing the features of modern and liberal Western civilisation, when there was growing interest in socialism and fascism among the intelligentsia in Turkey. In his *Üç Medeniyet* (Three Civilisations), which he published in 1927, he launched a

Westernist programme in which he suggested a wholesale (philosophical, political, economic and moral) liberal and westward transformation of Turkey. He wanted this because, particularly after the war, he believed that adopting the political, economic, scientific and moral systems on which the modern West was founded would secure Turkey's survival.

Until his death in 1939, his ideas mostly revolved around the main arguments of his programme. Setting out his liberal ideas in the 1920s and '30s, alongside other sources (especially the *oeuvres* of French Enlightenment thinkers), he began to invoke Durkheim's sociology, which the French thinker had himself proclaimed as the French Third Republic's liberal and secular ideology.[30] Moreover, Petr Kropotkin's 'science of ethics' loomed large in Ağaoğlu's later writings, forming, in place of the moral teachings of Islam, the intellectual basis of his suggestion for the moral reconstitution of society. Ağaoğlu's developing programme of political, economic and moral liberation of society by means of Westernisation, with deep Durkheimian, Kropotkinian and Enlightenment influences, contained and displayed the fundamental elements of his republican, nationalist and secular liberalism.

The reason for selecting Ağaoğlu as the subject of this study is not limited to the fact that he was the most prominent liberal in early Republican Turkey; he was an important figure in modern Turkish history for a variety of reasons. He made his fame in Turkey first as a pioneer of Turkish nationalism in the 1910s, when he became a member of the founding board of the nationalist organisation Turkish Hearths (*Türk Ocakları*). Together with Ziya Gökalp and other leading nationalists of the time, he ardently wrote about Turkish nationalism in the 1910s and '20s. A decade later, he appeared as a spokesman of the Kemalist revolutionaries and an ardent defender of Westernisation, as his various public debates and especially his *Three Civilisations* reveal. As noted above, he became a member of the committees which penned the first programme of the People's Party and which drafted the first constitution of the Republic. In the 1920s, he was a party man and an advocate of the Kemalist Revolution. He served as a member of parliament between 1923 and 1931. Yet with his 1926 report to Kemal Atatürk where he criticised the RPP's actions and particularly during the Free Party experience and in his 1933 writings he appeared as an opponent of authoritarianism. After the short-lived Free Party (FP) experience in 1930, he never returned to active politics.

In 1932–33, he publicly discussed with the writers of the patriotic-leftist journal *Kadro* the economic model Turkey should employ for its development

---

30   Steven Lukes, *Emile Durkheim, His Life and Work: A Historical and Critical Study*, London: Allen Lane, 1973, p. 77.

and later formed an intellectual group with such young scholars as Hilmi Ziya Ülken (1901–1974) and Mustafa Şekib Tunç (1886–1958) to start a new humanist movement in Turkey.[31] The group gathered at the famous oval room of Ağaoğlu's house every Monday evening and debated philosophical, political and social problems of the Republic, such as its Westernisation project, the moral reconstitution of Turkish society and the actions of the ruling party. Hence, one may say, Ağaoğlu came to form a bridge (like J.S. Mill who looked back to Jeremy Bentham and James Mill and looked forward to T.H. Green at one and the same time)[32] between the nationalist writer Ziya Gökalp and the young humanist scholars of early Republican Turkey who would heavily influence Turkish academic life throughout the twentieth century.

An analysis of Ağaoğlu's interpretations and adaptations of European liberalisms is also of importance in displaying the relationship of the liberal tradition with its sub-tradition (liberalism in Turkey) and an individual contributor (Ağaoğlu) to it. This tripartite relationship is significant for our understanding of all three elements, even if they are distinct. Contemporary Turkish liberals who have needed to look back to the history of liberalism in Turkey have considered Ağaoğlu as the only liberal of early Republican Turkey, although they describe him as a 'roughly liberal' figure.[33] It has been occasionally questioned whether his liberal thought was genuinely a defence of liberalism[34] and whether it was consistent, since the main features of his thought, which have been partly studied, do not match closely the main traits of the Anglo-American liberal tradition.[35] The differences between his liberal work and the stereotypical description of liberalism have led it, perhaps rightly so, to be classified as an unconventional liberal account.

Although it has often been argued that until the 1980s Turkey failed to provide a fertile political, economic and intellectual soil for liberals,[36] there has actually been a tradition of liberalism in the Turkish context that can be traced back to the constitutional movement of the Young Ottomans in the mid-nineteenth

---

31   Safa, "Ahmet Ağaoğlu".

32   H.S. Jones, "John Stuart Mill as Moralist," *Journal of the History of Ideas*, vol. 53, No. 2 (Apr.–Jun. 1992), pp. 287–308.

33   Atilla Yayla, "Liberalizme Bir Bakış," *Türkiye Günlüğü*, No. 17 (Winter 1991), pp. 32–63; Mustafa Erdoğan, "Liberalizm ve Türkiye'deki Serüveni," in *Liberalizm, Modern Türkiye'de Siyasal Düşünce*, ed. Murat Yılmaz, Istanbul: İletişim Yayınları, 2005, pp. 23–40.

34   Coşar, "Türk Liberalizminin Açmazlarına bir giriş".

35   Erdoğan, "Liberalizm ve Türkiye'deki Serüveni," p. 34.

36   Erdoğan, "Liberalizm ve Türkiye'deki Serüveni," pp. 35–36; Yayla, "Liberalizme Bir Bakış," p. 56.

century.[37] The liberalism in question has been empirical, a positioning against an autocratic sultan or an authoritarian Prime Minister, against the unconstitutional acts of the ruling elites, be it the Unionists, the Democrats or the military. It has been a struggle, since the late Ottoman Empire, to introduce constitutional rule and to ameliorate the constitution to the extent that the rights and freedom of the individuals and society be guaranteed by the rule of law.

It is also important to note that in modern Turkish politics and thought, liberalism has mostly been voiced and interpreted as an ideology pertaining to economic thought. For example, Çavdar's *Liberalism in Turkey* is a history of economic liberalism in Turkey only.[38] The political aspects of liberal thought have attracted far less attention in the Turkish context, while its moral components have been almost entirely overlooked.

This is due to the fact that the establishment and development of the capitalist economic system has tended to be a fundamental concern in the liberal tradition in Turkey. According to İnsel, there has been an inclination toward the idea that the rise of liberal thought was an outcome of the development of capitalist economic structure in the West.[39] One of the most vital differences of opinion among Turkish liberals has been as to how the Turkish economy could be integrated with the capitalist economic system. Broadly speaking, one group has tended to argue for the implementation of protectionist economic policies, at least temporarily, while the other has defended international free trade. These differing views have also triggered tensions between political and economic strands of liberalism in Turkey,[40] in both late Ottoman and Republican contexts. It is in the tenuous link between political and economic liberalisms that we can find one of the reasons why Ağaoğlu's liberalism has long been misinterpreted. This also invites us to look briefly at the history of liberal thought in Turkey up to the time of Ağaoğlu.

The birth of liberal thinking and practice in the Turkish context was a consequence of the pressures from the Great Powers on the Ottoman authorities to grant non-Muslims greater political rights, of the reception of French and Anglo-Saxon liberal ideas by the emerging intelligentsia and a growing awareness that the sharing of political and economic power in the late Ottoman Empire and Republican Turkey could hardly be secured through institutional reform to bring about the rule of law.

---

37   Ayşe Kadıoğlu, *Cumhuriyet İradesi, Demokrasi Muhakemesi*, Istanbul: Metis Yayınları, 1999, p. 9.

38   Tevfik Çavdar, *Türkiye'de Liberalizm, 1860–1990*, Ankara: İmge Kitabevi, 1992.

39   Ahmet İnsel, "Türkiye'de Liberalizmin Soyçizgisi," in *Liberalizm, Modern Türkiye'de Siyasal Düşünce*, ed. Murat Yılmaz, Istanbul: İletişim Yayınları, 2005, p. 47.

40   Ibid., p. 42.

Çavdar tells us that liberalism became an element of modern Turkish thought in the 1860s when the Young Ottomans—named after the youth movements in Europe (Young Italy, Young France, Young Spain)—initiated a constitutional movement.[41] This was approximately five decades after the term 'liberal' (*liberales*) had been made part of modern European political discourse in Spain by the struggles of the revolutionary Spaniards who were supporters of the aborted constitution (1812).[42] Influenced by Enlightenment ideas and the ideals of the French Revolution, the Young Ottomans were the first men to form a group of writers that propounded the European-oriented principles of rationality, individual rights, representative government, constitutionalism and nationalism in the Near East in the 1860s and '70s.[43]

Their work was more of an anachronistic imposition of European principles in the Ottoman context with an accompanying attempt to find Islamic or Ottoman counterparts to them. Although there were remarkable discrepancies between their ideas, their overall thought tended to be critical of the Tanzimat (regulations) era (1838–1876), during which a large number of Western-inspired political and social reforms were carried out.[44] In their eyes, the output of the Tanzimat reforms had dealt with individual rights and egalitarianism with a rather unclear vocabulary and the effectiveness of the subsequent Tanzimat reforms had been doubtful. "On the level of action as much as on that of ideas, the direction which the Tanzimat pointed for the future of Ottoman political life was not so much that of liberalism, as that of a melding of liberal and patrimonial elements."[45] For the Young Ottomans, the Tanzimat statesmen went too far in Westernisation and created too dominant a bureaucracy. Like the constitutional movements of the West, their movement demanded the re-imposition of controls over bureaucracy, while at the same time urging Ottoman statesmen not to forget the resources of their own tradition.[46] In so doing, they established a new mode of thinking in the Ottoman Empire that marked the beginning of the history of modern Turkish thought.

---

41 Çavdar, *Türkiye'de Liberalizm*, p. 14.
42 George Claeys, "Liberalism," in *Encyclopedia of Nineteenth-century Thought*, London: Routledge, 2005, p. 274.
43 Carter V. Findley, "The Advent of the Ideology in the Islamic Middle East (Part II)," *Studia Islamica*, No. 56 (1982), p. 148.
44 For a detailed account of the Young Ottoman thought please see, Şerif Mardin, *The Genesis of Young Ottoman Thought: A Study in the Modernization of Turkish Political Ideas*, Syracuse: Syracuse University Press, 2000.
45 Ibid., p. 166.
46 Ibid., p. 149.

İbrahim Şinasi (1826–71) was not only the first leader of the Young Ottomans but also the first modern Turkish enlightener and the first outstanding advocate of Westernisation in the Ottoman Empire.[47] He made huge innovations in Ottoman language, literature and journalism. For the first time with Şinasi, new terms such as citizens' rights, freedom of expression, constitutional government, liberty, natural rights of the people, etc. were used in Ottoman newspapers.[48] In using this new vocabulary, it was especially reference to the concept of liberty which marked the difference between political and economic liberalism in the Ottoman Empire. There were two words in Ottoman Turkish that served as the counterparts of the French word *liberté*,[49] the first being *serbestî*, a word of Persian origin which refers to being free, acting as one wishes without obstacle. As İnsel points out, the word *serbestî* was generally used to refer to material liberties such as freedom of trade (*serbest-i ticaret*), of education (*serbest-i tedrisat*) and of information (*serbest-i muhaberat*).[50] The second word was *hürriyet*, of Arabic origin and derived from *hürr*, which means 'to be set free'. Compared with *serbestî*, *hürriyet* more often expressed broader and abstract notions of liberty such as individual freedom and national freedom.[51] The Young Ottomans and the following generations generally used *serbestî* when they were speaking about elements of economic liberalism, while *hürriyet* was generally employed to refer to political liberties.

After Şinasi fled to Europe, Namık Kemal (1840–88) took up the role of the leader of the Young Ottomans and became the most famous of all. It was in the works of Kemal that the concepts that Şinasi had introduced were put into a theoretical framework. Kemal's series of articles entitled *Usul-ü Meşveret Hakkında Mektuplar* (Letters on a Constitutional Regime) were the first attempts to describe to Turkish readers the theory underlying liberalism and constitutionalism.[52] Moreover, his doctrine of natural rights and the sovereignty of the people was "a milestone in the struggles of the Turkish intellectuals to strike a new course in that maze leading from the medieval to the modern world" and the first tangible evidence of the impact of the Western mind.[53] He employed the word *hürriyet* as a very prominent feature of his political thought. Kemal's work, broadly speaking, was an attempt to synthesize European theories of the responsible state with the teachings of Islam.

47   Mardin, *The Genesis of Young Ottoman Thought*, p. 256.
48   Niyazi Berkes, *The Development of Secularism in Turkey*, London: C. Hurst, 1998, pp. 197–198.
49   İnsel, "Türkiye'de Liberalizm Kavramının Soyçizgisi," pp. 42.
50   Ibid., p. 41.
51   Ibid., p. 41.
52   Berkes, *Development of Secularism*, p. 210.
53   Ibid., pp. 210–211.

The ideas of the Young Ottomans had wider implications than political liberalism, as revealed by their explicit promotion of economic liberties. They identified the Anglo-Ottoman Commercial Convention of Balta Limanı (1838), which promoted free trade, as a threat to Ottoman economic development. This commercial convention and the Tanzimat reforms, as Findley argues, had been the outcomes of the strong influences exerted by European liberalism almost by force.[54] The European liberalism in question here was one inspired by the Manchester School that pleaded for international free trade. When the Ottoman Empire had needed British aid for the settlement of the conflict with Muhammed Ali Paşa of Egypt in the late 1830s, it had agreed on the Balta Limanı commercial convention and on the proclamation of the Gülhane Decree (1839), which had marked the beginning of the Tanzimat reforms. After 1839, the Ottoman economy had been practically deprived of its last defence against the growing industrial might of Europe, with the politically mandated adoption of free trade.[55] The Young Ottomans, therefore, called for a full-scale development of the Ottoman economy by giving priority to the amelioration of domestic elements. Although they were uneasy with state interference in economic activity and although many, especially Namık Kemal, supported international free trade as necessary for the development of local economies, they also believed that the Ottoman economic structure was not ready for it.[56] Comparative advantage was important, but equally important was the necessity to establish a domestic bourgeoisie, domestic banks and solid domestic industry. Kemal believed that protectionist economic policies should be implemented until a strong Ottoman economy capable of competing with foreign economies was built up. His concurrent defence of free trade and unconditional independence was an intrinsic paradox, but Çavdar argues that it is this very paradox of suggesting both further capitalism and the protection of the economy, both integrating with the world economy and preserving independence, which has formed one of the prominent features of economic liberalism in Turkey since the time of Namık Kemal.[57] To reiterate, the Young Ottomans' appeal for state intervention was limited to the imposition of protectionist customs policies. Otherwise, they were deeply attracted to economic liberalism and to the idea of a capitalist recovery of the Ottoman economy, because of their belief that the liberal institutions to which they aspired were based on this economic system.[58]

---

54   Carter V. Findley, "The Advent of the Ideology in the Islamic Middle East (Part 1)," *Studia Islamica*, No. 55 (1982), p. 163.
55   Ibid., p. 164.
56   İnsel, "Türkiye'de Liberalizm Kavramının Soyçizgisi," p. 45.
57   Çavdar, *Türkiye'de Liberalizm*, p. 52.
58   İnsel, "Türkiye'de Liberalizm Kavramının Soyçizgisi," p. 47.

The Young Turks, who succeeded the Young Ottomans, were also supporters of capitalism; they also suggested the creation of a local bourgeoisie and their ultimate aim was to reintroduce the constitution aborted by Abdulhamid II in 1878. Since, especially after 1870, the Western powers had begun to pose threats to Ottoman sovereignty, a sharp version of anti-imperialism formed an important component of their thought.[59] While the Young Ottomans had stressed Ottomanism (*Osmanlılık*) as a supranational identity, Turkish nationalism began its rise with the Young Turks, although they did not completely give up the idea of Ottomanism. The Young Turks' *Weltanschauung*, which aimed to liberate Ottoman society, therefore concurrently embraced anti-imperialism, nationalism and capitalism.

At the 1902 Congress of the Ottoman Opposition, the Young Turks split into two groups. This split is important to note because it is regarded as the starting point of the separation of the routes of the liberals and the Turkists in Turkey. The division was a result of the differences of opinion with regard to whether Sultan Abdulhamid II should be overthrown with the aid of foreign powers. Those who supported foreign intervention, including the Armenians and Greeks, it has been argued, gathered around the 'liberal' leadership of Mehmed (Prince) Sabahaddin (1877–1948). The others, led by Ahmet Rıza (1859–1930), were against foreign intervention and preferred a centralist government, while Sabahaddin's programme advocated decentralisation.

Translating the teachings of Frédéric Le Play's Catholic school of sociology into the Ottoman context, Sabahaddin's social thought revolved around the ideas of private initiative and decentralisation. He often needed to underline that he was not a supporter of any political or economic ideologies, but the scientific teachings of *La Science Sociale*.[60] With the works of Sabahaddin, the idea of the scientific study of society in restructuring Ottoman politics and society became popular in the Ottoman Empire. The school whose teachings he absorbed was mainly concerned with ending the cycle of revolutions taking place in France in the nineteenth century, whereas Sabahaddin's programme aimed to create a new social system following a political revolution in the Ottoman Empire.[61] In the light especially of the social theories of the second generation of the School of Le Play (the leading figures of which were Edmond Demolins and Paul de Rousiers), Sabahaddin asserted that the communitarian social structure of Ottoman society should be replaced by a particularistic

59   M. Şükrü Hanioğlu, *Preparation for a Revolution: The Young Turks, 1902–1908*, New York: Oxford University Press, 2002, p. 302.
60   Mehmed Sabahaddin, *Türkiye Nasıl Kurtarılabilir?* Istanbul: Ayraç Yayınları, 1999, pp. 22–23.
61   Hanioğlu, *Preparation for a Revolution*, p. 93.

structure as found in Anglo-Saxon countries. Individuals should be allowed and encouraged to develop their faculties of initiative, perseverance and industry. The entire social system should be organised to serve the strengthening of individuals. Therefore, he wanted local governments and municipalities to be given further rights in his programme.[62]

Like Sabahaddin, Ahmet Rıza, the leader of the coalition group within the Young Turks,[63] was fascinated by the teachings of a French school of sociology, in this case Saint-Simonianism; he closely followed the works of 'the liberal Saint-Simonian' Pierre Laffitte.[64] Ahmet Rıza also suggested the creation of a new educated individual, despite regarding the state as the engine of progress. His emphasis on the strengthening of the individual was not as strong, although the attention paid in his thought to public education was remarkable. It was Sabahaddin who for the first time accentuated the individual as the most important social, political and economic actor in modern Turkish social and political thought. With him, the individual became an important element of public discourse in the Ottoman Empire. Probably because Turkish political thought has been so unaccustomed to emphases to this effect, those who spoke of the importance of the individual in the Ottoman Empire or the Republic of Turkey, including Sabahaddin, Baha Tevfik (1884–1914), who, following Nietzsche's work, defended anarchist individualism, and Ahmet Ağaoğlu, have been insistently identified as 'liberal individualists'.[65]

Given this framework, it will not do to maintain, with the existing literature on liberalism in Turkey, that the intellectual schisms emanating from the arguments around centralisation and decentralisation provide us with a practical

---

62   Cenk Reyhan, *Türkiye'de Liberalizmin Kökenleri: Prens Sabahattin*, Ankara: İmge Yayınevi, 2008.

63   Hanioğlu, *Preparation for a Revolution*, p. 28.

64   H.S. Jones, "French Liberalism and the Legacy of the Revolution," in *Historicising the French Revolution*, ed. C. Armenteros, I. DiVanna, T. Blanning, Newcastle-upon-Tyne: Cambridge Scholars Publishing, p. 201. Jones explains this paradoxical description (because there was a strong strain of authoritarianism in the Saint-Simonian tradition) by pointing out the overlap between the Saint-Simonian and liberal traditions in France, which appeared in the shape of their common desire to 'close the French Revolution' and their acknowledgement of 'organization' as the key to social reconstruction. Moreover, it was a common characteristic of the Saint-Simonians, French liberals and Le Playists to consider 'individualism' to be the central ill of society.

65   Cavit O. Tütengil, *Prens Sabahattin*, Istanbul: Istanbul Matbaası, 1954; Ali Erkul, "Prens Sabahattin," Kongar, Emre (Ed.), *Türk Toplum Bilimcileri*, Istanbul: Remzi Kitabevi, 2003; Rukiye Akkaya, *Prens Sabahaddin*, Istanbul: Liberte Yayınları, 2005; Mehmet Alkan, "Düşünce Tarihimizde Önemli Bir İsim: Baha Tevfik," *Tarih ve Toplum*, (Apr., 1988), pp. 41–49.

demarcation line between liberalism and its opponents. As seen in the case of some variants of liberalism in France (most prominently the Doctrinaires), for example, liberalism could well employ centralist theories, and to advocate decentralisation does not necessarily mean to advocate liberalism. It was true that the centralisation-decentralisation dichotomy was the main issue leading to schisms in the Young Turk movement after the question of the intervention of foreign powers. But the schism was not as sharp. If one needs to regard the Young Turk movement as a liberal movement and an integral part of the history of liberalism in Turkey, it should be done by taking into account Ahmet Rıza's Laffittist organisation-oriented ideas as much as Sabahaddin's individual-based social programme.

As concerns the economy, during the Hamidian (1876–1909) and the Second Constitutional (1908–1919) periods, debates centred on the old question of protectionism versus *laissez faire*. The conservative writer Ahmet Midhat (1844–1912) was the most important critic of the latter.[66] Although most of his social and political views noticeably differed from Namık Kemal's political ideas (Ahmed Midhat was a supporter of Hamidian rule), the opinions of the two regarding the means of the development of the Ottoman economy were similar. In *Ekonomi Politik* (1880), arguing that economic liberalism was giving rise to an intellectual anarchy and triggering increasingly deteriorating conditions for the Ottoman economy, Midhat suggested that Ottoman trade should not be left in the hands of the non-Muslims and foreigners only. For him, it should also be undertaken by Ottoman Turks and Muslims.[67]

The chief opponent of Midhat's views was Sakızlı Ohannes Paşa (1830-1912), an Armenian professor of finance and Minister of the Civil List. As the champion of *laissez faire* economics in the late nineteenth century, Ohannes Paşa taught the principles of economic liberalism at the *Mekteb-i Mülkiye*, where Ottoman bureaucrats were educated. He believed that protection of a certain industrial field would channel limited capital to this field and lead to a disequilibrium in the allocation of investments. Therefore, no industrial field should be protected and the economy should be left to the natural course of the principle of comparative advantage.[68]

One of his students, Kazanlı Akyiğitzade Musa (1865–1923), turned away from Ohannes's teachings and joined the 'protectionist' camp in the 1890s. He

---

66   V. Necla Geyikdağı, "The Relationship between Trade and Foreign Direct Investment: Testing Ahmed Midhat Efendi's Hypothesis," *International Journal of Middle East Studies*, vol. 40, (2008), pp. 547–549.
67   İnsel, "Türkiye'de Liberalizmin Soyçizgisi," p. 47.
68   Çavdar, *Türkiye'de Liberalizm*, p. 69.

was fascinated by the protectionist teachings of the German economic theorist
Friedrich List, but like Kemal, he saw economic protectionism as a transitional
economic policy which should be lifted with the strengthening of the economy. Musa later wrote an economics text based on Listian teachings and began
to teach at the Imperial War College.[69] Hence, Ottoman officers' education in
economics came to be based on Listian principles and protectionist policies,
while Ottoman bureaucrats were taught the main principles of *laissez faire*
economy by an ardent defender of economic liberalism.[70]

In spite of this, after the 1908 Revolution, which was the work of middle-
ranking officers in the Ottoman army, it was Mehmet Cavid Bey (1875–1926),
who has been believed to be another advocate of *laissez faire* economics, who
took control of Ottoman economic policy as the finance minister of the Young
Turk era. This was due mainly to Cavid's central role within the inner circle of
the Unionists, to the fact that he was perhaps the only *financier* among them
and to his strong foreign connections in the financial circles in Europe. According
to Toprak, in the Second Constitutional period, thanks to Cavid Bey, the concept
of *serbestî* became an integral element of Ottoman economic thought.[71]
Together with Rıza Tevfik (1869–1949) and Ahmet Şuayb (1876–1910), Cavid published *Ulûm-u İktisadiyye ve İctimaiyye Mecmuası* (the Journal of Economic and
Social Sciences), in which the group advocated liberal teachings such as international free trade, cosmopolitanism and individualism in economic affairs.[72]

Cavid argued that trade played a major role in the development of economies and the role of the government must be to facilitate it:

> The thing to expect from the governments is to inform the tradesmen
> of the intelligence information acquired through its consulates, to pro-
> tect the rights of its subjects in foreign countries, to remove all methods
> and laws that prevent freedom of trade, and especially in those countries
> which are not advanced in sciences and education, it is to guide the
> tradesman in every field and to use its own power in fields where the
> individuals [cannot make any initiatives]. But in developed countries
> and, partially in developing countries, tradesmen must rely only on

---

69   Akyiğitzade Musa, *İlm-i Servet veyahut İlm-i İktisat: Azâde-gi Ticaret ve Usul-I Himâye*,
      Istanbul: Mekteb-i Harbiye, 1316.
70   İnsel, "Türkiye'de Liberalizmin Soyçizgisi," p. 49.
71   Zafer Toprak, *Türkiye'de Milli İktisat, 1908–1918*, Ankara: Yurt Yayınları, 1982, p. 23.
72   Nazmi Eroğlu, "Mehmed Cavid Bey'in İktisadi Görüşleri," *İstanbul Universitesi Ataturk
      İlkeleri ve İnkılap Tarihi Enstitüsü Dergisi: Yakin Dönem Türkiye Araştırmaları* (2002), 163–
      183, p. 164.

themselves for success, rather than seeking the guidance of the government; they enlighten civil servants of the government who lack commercial skills. The government does not intervene [in these countries] in the direction of the commercial path of the country with other nations.[73]

Cavid suggests that the government should take the opinion of those who are knowledgeable such as tradesmen for the laws and conditions that the government prepares, for its public works policies, for the taxes that are related to commerce, in short, for all its actions that directly or indirectly affect the nations' economic life.[74]

Although İnsel argues that Cavid hardly mentioned the possibility of exploiting economically weak countries in the international economy, where there was unequal trade between strong and weak economies,[75] Cavid's writings reveal that he in fact had reservations, like the Young Ottomans, in suggesting international trade and limited state interference in the economy.[76] Cavid maintained that as long as the Great Powers sought to exploit the system a full international free trade would have dangerous consequences for economies such the Ottoman economy. Nor was he completely against the establishment of state monopolies especially if they would be profitable as in the case of oil production and export.[77]

Despite these ideas and yet his much more nationalist financial practice as the Minister of Finance,[78] he has come to be known, at the hands of later commentators, as the owner of extremely materialistic (*maddeci*) views in economics. Ağaoğlu was once 'accused of' advocating the liberalism of Cavid Bey in the 1930s and he would reject these accusations,[79] which was in a sense an indicator of the fact that the hatred for the economic brand of liberalism was what gave liberalism a deragotary connotation in the Turkish context.

This one can seek in the writings of such Listian writers as Akyiğitzade Musa and perhaps more importantly Ziya Gökalp. The latter also criticised materialism and laid the seeds of economic nationalism and corporatism, with which economic protectionism and the creation of a Turkish bourgeoisie were defended.

---

73 Mehmed Cavid, "Ticaret Odaları," *Ulum-i İktisadiye ve İçtimaiye Mecmuasi*, No. 2 (1908), pp. 199.

74 Ibid., p. 200.

75 İnsel, "Türkiye"de Liberalizmin Soyçizgisi," p. 53.

76 Deniz Karaman, "Ulum-i İktisadiye Mecmuasi," *C.U. Sosyal Bilimler Dergisi*, 28/1 (May, 2004), pp. 65–87, p. 73.

77 Mehmed Cavid, "1327 Senesi Esbab-i Mucibe Lahiyasi," *Ulum-i İktisadiye ve İçtimaiye Mecmuası*, No. 23, (1911), pp. 1144.

78 "Maliye Nazırı," *Tanin*, July 1, 1909.

79 Şevket Süreyya, "Darülfinun İnkılap Hassasiyeti ve Cavid Bey İktisatçılığı," *Kadro*, vol. 1, No. 12 (1932), pp. 38–43.

Gökalp argued that international free trade and cosmopolitanism were nothing but components of the national economy of Britain.[80] The Turks should free themselves from the yoke of the British economy and claim their own national economy, morality, legality and literature.

Harbouring the teachings of the Durkheimian philosophy of solidarism and the German view of *Sozialpolitik*, he asserted that the Turks could be inspired by the Germans, who had achieved order and unity (*Alman ittihâtı*) in three stages: cultural, economic and political unity.[81] The Turks had initiated the process of cultural unity; now it was time to sow the seeds of economic unity. Economic nationalists did not defend state interference in the economy, but only the nationalisation of economic actors.

Hence, one can argue, in contrast to mainstream arguments, it would be false to say that, throughout the 1910s, Cavidian liberalism and economic nationalism formed two main strands of economic thought in the late Ottoman Empire. Even Cavidian liberalism was imbued with nationalist sentiments, and he could well suggest protectionism and state monopolies. On the other hand, the leading nationalist figures actually wanted the creation of a strong bourgeoisie.[82] For Gökalp, for example, the reason for the lagging behind of the Empire was the non-existence of economic classes among the Turks,[83] while Akçura was of the opinion that the development of the Empire was dependent upon the emergence of a Turkish bourgeoisie.[84] That being said, those who associated themselves with political liberalism would at times feel the urge to make a distinction between economic and political liberalism, for there was an apparent suspicion for unfettered economic liberalism. Ağaoğlu was one of these political liberals.

In a similar vein, it has perhaps falsely been argued that the problem that led to ideological clashes among the late Ottoman intelligentsia was the question of whether political rights and equality should be based on the bonds of nationality, religion or the identity of Ottoman citizenship. This question gave rise to a so-called intellectual polarisation between the Islamists (*İslamcılar*), the Turkists (*Türkçüler*) and the Ottomanists (*Osmanlıcılar*).[85] The schisms

80   Ziya Gökalp, "İktisadi vatanperverlik," *Yeni Mecmua*, May 5, 1918. pp. 322–323; cf. Toprak, *Türkiye'de Milli İktisat*, p. 25.
81   Ibid., p. 28.
82   The liberal traits in the writings of the Turkists have already been shown in two important studies of the social and political thought of Gökalp and Akçura. Taha Parla, *The Social and Political Thought of Ziya Gökalp*, Leiden: E.J. Brill, 1985; François Georgeon, *Aux Origines du Nationalisme Turc, Yusuf Akçura, 1876–1935*, Paris: Éditions ADPF, 1980.
83   Toprak, *Türkiye'de Milli İktisat*, p. 32.
84   Ibid., p. 33.
85   Peyami Safa, *Türk İnkılâbına Bakışlar*, Istanbul: İnkılâp Yayınevi, 1938.

between these groups amounted no more than to differing emphases in their writings so that at times it was impossible to distinguish the views of one from another. A rough account of ideological divides among these three groups would suggest that the Islamists believed that the Empire could be empowered by emphasising the role of the Sultan Caliph as the leader of the Islamic world and strengthening the ties between various Muslim elements in the empire; that the Turkist emphasis was on the creation of a community of national communities with equal rights, whereas the Ottomanists wanted to appease the nationalist movements for fear of the disintegration of the empire, which had threatened to occur since the start of the secessionist movements of different ethnic groups in the early nineteenth century. For them, the empire should be regarded as an assembly of individuals enjoying equal citizenship rights. The above-mentioned historiographical flaw of discussing the existence of binary oppositions within the Young Turk movement as liberals (Sabahaddinians) and illiberals (Unionists), and the men of the 1910s as Cavidian liberals and Gökalpian nationalists passes on when it is claimed that late Ottoman thought had three major groups, the Ottomanists, Islamists and the Turkists.

Liberal historiography has often identified early Republican Turkey as one of the periods least hospitable to liberalism in Turkish history.[86] According to this account, during and after the War of Independence, when all groups opposing the Kemalist Revolutionaries were eradicated from political and intellectual circles, liberalism as a political ideology virtually withered away. According to İnsel, political liberalism then came to mean 'reactionism' (*gericilik*), which the authoritarian reformists associated with traditionalism.[87] However, when one looks at the political lexicon of the time, it will be seen that the legislation and actions of the Republican People's Party, such as the abolition of the Caliphate and religious orders in 1924, were portrayed in the contemporary press as 'liberal' acts.[88] Moreover, in the matrix of Gökalp's political thought, the Republican People's Party was classified as a liberal party.[89]

In the 1920s, the terms 'liberal' (*liberal*) and 'left' (*sol*) were almost synonymous in political vocabulary and stood for the liberation of society from the social ills associated with the old regime. They also referred to 'modernisation' or 'Westernisation', which were used interchangeably throughout the decade.

---

86   Murat Belge, "Mustafa Kemal ve Kemalizm," *Kemalizm* volume in *Modern Türkiye'de Siyasi Düşünce,* Istanbul: İletişim Yayınları, p. 34; Erdoğan, "Liberalizm ve Türkiye'deki Serüveni," p. 33; Yayla, "Liberalizme Bir Bakış," p. 57.
87   İnsel, "Türkiye'de Liberalizmin Soyçizgisi," p. 68.
88   "Liberal Partisi Hilâfet'in külliyen ilgâsına karar Verdi," *Tevhid-i Efkâr*, February 29, 1924.
89   Ziya Gökalp, "Fırkaların Siyâsî Tasnifi," *Hâkimiyet-i Milliye*, April 19, 1923.

Being a liberal or a leftist meant, for contemporary thinkers and politicians, to be a revolutionary progressivist (as opposed to a conservative).

It is in this period that Ağaoğlu, as the spokesman of the Revolutionaries, made his name as a liberal in Turkey. He saw the Kemalist Revolution as an Eastern counterpart of the 'liberal' French Revolution.[90] Influenced by the teachings of Enlightenment thinkers, the ideas of Renan and Durkheim, he played an important role in integrating French Republican culture into Turkey with his political writings of the 1920s; and by 1930 he had become known as the most ardent and prominent liberal in early Republican Turkey.[91] Yet, in the 1930s, he felt the need to write explicitly against economic liberalism, concurrently asserting the importance of liberal democracy.

His later liberal work thus wrestled with the tensions of economic liberalism (and its most disliked individualism) and political liberalism, despite its undemocratic propensities. He attempted to resolve the problems of individualism and poverty in democratic culture by means of a campaign which suggested the moral reconstitution of society in a communitarian direction. In his view, such reconstitution was a pre-requisite for a functioning democracy which Turkey lacked at the time.

1.2   Ideas and Contexts

The present study draws upon a range of approaches and disciplines, and therefore, will have to cope with the methodological difficulties that each brings. In the first place, it is a study of intellectual history. It will attempt to occupy the middle ground between two different, even opposing, traditions in the writing of intellectual history: contextualism and intellectualism.[92] With the linguistic movement of the 1970s,[93] Quentin Skinner and the new historians of the Cambridge school invited intellectual historians to "focus not merely or even mainly on the canon of so-called classic texts, but rather on the place

90   H. Ozan Özavcı, "The French Revolution from a Turkish Perspective: Ahmet Ağaoğlu and High Individualism," in *Historicising the French Revolution*, ed. C. Armenteros, I. DiVanna, T. Blanning, Newcastle-upon-Tyne: Cambridge Scholars Publishing, pp. 146–168.

91   Ahmet Ağaoğlu, *Serbest Fırka Hatıraları*, Istanbul: İletişim Yayınları, 1994, p. 16.

92   Donald Kelly, "Intellectual History in a Global Age," *Journal of the History of Ideas*, Vol. 66, No. 2 (Apr., 2005), pp. 155–167.

93   J.G.A. Pocock, "Languages and Their Implications: The Transformation of the Study of Political Thought," *Politics, Language and Time: Essays on Political Thought and History*, New York: Atheneum, 1971.

occupied by such texts in broader traditions and frameworks of thought."[94] Known as the revisionists, they rejected the widespread (intellectualist) notion that "the whole point of studying 'great' works of philosophy is to extract 'time-less elements' or 'dateless ideas' with universal (and therefore contemporary) application."[95] According to this account, by treating ideas, in Lovejoy's words, as 'isolated units' or 'unit ideas'[96] with the intent of appropriating them to present problems, the intellectualists neglected "the uniquely historical ques-tion of what the various thinkers intended to say and have."[97] In the eyes of the revisionists, the interpretative techniques deployed by the intellectualists were not properly historical. Following the warnings of the revisionist school, I will focus on the ideological meaning in the immediate discursive environment in which the texts that will be examined here were produced. To this end, I will take into consideration the complex intentions of the writer and what he was actually doing in pursuing that linguistic act whilst seeking meaning in his writings.[98] I will thus employ a historicist or contextualist approach by paying attention to the context and trying to identify the multiple connections between the writer's inner convictions, his textual output, his political and intellectual surroundings and his biographical experience.

Neither do I ignore the broader relevance of ideas propounded in these texts. Ağaoğlu's linguistic act will also be placed within the fields of the history and sociology of ideas, and of the history of intellectuals, with an intellectual-ist approach, given that what he was doing as an author was to adopt ideas of Western origin and adapt them to the Turkish context, thus serving as a con-duit in the transmission of those ideas. In so doing, neither Ağaoğlu nor other contemporary Turkish thinkers were particularly concerned with the con-texts within which the migrant ideas they dealt with were produced, but treated ideas as independent units. Regarding all ideas as omnipotent tools to help them understand and transform their societies, they sincerely believed that an idea of Western European origin could well be used in the peculiar

---

94   Quentin Skinner, *Liberty before Liberalism*, Cambridge: Cambridge University Press, 1998, p. 101. For an important account of the main views of Quentin Skinner, one of the most prominent figures of the Cambridge School, and his critics, *Meaning and Context*, James Tully, ed., Princeton, N.J.: Princeton University Press, 1988.

95   Joseph V. Femia, "A Historicist Critique of "Revisionist" Methods for Studying the History of Ideas," *History and Theory*, Vol. 20, No. 2 (May, 1981), pp. 113–134.

96   Arthur O. Lovejoy, *The Great Chain of Being: A Study of the History of an Idea*, Cambridge, Mass.: Harvard University Press, 1936.

97   Femia, "A Historicist Critique," p. 113.

98   Skinner, "Meaning and Understanding in the History of Ideas," *History and Theory*, 8:1 (1969), p. 45.

conditions of Turkish social and political life. In their view, ideas contained meanings transcending all boundaries. I will therefore give credit equally to the traditional intellectualist school, treating ideas as units that operate beyond contexts.

Another essential concern I have here is to display the links between Ağaoğlu's work and the intellectual traditions of which he was part. I will attempt to demonstrate that some of the views credited to Ağaoğlu at different times of his life were in effect more widely shared across a variety of Turkish thinkers (liberal advocates of Pan-Islamism, Turkish nationalists and revolutionary republicans). To what extent then were Ağaoğlu's ideas distinguishable from those of other important Turkish thinkers of his time? This question will also entail paying attention to the intellectual context(s) within which Ağaoğlu lived and wrote, although it will not always be easy, or even possible, to identify the direct or indirect influences of those contexts on his intellectual tendencies.

With these methodological concerns in mind, I tried to exploit a wide range of materials. The primary sources were of course Ağaoğlu's writings: all his books and a wide range of his journalistic articles that appeared in French, Russian, Ottoman and Turkish journals. Besides these, his autobiographical scripts, personal letters, unpublished articles and his conference papers were examined. My contextualist concerns also led me to exploit a large number of secondary sources to map the political, economic and intellectual milieux and biographical experiences of Ağaoğlu in order to exhibit links between textual output and biographical events. Since Ağaoğlu was a prolific writer, his journalistic writings that will be examined and cited in this study will be selected from distinct periods of his lifetime by their relevance to the central subject of the present study. My intellectualist aims, on the other hand, make it necessary to look at the works of those who inspired Ağaoğlu intellectually or at secondary sources concerning their lives and thoughts. Because of their direct influence on Ağaoğlu, I devoted particular attention to the main teachings of Renan, Durkheim and Kropotkin. Since there was sometimes no general acknowledgement of these sources or citations, their effective influence will be uncovered, to borrow from Hazereesingh, "by identifying key conceptual overlaps and substantive patterns of repetition."[99]

Among the most important secondary sources that I exploited in this study were of course works about Ağaoğlu's life and thought and particularly his liberalism. Some of these studies have already been cited above while underscoring

---

99   In employing this approach one of my inspirations was Sudhir Hazareesingh's *Intellectual Founders of the Republic, Five Studies in Nineteenth Century French Republican Political Thought*, Oxford; New York: Oxford University Press, 2001. p. 11.

why it is important to study Ağaoğlu's liberalism and when referring to the existence of misinterpretations. But there are still a few points that should be made here about the existing literature, as this is the only means by which I can pay my debt to this material, from which I have benefited vastly.

1.2.1 Ağaoğlu in Literature

With the rise of the liberal Motherland Party in the 1980s and the neoliberal transformation in the following decades, liberalism has become an object of enormous scholarly attention in Turkey. Although only a few very short monographs and one anthological study have until now been published on the nearly two hundred year long history of liberalism in the Turkish context, as the most prominent liberal thinker in the early republican era, Ağaoğlu has attracted great interest as an individual thinker.[100] It was first with François Georgeon's 1986 article on Ağaoğlu's French sojourn (1888–1894) that his life and work became the sole subject of a scholarly study.[101] In the two decades following Georgeon, insofar as the present study has been able to establish, six books (four in Turkish, one in Azerbaijani and one in English) and approximately twenty articles specifically about Ağaoğlu's life and thought have been published. Although none of the books has particularly focused on his liberalism, all were important in shedding some light on different aspects of his intellectual career.

The first book that examined Ağaoğlu's life and thought was Fahri Sakal's *Ağaoğlu Ahmed Bey* of 1999.[102] In this study, Sakal first provides the reader with biographical information and brief accounts of some phases of Ağaoğlu's intellectual life between 1891 and 1939. Sakal's work depicts his intellectual evolution as beginning with his departure from Persian nationalism for Islamism, continuing with his leaving behind Islamism for Turkish nationalism and culminating in his appearance as a 'liberal individualist'. Although Ağaoğlu is described as a liberal individualist thinker and it is argued that his liberal individualism makes him relatively close to the school of Mehmed Sabahaddin, in a book of more than two hundred pages, only a few are devoted to Ağaoğlu's liberalism and his notions of the state, society and the individual, probably because the study was not primarily concerned with his liberal work. Sakal's

---

100 The anthological volume on liberalism in the anthological series on modern Turkish political thought of the İletişim Publications has been the richest study of the history of liberalism in Turkey, even though it suffers from a lack of coherence, like most other anthologies.

101 François Georgeon, "Ahmet Ağaoğlu, un Intellectuel Turc Admirateur des Lumières et de la Révolution," *Revue du Monde Musulman et de la Méditerranée*, vol. 52–53, (1989), pp. 186–197.

102 Fahri Sakal, *Ağaoğlu Ahmed Bey*, Ankara: Türk Tarih Kurumu Basımevi, 1999.

work is nonetheless of great importance as the first monographic study of Ağaoğlu which has made available for later students of Ağaoğlu's thought a map of the thinker's life and a detailed account of sources—most notably the first account of the journals and newspapers in the late Ottoman Empire and early Republican Turkey to which Ağaoğlu contributed.

Ufuk Özcan's *Ahmet Ağaoğlu ve Rol Değişikliği: Yüzyıl Dönümünde Batıcı Bir Aydın* (*Ahmet Ağaoğlu and the Change of Roles: A Westernist Intellectual at the Turn of the Century*)[103] was the second book to be published on Ağaoğlu's life. The emphasis of this study, as is evident from its title, is on the changing roles of Ağaoğlu in Azerbaijani and Turkish intellectual and political life in the late nineteenth and early twentieth centuries. Like Sakal, Özcan introduces Ağaoğlu as a liberal individualist thinker, whose economic views are along the lines of *laissez faire* liberalism and who totally rejects Ziya Gökalp's communitarian views. The same arguments run through Gülseren Akalın's *Türk Düşünce ve Siyasi Hayatında Ahmet Ağaoğlu* (*Ahmet Ağaoğlu in Turkish Intellectual and Political Life*).[104] However, none of these studies examines in depth Ağaoğlu's communitarian propensities in reference to the works of Petr Kropotkin and Émile Durkheim, his understanding of the state or his thoughts on the relationship between society and the individual; yet Ağaoğlu is usually described as a representative of the strongly individualist Anglo-American tradition of liberalism in early Republican Turkey.[105]

Holly Shissler's *Between Two Empires: Ahmet Ağaoğlu and the New Turkey*, which is the only English monograph about Ağaoğlu, focuses on Ağaoğlu's activities and ideas until 1919.[106] In this study, which comes from Shissler's doctoral thesis, she successfully traces the intellectual evolution of Ağaoğlu with a close examination of the impacts of his early education and the early French influences (Renan and Darmesteter) on his thinking. Her analysis of Ağaoğlu's studentship year in Paris and his notion of nationalism are very convincing.

---

103   Özcan, *Ahmet Ağaoğlu ve Rol Değişikliği*.

104   Gülseren Akalın, *Türk Düşünce ve Siyasi Hayatında Ahmet Ağaoğlu*, Baku: Azatam, 2004.

105   The most recent book to be published in Turkish on Ağaoğlu's life and thoughts, Abdullah Gündoğdu's *Ümmetten Millete: Ahmet Ağaoğlu'nun Sırat-ı Müstakim ve Sebilürreşad Dergilerindeki Yazıları Üzerine Bir İnceleme* (*From Religous Community to Nation: A Study on Ağaoğlu's Writings in the Journals Sırat-ı Müstakim and Sebilürreşad*) of 2007, on the other hand, is about Ağaoğlu's writings in Islamist journals between 1909 and 1914, which mostly focused on high politics. Therefore, it is of little relevance to our concerns in the present thesis. Abdullah Gündoğdu, *Ümmetten Millete: Ahmet Ağaoğlu'nun Sırat-ı Müstakim ve Sebilürreşad Dergilerindeki Yazıları Üzerine Bir İnceleme*, Istanbul: IQ Yayıncılık, 2007.

106   Shissler, *Between Two Empires*, p. 5.

Together with the other study on Ağaoğlu's French sojourn, Georgeon's "Les Debuts d'un intellectuel Azerbaidjanais: Ahmet Ağaoğlu en France, 1888–1894,"[107] Shissler exploits a large amount of sources on Ağaoğlu's early education and writings. She successfully displays some of the possible influences on his thought of his teachers, James Darmesteter and Ernest Renan, and offers equally successful interpretations of his early French writings. The present book has therefore benefited greatly from these works in studying the early phases of Ağaoğlu's life and thought.

Shissler also devotes a chapter to Ağaoğlu's activities and writings in the early Republican era. However, this forms the Achilles' heel of her book, because in that chapter, some of Ağaoğlu's most important works in early Republican Turkey such as *Serbest İnsanlar Ülkesinde* (*In the Land of Free Men*) and *Ben Neyim*? (*What am I?*) are neither examined nor even mentioned. Moreover, nowhere in Shissler's work do the names of Durkheim or Kropotkin appear, despite the tremendous influence of these two thinkers on Ağaoğlu. Shissler also describes Ağaoğlu as a liberal individualist and a lifelong opponent of étatism, and devotes no space to his moralist project.

There is not enough space here to review all the articles written about Ağaoğlu's thought, some of which will be mentioned in the body of the book. All these articles were of course of a certain importance in the sense of contributing to our knowledge of Ağaoğlu's liberal work. To name a few, it was Georgeon who first argued that the notion of the individual was of central importance to Ağaoğlu's work, which was heavily influenced by Enlightenment thinkers and the ideals of the French Revolution.[108] Georgeon rightly asserts that Ağaoğlu believed in the theory of progressive evolution towards modern society and that the French Revolution was a milestone in this process, which gave birth to individualism. He underlines this point by referring to "individualism, but at the same time mutual aid. For Ağaoğlu, individualism does not mean the supremacy of individual ambition and egoism; in contrast, it is the supremacy of solidarism and mutual aid. Only strong individuals can bring aid

---

107 François Georgeon, "Les Débuts d'un Intellectuel Azerbaidjanais: Ahmed Ağaoğlu en France 1888–1894", in Ch. Lemercier-Quelquejay, G. Veinstein and S.E. Wimbush ed., *Passé Turco-Tatar, Présent Soviétique*, Etudes offertes à Alexandre Bennigsen, Louvain and Paris: Editions Peeters, 1986. See also, Ada H. Shissler, "A Student Abroad in Late Ottoman Times: Ahmet Ağaoğlu and French Paradigms in Turkish Thought," in *Iran and Beyond: Essays in Middle Eastern History in Honor of Nikki Keddie*, edited by Rudi Mathee and Beth Baon, CA: Mazda, 2000.

108 Georgeon, "Ahmet Ağaoğlu, un Intellectuel Turc Admirateur des Lumières et de la Révolution".

to others."[109] However, Georgeon's interpretation overlooks those writings of Ağaoğlu in which the term 'individualism' refers also to a cancerous trait: egoism. That is, he provides no account of how Ağaoğlu used the term in his writings (sometimes even on the same page) with two distinct meanings. Another major drawback of Georgeon's work is that it devotes little space to the political, economic and intellectual contexts within which Ağaoğlu put forward his social and political ideals.

Of all the studies of Ağaoğlu's ideas, only in Coşar's work do the deep parallels between the communitarian tendencies of Continental liberalism and Ağaoğlu's thought receive mention.[110] But Coşar attempts no excavation of Ağaoğlu's intellectual sources, which prevents her articles from uncovering the Renanian, Durkheimian and especially Kropotkinian influences. Yet, she too identifies Bergson as an important later influence on Ağaoğlu's thought, whereas, as will be demonstrated, it is hardly possible to cite Bergson's works among the intellectual sources that Ağaoğlu exploited in propounding his arguments.

A few methodological points about articles on Ağaoğlu's thought also need to be made before moving onto the outline of the present book. First of all, in some of these studies, Ağaoğlu's ideas and his use of certain concepts have been furnished with a coherence and congruence that he actually did not achieve, or achieved in a different way. For example, it has been argued that Ağaoğlu absorbed the teachings of Henri Bergson in the latter's *L'évolution créatrice* of 1907.[111] It was true that when Mustafa Şekib Tunç translated this book into Turkish in 1936, Ağaoğlu read the preface of Tunç's translation, then wrote a short article about the book which reveals that Bergson's division of the inner and outer selves of the individual, one representing the will (inner self) and the other, reason (outer self), captured his interest. In his *Ben Neyim? (What am I?)*,[112] perhaps inspired by this notion of the divided self, he attempts to provide an account of the struggles between the inner and outer selves of the individual. Although Bergson's influence on Ağaoğlu was limited to this shallow inspiration, it has been argued that Ağaoğlu's notions of inner and outer selves also represented the will and reason of an individual,[113] whereas what Ağaoğlu actually meant was different. As is shown in Chapter 9, while the inner self in Ağaoğlu's work stood for the individual's realm of thoughts and sentiments (*söz alemi*),

109   Ibid.
110   Coşar, "Türk Liberalizminin Açmazlarına Giriş," p. 168.
111   Nazmi İrem, "Turkish Conservative Modernism: Birth of a Nationalist Quest for Cultural Renewal," *International Journal of Middle Eastern Studies*, vol. 34, 2002, pp. 87–112.
112   Ahmet Ağaoğlu, *Ben Neyim?* Istanbul: Ağaoğlu Yayınevi, 1939.
113   Kadıoğlu, "Citizenship and Individuation in Turkey," p. 209.

the outer self referred to his realm of action (*iş alemi*). Moreover, there is no evidence that Ağaoğlu ever read any of Bergson's books. Although in his various studies in the 1920s and '30s he at times cited and often mentioned the books of various Western European thinkers that he had read, and from which he drew his ideas, none of Bergson's works received mention. Therefore, the argument that Ağaoğlu turned to the teachings of Bergson in his later work and became a Bergsonian seems misleading.[114] One may well argue here that the absence of evidence is not necessarily the evidence of absence. But existing studies which argue the existence of such an influence take it almost for granted, pointing out nothing more than Ağaoğlu's use of the concepts of inner and outer selves, which carried different connotations from those of Bergson, and his notion of dialectical evolution (with the belief that he borrowed it from *L'évolution créatrice*), which was essentially a reflection of his readings on historical materialism, Hegelian dialectics and Renanian conception of history in his early youth.[115]

Moreover, with the exception of Shissler's book, all existing studies have been inclined to approach Ağaoğlu's liberalism with a conceptual and inherently static form of analysis. Few have paid close attention to the evolution in his ideas and to the fact that the subject matter of their study, Ağaoğlu, was also an evolving being: there were different Ağaoğlus and likewise different nationalisms and liberalisms of Ağaoğlu at distinct times (which is not to say that there were no constants in his thought). This is precisely why repeated emphasis has been made of the fact that one of the major objectives of the present study is to display the thinker's intellectual evolution. The dynamic relationship between his inner convictions and outer conditions is of importance for both the contextualist and intellectualist purposes of this book.

The study combines four types of narrative. First, at an immediate level, it offers an analysis of Ağaoğlu's liberal thought, seeking to uncover the main characteristics of his liberalism in connection with his Western European inspirers and with the immediate discursive environments and biographical events. In the context of the history of political thought, it examines the relationship between nationalism and liberalism in Turkey and seeks to address the ideological origins of the Republic. From the viewpoint of the sociology of ideas, it will highlight the two-way transformation of migrant ideas and host contexts, and the roles played by intellectuals in conveying ideas. Finally, from a historical perspective, it narrates a brief political and economic history of the Caucasus region of the Russian Empire, late Ottoman Empire and the Republic of Turkey, with a focus on the multiple roles played by Turkish intellectuals in

---

114   İrem, "Turkish Conservative Modernism".
115   Ahmet Ağaoğlu, *İhtilal mi İnkılap mı?* Ankara: Alaeddin Kıral Basımevi, 1942.

these contexts in the late nineteenth and early twentieth centuries. These narratives are embodied in ten chapters, including this introduction and the conclusion.

The first two chapters following the introduction, and Chapter 5, are intended to provide the reader with biographical/contextual information. Chapter 2 considers Ağaoğlu's early family life and education (1869–1894), his encounter with the questions that became his lifetime quest, and the Russian and early French influences on his thought. The closing section of the chapter is devoted to his early French writings, which form the nucleus of Ağaoğlu's liberal and nationalist thought. Chapter 3 describes Ağaoğlu's life and activities in the Russian and Ottoman imperial contexts (1894–1919) and sketches their overall social, political and intellectual ambiances.

After these two mainly biographical chapters, Chapter 4 lays out Ağaoğlu's views on the relationship between Islam and liberalism and the question of women in the Islamic world; it examines his liberal account of Pan-Islamism and his Turkish nationalist ideas, giving an account of his early ideas up to the late 1910s.

Chapter 5 presents background information on the social, political and intellectual context in early Republican Turkey for a better understanding of the following four chapters, which approach Ağaoğlu's liberal value commitments, theory of history and social ontology from different angles. His Malta years, his role in the National Liberation Movement of Mustafa Kemal, his activities in the first years of the Republic and a detailed description of the Free Party era are investigated in this chapter, which also examines the last decade of Ağaoğlu's life and his activities as an independent writer in this decade.

The subject of Chapter 6 is Ağaoğlu's interpretation of the Kemalist Revolution from a liberal perspective, and his views of democracy, liberalism, and the question of women.

Chapter 7 aims to analyse Ağaoğlu's idea of a liberal social and political order and his theories of the state and the individual, and the Durkheimian and Gökalpian influences on his ideas. In the last section of the chapter, some light is shed on the economic thought of Ağaoğlu, with a focus on his views on étatism in the 1930s. It draws mainly on the discussions between the *Kadro* group and Ağaoğlu about the economic development policies of Turkey.

Chapter 8 assesses Ağaoğlu's idea of Westernisation. His late views on this issue are examined with a focus on his 'hidden dialogue' with Ziya Gökalp and in comparison to the opinions of Hilmi Ziya Ülken on the subject. The focus of the chapter is on how Ağaoğlu used the terms 'civilisation' and 'culture', in order to understand the philosophical basis of his notion of Westernisation within which he embedded his liberal thought. His later nationalist thought and its relationship with his project of Westernisation are also addressed in this chapter.

The last chapter before the conclusion, Chapter 9, examines the moral project of Ağaoğlu. Following a brief look at the Kropotkian influences on his thought, Ağaoğlu's attempt to lay the moral ideology of the Republic is explored, with a close reading of his later works, including *In the Land of Free Men*, a utopian novella, and *What am I?*, his swansong.

CHAPTER 2

Between Two Worlds: Ideas in the Making

At the age of sixty-seven Ahmet Ağaoğlu wrote in his memoirs that since his early youth he had been struck by the question of why there existed such huge differences between what he called the Eastern and Western ways of life. "When I grew up," he noted, "this question would also grow; it would expand its meaning and character; it would surrender [me] and, by becoming a pain..., it would poison my entire life."[1] Ağaoğlu's memoirs, the 1936 version, read as the story of a heart and a mind torn between what he calls the East and West. On the one hand, it offers us a fascinating reading of how a man lived his life seeking to understand his life's quest. On the other, it invites to us to be cautious. The reader of Ağaoğlu's memoirs, which were written at a time when he was deeply preoccupied with the issue of East-West differences, must be aware, as Hayek once speculated, that "the existence of an autobiography may be the cause of our knowing less about its subject."[2]

Fortunately, there are two different autobiographies of Ağaoğlu. The first one was written at an uncertain time in the 1910s and was never published. It covers his early youth through until his arrival in Istanbul and his first years there in the early 1910s.[3] It shows some stark contrasts with the second one published initially in *Kültür Haftası*[4] in 1936 and later in his son Samet's *Babamdan Hatıralar* (1940)[5] and which cover only the period from his birth to his trip to Paris in 1888. The 1910s version of his autobiography does not mention the question of the differences between East and West at all. Nor does it entirely match with the 1936 version of Ağaoğlu's life story.

Even though there is strong need to avoid, while reading autobiographies, the snares which the writer lays for posterity and his subjectivity, his or her

---

1 Ahmet Ağaoğlu, "Altmış Yedi Yıl Sonra," *Kültür Haftası*, No. 3–7, January 29 – February 26, 1936.
2 F.A. Hayek, *John Stuart Mill and Harriet Taylor: Their Friendship and Subsequent Marriage*, London: Routledge & Kegan Paul, 1951, p. 16; cf. H.S. Jones, *Intellect and Character in Victorian England: Mark Pattison and the Invention of the Don*, Cambridge: Cambridge University Press, 2007, p. 15.
3 Ağaoğlu Ə. Tərcümeyi-hali-acizanəm. AMEA-nın M. Füzuli adına Əlyazmalar İnstitutu, f.21; Yusuf Akçura's 1928 book covers Ağaoğlu's life mainly in reference to this early account, Yusuf Akçura, *Türk Yılı*, Istanbul: Yeni Matbaa, 1928.
4 Ahmet Ağaoğlu, "Altmış Yedi Yıl Sonra".
5 Samet Ağaoğlu, *Babamdan Hatıralar*, Ankara: Ağaoğlu Külliyatı, 1940.

own version of the story also needs to be respected.[6] This is because, as Jones underlines, "if a real confession is to be wrought from the author's testimony, the first step must be to listen to the story [she or] he wants to tell us."[7] This chapter aims to critically read the stories that Ağaoğlu wants to tell us about his early life. It will attempt to show Russian and early French influences on his thought, which helped him to form the nucleus of his later liberal ideas, before reviewing his early writings that appeared in French journals in the 1890s.

2.1   Family Life and Education

According to the 1910s version of his autobiography, Ağaoğlu was born in 1868 in Shusha, in Russian-controlled Azerbaijan with the family name Aghayef.[8] His family was originally from the Kurtlareli tribe, which had emigrated from Erzurum to Karabagh in the eighteenth century.[9] Their native tongue was Azerbaijani (a language of Turkic origin, but more ancient than standard Ottoman Turkish), but they could also speak Arabic and Persian.[10] A wealthy landowner family, they gained the nobility title of "bey" which, as Ağaoğlu notes, was officially recognised by the Russian authorities. Along with other major landowners, his family had been positively affected by Russian control in the region, gaining private ownership of lands that had once belonged to the khan.[11]

In the Caucasus, Muslim people of the time, no matter what their ethnic origins, identified themselves with the religion and culture of Islam. Ağaoğlu's

---

6   Ibid., p. 15.

7   Jones notes that "reading autobiographies critically is an everyday task for the historian, who has to address not only the fallibility of memory but also the desire of their subjects to present their own lives in the most favourable possible light and so to weave webs of myth in which later generations have become entangled," Ibid., pp. 15–16.

8   Ağaoğlu Ə. Tərcümeyi-hali-acizanəm. AMEA-nın M. Füzuli adına Əlyazmalar İnstitutu, f.21.

9   Akçura, *Türk Yılı*, p. 420.

10   Ibid., p. 420. This was due to the fact that Azerbaijan had been torn for a few centuries between different identities under the concomitant influences of Iran, Russia and the Ottoman Empire. The Persian language was highly predominant in the countryside and Azeri was limited to more intellectual parts of the population in urbanized zones; for more detail see, Charles van der Leeuw, *Azerbaijan: A Quest for Identity, A Short History*, Surrey: Curzon Press, 2000.

11   Serge A. Zenkovsky, *Pan-Turkism and Islam in Russia*, Cambridge; Massachusets: Harvard University Press, 1960, p. 9. For more detailed information, see Shissler, *Between Two Empires*, pp. 58–59.

family was a patriarchal Shi'ite family. As he himself notes, if someone were to ask his father, Mirza Hasan, "Who are you?" he would say he was "of the community of Blessed Mohammed", a follower of Ali and son of Mirza İbrahim from Kurtlareli, but he would never think or say that he was a Turk.[12]

Both his maternal and paternal sides were well educated and respected in Shusha. Mirza Hasan (Agayef) was a literate man, but he had no interest in contemporary political developments (Russian domination) in the region.[13] Ağaoğlu's mother Taze Hanım was an ambitious woman who, along with Hajji Mirza Mehmet (Ağaoğlu's elder uncle and the head of the family), was responsible for Ağaoğlu's care and education. Ağaoğlu identifies his mother as the person who "changed the direction of his life, placing him at the very centre of two different worlds and into a life of dilemmas."[14] This was because Taze Hanım entered a hidden struggle with Mirza Mehmet over his education, which Ağaoğlu reflects as a first turning point in his life.[15]

Mirza Mehmet was responsible for approximately fifty people who formed the family household. He was a zealous Muslim, knew Arabic and Persian very well and had studied Shari'a in depth. He regularly organised meetings at his house, where theological and metaphysical issues were discussed by the local ulema. Ağaoğlu sometimes attended these gatherings, but he found it difficult to understand "the erudite and obscure Turkish spoken in these discussions."[16] While he longed to become like the religious scholars who attended these meetings, Mirza Mehmet envisioned his future as taking place in Iran, where he would study to become a mujtahid.[17] In pursuit of this goal, when Ağaoğlu was six, he began to receive private Arabic and Persian lessons from an ahund (Islamic teacher). He was later enrolled in the local madrasa (mosque school), where he was taught in Persian and Turkish, while continuing Arabic lessons.[18] Thus, his educational life began according to his uncle's expectations.

However, Ağaoğlu's mother was discontented with the type of education he was receiving and was unhappy with the boy's future as envisioned by the uncle. Taze Hanım despised the ahunds' lifestyle, but not because she was secular. Rather, as Ağaoğlu notes, she was a religious woman, but her pursuit of religion

---

12   Ağaoğlu, "Altmış Yedi Yıl Sonra," in *Babamdan Hatıralar*, ed. Samet Ağaoğlu, p. 64; Shissler, p. 44.

13   Ibid., p. 64.

14   Ibid., p. 67.

15   Ibid., p. 67.

16   Ibid., p. 46.

17   Samet Ağaoğlu, *Babamdan,* p. 65.

18   Akçura, *Türk Yılı,* p. 422; Shissler, *Between Two Empires,* p. 46.

"was fitting the pattern of the nomadic Turkic tribes. She wished to view God, the prophet and the clergy as lucid and crystal clear as the rivers and mountains she saw."[19] She felt that the 'weird' clothes of mullahs and ahunds were deceptive and detested any intermediary between God and the individual.[20]

Taze Hanım had a secret alternative plan for her son's education, different from that of the uncle.[21] This plan was inspired by the life of one of Taze Hanım's relatives who had served with the Russians in a war in Poland. After spending a few years abroad, her relative had returned to Karabagh with an impressive uniform and great local prestige. Thereafter, he would be called on by all the visiting dignitaries who came to town. Taze Hanım desired her son to be like him so that those people of Shusha who had problems to be solved would seek her hospitality to ask Ahmet's help. To this end, she secretly arranged Russian lessons for him when he was eight.[22]

When Ağaoğlu began receiving Russian lessons, a struggle over his education erupted between "the head of the family, the huge uncle Mirza Mehmed, and [the] small mother, Taze Hanım who could not even sit or unveil next to him."[23] Even after the fourth year Ağaoğlu was finding Arabic and Persian very difficult because the techniques of his Arabic and Persian teachers—as compared to those of his Russian teacher—were not facilitating his work.[24] Under pressure from Taze Hanım and the governor of Shusha, who believed that Ağaoğlu could be an example and encouragement to other Muslim families, Mirza Hasan agreed to enrol Ağaoğlu in a Russian gymnasium, when Mirza Mehmed went to Tiflis to receive treatment for his health.[25] Ağaoğlu thus began to receive a secular education in his early teens.

---

19   Ağaoğlu, "Altmış Yedi Yıl," p. 67.

20   Ibid., p. 67.

21   Ibid., p. 67.

22   Ibid., p. 68. Ağaoğlu Ə. Tərcümeyi-hali-acizanəm. AMEA-nın M. Füzuli adına Əlyazmalar İnstitutu, f.21.

23   Ibid., p. 67.

24   Ibid., p. 69. "It was the fourth year. I still hadn't managed to master Fuzuli's *Leyla and Mecnun*. When it came to *Gülistan* and *Bostan*, the teacher would still read out a segment each day, explain its meaning and then I would read it, sounding it out, after him... However, I mastered Russian writing in three months. I was already able to read any type of book which was put into my hands. Then too, those Russian books were so appealing; they were all diagrams and illustrations and oh so strange stories and tales...while the others were a bone dry set of things that rattled around in my brain. They didn't entice me at all." Ağaoğlu, "Altmış Yedi Yıl," p. 69, trans. Shissler, *Between Two Empires,* p. 46.

25   Mirza Mehmet would later agree to enrol Ağaoğlu in a Russian gymnasium and would take Ahmet to register for the school himself. However, in Ağaoğlu's 1910s autobiography,

2.1.1   *Encounter with Russian Radicalism*

Ağaoğlu first studied at the newly created Russian middle school, and two years later passed exams in French, history and geometry to enter Shusha's Russian Realschule. He then went to Tiflis to continue his education.[26] Having been able to compare the education offered in traditional ways in the madrasa[27] with the modern methods in Russian schools,[28] he was struck by the question of why there existed such huge differences between the two. This was, Ağaoğlu relates, when he began to question 'the Eastern or Islamic way of life' and what led in the 1880s, when still in his teens, to an extraordinary ferment of ideas and emotions in his mind and heart.[29] The new ideas he encountered during his education in Russian schools began to change his worldview and opened doors on foreign streams of thought he would probably never have noticed otherwise.

At school Ağaoğlu became a member of the Russian progressive youth,[30] while at home he saw, and over time became alienated from, the traditional life of his family. This dichotomy in his life resulted mainly from his contact with radicalism in Russian schools through his teachers, who were conduits for the ideas of the Russian intelligentsia and who, according to Ağaoğlu, were carrying intellectual trends and revolutionary ideas to Karabagh.[31]

Although there is insufficient evidence to be certain, his teachers were most probably followers of the Narodnik or 'going to the people' campaign, which sent young people "to settle in villages to work as doctors, teachers, or artisans and to do the work of revolutionary propaganda by making the message relevant to the lives of the people."[32] His fascination with the Russian revolutionary movement, which found its roots in radicalism, made him receptive to the ideas of Russian radicals.[33]

---

he writes that his father enrolled him Russian schools, seeing that he was more successful in learning Russian, without mentioning the struggle between Taze Hanım and the uncle.

26   Vilayet Quliyev, Foreword to *Ahmed Bey Ağaoğlu: Seçme Eserleri*, Baku: Şarq-Garp, 2007, p. 5.
27   Akçura, *Türk Yılı*, p. 422; Shissler, *Between Two Empires*, p. 46.
28   Samet Ağaoğlu, *Babamdan Hatıralar*, p. 71.
29   Ibid., p. 71.
30   Judith E. Zimmerman, "The Uses and Misuses of Tsarist Educational Policy," *History of Education Quarterly*, vol. 16, No. 4 (Winter 1976), pp. 487–494.
31   Scott J. Seregny, "Russian Teachers and Peasant Revolution, 1895–1917," in *Modernisation and Revolution: Dilemmas of Progress in Late Imperial Russia*, eds Edward H. Judge and James Y. Simms, New York: East European Monographs, 1992, pp. 59–67; Ağaoğlu, "Altmış Yedi Yıl," p. 73; trans. Shissler, *Between Two Empires*, pp. 52–53.
32   Shissler, *Between Two Empires*, p. 55.
33   Ağaoğlu, "Altmış Yedi Yıl," pp. 73–74.

In the second half of the century, the revolutionary democratic movement or radicalism, a strand of the Russian Westerner movement, had dominated Russian intellectual life. Given the appellation of nihilism by Ivan Turgenev in his *Fathers and Sons*, Russian radicalism at the time was defined, in Kotlyarevski's words, as "a complete rejection of all the previously dominant views regarding the abstract fundamentals of life and an attempt to replace these views by a new outlook based upon a materialist and utilitarian interpretation of all the problems of life and the spirit."[34] It had become popular among the young generation with the dissatisfaction with the emancipation of the peasants.[35]

Even though the new Russian radicals' views had varied, with respect either to the periods in which they had lived or to their social origins, their outlook had usually seemed to be a mixture of nihilism and utopianism with a positivist and materialist tendency.[36] Captivated by the European revolutions of 1848 and maybe more by the French Revolution of 1789, they had simultaneously rejected "sentimental romanticism for hard-headed realism [and] the status quo, ...and displayed an unparalleled capacity for faith in various fantastic formulae for the individual or collective salvation of humanity."[37] Since the nihilists were aware that they would not be able to overthrow autocracy alone, in the late 1870s they had developed the idea of 'going among the people'.[38]

The chief representative of the radical/nihilist strand of Westernism in Russia was Nikolai Gavrilovich Chernyshevskii (1828–1889). His banned novel *Chto Delat?* (*What is to be Done?*) of 1863, a powerful source of inspiration for several generations of progressive Russian youth, reached the hands of Ağaoğlu in his high school years by means of his teachers.[39] A major figure of women's emancipation in nineteenth century Russia, Chernyshevskii paid particular attention to the question of women in Russian society in this novel.[40]

---

34   Nestor Kotlyarevski, *Kanun osvobozhderiya*, Petergrad, 1916, VIII, cf. Frederick C. Banghorn, "D.I. Pisarev: A Representative of Russian Nihilism," in *The Review of Politics*, vol. 10, No. 2 (April 1948), pp. 190–211.

35   Sergei K. Stepniak, *Nihilism As it is*, London: T. Fisher Unwin Paternoster Square, 1895, p. 15.

36   Daniel R. Brower, "Fathers, Sons and Grandfathers: Social Origins of Radical Intellectuals in the Nineteenth Century in Russia," *Journal of Social History*, vol. 2, No. 4 (Summer 1969), pp. 333–355, p. 342.

37   Banghorn, "D.I. Pisarev," p. 193.

38   Stepniak, *Nihilists*, p. 17.

39   Ağaoğlu, "Altmış Yedi Yıl," p. 74

40   Andrew M. Drozd, *Chernishevskii's What Is to Be Done?: A Reevaluation*, Evanston, Illinois: Northwestern University Press, 2001, p. 80.

Drozd writes that "many young men and women consciously began to model their lives on the main characters of the [novel]."[41] Under its influence, fictitious marriages blossomed as they were "stages so that young women could escape an oppressive familial home or seek higher education."

At about the same time Ağaoğlu read *Chto Delat?*, he became tutor to an Armenian girl in Tiflis, to whom he taught mathematics, in return receiving advanced Russian lessons from her. This first-hand contact with a non-Muslim female student, he writes in his 1936 memoirs, led him to pour scorn on his female relatives in Shusha, who spent all their lives, in his words, "reading and memorizing the Qur'an and learning virtually nothing."[42] The novel and the importance devoted to the women's question by its author, and his experience in a non-Muslim environment in Tiflis were perhaps what for the first time in his life made him think consciously of the situation of women in the Islamic world.

One must also note that Russian nihilists combined in their ethics an individualism seeking "the removal of all shackles on the natural rights of individual human development—but not individualism in the sense of setting up any sharp opposition between society and the individual—and a socialist tendency emphasizing the necessity of distributing among all mankind the blessings hitherto enjoyed only by the privileged."[43] There was a congruency between their ethics and their social doctrine born of a hatred for the alleged perpetration of exploitation by the Russian autocracy and aristocracy or by the Western bourgeoisie.

In his school years, Ağaoğlu also read pamphlets on historical materialism and encountered at the time the ideas of the predecessors of the new Russian radicals, namely, the 'men of the 1840s', a group to which Bakunin, Herzen, Turgenev and Belinski, despite their many differences, all belonged.[44] Their influence on Ağaoğlu's thought is rather difficult to demonstrate, because Ağaoğlu hardly cited these thinkers in his work, but only spoke of the fact, in his 1936 memoirs, that he was fascinated and inspired by his contact with their artefacts.

At that time Russian illuminati were inspired by the idealists, especially [figures] like Tolstoy, Dostoyevsky, and Turgenev. They were implacable enemies of the crown, of autocracy, of cruelty and force, of religious zeal

41   Ibid., p. 10.
42   Ibid., p. 81.
43   Banghorn, "D.I. Pisarev," p. 192.
44   Ağaoğlu, "Altmış Yedi Yıl," p. 74.

and ignorance. Despite all the vigilance and all the efforts of a tyrannical Tsar like Alexander III, these teachers found a way to inculcate in the students a love of learning, culture, beauty and freedom. They showed their students how to gain education and maturity on their own.[45]

Ağaoğlu's memoirs suggest that he had access to the works of both the men of the forties and the men of the sixties (or later Russian radicals, known as nihilists), yet it is hard to prove whether the idealist motifs in his later writings and his appeal to liberal constitutionalism were derived from the influences of the men of the forties, who admired constitutional Western liberalism and Hegelian idealism (as seen in Turgenev). He states in his memoirs that his contact with the works and activities of the Narodniks led to his eventual estrangement from the patriarchal society to which he belonged.[46]

When Ağaoğlu went to Tiflis to pursue the final year of his high school education, he was frequently invited to join the meetings of a branch of the Narodnik society. The clandestinely delivered speeches of the revolutionary spokesmen shook him spiritually and intellectually and led him to see how very different the two worlds, East and West, were.[47] He tells us that he never forgot one of the revolutionary propagandists' speech and enthusiasm to help the Russian people solve their problems (of distress and suffering, autocracy, corruption of governors, ruthlessness of landowners) at the first meeting of the society he attended.[48]

After being awarded his diploma in Tiflis in 1887, Ağaoğlu returned to Shusha to spend his last summer with his parents. His success in Tiflis was rewarded with a grant which procured him the chance to pursue his higher education in St. Petersburg. Now feeling alien to what he called the Eastern way of life, he decided to leave Azerbaijan. In August of 1887, imbued with radical views, he set off for St. Petersburg to pursue his university education. Ağaoğlu notes his feelings during his departure from Shusha as follows:

> Now we were descending a great mountain. With every turn of the wheels I was growing a little more distant from these lands where I was born and raised, from the people who had given me life and breath. I was growing more distant not only physically but spiritually. But to draw near to whom? To what? It is as unclear on this day as it was on that... I was to

---

45   Akçura, *Türk Yılı*, pp. 422–423, trans. by Shissler, *Between Two Empires*, p. 54.

46   Ağaoğlu, "Altmış Yedi Yıl," p. 74.

47   Ibid., pp. 79–80.

48   Ibid., pp. 80–81.

lose the wholeness with which history and nature had endowed me. But I was not to acquire a new wholeness.[49]

At nineteen, Ağaoğlu arrived in St. Petersburg to study at the Polytechnic Institute. There he found the opportunity to pursue the student life he had dreamed of while reading the novels of Turgenev and Dostoyevsky in his teens. He also met Hüseyinzade Ali (1864–1941) and Ali Merdan Topçubaşı (1865–1934) who were also students there at the time. As will be shown in the following chapter, the three would form a new generation of intelligentsia in Azerbaijan in the late 1890s to defend the rights of Azerbaijanis against the Tsarist government. In St. Petersburg Ağaoğlu occasionally participated in the activities of the Revolutionary People's Party through the introduction of a fellow student. He was very happy and impressed by the charms of the city, particularly by Nevsky Prospekt, which he had taken to be a centre of intellectual activity 'in his Oriental fantasies'.[50] However, he found himself having to leave St. Petersburg in a few months. According to his three different accounts, he left either because he failed a trigonometry exam and started to cry in the middle of the class belittling and humiliating himself in front of his teacher and classmates and wanted to go away next day[51] or because he could not get used to the new climate and had health problems[52] or because one of his teachers, an anti-Semite, mistaking Ağaoğlu for a Jew, deliberately made him fail his exam and so forced him to leave the school.[53] In either case, his new destination became Paris.

2.1.2   Paris

Ağaoğlu arrived in Paris on January of 1888 with enthusiasm, conscious that he was going to live in the city where the Great Revolution had taken place. The first Muslim student to come to Paris from the Caucasus,[54] he stayed in France for six years. In the beginning, he could speak virtually no French and was seriously short of money. Because he wanted to spend as little as possible, during his first few months in Paris he only studied French on his own (by reading and

---

49   Ibid., p. 89, trans. Shissler, *Between Two Empires,* p. 44.

50   A. Agaev, "Vospominanija o Peterburge," *Kaspii,* March 14, 1903.

51   Ibid.

52   Ağaoğlu Ə., Tərcümeyi-hali-acizanəm. AMEA-nın M.Füzuli adına Əlyazmalar İnstitutu, f.21.

53   Ağaoğlu, "Altmış Yedi Yıl," p. 90.

54   Ibid., p. 103.

taking notes from Musset's novels) while awaiting a supply of money from his parents.

After May 1888, when Ağaoğlu finally received financial support from his family, he started to consider his educational prospects and decided first to attend a public lecture delivered at the Collège de France. The lecture, on Zendavesta and Shahname, was by James Darmesteter (1849–1894), whose discussion on the origins, development and significance of the word *gül* (rose) impressed him. Shortly thereafter, Darmesteter became his mentor.[55]

Living in one of the West's major cities, at the heart of a civilisation he admired, Ağaoğlu studied Oriental languages at the Ecoles des Langues Orientales and attended classes at the Collège de France.[56] He took classes from Barbier de Maynard and Darmesteter and concentrated in his studies on Persian history, culture and religion. Through Darmesteter, Ağaoğlu was introduced to the famous philosopher Ernest Renan (1823–1892) and to Madame Juliette Adam (1836–1936),[57] a powerful figure in the intellectual circles of Paris and the editor of *La Nouvelle Revue*.[58] Through these connections he was able to meet such prominent French intellectuals as Hyppolite Taine (1828–93), Gaston Paris (1839–1903) and Jules Lemaître (1853–1914), and embarked upon a writing career, his essays appearing regularly in *La Nouvelle Revue* between 1891 and 1893. During his stay in France, he also contributed to *La revue bleue* and to *Le Journal des Débats*. Moreover, in 1892, he went to Britain to deliver a speech about his studies at the Ninth International Orientalist Congress

---

55   Ibid., p. 122.
56   Georgeon, "Les Débuts,", p. 376.
57   Renan introduced Ağaoğlu to Juliette Adam with the following letter:
     "Will you permit me to introduce you for *La Nouvelle Revue*, Mr. Ahmed Bey Agheff, a young Persian of great worth who is studying in our program and who has been recommended to me by Mr. James Darmesteter? I believe that Mr. Agheff could furnish you with very interesting studies about his country. He knows it extremely well and Mr. Darmesteter tells me that his French style won't require more than slight work to become remarkable for its originality. Let me add, dear Madame, the expression of my best wishes. E. Renan," cf. Shissler, *Between Two Empires*, p. 77.
58   Madam Adam's *La Nouvelle Revue* was a bi-monthly journal founded in 1879. It encouraged young writers to publish and accepted articles from various young scholars with the aim of bringing fresher approaches to contemporary political issues in the world. For more detailed information on the journal, see Marie-France Hilgar, "Juliette Adam et la Nouvelle Revue," *Rocky Mountain Review of Language and Literature,* vol. 51, no. 2, 1997, pp. 11–18.

in London.[59] He also met in Paris the leading figures of the Young Turk movement, Ahmet Rıza, Dr. Nazım (1870–1926) and Esat Paşa (1862–1952).[60]

Especially with Ahmet Rıza he regularly discussed the social and political problems of the Muslim world and formed a good friendship.[61] The two met in 1889 when G. Ferrari's magazine *Le revue bleue* got his critical article on the newly emergent major work of Lord Curzon published with a preface by Ferrari. After reading this article, Ahmet Rıza came to meet Ağaoğlu. The former, in exile and fighting against the despotism of Sultan Abdulhamid II as a Young Turk leader, was suffering, Ağaoğlu notes, great hardships and difficulties at the time. He was far distant from the present of his world but devoted to his cause. "From the first meeting, we had differing tastes, trends and ideas." Ahmet Rıza was a positivist. It would take Ağaoğlu about three decades to embrace the ideas of Durkheim who gave a new direction to the teachings of the positivistic school. The Azerbaijani moved in the professorial environment, while Ahmet Rıza remained active in the realm of politics.[62] Even though Ağaoğlu did not share Ahmet Rıza's positivistic scientist views at the time, he writes that he was impressed by the latter's optimistic belief in the awakening of the East and its liberation from the West.[63]

In France, confronted, perhaps for the first time in his life, with the question of his nationality, Ağaoğlu introduced himself as a Persian. According to Shissler, there are two possible explanations for this:

> [T]he first is that as a Shi'ite from the Caucasus he came from a strongly Persian cultural milieu with which he identified; the second is that as a Middle Easterner, moving in academic circles in a Western capital in the late nineteenth century, he saw some value in identifying himself with an 'Aryan' nationality.[64]

Also, since his mentor at the Collège was an expert in Persian studies, he may have thought that emphasizing his Persian identity would increase Darmesteter's interest in his academic studies. Shissler underlines that in

---

59   Ahmed-Bey Agaeff, "Les Croyances mazdéennes dans la religion chiîte," in *Transactions of the Ninth International Congress of Orientalists, vol. 2*, ed. Delmar Morgan, London: Kraus Reprints, 1893, pp. 505–515.

60   Ağaoğlu Ə. Tərcümeyi-hali-acizanəm. AMEA-nın Mgggg adına Əlyazmalar İnstitutu, f.21, Süreyya Ağaoğlu, *Bir Ömür*, p. 7.

61   Ahmed-bek Agaev, "Tureckij parlament i Ahmed Rza-bek," *Vestnik Baku*, 21 December 1908.

62   Ibid.

63   Ibid.

64   Shissler, *Between Two Empires*, p. 82.

Akçura's account of Ağaoğlu's Paris sojourn, "Ağaoğlu comments that when he heard Darmesteter's lecture on the history and development of Persian language and poetry, he was blown over and amazed by the depth and quality of the scholarship and immediately wondered if work of this kind existed for Turkish."[65] It is, therefore, uncertain whether Ağaoğlu genuinely regarded himself as a Persian at the time or if he later reconstructed his past, as he apparently did in some other cases, with a Turkish identity, denying the years when he had embraced Persian identity. According to Georgeon, during his stay in Europe between 1888 and 1894, he identified himself interchangeably as Muslim, Shi'ite, and Persian but not as a Turk.[66]

2.2   Early French Influences

Ağaoğlu's encounter with eminent French figures, the social and political ideas of his immediate teachers Darmesteter and Renan, their methods, and the Western way of life he observed during his French sojourn all affected his early thoughts and left lasting marks on him. The six years that he spent in Paris (1888–1894) coincided with a period of political struggle and disputes that centred on the type of regime and the constitution. These dominated the foreground of public life in the Third Republic. The defeat of the French at the hands of the Prussians in 1870 had caused a deep wound in the psyche of many Frenchmen and led to a strong sense of humiliation, to nationalism and to the fear that some deep moral weakness had brought them to failure. Numerous intellectuals, including Darmesteter and Renan, had tried to explain the defeat of France by the superiority of German scientists over their French counterparts and stressed that it was only the savant that should initiate an enterprise to resolve the problems of France.[67] Moreover, according to Lehning, in French Third Republican thought, all strands of republicanism accepted the essentials of political liberalism.[68] There was a compromise among the republicans and the liberals over the rights of citizens, over "a wide or universal suffrage, and parliamentary government through a ministry responsible to the legislature."[69]

---

65   Ibid., p. 83.
66   François Georgeon, "Les Débuts," p. 377.
67   James Lehning, *To be a citizen: The Political Culture of the Early French Republic,* Ithaca, London: Cornell University Press, 2001, p. 2.
68   Ibid., p. 5.
69   Paul Farmer, *France Reviews Its Revolutionary Origins: Social Politics and Historical Opinions in the Third Republic,* New York: Octagon Books, 1973, p. 25.

But this was complemented by the rejection of the right of the lower classes to dominate politics.

During the centenary of the French Revolution, which was celebrated with an international exhibition and the building of the Eiffel Tower in 1889, Ağaoğlu was in Paris, fascinated by his observations. In the same year, when the Iranian Shah Nasr'eddin visited France for the Universal Exhibition, as he tells us, he found the opportunity to observe closely this incident, which he recalls as the juxtaposition of one leader who represents despotism with another (the President of France) who represents a free nation.[70] The humble, smart and plain suit of the French President and his modest behaviour compared favourably with the imposing jewellery and dress of the Shah of Iran, whose arrogant attitude toward his subjects convinced Ağaoğlu of the superiority of the Western way of life.[71] Influenced by his readings and experiences, he began to form a clearer opinion of the differences between two worlds, that which he came from and that in which he was now living.

2.2.1   *James Darmesteter and Ernest Renan*

For his early writings Ağaoğlu found inspiration as much in the ideas and teachings of his teachers as in his everyday observations. Darmesteter and Renan were two of the most prominent Orientalists in France in the late nineteenth century. When Darmesteter succeeded Renan as secretary of the Societe Asiatique in 1882, he was thirty-three years old.[72] In the next twelve years through until his death in 1894, he produced a vast literature in Hellenic studies, the history of Judaism, Perso-Indian culture and methodologies of Orientalism.[73] Unlike Renan, he was not a public political figure in the Third Republic. He owed his fame as an eminent Orientalist to the painstaking research and analysis he undertook throughout his career, which Muller once described as 'primus inter pares' in the rich Orientalist tradition in France.[74]

Darmesteter excelled and interested himself in a wide range of other issues also. A critic and exponent of modern life and literature, he published a volume of essays on English literature, of Afghan songs and of original poems.[75]

---

70   Akçura, *Türk Yılı*, p. 424.

71   Ibid.

72   Salomon Reinach, *James Darmesteter*, Paris: Les cahiers d"etudes juives, 1932, p. 18.

73   Josephine Lazarus, "Book Review: Selected Essays of James Darmesteter," *International Journal of Ethics*, vol. 6, no. 2 (Jan., 1896), pp. 261–264.

74   Gaston Paris, *Penseurs et Poetes: James Darmesteter, Frederic Mistral, Sully Prudhomme, Alexandre Bida, Ernest Renan, Albert Sorel*, Paris: Ancienne Maison Michel Levy Freres, 1896, p. 2.

75   Darmesteter was a sincere admirer of the British culture, Reinach, p. 17.

Simultaneously, he translated the poems of the English poet, Mary Robinson, his wife to be, who had also written criticism and history, including a detailed biography of Ernest Renan.[76] Darmesteter's most famous work was the French translation of the traditional interpretative commentary of the sacred texts of Zoroastrianism, the Avesta (Zend Avesta). He went to Bombay in 1887 in order to study Oriental languages and collected a large amount of material. His original methods in Oriental studies led him to dominate the field with his more modern approach.

Believing that philological methods at the time had certain shortcomings, aside from rigorously applying all the tools of nineteenth-century historical linguistics, Darmesteter tried to "introduce the careful assessment of historical information and local tradition, of cultural context...to his analyses."[77] He attempted to "trace a history of mentalities, to bring all kinds of evidence to bear on a text or problem in order to really reveal something about how people in a given time and place thought about something and how those ideas evolved over time," and employed a step-by-step approach. Ağaoğlu's writings showed that the latter employed similar methods in understanding social phenomena. He discussed social and political problems through a detailed historical analysis of their development, citing a large corpus of literature, which was "an Ağaoğlu trademark."[78]

Where politics were concerned, Darmesteter was a patriotic, extolling the France of all time, but especially the French Revolution of 1789. As I shall discuss below, Renan stood as a more anti-revolutionary figure, while Paris notes that Darmesteter saw the revolution and its ideals as highest and purest.[79] According to his account, Jews had seen the revolution as a means for their emancipation and dignity bringing justice and peace. While condemning its horror crimes and extravagances, Darmesteter recognized it as an almost divine character.[80]

In a similar vein to Renan, Darmesteter believed in the existence of a national mentality as a product of historico-cultural processes.[81] And just as Renan, he attributed a great role to heroic figures in the formation of the souls of the nations, tying a version of romantic individualism with patriotism.[82] This was

---

76   Mary Robinson Darmesteter, *The Life of Ernest Renan*, London: Methuen & Co., 1898.

77   Shissler, *Between Two Empires*, p. 79.

78   Ibid., p. 80.

79   Paris, *Penseurs et Poets*, p. 44.

80   Ibid., p. 44.

81   Shissler, 79.

82   James Darmesteter, *Critique et politique*, Paris : Ancienne Maison Mchel Levy Freres, 1895, pp. viii–ix.

most obvious when he published, under the influence of the defeat in the Franco-Prussian War, a textbook of patriotic readings for schoolchildren under the pseudonym of J.D. Lefrançais. The book contained stories about heroic French figures.[83] He teamed up with the cult of Jeanne d'Arc, who was perhaps the first sublime revelation of the consciousness of the people of France, and with the French Revolution, "one of the two major things that ever happened on earth."[84] As I shall demonstrate, the cult of heroic figures (especially Jeanne d'Arc) or romantic individualism and the defining role of the French Revolution in Western history would loom large in Ağaoğlu's writings also.

In an 1893 address at the Societe Asiatique, one year after Ernest Renan passed away, Darmesteter would say that as a philosopher Renan left a set of ideas from which he did not care to gather a body of doctrine, and yet which formed a coherent whole.[85] The difficulty of tracing Renan's intellectual influence on Ağaoğlu stems partially from this. Also the latter ceased citing the works of his teacher in his later work. Even then, there are noticeable overlaps of thought patterns as far as their romantic individualism, their accentuation of the role of the individual for social progress, and, to a certain extent, their conceptions of nation and their theories of history were concerned. That being said, there will be an inevitable degree of speculation in speaking of such influences, which is why the following paragraphs should perhaps be read as outlining the parallels (and differences) between the writings of the two.

Renan was one of the most renowned and controversial figures of nineteenth-century France. He was a social radical who tried to stay aloof from contemporary politics, but at the same time heavily influenced it.[86] As Jones argues, he became one of the most important figures of a certain kind of liberal tradition in the Third Republic, which attempted to transcend the tensions between constitutionalism and republicanism.[87] Renan renounced 'the cult of the [French] Revolution' arguing that its "materialistic conception of property, its contempt for personal rights, its attention to the individual only," and its taking "the individual as a being unconnected with yesterday or tomorrow and without any moral ties"[88] were vital considerations. Yet his *Vie de Jésus* of 1863

---

83   J.D. Lefrançais, *Lectures Patriotique sur l'histoire de France A l'usage des écoles primaires*, Paris: Librairie Ch. Delagrave, 1882.

84   Paris, p. 44.

85   Darmesteter, *Critique et politique*, pp. 70–71.

86   Gary Shapiro, "Nietzsche contra Renan," *History and Theory*, vol. 21, No.2, (May, 1982), pp. 193–222.

87   H.S. Jones, "French Liberalism and the Legacy of the French Revolution," p. 194.

88   Ibid., p. 198.

had made him a high priest of the dominant creed which suggested that science was the mighty ally of the Republic, because both were rational and both accentuated equality and worked for development.[89]

The fundamental guiding principle of Renan's intellectual activity was to grasp the present by way of the past, particularly the ancient past.[90] Lenoir tells us that his theory of history was based on the Hegelian belief that "there is in history a spontaneous tendency and a vital force."[91] This conception of history drew upon Herder's theory of spontaneous generation, which Renan believed, was a near true, but still vague, approach to the philosophy. Discussing that history was seen by Bousset as a specific plan designed and directed by a superior force of man, by Montesquieu as a sequence of events and causes, and by Vico as a movement almost lifeless and without reason, he noted:

> Ce sera l'histoire d'un être, se développant par sa force intime, se crevant et arrivant par des degrés divers a la pleine possession de lui-même. Sans doute il y a mouvement, comme le voulait Vico; sans doute il y a des causes, comme le voulait Montesquieu; sans doute il y a un plan impose, comme le voulait Bossuet. Mais ce qu'ils n'avaient pas aperçu, c'est la force active et vivante, qui produit ce mouvement, qui anime ces causes, et qui, sans aucune coaction extérieure, par sa seule tendance au parfait, accomplit le plan providentiel. Autonomie parfaite, création intime, vie en un mot: telle est la loi de l'humanité.[92]

As I shall demonstrate, Ağaoğlu's reading of history would be based on a similar approach drawing upon spontaneous tendency and Hegelian dialectics.

Another fundamental aspect of Renan's thought was that he defended an elitist and heroic strand of individualism accentuating the divinity within oneself. He was a positivist, but like many of his contemporaries the outlook of his positivism was deeply coloured by romanticism.[93] That is, he conceptualized science as stemming not from Comte's work, but from a type of pantheism that emphasized self-development as a means of realizing God within oneself.[94]

---

89   Ibid., p. 386.

90   Raymond Lenoir, "Renan and the Study of Humanity," *The American Journal of Sociology*, vol. 31, no. 3 (Nov., 1925), pp. 289–317.

91   Ibid., p. 294.

92   Ernest Renan, *L'Avenir de science pensees*, 173.

93   Alan Pitt, "The Cultural Impact of Science in France: Ernest Renan and *Vie de Jésus*," *The Historical Journal*, Vol. 43, No. 1, (Mar. 2000), pp. 79–101.

94   Chadbourne, *Ernest Renan*, p. 7; Mariette Soman, *La formation philosophique d'Ernest Renan*, pp. 72–73.

Concerned with the rapid changes in society and the emergence of a new way of life (thanks to the rise of capitalism and industrialisation in France), he drew parallels between the lives of Christ and the savant (or himself) and imputed a special role to the latter, not merely as a pure scholar but also as a moralist.[95] By the moralist of the nineteenth century, however, he referred to a selfless researcher or a serious worker, self-developed in the widest sense. It was in the perfection and personality of the savant himself, Renan believed, that lay the identity of science, rather than in its subject matter. Realizing in their work something more important, something quasi-divine, it was the bravery and independence of the savants which made science appealing, not the fact that it represented enlightenment for all. That is, the romantic and heroic individualism accentuated in Renan's work had resulted fundamentally from a pantheistic view that represented a transitional philosophy between traditional views and modern secularism. This pantheist view revealed that divinity entered society "through the work of the creative individual, be it through the teachings of Christ or through the researches of the contemporary savant."[96]

For Renan, the only source of value in social matters was the fullest elevation of the individual's intellectual and spiritual faculties. "There will be no happiness until all are equal," he wrote, "but there will be no equality until all are perfect."[97] "The object of man is not to know, to feel, to imagine, but to be perfect, that is to say, to be a man in every sense of the word."[98] He believed that the model of perfection was given by mankind itself; the most perfect life was that which best represented all mankind; cultivated humanity was not only moral; it was also "clever, curious, poetic, passionate."[99]

In his eyes, the capital problem of the nineteenth century was to elevate and ennoble the people, and it was due as much to the intellectual and moral conditions of society as to political and economic regulations. Renan's main concern was the expansion of the limits of man's relationship with man, or, as he puts it, "the pursuit of perfection through criticism, disinterestedness and self-sacrifice,"[100]

> for man shall not live by bread alone…Disinterestedly to pursue truth, beauty and good, to realize science, art and morality—these are for him

---

95   Renan, *L'Avenir de Science*, p. 13.

96   Pitt, p. 97.

97   Lenoir, "Renan and the Study of Humanity," p. 303.

98   Renan, *L'Avenir de Science*, p. 12.

99   Ibid., p. 12.

100   Alaya, "Arnold and Renan," p. 551.

a need as imperious as that which impels him to satisfy his hunger and his thirst.[101]

On the issue of the spiritual satisfaction and elevation of the individual, Renan's views appear to display similarities with those of the Catholic social scientist Frédéric Le Play. Considering that religion satisfies the spiritual needs of people and reunites them by its superiority with their finite existence, Renan, like Le Play (whose teachings Sabahaddin Bey thoroughly studied), viewed religion as a tool that would enable the common man to resist the attractions of moral and social anarchy in the democratic world he saw coming. For him, religion should be a public entity to serve as a spiritual bond uniting men. However, unlike Le Play, he ardently defended the separation of Church and state, and there was an unequivocal anti-clericalism in his writings, but for efforts towards the public welfare to have a solid basis, he regarded a fundamentally religious implementation of the concept of human sympathy and solidarity as essential.[102] Moreover, Renan found Le Play's sociological methods insufficient, as he believed that Le Play could "only ever see workers: as if, in a great house, we only saw the servants. The purpose is not there."[103] Like most nineteenth century liberals, Renan feared mob rule.[104] In this context, the Turkish followers of the two French thinkers, Sabahaddin and, as will be demonstrated, Ağaoğlu, also had parallel views up to the late 1920s, especially with regard to the importance of the individual for social progress and the function of religion as a spiritual bond and progressive moral force.[105]

Before identifying or speculating on the intellectual links between Renan and Ağaoğlu, I shall also mention that, as a reluctant democrat, the former developed his own concept of nation as we most obstinately see in his famous address given at the Sorbonne in 1882 on the topic *Qu'est-ce qu'une Nation?* He asserted that a nation was "a soul, a spiritual principle."

> Two things, which in truth are but one, constitute this soul or spiritual principle. One lies in the past, one in the present. One is the possession in common of a rich legacy of memories; the other is present-day consent,

---

101   Lenoir, "Renan and the Study of Humanity," pp. 302–303.

102   Alaya, "Arnold and Renan," p. 568.

103   Ernest Renan, *Notes de la fin de sa vie,* Bibliothèque Nationale, NAF 14201, f. 79, cf. Pitt, "The Cultural Impact of Science in France," p. 99.

104   Dana Bierer, "Renan and His Interpreters: A Study in French Intellectual Warfare," *The Journal of Modern History,* vol. 25, no. 4 (December 1953), p. 384.

105   Sabahaddin, *Türkiye Nasıl Kurtarılabilir? Ve İzahlar,* p. 72.

the desire to live together, the will to perpetuate the value of the heritage that one has received in an undivided form...The nation, like the individual, is the culmination of a long past of endeavours, sacrifice, and devotion.[106]

Although Bierer argues that Renan's views were most unlikely to have introduced the racial theory and have endorsed the programme of Action Française,[107] Shissler shows the essentialist racial distinction he made between Aryans (the Indo-European race embracing the noble people of India, Persia, the Caucasus and all of Europe) and Semites (the people of the native populations of western and southern Asia below the Euphrates).[108] She maintains that, according to Renan, the Aryans or Indo-Europeans owned "almost all the great military, political and intellectual movements in the history of the world," while the Semitic race owned religious movements. The Indo-Europeans were too engaged with the world and its variety to come up with monotheism, while the Semitic race stripped divinity of its trappings and "without reflection or reasoning attain[ed] the purest religious form humanity has ever known."[109]

In Shissler's account, Renan argued that Semites were naturally intolerant, had never known "civilisation or an intermediate milieu between the complete anarchy of desert nomads and bloody and unmitigated despotism."[110] Indo-Europeans, on the other hand, possessed the traits of aristocracy, democracy and feudalism, discipline and military organisation; they had been the only "ones who [had] known liberty and who [had] accommodated the state and the independence of the individual at the same time."[111] The essentialist distinction between the Aryans and the Semites in Renan's work may have been an inspiration for Ağaoğlu's equally essentialist views on, as Shissler shows us, the characteristics of the Aryan Shi'ites. That being said, where Ağaoğlu's conception of the differences between Western and Eastern civilisations were

---

106   Ernest Renan, *What is a Nation?*, a Lecture delivered at Sorbonne University, March 11, 1882, pp. 906–907.

107   Bierer, "Renan and His Interpreters," p. 384.

108   Shissler, *Between Two Empires*, p. 88.

109   Renan, "Histoire du peuple d'Israël," in *Oeuvres complètes d'Ernest Renan*, vol. 6, ed. Henriette Psichari, Paris : Calmann-Lévy, 1947, pp. 86 ff; cf. Shissler, *Between Two Empires*, p. 88.

110   Renan, "De la part des peuples sémitiques dans l'histoire de la civilisation," in *Oeuvres complètes d'Ernest Renan*, vol. 2, ed. Henriette Psichari, Paris: Calmann-Lévy, 1947, p. 324; cf. Shissler, *Between Two Empires*, p. 89.

111   Renan, "Histoire du peuple d'Israël"; cf. Shissler, *Between Two Empires*, pp. 88–89.

concerned, as I shall demonstrate, one does not find a similar essentialism but instead an attempt to draw upon a developing theory of history.

Renan's concept of nationalism was not based on a racial doctrine of any sort. As he wrote elsewhere,

> The truth is that there is no pure race, and to base politics on ethno-graphic analysis means basing it on an illusion…In the beginning the racial factor has tremendous importance, but this gradually wanes, and sometimes, as in France, it disappears completely…I conceive the future will see a homogenous humanity in which all the native rivulets will coalesce into a great stream, and all memory of diverse origins will be lost.[112]

Renan was more of a civic nationalist, attaching greater importance to common history than to race and defining the nation as a plebiscite tous les jours, thus introducing a strong voluntary element into nationalism.

With regard to nationalism, Ağaoğlu, like Renan, attached greater importance to common history and culture than to race. However, Ağaoğlu's brand of early nationalism was akin to ethno-cultural nationalism. He eventually began to introduce into his nationalism civic features when he argued in the 1920s that further individual liberties would unite individuals together into a nation. Moreover, the type of liberalism Renan defended was only slightly congruent with Ağaoğlu's liberalism. In Renan's thought, there was an explicit defence of individualism against any imposition of state authority over the individual, whereas Ağaoğlu would turn to Durkheim and consider the state a moral agent which had to expand in parallel with the progress of its individuals and their more complex needs.[113] Renan's antagonism toward revolutions and his desire to end the French Revolution culminated in his taking the terms 'liberal' and 'revolutionary' as antonyms, whereas in Ağaoğlu's thinking, as will be demonstrated in Chapter 6, they were virtual synonyms.[114]

Despite this, from his early writings, Ağaoğlu's main tool of analysis, like that of Renan and Darmesteter, was to refer to history in understanding present problems. Like most other contemporary Turkish nationalists, Ağaoğlu would turn to the ancient past of the Turkic nations and seek to understand their real character, stripped from Islamic influences, by this means. His explanation of history tended to be more confined to Hegelian dialectical

---

112   Renan, *What is a nation?*, pp. 120–121.
113   For more detail, see Chapter 7.
114   Jones, "French Liberalism," p. 194.

determinism. It was perhaps also an echo of his reading of pamphlets on historical materialism during his contact with the Russian radicals together with
Renanian influences on his thought, but it ran through his entire intellectual
career.

The fullest elevation of the individual was likewise a central concern in
Ağaoğlu's thought. With his first writings, he would address the predicament of
the individual as the fundamental problem of Eastern societies. Again like
Renan, he not only sought the material elevation of individuals but also
stressed the development of their intellectual and spiritual faculties. In 1921, he
wrote:

> Society is composed of individuals. Individuals…have a heart and a mind
> as well as a stomach. They need to satisfy the needs of their hearts and
> minds as much as the needs of their stomachs. If we observe ourselves in
> isolation from our society…, we admit that our interests are related not
> only to materiality, but also to spirituality. Such spiritual values as honour
> and dignity sometimes give pain as much as the need for bread and water
> does, and we do everything to satisfy them; we even die.[115]

As will be demonstrated, a brand of heroic and selfless individualism would be
observed in his writings when he argued that the moral strength of modern
Western societies depended not on their religions but on the selfless and heroic
struggles of such individuals as Jeanne d'Arc and Galileo, whose life stories
heightened the moral awareness of entire civilisations. For the same reason, he
would attribute a special role to the intellectuals in the Turkish context in
instilling strong moral values into the hearts of individuals—another argument running throughout his intellectual career.

2.3   Early Writings

Ağaoğlu's early work was not a mere reflection of what he learned from the
Russian radicals, from Darmesteter or from Renan. There were deep motifs of
each, but his concerns were different. When he embarked upon his writing
career at the age of twenty with his essays appearing in *La Nouvelle Revue* and
eventually in *La Revue bleue* and *Le Journal des Débats*, his principal aims were
first to introduce the Muslim world in general and Persia in particular to the
French public, which had little knowledge of them, and second to find the

---

115   Ahmet Ağaoğlu, *İhtilâl mi, İnkılâp mı?*, p. 54.

means to strengthen his society.[116] The first objective is of importance in show-ing how he understood the Eastern world, or how he wanted Western nations to understand it, while it is in the second aim that we find the nucleus of his liberal thought.

The main subject of Ağaoğlu's French writings was Iran and Persian culture. While trying to attract public attention to the threats posed to Persia by British Imperialism, he intrinsically and systematically aimed to challenge the preju-dices against Islam and Iran that he witnessed in the salons of Paris[117] by offer-ing his own insider's perspective[118] and constructing "a Middle Eastern identity for himself that was not hopeless—that was capable of self-strengthening and advancement, that was capable of success within his adopted framework."[119]

Ağaoğlu portrayed Persian culture and society in his French writings as markedly different from those of other Muslim nations. There is no evidence that he had ever been to Iran, but his knowledge of its culture through his homeland was remarkable. As a matter of fact, he often spoke of the entire Islamic world in describing the state of Persian society and at times used the terms 'Persian' and 'Muslim' interchangeably, perhaps under the influence of Renan,[120] he pointed to Persians as constituting a unique nation in the Islamic world, because Shi'ism was the dominant religion there. For Ağaoğlu, Shi'ism, being a "religion à part, essentiellement nationale," led Persia to have a national soul (l'âme de la Perse) and a national expression serving to cement and unify its people against external threats. By 'external threats' Ağaoğlu meant the establishment of Russian and British domination of Iran and the activities of American Protestant missionaries based in Iran who published a journal in Persian (The Sunray).[121] But the national character of Persians, marked by

---

116 As Georgeon shows, in much of what he wrote about Persian society, particularly about the history and role of Shi'ism, Ağaoğlu directly followed (and cited) the works of Gobineau (*Trois en Asie, Les Religions et les philosophes dans l'Asie centrale*), Renan ("Les Teazies de la Perse," "L'Islamisme et la science") and Darmesteter (*Ormazd et Ahriman*, "Sketch of the Literature of Persia").

117 Ahmet Bey, "La Société Persane: les Européens en Perse," *La Nouvelle Revue,* No. 84 (1892), pp. 792–805.

118 François Georgeon, "Les Débuts," p. 377.

119 Shissler, *Between Two Empires,* p. 85.

120 According to Shissler and Georgeon, Renan, who had regarded the Persians as the Indo-Europeans of the Islamic world, having preserved many of their primitive genes over centuries and with their contributions to their geography, was an obvious influence for Ağaoğlu's arguments regarding Persia.

121 Ahmet Bey, "La Société Persane: les Européens en Perse".

Shi'ism, promised resistance to these external dangers.[122] He interpreted the collective reactions of merchants and Islamic scholars in Iran during the time of the British tobacco monopoly in 1890 as the emergence of a national soul with the capacity to resist.

For Ağaoğlu, a nation was an organic body and its capacity for resistance lay in the force of attraction which existed between its elements, otherwise put, between the individuals that compose it.[123] It was "les idées communes, les préjugés généraux, les croyances nationales" that attracted individuals to each other.[124] Despite anarchy and foreign domination in the Muslim world, Shi'ism in Iran had made it possible to produce collective rituals, plays and festivals which strengthened their communal bonds.[125] Despite the fact that "literature is dead, the rulers corrupted, and the peasants are bowed under the yoke of economic and political sufferings,"[126] by giving an intellectual and moral vigour to Persian society, Shi'ism served as a formative element of nationhood in Persia.[127]

> Religion [...] is in reality a compromise between the past and the present [...] which, adjusting itself therefore to the tastes and penchants of each, guarantees the spiritual unity of Iran in the future by reconnecting its present to the most remote periods of history.[128]

For Ağaoğlu, Shi'ism was a progressive sect, in contrast to the bigoted nature of Sunnism, which is based on an absolutist belief in God.[129] He sought to promote the idea of adjusting Islam to the contemporary needs of the people and to urge them to seek guidance in Islam.[130] With no intermediary between God and the individual, he believed, Sunnism distances the individual from God,

---

122   Georgeon, "Les Débuts," p. 379.
123   Ibid., p. 379.
124   Ahmed Bey, "La Société persane: La Religion et les Sectes religieuses," *La Nouvelle Revue*, No. 73 (1892), pp. 539–540.
125   Ahmed Bey, "La Société persane: le théâtre et ses fêtes," *La Nouvelle Revue*, No. 77 (1892), pp. 537–538.
126   Ahmed Bey, "La religion et les sectes religieuses," pp. 540–541.
127   In the same article, Ağaoğlu wrote: "Heuresement pour le Perse, il lui reste encore une source intacte où elle puise toute sa vie active soit morale, soit intellectuelle, c'est sa religion chiîte. Tout ce que la nation compte d'actif, d'intelligent afflue de ce côté-là; rien ne se fait en dehors d'elle."
128   Ahmed Bey, "Le théâtre et ses fêtes," p. 538, cf. Shissler, p. 96.
129   Ahmed Bey, "La religion et les sectes religieuses," p. 526.
130   Ibid., p. 111.

whereas the Mahdi, the imams and the mujtahids in Shi'ism, by interpreting Islam in a liberal fashion, not only serve as a bridge between the two but also reform the religion.[131]

Since his early writings one can see that Ağaoğlu was convinced that a radical change had to come into existence for the Islamic world, including Persia, not to vanish politically. The destinies of those Muslim states, which were losing their independence one by one, were telling enough. Then what could be done to change the course of this destiny? For the early Ağaoğlu, the alphabet, printing, and all other agents of civilisation were nothing more than tools; secondary conditions. The problems of the Eastern world must be sought in its deepest roots. In his review of Charles Mismer's work titled *Souvenirs du Monde Musulman*, he wrote:

> La condition premier et essentielle, c'est d'avoir des individus dans toute la force de ce mot, c'est-a-dire des êtres capables d'idéal et de dévouement; c'est la chef de la civilisation occidentale. Nul, malheureusement, ne peut contester que dans les classes dirigeantes du monde musulman, il y a aujourd'hui une pénurie déplorable de caractères et de volontés, a l'encontre de ce qui se produisait pendant les quatre premiers siècles de l'islam. Quelle est la cause de cette mort de l'individu?[132]

According to Ağaoğlu, it was the situation of women in Muslim families that killed the individual. It took away all his initiative and personal energy.[133] It imbued children with a sense of egoism, passiveness and inactivity, the most dangerous of all problems of the East. This could be clearly seen when one placed under scrutiny the situations of upper class women in Europe and Asia:

> En Europe, la femme en général est un élément de progrès; en Asie, elle est avilie au dernier degré par l'homme, et son avilissement se paye par une dégradation générale de la société tout entière. L'enfant qui sort de la famille pour devenir membre actif de la société a laquelle appartiennent ses parents ne présente, et dernière analyse, que le produit de deux influences; celle de son père qui agit sur sa raison et développe en lui les instincts de force, et celle de sa mère qui agit sur son cœur en développant en lui les sentiments de pitié et d'abnégation; de ces deux influences

131   François Georgeon, *Osmanlı-Türk Modernleşmesi, 1900–1930,* Istanbul: Yapı Kredi Yayınları, 2009, p. 111.
132   Ahmed Bey, "Le Monde musulman," *Revue bleue politique et littéraire,* No. 50 (1892), p. 319.
133   Ahmed Bey, "La Société Persane: le clergé," *La Nouvelle Revue,* No. 70 (1891), p. 804.

sort l'individu équilibre, égoïste dans les justes limites que réclame sa conservation, et capable des grands actes d'abnégation que lui dicte son cœur. En Europe, garce aux rapports plus justes plus ou moins bien combines, et de la ces contradictions dans la conduite de l'individu, qui passe de l'égoïsme a la générosité et que ne sont au fond qu'une parfaite harmonie. Chez nous, au contraire, la femme des hautes classes, réduite a l'état d'instrument passif pour les plaisirs de son mari, et d'ailleurs rarement en communication avec ses enfants males, est incapable d'inspirer des sentiments quelque peu élevés, et l'enfant se trouve entièrement sous l'influence du père, qui, de par sa fonction naturelle, ne peut lui inspirer que des sentiments de pur égoïsme et l'adoration de la force brutale.[134]

In his account, in order for the individual to revitalise, the Eastern women should be able to completely enjoy the rights with which the religion of Islam has endowed them.[135] That is, it was not in the teachings of Islam that one should have sought the real reasons for the situation of Eastern women. The early Ağaoğlu laid the historical blame instead at the door of the Turks, the lower clergy of Arab origin and the lack of a hierarchical organisation and a strong state to control it.[136]

With the Turkish domination of Islamic lands, he argued, the role of the caliphate was demoted, while reducing state authority over religion weakened Islamic hierarchical organisation. The weakness of the state, which was unable to impose its authority on the clergy, resulted in unfettered powers for the lower clergy (who were mostly Arab) and their corruption. The lower clergy impeded almost all attempts at change in order to secure their position in society. By using this as an instrument and exploiting it, they engendered increasing moral degradation in society and the eventual weakness of the individual. Otherwise, Ağaoğlu firmly rejected the argument that Islamic teachings (especially polygamy) led to the degradation of Muslims in general and women in particular. As will be discussed in detail in Chapter 4, in his view, at least until the 1920s, the Islamic mentality was essentially congruent with modernity and liberalism.[137] The main problem was to create the necessary circumstances in the East for the elevation of the individual, because the death of the individual in the East, both in Iran and Turkey, rendered and would render futile all efforts

---

134   Ahmed Bey, "Le Monde musulman," p. 319 (Emphasis mine).
135   Ahmed Bey, "La Société Persane: le clergé," *La Nouvelle Revue,* No. 70 (1891), p. 804.
136   Ahmet Bey, "La Société Persane: la femme persane," *La Nouvelle Revue,* No. 69 (1891), pp. 376–389.
137   Georgeon, "Les Débuts," p. 383.

at political reform, because the question of the individual, the key to all the problems of the East, was yet unsolved.[138]

Little is known as to whether Ağaoğlu had come to France already imbued with this idea under the influence of Russian radicals or whether his observations in the West and the influences exerted on him, especially by Renan, led him to think so. His reading of Charles Mismer, who in his book also covers the situation of women as a source of social problems in the Ottoman Empire, may have influenced him as well.[139] There may be more than one answer to this question, but what is clear is that in France Ağaoğlu became convinced, as some sections of his French writings suggest, that there were clear differences between the social and individual practices of life in what he calls the East and the West.

In the West, Ağaoğlu did not see the contradictions that he witnessed in the East between the individual and society.[140] He seems to have been impressed by the fact that people were judged in the West according to their merits.

> [The Western individual] has understood perfectly that hopes and ideals are two things almost as necessary for life as air and bread; they are the motive forces which push forward both the individual and society...The goal which he assigns himself demands activity, energy, progress...[141]

He wrote, perhaps a little exaggeratedly, that the Western individual's ideals have changed over time: "yesterday [it was] religion, today liberty and equality, soon socialism."[142] The West owed its superiority over the East to its traits of emulation and competition.[143]

Ağaoğlu left France in January 1894. Before his return to the Caucasus he had thus gone through an intellectual transformation, partly shaped by his crisis of conscience when he had been a student in Russian secondary and high schools. He had felt in a sense alien to the Islamic world from which he originated, but at the same time, as his French writings reveal, he was antagonized by the Western misperceptions of the very same world. Ağaoğlu's intellectual endeavour subsequently became a struggle to find a way to ameliorate the

---

138   Georgeon, *Osmanlı-Türk,* p. 110.
139   See, Charles Mismer, *Souvenirs du Monde musulman,* pp. 119–127.
140   Georgeon, "Les Débuts," p. 383.
141   Ahmed Bey, "La Société Persane : l'instruction publique et la littérature," *La Nouvelle Revue,* No. 79 (1892), pp. 291–292, cf. Shissler, p. 91.
142   Ahmed Bey, "La Société Persane: le clergé," p. 804.
143   Georgeon, "Les Débuts," p. 383.

situation of Islamic nations by concurrently employing an evolving nationalist (he would become a Turkish nationalist shortly after his return to the Near East) and liberal programme. The constant evolution of his ideas reveals the fact that while he always felt sandwiched between East and West, the making of his ideas in fact never came to an end.

In leaving France, besides a certain understanding of nationalism and historicism, he also carried with him the idea that the only source of value in social matters was the fullest elevation of the individual's intellectual and spiritual faculties and that the most important problem of the East was the moral weakness of its individuals, particularly their egoism. The cause of this, he thought, was the demeaning role of women in social life. Therefore, on his return to the Near East, he would continue to write about the question of women in the Islamic world, yet he would also involve in a struggle to defend the rights of local Muslims.

CHAPTER 3

Return to the Near East

In the 1910s version of his autobiography, Ağaoğlu writes that he had to return
to his homeland after receiving the news of his father's passing away.[1] In the
quarter century he spent in the Near East until his deportation to Malta in 1919,
he made important contributions to defend the rights of Muslims in the
Russian Empire and to the birth of Turkish nationalism in both Russian and
Ottoman empires. He appeared in this period more as a political agitator than
as a political thinker. Most of his writings at the time were driven by the desire
to complement his political actions or popularize the aims of political groups
he was associated with. In the Caucasus, he struggled for the political and economic rights of local Muslims, who felt themselves underprivileged under
Russian rule.[2] In the Ottoman context, whilst agitating for Turkish nationalism, he acted as a mouthpiece of the Young Turks' Committee of Union and
Progress (CUP). It was in this period that he turned to the idea of nationalism
and the significance of collective action, encompassing both a commitment to
the common good and a notion of freedom.

3.1   The Caucasus

Ağaoğlu arrived in the Caucasus in May 1894. Soon after his visit to Shusha, he
went to Tiflis, the capital of the region, where he worked as a gymnasium
teacher and contributed to the journal of *Kavkaz* (Caucasia) with his articles in
Russian.[3] When he realised that the journal had little follower among the
Muslims, he wanted to publish a journal in his native, but he could not get
permission from Russian authorities. He later went to Baku, where he worked
as a civil servant at the office of the Baku governor. A few months later he
returned to Shusha to teach French.[4] He also contributed to the creation of
the first library in his hometown.[5] In 1897, he returned to Baku to become one

1   Ağaoğlu Ə. Tərcümeyi-hali-acizanəm. AMEA-nın M. Füzuli adına Əlyazmalar İnstitutu, f.21.
2   Tadeusz Swietochowski, *Russian Azerbaijan, 1905–1920: The Shaping of a National Identity in
    a Muslim Country,* Cambridge: Cambridge University Press, 1985, p. 23.
3   Ağaoğlu Ə. Tərcümeyi-hali-acizanəm. AMEA-nın M. Füzuli adına Əlyazmalar İnstitutu, f.21.
4   Lale Osmanqizi, *Ahmedbey Ağaoğlu'nun Publisistikasi*, Baki: Elm ve Tahsil, 2012, p. 35.
5   Ibid., p. 36.

© KONINKLIJKE BRILL NV, LEIDEN, 2015 | DOI 10.1163/9789004297364_004

the central figures of the Russian Muslim political elite. Meanwhile he got married to Sitare Hanım, the daughter of a wealthy and noble family of the region. The two had five children while in the Caucasus but they lost one at infacy. Their last child Gültekin was born after they moved to Istanbul.[6]

The Caucasus Ağaoğlu returned to was in rapid economic and political transformation in the fin de siècle. Its oil industry accounted for half the total world output of crude oil in 1902, which made the region a centre of attraction for not only the big capital, but also for thousands of workers and their families. It led to fierce competitions over the oil-rich lands and means of transportation, extraction and delivery of petroleum.

The political and cultural capital of the region was Tiflis. Yet the centre of the oil activity was the city of Baku. A small town in the early 1870s with a population of 13,392, Baku became a global attraction centre by 1909 with 222,694 inhabitants from different ethnic groups, the majority being Russians and Azerbaijani Muslims. It saw a rapid urban growth through the influx of foreign and Caucasian entrepreneurs in the oil business and non-agricultural workers and with its European-style buildings, telephone system and its active City Council.[7] A young voyager back then, Calouste S. Gulbenkian would write in his travelogue about Baku that, "je trouvais une ville moderne, avec des rues bien larges, bien aérées, bordées de maisons assez basses, comme dans toute la Russie, mais très commodes et très saines; bref, entre Bakou et Petersburg ou Odessa, je n'apercevais d'abord aucune différence..."[8] Aleksandr Ivanovič Novikov, the mayor of Baku between 1902 and 1904, would describe the city as "a unique blend of Pennsylvania's industry, Russia's bureaucracy and Persia's culture."[9] By all means, Baku was turning into a global city whose transformation would play an important role in the rise of Turkish nationalism.

The region's rapid change began in 1872, one might say, when Russian authorities decided to liberalize the oil industry. Until that year, Russian policies had alternated between the monopoly lease system and direct state use of Baku's oil wells, using traditional methods to dig out oil.[10] During the forty-year

---

6   Interview with Tektaş Ağaoğlu, November 27, 2014.

7   Audrey Alstadt, "Baku: Transformation of a Muslim Town," in *The City in Late Imperial Russia*, ed. Michael F. Hamm. Bloomington: Indiana University Press, 1986.

8   Calouste S. Gulbenkian, *La Transcaucasie et la Péninsule d'Apchéron: Souvenirs de Voyage*, Paris: Libraire Hachette *etC^{ie}*, 1891, p. 186.

9   A.I. Novikov, *Zapiski gorodskogo golovy*, SPb: n.p. 1905, cf. Samuel C. Ramer, "Democracy versus the Rule of a Civic Elite: Alexandr Ivanovič Novikov and the Fate of Self-government in Russia," *Cahiers du monde russe et soviétique*, 22 (Apr.–Sep., 1981), p. 172.

10   Joseph A. Martellaro, "The Acquisition and Leasing of the Baku Oilfields by the Russian Crown," *Middle Eastern Studies*, Vol. 21, No.1 (Jan., 1985), pp. 80–88; Miryusif Mirbabayev,

long lease system, the entire oil extraction had been limited to 17 million poods and eighty-eight per cent of the oil fields had belonged to Azerbaijani Muslims. When it became clear that Russian oil industry was unable to cope with American industry, the ownership of Baku's petroleum deposits were relinquished and auctioned off as semi-permanent leasehold to private entrepreneurs in November 1872.[11]

At the end of the first auction those who became owners of oil fields in Baku included twelve Russian industrialists and eleven Armenian companies. As compared to the Russians and Armenians, Muslim industrialists far lagged behind. There were only two Azerbaijani figures with much smaller capital, Gasim Selimkhanov and Hajji Zeynel Abidin Taghiev. The Azerbaijani share of the entire oil fields was less than to thirteen per cent at the end of the 1870s.[12]

The main figures of the Azerbaijani oil bourgeoisie such as H.Z. Taghiev and Musa Naghiev, forming minor to middle-rank industrialists, suffered from the rapid growth of the big Russian and Western capital such as the Nobel Brothers Co. and the Rothschilds, which undercapitalized them by decreasing oil prices and monopolizing most fields.[13] In 1906, while 135 companies controlled more than three hundred enterprises in extraction and refining, six of them dominated the industry. None were Azerbaijanis.[14]

Moreover, the population of a diverse group of workers (Russians, Armenians, Tatars and Persians) increased from 3,800 in 1885 to 26,000 in 1909.[15] Unlike the changes in Asia Minor, which became demographically less heterogeneous after the Russo-Ottoman and the Balkan Wars, the Apsheron peninsula became more cosmopolitan and diverse with the oil revolution. But the city of Baku

*Azerbaycan Neftinin Qısa Tarixi,*Bakı: Azerneşr, 2007; John P. McKay, "Baku Oil and Transcaucasian Pipelines, 1883–1891: A Study in Tsarist Economic Policy," *Slavic Review,* Vol. 43, No. 4 (Winter, 1984), p. 606.

11 Xachatur Dadayan, *Armyani i Baku 1850–1920,* Erevan: Nof Norabank, 2007, p. 12. This was mainly because of the struggle flared up between the two industrialists Vasilii A. Kokorev and Ivan Mirzoev; see, V.A. Matichev, I.G. Fuks, Merchandising and the oil business in Russia (review), *Chemistry and Technology of Fuels and Oils,* 29/8 (Aug., 1993), p. 404.

12 Manaf Süleymanov, *Azerbaycan Milyonçuları: Haci Zeynalabdin Tağıyev,* Baku: Gençlik, 1996; Okan Yeşilot, *Hacı Zeynelabidin Tagiyev: Azerbaycan'da Birçok İlki Gerçekleştirmiş Efsanevi Petrol Kralının Hazin Son, Şöhreti, Serveti ve Hayırseverliği,* Istanbul: Kaktüs Yayınları, 2004; Idris Aliyev&Orkhan Mamedzade, "History of the Baku "Black Gold": Fate of the Communities and Formation of National Bourgeoisie," in Leila Alieva ed., *The Baku Oil and Local Communities: A History,* Baku: Qanun, 2009, p. 127.

13 Dadayan, *Armyani,* p. 21.

14 Christopher Rice, "Party Rivalry in the Caucasus: SRs, Armenians and the Baku Union of Oil Workers, 1907–1908," *The Slavonic and East European Review,* vol. 67, No. 2 (Apr. 1989), p. 230.

15 P. Petrovic, *Rabochie Bakinskaga Neftepromishlennago Raiona,* Tiflis, 1911, p. 7.

was hardly a melting pot. Most being immigrants, the oilmen constituted sixty per cent of the total labour force in the city at the time.[16] More than half (fifty-four per cent) of these were Azerbaijanis, whilst Russian and Armenian workers constituted twenty per cent each. Russian workers were mainly educated and skilled workers with better-paid jobs.[17] Azerbaijani workers, on the other hand, with a literacy rate of less than ten per cent, engaged in menial jobs mostly in drilling and oil extraction.[18]

Petrovic tells us that, despite all the diversity in the Baku oil industry at the time, among Armenian industrialists a national romanticism was easily noticed, as they, but particularly Alexander Mantashev, tended to hire trustable Armenians to work with them and they started to act collaboratively.[19] Azerbaijani companies, on the other hand, were disorganized and struggling in the oil industry against the collaboration of the big capital, just as Azerbaijani Muslim workers against the educated and skilled Russian and Armenian workers. Muslim entrepreneurs were all registered to the Baku Oil Factories Association in 1893, but when it was divided into two camps, the leading two Azerbaijani industrialists Taghiev and Naghiev would remain in rival groups.[20]

In 1897, Taghiev sold his business to Evelyn Hubbard, the head of the Bank of England. The same year he bought the journal of *Kaspii*, which would voice under its new owner Russian Muslim concerns. Having not given up all his shares, he kept his foot in the oil business to return back again the early 1910s. Meanwhile, he concentrated on new ventures in such fields as textiles and fishing. He was complainant of great difficulties in granting permissions, let alone concessions, to start new businesses or to expand the existing ones just as he had experienced during his oil venture.[21]

By 1900, the local Azerbaijani elite could see that local Azerbaijani Muslims were not only less skilled, poured scorn by Russian and foreign authorities and enjoyed lesser freedoms. The lands of local peasants were confiscated by the state and handed over to the big capital.[22] As in the case of Taghiev, the growing middle-class was clearly feeling under-privileged in starting enterprises.

---

16   Rice, "Party Rivalry," p. 229.

17   Petrovic, *Rabochie*, p. 18.

18   Rice, "Party Rivalry," p. 229; Petrovic, *Rabochie*, p. 20.

19   Petrovic, *Rabochie*, p. 19. That said, Petrovic also notes that, toward the mid-1910s the national romanticism of Armenian would be replaced by cosmopolitan attitudes among them.

20   Yeşilot, *Tagiyev*, p. 47.

21   Seyitzade, *The Roads*, p. 9.

22   *Kaspii*, October 27, 1905, cf. Dilara Seyid-zade, *Azerbaijan in the Beginning of xxth Century: Roads Leading to Independence*, trans. G. Bayramov, Baku: OKA Offset, 2010, p. 48.

The actions of the Russian government in bureaucratic and socio-political spheres would further lead them to feel themselves subject to persecutions and more than the other people of the region.[23]

Perhaps it would not be false to say that political and economic discrimination and the rise of the oil industry among Azeribaijani Muslims would lead to the rise of the second generation of the Azerbaijani intelligentsia. As the nationalist writer Yusuf Akçura explained in 1912:

> ...with the arrival of Europeans, [the small artisans, manufacturers and farmers] started to invest in new industries and trades through the methods they learned from [them]...As a new social force, a rich bourgeois class thus emerged in the Turkish world. Its examples are the rich bourgeoisie formed by big merchants, industrialists and miners in...Baku. The bourgeois class is nationalist; its economic interests suggest the emergence and development of nationalist ideas and sentiments. Many theorists of nationalism rapidly gathered around the bourgeoisie...[24]

Although to say that Azerbaijani elites immediately realized that they had common concerns and acted collectively for national interests would be to exaggerate somewhat, there was an element of truth in Akçura's account. Since the early 1890s, they began to form alliances in the shape of journals and political campaigns to defend their rights against the restrictions imposed upon non-Christians by the Tsarist government.[25]

3.1.1 The 1905 Petition, Violence and the End of the Oil Revolution
Ağaoğlu's appearance in Azerbaijani political and intellectual history coincided with the rise of the new intelligentsia. In 1897, Taghiev invited him to Baku to contribute to his *Kaspii*,[26] which marked the beginning of a new episode in his life. He found the opportunity to meet important figures of the liberal Azerbaijani intelligentsia, the bourgeoisie and members of the Baku duma.[27] While teaching at the local gymnasium, he also joined the duma.

---

23 *Revendications de la Délégation de Paix de la République de l'Azerbaijan du Caucause présentées à la Conférence de la Paix, à Paris*, p. 9.
24 Yusuf Akçura, "Türklük," *Salname-i Servet-i Fünun*, February 16, 1912.
25 Audrey L. Altstadt, *The Azerbaijani Turks: Power and Identity under Russian Rule*, Stanford: Hoover Institution Press, 1992, pp. 24–25.
26 Quliyev, *Foreword*, p. 8.
27 Ibid., p. 35. The City Duma in Baku was established in 1878 according to the provisions of the Urban Reform in 1870; Audrey Aldstadt, "The Baku city duma—an arena of conflict," *Central Asian Survey*, vol. 5, No. 3 (1986), p. 50.

Although published in Russian (because of the restrictions of the Tsarist government), *Kaspii* was the only Azerbaijani newspaper in Baku.[28] Its editor-in-chief (when Ağaoğlu started to work for the newspaper) was Ali Merdan Bey Topçubaşı, now a lawyer with close links to the Russian constitutionalist liberals (the Kadets) and a friend of Ağaoğlu since their student years in St. Petersburg. Such figures as Hasan Zerdabi and Neriman Nerimanov (1870–1925), future president of the Azerbaijani Republic, were also writing in the *Kaspii* at the time. The journal had an eclectic structure giving space to writers of the three main ideologies in Azerbaijan at the time: liberalism, Pan-Islamism and Pan-Turkism.[29] Yet its main occupation was with more immediate issues, which revolved around Muslims' absence of political, social and cultural rights.[30]

As the city of Baku grew into an urban metropolis in the last quarter of the nineteenth century, Tsarist authorities developed new migration and administrative policies for the viceroyalty of the Caucasus. Local Azerbaijani Muslims had already been deprived, unlike Armenians and Georgians, of having their national schools, religious buildings and benevolent societies, and the Muslim clergy was appointed by the Russian authorities.[31] The demographic structure of the region had also changed as peasants of Russian origins and Orthodox believers were settled in the Caucasus as of 1899. By 1903, while Baku's population equalled 155,876, only twenty-eight per cent of the population consisted of the Azerbaijanis. Russians outnumbered them forming some thirty-six per cent of the population.

Alexander II's Urban Reform of 1870 had been extended to the Caucasus in 1874 and a city council (*gorodskaia duma*) had been established in Baku in 1878. The Urban Reform in effect had "reaffirmed imperial jurisdiction over Muslim subjects by further limiting the already restricted purview of religious courts to family matters."[32] As an offshoot of the imperial Russification policies, one of its central objectives had been to guarantee the predominance of ethnic Russians in all administrative institutions. Ethnic Russians

---

28   Ibid., p. 35. For an overview of the press of this era, see Alexandre Benningsen and Chantal Lemercier-Quelquejay, *La Presse et le Mouvement National Musulman de Russie avant 1920*, Paris: Mouton, 1964.

29   Swietochowski, *Russian Azerbaijan*, p. 35.

30   Leyla Hajiyeva, *Ağaoğlu Ahmet Bey Publisistikası*, p. 8.

31   Quliyev., p. 9.

32   Audrey Alstadt, "The Baku city duma—an arena of conflict," *Central Asian Survey*, vol. 5, No. 3 (1986), p. 50.

secured a privileged position in the administrative and legal structure of the viceroyalty. Ramer writes:

> National considerations also played a role here. The higher standards on which [the Baku mayor Novikov] insisted virtually precluded hiring Moslems, and Moslem leaders in the duma were not impressed by his arguments that he sought only quality. (The hiring of some local Armenians under these new standards only heightened their perception of ethnic discrimination)...Finally, a wholesale preference for outsiders, whatever its justification, tended to offend local pride. Such Baku "patriotism," as it was called, was hardly mollified by Novikov's attempts to "prove the superiority of the new...people over the local swamp."[33]

Russians were holding sixty-five per cent of the positions in administration. Jobs within the armed forces and in judiciary were predominantly at the hands of the Slavs, while Azerbaijanis, together with Armenians, held few and only minor administrative positions.[34] That said, they were numerous in industries other than oil and possessed most of the land, a key factor in determining the electorates for the City Duma.[35]

The City Duma was an important platform to bring into Tsarist government's attention major issues and problems in the city, even though Russian authorities were finding its suggestions and actions unwise, ungrateful and as products of narrowly conceived political motivations.[36] The Duma elections were indirect. Only those with a specified amount of immovable land or a certain amount of trade income per year were granted suffrage. Despite the fact that in 1897, for example, Azerbaijanis formed only forty per cent of the population of the Baku city, they constituted the majority of the electorates. To prevent Azerbaijani control in the City Duma, Russians put restrictions on non-Christian representation. Between 1878 and 1890, no more than one-half; between 1890 and 1900, one third; and after 1900, again one-half of the seats in the Duma were allocated to non-Christians.

On February 18, 1905, just after the Bloody Sunday, to offer a respite against growing political, economic and ideological tensions, the Tsarist authorities read an edict with which they publicly announced that they gave all loyal

---

33   Ramer, "Novikov," p. 176.
34   Alstadt, *The Azerbaijani Turks*, p. 29.
35   Ibid., p. 31.
36   Ramer, "Novikov," p. 176.

subjects the opportunity "to be heard by them" in public matters.[37] One month later, on March 15, 1905 Azerbaijani local elite arranged a meeting at Taghiyev's resident to voice their concerns collectively.

As noted above, the local bourgeoisie and intelligentsia had already been working together in the Baku *duma* and in the *Kaspii*. The major Azeri oil magnates Taghiyev, Naghiyev, and other figures such as Mirza Asadullayev, and Murtuza Mukhtarov and leading members of the intelligentsia including Ali Mardan Topçubaşı, Nejef Vezirov and Ahmed Ağaoğlu were all taking seats at the City Duma. In March 1905, they agreed to prepare a collective petition to be submitted to the Tsarist government for the first time. An educated lawyer and an editor of *Kaspi*,[38] Topçubaşı was given the task of penning the petition, which enlisted the political and social problems of the Muslims of the Caucasus.[39]

The petition was presented on April 12 in St. Petersburg. Opening with the lamentation that a century long Russian rule in the Caucasus brought no development for the Muslims, it maintained that Caucasian Muslims were the single most disenfranchised group and considered by the administration as if they were the inferior race.[40] Together with other Muslims of Russia, the petition added, they were treated as the aliens of the empire, excluded from the family of Russian citizens. They had the same duties and obligations like other subjects, but not the same rights.

The petition suggested democratic liberties for the Caucasian Muslims; freedom of expression and conscience, freedom of press (in Russian and native languages), freedom of association, and the right to free primary education. It proposed the lifting of restrictions imposed upon the Muslims such as their limited representation in the City Duma and other inequalities: as noted above, Muslims were restricted from occupying senior positions in civil and military administration; secondary school and high school Muslim graduates were not allowed to choose liberal professions; Muslim students were unable to receive state bursaries and enrol in a number of Russian high schools; Muslim industrialists were deprived of the property laws of Russian nobility

37   Édith Ybert-Chabrier, "La pétition des musulmans du Caucase en réponse á l'oukase du 18 février 1905," Cahiers du Monde russe, Vol. 48, No. 2/3, Les résonances de 1905 (Apr.–Sep., 2007), p. 244.

38   C.M. Ishakhov, *A.M. Topchubashi: Dokumenty iz Lichnykh Arkhivov, 1903–1934*, Moscow: Izdatelstvo, 2012, p. 11.

39   *Kaspii*, March 17, 1905, cf. Dilara Seyitzade, *Azerbaycan Burjuvazisi ve İdeoloji Savunucuları*, Ankara: Türk Tarih Kurumu, 1994, p. 2243.

40   Ybert-Chabrier, "La pétition," p. 249.

and merchants.[41] Caucasian Muslims were of the opinion that without introducing civil liberties and giving an end to inequalities, the implementation of the self-government (*zemstvo*) system in the Caucasus, which the Russian authorities had been planning (and put into practice in August 1905), would bring no good to the region.

Even though it was only one of the more than seven hundred petitions submitted to the Tsarist authorities in that month, on July 10, Count II Vorontsov Dashkov, the governor of the Caucasus, accepted a Muslim delegate led by Topçubaşı. In this meeting, acknowledging the overall problems of the Muslims, he promised to "pay special attention to the opening of schools in their native language, the establishment of educational institutions for girls and Muslim religious schools, and to provide support to the publication of newspapers, magazines and books in their native languages."[42] However, they would have to wait about one year to see their collective struggles to bore their first fruits.

Meanwhile, with the fervent of the revolution following the defeat of Russians at the hands of the Japanese, strikes and open rebellion had spread throughout the empire. In the Caucasus, instigated strikes and agrarian disorders were coupled with increasing tensions between Tatars and Armenians. Azizov tells us that the frictions between the two stemmed mainly from centuries long hostility between Tatars and Armenians, ignorance, the growing bitter feeling among the Tatars that Armenians were better controlling the trade and industry in the region, the former's lack of education, and provocations by extreme groups of each ethno-religious group.[43] These turned into reciprocal attacks in February 1905, when Agharza Babayev, an Azerbaijani businessman, was killed by Armenians.[44]

The violence went beyond control in the second half of 1905. Between August and September 1905, there were not only large number of reciprocal murders; each group also attacked the others' oil refineries and sites, destroying fifty seven per cent of the wells of the Armenians and Muslims. In February 1906, rhe British Consul Stevens reported:

> It is much feared that the Government will never be able to bring about permanent peace between these two races. Mutual enmity has increased

41   USSR State Central History Archives, f. 1276, List 1, No. 107, p. 63, cf. Seyitzade, *Azerbaycan Burjuvazisi*, p. 2244.

42   Ishakhov, *A.M. Topchubasi*, p. 11; Nazile Abbaslı, *Azerbaycanda Özgürlük Mücadelesi*, Istanbul: Beyaz Balina Yayınları, 2001.

43   Eldar Azizov, *Difai: XX. Asrin evvellerinde ermeni-azerbaycanli münakişesinin ilkin tarihi şartleri ve sebepleri*, Bakı: n.p., 2009, p. 65.

44   Ibid., p. 56.

so much latterly, and their hatred of each other has assumed such dangerous proportions that it is generally believed the Tatars, who in the eastern and southern provinces ... number as many as six to one, will continue the struggle until such time as they succeed in exterminating the Armenians.[45]

The Armeno-Tatar massacres, the decreasing efficiency of oil fields and the departure of foreign capital from Baku would bring about the end of the Baku oil revolution.[46] By 1913, Russian share in the oil industry fell from fifty-two (1902) to only nine per cent.[47]

With the belief that Russian Muslims lacked coordination in their actions against the Armenians, the Azerbaijanis established the *Difai* (Defence) in early 1906, to protect the Caucasian Muslims politically and militarily. Also known as the Defence Committee of the Caucasian Muslims, it set its main objective as defending Muslim villages from the violent attacks of the Dashnaktsutiun and to establish "an effective fraternity and union among the various peoples of the Caucasus," including a relationship of solidarity with the Dashnaktsutiun party.[48] Penned and published in *İrşad* (Guidance) by Ahmet Ağaoğlu, its programme also called for internal strengthening of the Muslims through education and national unification.[49]

Its 52-point programme issued by its Karabagh Union Assembly in October 1907 presented the characteristics of "more of a moral code of conduct, puritan and uncompromising" and providing for the persecution of any breaches of strict moral code, from the abduction of young girls to adultery and homosexuality.[50] As I shall discuss below, the strict nature of the constitution of Ağaoğlu's utopian country *The Land of the Free Men* can be likened to this.

That being said, the *Difai* acted more than a defense and moralist organisation. It "carried out terrorist acts targeting representatives of the tsarist

---

45   P. Stevens to Sir Edward Grey, February 16, 1906, FO 371/120/121.
46   In this period, an estimated 128 Armenian and 158 Muslim villages were pillaged or destroyed, while estimates of lives lost range from 3,100 to 10,000; Swietochowsky, *Russian Azerbaijan*, p. 41; Nesrin Sarıahmetoğlu Karagür, *Petrolün Sihirli Dünyası Bakü*, Istanbul: IQ Yayıncılık, 2007, p. 43.
47   Yergin, *The Prize*, p. 133.
48   Nadir Devlet, *Rusya Türklerinin Milli Mücadele Tarihi, 1905–1917*, Ankara: Türk Kültürünü Araştırma Enstitüsü, 1985, pp. 132–133; Edyth Ybert, "Islam, Nationalism and Socialism in the Parties and Political Organisations of Azerbaijani Muslims in the Early Twentieth Century," *Caucasus Survey*, 1:1 (Oct., 2013), p. 49.
49   Vilayet Quliyev, *Ahmed Bey Ağaoğlu: Seçme Eserleri*, Baku: Şarq-Garp, 2007, p. 15.
50   Ybert, "Islam, Nationalism and Socialism," p. 48.

government and Muslims considered traitors of their community."[51] Notably, its terrorist activities never targeted Armenian personalities, and according to Russian authorities, including "militias established around local committees gathered together brigands, fugitives from penal colonies and outlaws of every description. These militias seemed to play a deterrent role: there would be no further Armenian-Muslim clashes after autumn 1906."[52]

The *Difai* was partially a fruit of the the October Manifesto which brought new constitutional freedoms and civil liberties,[53] and the lifting of censorship led to a proliferation of all types of publications.[54] The people were also allowed to organise meetings, to establish legal political parties and occupational groupings and unions.[55] While the Caucasus saw the establishment of its first political unit, at a broader scale Russian Muslims gradually turned to an autonomist direction at the time.

When twenty-five Muslim representatives were elected to the First State Duma in April 1906, with the initiative of Topçubaşı, they formed a faction together with other non-Russian representatives called the Parliamentary Group of the Union of Autonomists.[56] Russian public opinion was troubled by this, as they began to think that the unity of the empire was now under threat. The First Duma was dissolved shortly in July 1906. As the counter-revolutionary movement was gaining strength, the reform projects that targeted the introduction of further rights for Muslims were put on hold. Muslims, together with many other non-Russian and/or non-Christian groups, would see increasing pressures and restrictions on their communities in the late 1900s. With the 1907 electoral system law amendments, for example, non-Russians votes were given lower weight and Muslim publications were placed under tighter state controls.[57] As the prosperity of the Transcaucasia was turning upside down and Muslim rights put on hold, Russian Muslims would turn to nationalism.

In this period, Ağaoğlu was actively involved in the struggles of the Caucasian Muslims. In August 1905, he attended the First All-Russian Muslim Congress at

---

51   Ibid., p. 49.

52   Ibid., p. 49.

53   T.H. von Laue, "Count Witte and the Russian Revolution of 1905," *American Slavic and East European Review,* vol. 17, No. 1 (Feb., 1958), p. 28.

54   Nader Sohrabi, "Historicizing the Revolutions: Constitutional Revolutions in the Ottoman Empire, Iran and Russia, 1905–1908," *The American Journal of Sociology,* vol. 100, No. 6 (May 1995), p. 1407.

55   Jutta Schrerrer, "Intelligentsia, religion, révolution: Prèmier manifestation d'un socialisme chrétien en Russie, 1905–1907," *Cahiers du Monde russe et soviétique,* vol. 17, No. 4 (Oct.–Dec., 1976), pp. 427–466.

56   Ibid., p. 13.

57   Ibid., pp. 15–18.

Nizhni Novgorod. Chaired by Gasprinsky, the congress resolved to create a
Muslim organisation called the Union of Russian Muslims (*İttifaq-ı Müslimin*)
with the objectives of the unification of Muslims in Russia within one movement; the establishment of a constitutional monarchy based on proportional
representation of nationalities; the legal equality of the Muslim and Russian
populations; the abrogation of all laws and administrative practices that dis-
criminated against Muslims; and the cultural and educational progress of the
Muslims.[58] This congress was followed by another in January 1906, at which it
was decided to form an electoral alliance with the Constitutional Democrats
(Kadets), the hard core of Russian liberalism. At the third, the union was transformed into a political party.

In his writings of the day, Ağaoğlu's aims appeared to consist of defending
the collective rights of Muslims against the Tsarist government, criticising
clericalism, Sunni-Shi'ite conflicts and the traditional and obstructive mentality of Islamic scholars, and displaying the means to improve the situation of
Muslim nations with special emphasis on reform of the alphabet and the situation of women. The last was the subject of his first book published in Russian
in 1902 under the title of *Zhenshchina po Islamu i v Islame* (*Women according to
Islam and in Islam*).[59] In 1904 he also published a play, *İslam ve Ahund* (*Islam
and Teacher*) in the *Kaspii*, in which he satirically criticised the ignorance of
Islamic scholars and the fallacies of their teachings.[60]

While Russian Muslims benefited from the increasing intellectual and journalistic freedom in the aftermath of the 1905 Revolution in terms of getting
permission to propound the objectives of their communities, they were at
the same time strictly monitored by the Tsarist government, which not infre-
quently closed Muslim journals when their contents went against its grain.
Ağaoğlu actively contributed to the vigorous intellectual environment in
Azerbaijan between 1905 and 1908: at Taghiev's initiative, he began to publish
the daily *Hayat* (*Life*) on June 6, 1905 with Hüseyinzade Ali and Topçubaşı.
Hayat was the first newspaper that Ağaoğlu had brought out in Turkish. In its
first issue its editors identified it as primarily a Muslim and Turkish journal.[61]

---

58   Devlet, *Rusya Türklerinin,* p. 92; Swietochowski, *Russian Azerbaijan,* p. 49.
59   Ahmet Aghayev, *Zhenshchina po Islamu i v Islame,* Tiflis: Martirosyans, 1901. This book was
      translated into Turkish in 1959 with the title *İslamlıkta Kadın.* Ahmet Ağaoğlu, *İslamlıkta
      Kadın,* trans. Hasan Ali Ediz, İstanbul: Nebioğlu Yayınevi, 1959. I did not have the chance
      to see the Russian version of the book, which is why I will rely on the latter version in this
      study.
60   Ahmed Aghayev, *İslam va Akhund,* Baku: Hadim-i Millat, 1904.
61   Hüseyinzade Ali, "Gazetemizin Mesleki," *Hayat,* No. 1, 1905; cf. Cengiz Çağla, *Azerbaycan'da
      Milliyetçilik ve Politika,* İstanbul: Bağlam Yayınları, 2002, p. 52.

It published articles "representing and revealing religious idealism, conservatism and at times nationalism."[62] In a short time, it became one of the most popular journals in Baku. Its issues were delivered to Iran, Turkey and the Central Asia.[63] Ağaoğlu left *Hayat* when he began to feel uncomfortable with Taghiev's attempts to direct its policies.[64]

In February 1906, with the financial support of the young aristocratic landowner Isa Ashurbakov, he brought out another journal, this time in Persian. It was called *İrşad* with the motto of "Freedom, Equality, Justice".[65] Among contributors to the journal were Narimanov and Mehmed Emin Resulzade, as well as Young Turk leaders whom Ağaoğlu had met in Paris and Istanbul, including Abdullah Cevdet (1869–1932).[66] Despite receiving a subsidy from members of the native Azerbaijani bourgeoisie for the publication of *İrşad*, Ağaoğlu took an anti-capitalist stance in his writings in it, encouraging discussions on daily topics.[67] As he notes in his autobiography, in order to counterbalance Russification, he turned once again to Persia and promoted the discourse that "Persia belongs to Persians."[68] Furthermore, he persistently drew attention to the harm caused by the denominational conflicts between Sunnis and Shi'ites in the Caucasus, calling for union between Muslims.[69] When *İrşad* was closed by the Tsarist government in 1907, he published its successor, *Terakki* (*Progress*), with the financial support of Murtaza Mukhtarov and with virtually the same contributors.[70]

Since Ağaoğlu's attempts to promote nationalism and Pan-Islamism went against the grain of the Tsarist government, he was eventually put under surveillance by the Russian intelligence agencies.[71] When some members of the *Difai* were picked up by the police under Stolypin's regime and deported to Turkistan in 1908, many remaining members were absorbed into the newly founded Müsavat (Equality) Party of Azerbaijani Muslims for their protection.[72]

---

62   Ibid., p. 53.

63   Quliyev, *Ağaoğlu Ahmed Bey*, p. 10.

64   Swietochowski, *Russian Azerbaijan*, p. 57.

65   Çağla, *Azerbaycan'da Milliyetçilik ve Politika*, p. 56.

66   Akçura, *Türk Yılı*, p. 433.

67   Swietochowski, *Russian Azerbaijan*, p. 58.

68   Ağaoğlu Ə. Tərcümeyi-hali-acizanəm. AMEA-nın M. Füzuli adına Əlyazmalar İnstitutu, f.21.

69   He also mentions in his memoirs his support to committees that sought an Islamic union between Caucasian, Persian and Ottomans Muslims but does not name these. Ibid.

70   Devlet, *Rusya Türklerinin*, p. 207.

71   Akçura, *Türk Yılı*, p. 433.

72   Ibid., p. 433.

Feeling heavy pressure from the Russian government at the time, he decided to leave Azerbaijan.

When the middle-ranking officers and the Committee of Progress and Union of the Young Turks had forced Sultan Abdulhamid II to re-proclaim the constitution and parliamentary rule, which went down in history as the Young Turk Revolution of 1908, Istanbul had become an attractive destination for Russian Muslims. Ağaoğlu had maintained his correspondence with the Young Turks, with whom he had been in contact since he was a student in Paris. As a matter of fact, in 1894, en route to the Caucasus, he had stayed in Istanbul in order to make further connections with the Young Turks.[73] There he had also found the opportunity to make an interview with the Pan-Islamist thinker Jamal ad-Din al-Afghani (1838–1897) at the guesthouse of Abdulhamid II, which may partly explain the latter's influence on his writings until the late 1910s.[74]

The Young Turks' publications in *İrşad* and the exchanges of letters procured the maintenance of this contact.[75] In 1907, the CUP leaders approached Ağaoğlu with a letter, saying, "[o]ur ideas are directed to the same point. The same sun shines upon our paths. Let us achieve our aim by working together and being attached to each other."[76] After the Revolution in Istanbul, when a large number of Crimean and Caucasian thinkers, including Akçura, Gasprinsky and later Hüseyinzade Ali, began to migrate there in the hope of finding a freer intellectual atmosphere in the Ottoman Empire, Ağaoğlu went to Istanbul in early 1909 with the same hopes.[77]

---

73   Yusuf Akçura, *Türk Yılı*, p. 427.

74   Ağaoğlu Ə. Tərcümeyi-hali-acizanəm. AMEA-nın M. Füzuli adına Əlyazmalar İnstitutu, f.21.

75   Ahmedbek Agaef, "Tureckij parlament i Ahmed Rza-bek," *Vestnik Baku*, December 21, 1908. Hanioğlu notes that when some Caucasian Muslims sent a letter to Ahmet Rıza in 1906 complaining about Armenian encroachment, Bahaeddin Şakir "had seized the opportunity to approach to the region with the aim of flooding Eastern Anatolia and the Black Sea coast with revolutionary propaganda and disseminating their ideas through journals in the Caucasus (especially those to which Ağaoğlu was contributing). He sent a response on behalf of the Committee of Progress and Union stating that "the authors of the detestable massacres are not you, but those Armenian revolutionaries who are enjoying themselves by offending humanity." Hanioğlu, *Preparation for a Revolution*, p. 158.

76   Letter of Dr Bahaeddin Şakir to Agayef, "İrşad Ceride-i Muhteremesi Sermuharrerliğine," July 3, 1907. The Committee of Progress and Union also set him FFr 50 as a gesture, when Ağaoğlu was considering terminating his journal *İrşad* because of financial problems; cf. Hanioğlu, *Preparation for a* Revolution, p. 159.

77   Ahmet Agaeff to British High Commissioner, June 5, 1919, FO 371/4174/301; *Tercüme-i-hali-acizanem*, Respublika Alyazmalar Institute, f. 21, 403; for a detailed and interesting study on Russian Muslim emigration to the Ottoman Empire, see, James Meyer, "Immigration,

3.2   Istanbul

While Ağaoğlu was one of the central political and intellectual figures in the periphery of the Russian Empire, he appeared to be a peripheral actor in the centre of the Ottoman Empire at least in his first years in Istanbul. The half a decade after the Young Turk Revolution was a period of relative liberty and political turmoil.[78] The constitutional regime had enabled the opening of the parliament, the foundation of political parties and the introduction of further political, economic, intellectual and educational freedoms.[79] The sudden advent of a free press in this period had created a torrent of publications, currents of thought and ideas. Just before the revolution there had been around 120 newspapers and magazines being published in the Ottoman Empire. After the introduction of the constitution, with the lifting of censorship, this number shot up to 730 within a year. 377 were published in Istanbul.[80]

Ahmet Rıza Bey, one of Ağaoğlu's closest connections within the Young Turks, had become the president of the new parliament. Yet the CUP had refrained from placing its men in ministerial positions after the revolution. Its key men such as Cavid Bey and Talat Bey, for example, had acted until mid-1909, as under-secretaries. The 1909 counter-revolution would change the course of action and policy followed by the Committee. Its men were driven out of Istanbul during the counter-revolution. The suppression of the counter-revolutionaries by Mahmud Şevket Paşa's army would temporarily consolidate the power of the CUP. It had the backing of the army. Yet the destinies of the empire in the early 1910s would come to be conditioned partially by the strained relations between military leaders and civilian political elites thereafter.

After the counter-revolution, the CUP sought to have a greater control over the government. In June, Cavid Bey was appointed as the Minister of Finance

---

   Return and the Politics of Citizenship: Russian Muslims in the Ottoman Empire, 1860–1914," *International Journal of Middle Eastern Studies*, 39 (2007), 15–32.

78 Zafer Toprak, *Türkiye'de Milli İktisat, 1908–1918,* Ankara: Yurt Yayınları, 1982, pp. 18–22; Sina Akşin, *Jöntürkler ve İttihat ve Terakki,* İstanbul: Remzi Kitabevi, 1987, pp. 245–248. Feroz Ahmad, *The Young Turks; The Committee of Union and Progress in Turkish Politics, 1908–1914,* Oxford: Clarendon Press, 1969.

79 Sina Akşin, "The Place of the Young Turk Revolution in Turkish History," *Young Turks Symposium,* University of Manchester, 1988, pp. 13–29, also see Tarık Z. Tunaya, *Türkiye'de Siyasi Partiler,* vol. I-II-III, İstanbul: Hürriyet Vakfı Yayınları, 1989; Ali Birinci, *Hürriyet ve İtilaf Fırkası, II. Meşrutiyet Devrinde İttihat ve Terakki'ye Karşı Çıkanlar,* Istanbul: Dergah Yayınları, 1990.

80 Orhan Koloğlu, *Aydınlarımızın Bunalım Yılı 1918: Zafer-i Nihaiyeden Tam Teslimiyete,* Istanbul: Boyut Yayınları, 2000, p. 59.

at age thirty-two. This was followed by the appointment of Talat Bey as Minister of Interior.[81] That being said, until 1913, the CUP could not maintain its stronghold in office. The factionalisation within the military and the growing political power of the anti-Unionist groups such as the followers of Sabahaddin who founded the Liberal Party would lead the CUP to be ousted from government by the British backed Kamil Paşa and by the Saviour Officers led by Sadık Paşa. The Unionists returned to power with the 1913 *Bab-ı Âli* coup and remained in office until the end of Word War I.

Besides domestic instability, the 1910s saw endless international crises and wars for the Ottoman Empire. Ottoman troops fought the Tripoli War in 1911–1912; the Balkan Wars in 1912–1913, and the World War I. The first two had as substantial effects on Ottoman social, political and intellectual life. By the end of 1913, it had lost all its lands in North Africa and eighty-three per cent of its lands in Europe and suffered deep economic problems as a consequence of wartime expenses. The devastating defeat at the First Balkan War with thousands of Muslims emigrating to Istanbul and Asia Minor opened deep wounds in the psyches of many.

All these events and complications in domestic and international politics led to changes in the type of governance and the political atmosphere of the empire. After the 1908 revolution, the Unionists appeared to hold more liberal ideas and a romantic belief in upholding Ottomanness as an identity for all subjects of the empire.[82] They pragmatically sought to get the support of the Armenians and the Greeks in their struggle for political power in the first years of the new regime. Although it is difficult to pinpoint the Ottomanist ideas of the CUP, a speech delivered by Talat Paşa in a secret meeting of the Unionists in Monastir in 1910 reveals much about the means it was conceptualised and the obstacles ahead it:

> You are aware that by the terms of the constitution equality of Mussulman and Giaour was affirmed, but you, one and all, know and feel that this is an unrealizable ideal. The Sheriat, our whole past history, and the sentiments of hundreds of thousands of Mussulmans, and even the sentiments of the Giaours themselves, who stubbornly resist every attempt to Ottomanise them, present an impenetrable barrier to the establishment of real equality. We have made unsuccessful attempts to convert the Giaour into a loyal Osmanlı, and all such efforts must inevitably fail, as

81   Aykut Kansu, *Politics in Post-Revolutionary Turkey, 1908–1913*, Leiden: Brill, 1999, p. 153.
82   Ağaoğlu Ə. Tərcümeyi-hali-acizanəm. AMEA-nın M. Füzuli adına Əlyazmalar İnstitutu, f.21.

long as the small independent States in the Balkan Peninsula remain in a position to propagate ideas of separatism among the inhabitants of Macedonia. There can therefore be no question of equality until we succeeded in our task of Ottomanising the Empire—after we have at last put an end to the agitation and propaganda of the Balkan states.[83]

After the Balkan Wars, the changing demography of the empire and the political propensities of the ruling elites would further highlight the Turkist element within the CUP. All three most powerful political figures, Enver Paşa, the Minister of War (hailed as the second conqueror of Edirne), Talat Paşa, the Minister of Interior Affairs, and Cemal Paşa, Minister of the Navy, together with such lesser influential figures as the Grand Vizier Said Halim Paşa and Cavid Bey, were willing to adopt Turkish nationalism, promote economic nationalism and employ a more authoritarian mode of governance.[84]

In the run up to World War I and after, increasing censorship put an end to the relatively free intellectual atmosphere of the Second Constitutional era. By the end of the war, the number of newspapers and periodicals published in Istanbul dropped to fourteen.[85] Many publications and most political or non-political organisations were either closed or incorporated into the body of the CUP in the belief that only uniformity could enable the successful implementation of its growing nationalist policies. A militaristic nationalism, nurtured partly by Ziya Gökalp and other nationalist writers and by the Goltzian education young military officers had received before coming to power, began to rise in this period.[86]

Against this background did Ağaoğlu emerge as a pioneer of Turkish nationalism in Istanbul. After his arrival in the capital, he worked as the general inspector of some secondary schools in Istanbul.[87] Shortly afterwards, he was named director of the Süleymaniye Library. On September 24, 1910, he was naturalised as a subject of the Ottoman Empire and in October 1910, took up a post at the *Darülfünun* (which would later become the University of Istanbul) as professor of Turco-Mongolian history.[88] All the while he published essays in

83   Arthur B. Geary (Monastir) to G. Lowther, August 8, 1910, TNA FO 371/1014/33044.
84   Zafer Toprak, *Türkiye'de Milli İktisat,* p. 25.
85   Orhan Koloğlu, *Aydınlarımızın Bunalım Yılı 1918,* p. 59.
86   M. Naim Tufan, *Rise of the Young Turks,* N.Y., London: I.B. Tauris, 2000, p. 331; Feroze A.K. Yasamee, "Colmar Freiherr von der Goltz and the Rebirth of the Ottoman Empire," Diplomacy & Statecraft, vol.9, No. 2 (1998), pp. 91–128.
87   Catalogue note, BOA MF. MKT., 1157/3.
88   Catalogue note, BOA MF. MKT., 1162/31.

Ottoman and Caucasian journals including *Kaspii, Hagigat, Yeni Hagigat* (1910–1912), *İkdam* (1912–1915) and *Türk Sözü* (1918).[89] In the early 1910s, he regularly wrote in the *Kaspii* a column titled "Letters from Turkey" in which he gave detailed accounts of what went on Turkish politics at the time in a manner a diplomat would report to his capital.[90]

Ağaoğlu's first writings in the Ottoman Empire came in 1909 in the form of essays in the Islamist journals *Hikmet (Virtue)* and *Sırat-ı Müstakim (The Straight Path)*.[91] The latter hosted articles by writers with a wide range of views from different parts of the Near East, their common denominator being the aim of liberating Muslim nations from the encroachment of Western imperialism and the proposal of a substantial mental and moral reform in the Islamic world. Notably, such nationalist émigrés as Yusuf Akçura, İsmail Gasprinski and Ayaz İshaki also wrote for *Sırat-ı Müstakim* at the time. Since Ağaoğlu started to publish first in Islamist journals, later commentators have tended to depict his intellectual life in the late Ottoman Empire as an evolution from Islamism to Turkism.[92] However, as will be shown in the following chapter, Islamism and nationalism continued to be the intertwined components of his thought throughout the decade.

The journal to which Ağaoğlu contributed most frequently in this decade was *Tercümân-ı Hakikat (The Interpreter of Truth)*, which had been brought out since 1878 by the conservative man of letters and moralist Ahmet Midhat.[93] Ağaoğlu co-edited the journal with the latter between 1909 and 1911, though it is difficult to argue that there was any significant influence of Midhat over Ağaoğlu. He hardly mentioned the ideas or work of Midhat in his writings.

After Midhat died Ağaoğlu became the sole editor-in-chief of the journal and published in it numerous essays on high politics. Zealously supporting virtually all policies of the Committee of Union and Progress, the leaders of which procured him a new life in Istanbul, Ağaoğlu's *Tercümân-ı Hakikat* often seemed to be the mouthpiece of the Party in the 1910s. According to British intelligence sources, it was subventioned by the Germans during the war.[94]

In the second half of 1912 when, with the Young Turks being distanced from the government and with the start of the First Balkan War, he undertook an

89   Hajiyeva, "Ahmadbey Aghayev"in Publisistikası," p. 14.

90   Ahmdbek Agaev, "Pis'ma iz Turcii," *Kaspii,* January 5, 1910–February 2, 1914.

91   İsmail Kara, *Türkiye'de İslamcılık Düşüncesi, Metinler/Kişiler,* I, Istanbul: Kitabevi Yayınları, 1988, p. 311.

92   Sakal, *Ağaoğlu Ahmet Bey,* p. 94; Özcan, *Ahmet Ağaoğlu ve Rol Değişimi,* p. 112.

93   Ahmet Agayef, "Osmanlı Devriminin Şark Üzerindeki Tesiri," *Tercümân-ı Hakikat,* 1912.

94   Richard Webb to A.J. Balfaour, April 7, 1919, TNA Fo371/4173/296.

explicit campaign against the domestic and foreign policies of the government in his columns in *Tercümân-ı Hakikat*. On another occasion, he was arrested along with some other members of the Committee for his explicit defence of the actions of the Committee, which disturbed the Sublime Porte, and he spent approximately two weeks in prison in November 1912.[95] Under such conditions, as noted before, his ideas were at times informed by strong practical considerations; on certain occasions there was less conviction in his thought and more adaptability to circumstances. For example, although he had argued for further decentralisation in the Russian context in order for Russian Muslims to achieve further local rights, in the Ottoman context, as a member of the Unionists, he would strongly reject this policy.[96]

The other main journal to which Ağaoğlu was a frequent contributor in the 1910s was *Türk Yurdu* (*Turkish Homeland*). Together with *Genç Kalemler* (*Young Pens*), *Türk Yurdu* was a pioneering nationalist journal of the late Ottoman Empire.[97] It was launched by Yusuf Akçura and the famous nationalist Mehmet Emin Yurdakul (1969–1944) in Istanbul in May 1911, with the objective of working "to improve the intellectual standard of Turks and to make them strong-willed and enterprising."[98] The journal's editorial programme, penned by Akçura, suggested the use of simple language and the promotion of ideals acceptable to all Turks. The contributors were to deal mostly with subjects contributing to Turks' mutual awareness, their economic and moral improvement and their enrichment in scientific knowledge, and to give less room to political subjects in their writings. According to Dumont and Lewis, there was no other journal that was as significant as *Türk Yurdu* in shaping the fate of modern Turkey, because it literally provided the re-imagined roots of Turkish nationalism.[99]

In his *Türk Yurdu* writings, as will be demonstrated in the following chapter, Ağaoğlu laid out his views on Turkish nationalism, frequently pointing out the underprivileged position of the Turks in the Ottoman Empire and the importance of the Turkish component of the empire from a historical perspective.

---

95   Arsen Avagyan, *Ermeniler ve İttihat ve Terakki: İşbirliğinden Çatışmaya,* Istanbul: Aras Yayıncılık, 2005, p. 111; Süreyya Ağaoğlu, *Bir Ömür Böyle Geçti,* p. 11.

96   Ahmet Aghayef, "Adem-i Merkeziyet I, II, III," *Tercümân-ı Hakikat,* No. 11283, 11284, 11285, (Sep., 1912).

97   Masimo Arai, *Turkish Nationalism in the Young Turk Era,* Leiden; New York: E.J. Brill, 1991.

98   Yusuf Akçura, *Türk Yılı,* p. 437.

99   Paul Dumont, "La Revue *Turk Yurdu* et les musulmans de l'empire russe: 1908–1914", *Cahiers du monde russe et soviétique,* Vol. 15, No. 3–4 (1974), pp. 315–331; Bernard Lewis, "History-Writing and National Revival in Turkey", *Middle East Affairs,* Vol. 4, No. 6–7 (1953), 227–228; cf. Hakan Yavuz, "Nationalism and Islam: Yusuf Akçura and Üç Tarz-ı Siyaset," *Journal of Islamic Studies,* vol. 4, No. 2 (1993), p. 199.

In 1914, he left *Sebilürreşad* and started to write articles about the situation of the Islamic world in *İslam Mecmuası* (*Islamic Review*), which was issued by the contributors to *Türk Yurdu*.[100] They believed that their position in relation to Islam was given insufficient exposure, whereas religion was an important component of national spirit of their thought. Their new journal, whose slogan was "Life with Religion, Religion with Life," was therefore intended to benefit Islam and was itself a proof of the alliance between Islamism and nationalism in the Ottoman Turkish context. If nationalism was one ideal to be achieved for the salvation of the Ottoman people, Islam was one of its most important enabling components.

3.2.1   *The Turkish Hearths*

In 1912, one of the most important nationalist organisations in twentieth-century Turkey was founded after a number of meetings at Ağaoğlu's house in Fatih: *Türk Ocakları* (the Turkish Hearths). In fact, a group of medical students were the originators of the idea of founding such an organisation. The contributors of *Türk Yurdu* willingly helped this group and the Hearths was founded in March 1912.[101] The Russian émigrés Yusuf Akçura, İsmail Gasprinsky and Hüseyinzade Ali, together with Ağaoğlu, became members of its founding committee. The ultimate objectives of the Hearths were to elevate the educational, intellectual, social and economic situation of the Turks. The programme of the organisation insisted that it would not deal with politics. In effect, the society successfully followed the direction it had set itself in the beginning. It organised youth activities, set up clubs, instituted social activities and sports, held evening classes and provided free lectures, striving to educate the people in a nationalist spirit, "taught them to esteem their cultural heritage, [...] arranged literary and artistic soirées, published books and magazines, and assisted needy students with lodgings and medical care."[102] It made a great impact within and outside the Ottoman Empire and affiliated various nationalist groups all over Anatolia in a short time. Branches were established even in China and Turkistan. By 1914, the number of hearths in Anatolia became sixteen and they had a total membership of over 3000.[103]

---

100   Ahmet Aghayef, "İslam Aleminde Görülen İnhitatın Sebepleri," *İslam Mecmuası*, No. 2 (1914).

101   Yusuf Akçura, *Türk Yılı*, p. 354; also see, İbrahim Karaer, *Türk Ocakları, 1912–1931*, Ankara: Türk Yurdu Neşriyatı, 1992.

102   Jacob Landau, *Pan-Turkism: From Irredentism to Cooperation*, London: C. Hurst, 1995, p. 42.

103   Ibid., p. 30.

Ahmet Ağaoğlu worked vigorously for the Hearths until 1918, giving lectures in various branches and contributing to its publications. In the interim, he joined the CUP when they moved their headquarters from Salonika to Istanbul in 1912, after Salonika was annexed by the Greeks. Before his participation, other leading figures of the Turkish Hearths such as Gasprinsky and Hüseyinzade Ali had been elected as members of the central commission of the Committee of Union and Progress. This had secured close ties between the Unionists and the Hearths. The support of Gökalp for the Hearths after he came to Istanbul in 1912 fortified these ties. When the Unionists established an authoritarian rule, the Hearths became one of the few social and cultural organisations which was spared from being closed down.[104] Moreover, after 1913, it began to receive financial support from the Unionists and opened several new offices in Anatolia, in premises owned by the CUP.[105]

The Turkish Hearths implemented the cultural policies of the Unionists through its publications and its social and cultural activities.[106] It was no coincidence that organisations linked to the Unionists such as *Bilgi Derneği* (The Society of Knowledge)[107] and *Türk Gücü* (The Turkish Force) operated from the headquarters of the Hearths.[108] As part of the Unionists' "Towards the People" campaign, which aimed at social transformation by reaching out to as many people as possible, they established new journals such as *Halka Doğru* (*Towards the People*) and *Türk Sözü* (*Turkish Word*) in 1913 and 1914 with Ağaoğlu's contributions.

3.2.2 Activities during World War I
A couple of months after receiving a reader's letter in late 1914 questioning why he was still using a name of Russian origin (Aghayeff), he began to sign his

---

104   Akçuraoğlu Yusuf, "İttihat ve Terakki Cemiyeti'nin Yıllık Kongresi," *Türk Yurdu*, No., 49 (October 1913), p. 29, cf. Erol Köroğlu, *Ottoman Propaganda and Turkish Identity, Literature in Turkey During World War I*, London &N.Y.: I.B. Tauris & Co. Ltd., 2007, p. 64.

105   Enver Paşa provided a large amount of financial support for the society as understood from a note to his adjutant Kazım Orbay, in which he wants Rauf Paşa (Orbay) to give Ahmet Ağaoğlu a thousand lira; Füsun Üstel, *İmparatorlukta Ulus Devlete Türk Milliyetçiliği, Türk Ocakları, 1912–1931*, Istanbul: İletişim Yayınları, 1997, p. 74.

106   Köroğlu, *Ottoman Propaganda*, p. 65.

107   Ağaoğlu also wrote for their official periodical *Bilgi Mecmuası*; Ahmet Aghayef, "İslamiyetten Evvel Arablar," *Bilgi Mecmuası*, No. 1 (1915), pp. 53–62.

108   During World War I, with the support it received from the Unionists, the Turkish Hearths maintained its strong existence as a society under dictatorial rule and increased its number of offices from 16 to 25 in January 1916.

articles Ağaoğlu Ahmed.[109] Then, in 1915, he was elected to the Ottoman parliament from Karahisar and continued to represent it in the third and fourth terms.

During the war, Ağaoğlu was mainly preoccupied with producing propaganda against the Entente forces and with pressing the Turkist cause in and outside the Ottoman Empire. When he was added to the list of the British for imprisonment at the end of World War I, his activities during the war came to make him known as "a thoroughly most dangerous man".[110] He was noted to be consistently anti-British and a propagator of Pan-Islamism. The same source argues that he was very influential over the CUP during the war as a member of its central committee and was partially responsible for the Armenian massacres. His propaganda activities on behalf of the CUP were noted to have extended to Mecca from which place he got into touch with the Ulema of Al Azhar and became suspect to the British authorities in Egypt.[111]

When Ağaoğlu was informed of these while under detention in Mudros, he would send a petition to the British High Commissioner and reject the claims that his journal was German subventioned and that he was involved in the Armenian massacres. He would write, to prove that his imprisonment in mid-1919 was a mistake, that "[j]'affirme d'une manière absolue que ne j'ai jamais été en rapport avec les Allemands et n'ai jamais aime ce peuple." He also wrote that, although he was accused of having found a journal in Istanbul with German capital, he had in fact never established any journal throughout the 1910s.

Ağaoğlu also rejected the accusations for provoking the Armenian massacres. He argued that none of his writings during the war supported or appropriated the Armenian events.

> Au contraire, ..., j'ai fait mon possible a aider les Arméniens je suis en état de le prouver par les articles que j'ai écrit sur les Arméniens et par d'autres évènements et faits. Les Arménien étaient si pleins de reconnaissance envers moi qu'ils ont fait en mon honneur un banquet au Tokatlian ou assistaient entre autres les ministres actuels de l'Armenie-Khatissoff et Papadjanoff et membré de la délégation Arménienne a la Conférence de paix le poète Avronian.[112]

---

109   Sakal informs us that the first article that Ağaoğlu signed with his changed name was "Ergenekon ve Bozurt" which was published in *Tercümân-ı Hakikat*.

110   Minutes on the petition of Ahmed Agaeff, August 27, 1919, TNA FO 371/4174.

111   R. Webb to Curzon, August 26, 1919, TNA FO 371/4174/293.

112   Ahmed Agaeff to Lord Chancellor, April 16, 1919, TNA FO 371/4174/296.

During the war, besides his writings in *Tercümân-ı Hakikât* and *Türk Yurdu*, Ağaoğlu published two articles in the first two volumes of *Harb Mecmuası* (*The Journal of War*) and started to issue another propaganda journal, *Hilâl* (*The Crescent*). At the start of the war he wrote that the Ottoman Empire's geo-political importance as a country which controlled Istanbul and the Dardanelles was the inevitable cause of its entry into the war.[113] It was natural for the Ottomans to join the Central Powers, because these had no claims over Muslim nations, unlike the triple entente of Britain, France and Russia, which had long threatened the political existence of Muslim countries.[114] After his trip to Berlin in April 1915, he would also write very favourably on Germany and the Germans. He would maintain that with their disciplined social structure and with the admirable contributions of German women to politics and the national economy, Germany could hardly lose the battle.[115]

The pro-German tendencies in Ağaoğlu's writings of the time can be explained at a more immediate level as a wartime necessity. One supports and brags about his/her allies, not enemies. It can also be explained, at least in part, by means of re-constructing the details of his relationship with the Germans during World War I. I was unable to establish if his journals were indeed sub-ventioned by the Germans. But it was obvious that Ağaoğlu's rapprochement with the Germans during the war had reasons beyond the immediate aims of the CUP and the interests of the Ottoman Empire. This was linked to the broader goals of the Russian Muslims.

One can argue that Russian émigrés saw World War I as an opportunity to purge the people's bitter memories of the Balkan defeat and also to realise their dual program.[116] They were, first, working to strengthen the Turkish component of the empire; and secondly, struggling for further rights and the socio-economic elevation of Russian Muslims.

Before the war they had not sown hostility towards the Russian government. For example, they were underlining that *Türk Yurdu* was a "cultural, not political, journal, and more than once it praised Russian schools, literature and language."[117] In their view, there had been beneficial results of the coexistence of Russians and Muslims in Russia. This was not unknown to Russians in Istanbul. In 1913, their idea of taking a group of Ottoman professionals to Russia

---

113   Ağaoğlu Ahmed, "Türkiye'nin ve İslam Aleminin Kurtuluşu," *Harb Mecmuası*, No. 1, 1915.

114   Ibid.

115   BOA MF. MKT. 1207/58; Ağaoğlu Ahmet, "Almanya Seyahati İntibaatımdan: Alman Kadınlığı," *Türk Yurdu*, No. 84, 1331.

116   Ağaoğlu Ahmed, "Türkiye'nin ve İslam Aleminin Kurtuluşu," *Harb Mecmuası*, No. 1, 1915.

117   Zenkovsky, *Pan-Turkism and Islam in Russia*, p. 111.

on a tour and sending students to Russian had received support from Talat Bey, the Minister of Interior.[118] The Ministry of Education had assigned Ağaoğlu, who was serving for the ministry at the time, to draft a program on sending students to Russia. In March 1913, "a 'Turkish-Russian Committee' had been established in Istanbul for the development of closer cultural, economic and political ties."[119] According to Reynolds, it could be regarded even suspicious that the CUP and a figure like Ağaoğlu, who had long criticised the Tsarist Russian government in his writings and written in favour of Pan-Islamism, were enthusiastic about such a committee. In his view, it was possible that Ottomans were merely humouring the Russians with the committee, even though they provided financial support for it and wanted to open a branch office in St Petersburg perhaps even more than the Russians. For the Austro-Hungarian ambassador in Istanbul, the committee was mere window dressing. He excoriated its formation.[120]

When the war broke out, this rapproachment came to an end. Russian émigrés regarded the war as a chance for the Ottomans to bring succour to fellow Muslims living under Russian rule. Akçura interpreted the Ottomans' fight as a war of ideals, because they were fighting also for the rights of the Turkish people of the Caucasus Mountains, whose independence and freedom had been usurped by Russia.[121] Their ideals would "secure victory, because ideals are perpetual. Ideals never die; they live always by flourishing and developing, that is by moving from one victory to another."[122] In the same period, the Unionists sent out a circular to all of the local branches of their party:

> We pursue … an immediate goal—the realisation of our ideal … The national ideal of our people and our land drives us toward destroying the Muscovite foe and toward achieving in this manner the natural frontiers of the state in which our brothers in race will be included and united … Religious considerations drive us toward liberating the Islamic world from the domination of the infidel.[123]

This circular was a sign of the influence of the nationalists over the policies of the Party. During the war, the Turkish nationalists also dispatched agents to

---

118   Michael Reynolds, *Shattering Empires*, p. 42.

119   Ibd., p. 43.

120   Ibid., 43.

121   Akçuraoğlu Yusuf, "Geçen Yıl-1330 Senesi," *Türk Yurdu*, March 18, 1915; cf. Yusuf H. Bayur, *Türk İnkılabı Tarihi*, vol. 3, Ankara: Türk Tarih Kurumu Basımevi, 1983, p. 387.

122   Ibid., p. 387.

123   Swietochowski, *Russian Azerbaijan*, p. 76.

disseminate their ideals and mobilise support for Turkism, with the aim of strengthening the bonds between Ottoman Turks and Russian Muslims. Moreover, in 1915, the Hearths established *Rusya Müslümanları Türk-Tatar Milletleri Müdafaa-i Hukuk Cemiyeti* (The Society for the Defence of Rights of the Muslim Turco-Tatar Peoples of Russia). The organisation made demands from Russia on behalf of Russian Muslims, including equal representation in the Duma, full economic rights, religious freedom and cultural autonomy. In mid-1915 its members prepared a pamphlet and a memorandum, which they submitted to governments and published in their newspapers, and some delegates travelled to Vienna, Budapest, Berlin and Sofia. Ağaoğlu was one of the representatives of the Society. Their first pamphlets involved historical and demographic facts about the groups in question, while the second demanded independence for Russian Muslims and suggested that the Central Powers liberate them from the yoke of the Russians. The group also agitated inside the Ottoman Empire, pointing to the legal and national rights of Russian Muslim populations and simultaneously emphasizing their cultural and historical ties with the Ottoman Turks.[124]

This was not to say that they were defending Pan-Turkism, because until the 1917 Revolution few Turkish nationalists suggested the assembling of all Turks under a Turkish state or transforming the cultural-national brotherhood into a political unity. But they still placed their hopes both in the regenerative power of their nationalist sentiments and in the Ottoman-German alliance.[125]

After the 1917 Revolution in Russia, the disintegration of the Tsarist Empire raised hopes that the Ottomans would recover not only the territories lost in the Caucasus since 1914, but possibly also those that Russia had wrested from Turkey during the nineteenth century. Furthermore, immediately after the March Revolution, Talat Paşa explicitly stated that with the abolition of the Tsarist regime, the ideal of Turkey's eastern empire could be realised.[126] Hence, the Turanist ideal of uniting all Turkic nations under a single state was galvanized. The vision of the conquest of Turkic lands in Russia once again captivated

---

124   Paradoxically enough, Zenkovsky notes that during the war Topçubaşı's *Kaspii* called upon Russian Muslims to join Russia in the fight against Germany and Turkey, pointing out that they, like the Muslims of India, should not consider the Ottoman sultan-caliph head of all Muslims since he had not been chosen by the Muslims. Zenkovsky, *Pan-Islam,* pp. 125–126.

125   Akçura argued that a renewed alliance between the Ottoman Turks and the Germans was of the greatest importance for the successful development of the activities of Russian Turkic students in Istanbul.

126   Bülent Gökay, *A Clash of Empires: Turkey Between Russian Bolshevism and British Imperialism, 1918–1923,* London, N.Y.: I.B. Tauris, 1997, p. 17.

the mind of Enver Paşa.[127] For this reason, agents were sent to Baku to assemble a network and establish contacts with pro-Ottoman elements in Transcaucasia.

In the meantime, Hüseyinzade Ali delivered lectures on his native Transcaucasia envisaging three alternative resolutions to the situation of the region, the first being the formation of a federation of the Caucasus, the second the creation of separate Muslim and Georgian states, and the third the union of the Caucasus with Turkey in the form of a viceroyalty.[128] With the dissolution of the Federation of Transcaucasia, which was established after the disintegration of the Russian Empire, Azerbaijan proclaimed its independence in May 1918 and began its restructuring under the leadership of a pro-Russian Şura (Assembly).

The Ottomans clearly regarded Transcaucasia "as a part of the Turanian empire-in-the-making in 1918, which was also to include the North Caucasus, northern Persia and Turkistan."[129] The chief instrument of Enver Paşa's Pan-Turanian policy in Transcaucasia was a motley Ottoman-Azerbaijani force, the Army of Islam. Its commander was Enver's 25-year-old half-brother Nuri Paşa. At Enver Paşa's request, Ağaoğlu, who was critical of the passive role of the Ottoman Empire, particularly in the Brest-Litovsk negotiations,[130] went to Azerbaijan with the Ottoman Army as its adviser.[131] But he switched sides there. The same year, he was elected to the Azerbaijani parliament and started to work for the new Azeribaijani state.

At the end of World War I, when the Ottoman forces were required by the Armistice of Mudros to withdraw from the Caucasus, Ağaoğlu took on the role

---

127   Swietochowsky, *Russian Azerbaijan,* p. 118.

128   Ibid., p. 120.

129   Ibid., p. 130.

130   Bayur, *Türk İnkılâbı Tarihi,* pp. 139–141.

131   When there emerged a clash between the Ottoman foreign policy and the domestic policies of Azerbaijan, he found himself in the middle of a tension between Nuri Paşa, the commander of the Ottoman army, and Azerbaijani leaders. The cause of the problems was Nuri Paşa's interference in the politics of Azerbaijan. Nuri was not happy with the pro-Russian cabinet, therefore willing to form a new cabinet whose members would be appointed by him. Ağaoğlu asked the Azeri Şura to resign and establish a new government, indicating that they lacked popular support and it might lead to a revolt. In such a situation, he added, the Ottomans would not defend the Azeri government. This proposal was shocking to the Azeri leaders, who eventually rejected it, but still decided that the Şura should take a holiday. The decision taken by the Şura led to the resignation of leftist groups within it. Shortly thereafter, it was disbanded and a new government formed. This eventually triggered the emergence of an Azerbaijanist movement among some Azeri groups against the "friendly" interventions of Nuri Paşa.

of diplomat and struggled to preserve the independence of Azerbaijan against the Russian, Georgian and Armenian threats, including by asking Britain to recognize Azerbaijan as an independent state and to form an alliance at a meeting in Enzeli.[132] Suspecting that the Ottomans had an interest in this, the British authorities rejected his proposal. Therefore, Ağaoğlu sought the support of the Russians,[133] but this initiative also failed. In the end, he returned to Azerbaijan when the Azerbaijani government decided to argue its case before the Western Powers, in the belief that their support was the only option and thus vital, while its rivals, the Armenians and Georgians, had already made significant connections. To this end, a delegation was elected in early 1919 to represent Azerbaijani claims at the Paris Peace Conference. The delegation, of which Ağaoğlu was the leader, was forced to wait in Istanbul for three months en route to Paris, since the French government had denied visas to its members. During this delay, Ağaoğlu was arrested by the Ottoman police on the grounds that he was a Unionist and turned over to the British forces.[134]

---

132 Ahmed Agaeff to British High Commissioner, June 5, 1919, TNA FO371/4174/301.

133 Ağaoğlu Ahmet, "Berlin Müzakereleri," *Şule*, September 9, 1918; "Şark Konfederasyonu," *Şule*, September 17, 1918; Fahri Sakal, *Ağaoğlu Ahmed Bey*, p. 27.

134 Bilal Şimşir, *Malta Sürgünleri*, Ankara: Bilgi Yayınevi, 1985, p. 230.

CHAPTER 4

Rights, Religion and Nationalism

Pan-Islamism served as the ideological basis of Ağaoğlu's both liberal and nationalist work between 1894 and 1919. His attempts to defend the rights of Russian Muslims vis-à-vis the Russian state, his arguments for bringing a more modern interpretation to the religion of Islam, on the situation of women in the East, the emancipation of Muslims and their self-strengthening, and his work on the development of Turkish nationalism were all based on a Pan-Islamist foundation.

Mahmad Amin Resulzade (1884–1955), the first and only president of the Democratic Republic of Azerbaijan (1918–20), similarly argued that Pan-Islamism laid the ground for Russian Muslims on which to demand liberal reforms from the Russian authorities and to formulate a nationalist and modern worldview. Before and after the 1905 Revolution, he wrote, it set the goals of not only the Caucasians but all Russian Muslims.[1] Resulzade left us unanswered however what it meant for the Azerbaijani intelligentsia of the time.

According to Landau, the term Pan-Islamism had been coined by the Young Ottomans.[2] In an anonymous article in Ziya Paşa's *Hürriyet* (Liberty) in November 1868 and later in other articles by Ziya Paşa, the concept of *İttihad-ı İslam* (Union of Islam) was used for the first time. In January 1872, the Istanbul journal *Basiret* had used the term *İttihad-ı İslam* as an antidote to Pan-Slavism and Pan-Germanism, and in June of the same year, the prominent Young Ottoman Namık Kemal had maintained that only a union of all Muslims, led by the Ottomans, could save the Ottoman Empire.

Young Ottomans had desired to free the Ottoman Empire from its inferior (particularly economic) position in its relations with Western Powers.[3] Their successors the Young Turks had also exploited Pan-Islamism in their political struggles, along with Pan-Turkism and Ottomanism, at the end of the nineteenth century.[4] Yet its first extensive use was made in 1881 by Gabriel Charmes,

---

1 Lale Hadjievva, "Agir Mubarazalar Devri," p. 3.
2 Landau, *The Politics of Pan-Islam*, p. 2.
3 Mardin, *The Genesis of Young Ottoman Thought*, p. 60.
4 Hanioğlu, *Preparation for a Revolution*, p. 298.

© KONINKLIJKE BRILL NV, LEIDEN, 2015 | DOI 10.1163/9789004297364_005

a prolific French journalist, who developed an interest in the Ottoman Empire, visited parts of it and wrote about it repeatedly in the 1880s. It referred to creating a united Islamic front against the common threat.[5]

Among Pan-Islamist writers, there were variations in arguments adduced and conclusions reached. Of all these writers al-Afghani, although not its originator, was one of the best-known and most influential contributors and his account of Pan-Islamism was undeniably the one that caught Ağaoğlu's and other Russian Muslims' attention the most.[6] According to Resulzade, Afghani was the first to show that the emancipation of the Muslim work through liberal reforms required the awakening of national consciousness.[7] In his early writings, al-Afghani's approach was directed "to each Muslim country separately, emphasizing not solely the glory of Islam, but also the country's non-Islamic greatness."[8] In his later writings, however, he came to the conclusion that only a united Islamic world could match the physical force of any of the Western Powers. Therefore, markedly toning down his earlier attacks on the Ottoman Empire, he selected the Caliph as the most likely personality to direct a Pan-Islamic campaign.[9]

Al-Afghani's suggestions of a more rational interpretation of Islam and forming bonds of unity within and among different Muslim nations were the running themes in Ağaoğlu's writings throughout the period between the early 1890s and the late 1910s also. The latter's writings on equality and rights of Russian Muslims were nothing more than an echo of fellow Muslim intelligentsia's demands and writings. Yet his growing convictions on moral decay in Islamic society and his denouncement of individuality would markedly shape his work in early Republican Turkey. His formulation of Turkish nationalism, again along with fellow nationalists, would be the other most important heritage of his work in the imperial context.

4.1   Rights and Equality

In Ağaoğlu's view, Pan-Islamism was an eclectic current composed of three groups: the first consisted of the new Muslims, who believed that the survival

---

5   Jacob M. Landau, *The Politics of Pan-Islam*, p. 2; Mehrdad Kia, "Pan-Islamism in Late Nineteenth Century Iran," *Middle Eastern Studies*, vol. 32, No. 1 (Jan., 1996), p. 30.

6   Landau, *The Politics of Pan-Islam*, p. 13.

7   Hadjizade, "Agir Mubarazalar Devri," p. 3.

8   Landau, *The Politics of Pan-Islam*, Ibid., p. 14.

9   Jacob M. Landau, "al-Afghani's Pan-Islamist project," p. 50; cf. Landau, *The Politics of Pan-Islam*, p. 20.

of Muslims was dependent upon the unconditional adoption of the principles of the Western civilisation and the imitation of its lifestyle; the second called the conservatives argued that the main reason for the fallacy of Islamic societies was people's estrangement from their golden past, the decay of the ancient morality and individual freedoms, and the third sought to win the middle-way between the first two groups and wanted to interpret the words of God from a modern perspective offering serious reforms drawing from the teachings of Shari'a as exemplified in the work of al-Afghani.[10] The reform minded Russian Muslim intelligentsia and political and industrial elites who later formed the Union of Russian Muslims were falling into the third category. According to his account, they were also forming the liberals of Transcaucasia.

Swietochowski's arguments run parallel to this. Before the 1905 Revolution, he maintains, declarations in the Baku duma and articles in the *Kaspii* which demanded equality of rights for Muslims and Christians represented 'an attitude of mind' which one may call the Azerbaijani liberalism.[11] Its mouthpiece *Kaspii* launched a series of reformist campaigns with the aim of improving educational conditions, gaining Muslims the right to access to positions in the civil service, and alleviating the peasants' land hunger.[12]

As an elected member of the Baku duma and a writer for *Kaspii*, together with other liberals, Ağaoğlu participated in campaigns to gain concessions for Muslims in the Caucasus. The Muslim liberals demanded greater representation in the city dumas, access to high office in the civil service and military, trading privileges similar to those granted to Russian merchants, the right to publish and educate in their native, reform of the courts and provision for landless peasants.[13]

In his Russian and Turkish writings of the time, Ağaoğlu voiced these concerns repeatedly. While, on the one hand, he was critical of fellow Muslims to be too passive and lacking initiative to defend their rights and the rule of law, on the other, he, like other Russian Muslims, called for education and publication in native language, the opening of new schools, and permissions for local Muslims to work at these schools.[14] He also complained that those local

---

10   A. Agaev, "Panislamizm, ego kharakter i napravlenie," *Kaspii*, April 14, 1901; "Polozhenie musul'manskih narodov. Jeklektizm ili panislamistskoe dvizhenie," *Kaspii*, December 24, 1903.

11   Swietochowski, Russian Azerbaijan, p. 46.

12   Altstadt, "The Baku city duma–arena for elite conflict," pp. 49–66; Swietochowski, *Russian Azerbaijan*, pp. 35–36.

13   Akçura, *Türk Yılı*, p. 437.

14   Agaev A., "Neobhodimye raz'jasnenija k peticijam musul'man," *Kaspii*, April 1, 1905; "Peticija musul'man," *Kaspii*, April 15, 1905.

problems in education, services and judiciary could not be solved at their place, which was an impediment for the moral, intellectual and material progress of the local people.[15] Moreover, as concerns the under-representation of Muslims, he urged that "the elections of representatives must be made by community, meaning that only members of the community may run for the seats set aside for that community and only members of the community may vote for those seats."[16]

A member of the Baku duma, he wrote that Muslim representatives should be men of learning and experience, with extensive knowledge of the world, awareness of contemporary issues and a strong sense of service to the community. But in reality, he thought, the Muslim community was enslaved by the detrimental custom of giving greater weight to wealth, age, or inherited nobility than to merit. Centuries of autocratic rule, under Muslim regimes as well as Russian, had prevented the Muslim community of the Caucasus from participating in the management of common interests.[17] He was aware that it was as much because of the weakness of the Muslims as the oppression of the Tsarist government such inequalities in civil rights and imbalance between rights and duties were the case in the Caucasus at the time. Especially in his *Kaspii* writings, he therefore devoted more energy to understand and explain the reasons for the backwardness of Muslims and how this could be brought to an end.

4.2   Religion, Modernity and the Question of Women

The idea that the fundamental problem of the East was the moral predicament of the individual, an idea which Ağaoğlu had embraced and begun to propound during his Paris sojourn, loomed large in his Russian writings also. As in his French writings, he maintained that it was a consequence of the secondary role of women in Eastern societies. He also argued that it was the issue of the alphabet and the corruption of the clergy that prevented awakening in the Islamic world. His writings between 1894 and 1919 offered a historical explanation to these problems, placing the role of Islam and the clergy at its centre.

In Ağaoğlu's view, the religion of Islam, if interpreted accurately, could well provide Muslims with the moral norms that they needed in order to ensure

---

15   Ahmet Aghaeff, "Kafkasların Halihazırı," *Hayat*, 1905; cf. Shissler, pp. 151–156.
16   Ahmet Aghayef, "Adem-i Merkeziyet I, II, III".
17   Shissler, *Between Two Empires*, p. 153.

their social and individual development. He attempted to show in his writings
of the time that Islam had a progressive social function; it was not an impediment to modernity.

> It is incorrect to raise even in principle the question of the relationship of
> the three monotheistic religions—Christianity, Judaism, Islam—to con-
> temporary civilisation. They proceed from one another, they confess one
> and the same origin. Judaism created Christianity and both together cre-
> ated Islam; this was the last, emerging in a special historical medium and
> conditions. It created medieval Arab culture which through two chan-
> nels, Byzantium and Spain, influenced Europe, and having acquainted
> the Christian and Jewish world with ancient Greek culture, prepared the
> ground for the epoch of the renaissance of science and art.[18]

For Ağaoğlu, the historical role Islamic civilisation played in the service of
humanity was a testimony of how Islam could tolerate free and liberal institutions, how it could adapt itself to the demands of such institutions, and how it
could permit Muslims to mingle with other non-Muslim peoples.[19] He did not
devote any space in his writings to the characteristics of the institutions in
question. Instead, he saw it adequate to argue that what the Muslims needed
to do was to cast off the debased clergy, who had long undermined the importance of Islam with their misinterpretations of its teachings and their false
preaching tied to profane interests.

With these arguments, he differed remarkable from the ideas of Mirza Fath
Ali Akhundzade, the most prominent figure of the first generation of the modern Azerbaijani intelligentsia. Akhundzade had raised the question of women
in the Caucasus a few decades before Ağaoğlu, claiming that Islam was incom-
patible with women's rights, as "both Islamic laws and social norms sanctified
women's subordination with irrational, inhuman and stringent rules (infringe-
ments of which were severely punished)." For Akhundzade, the only solution
was a complete break with the Islamic past.[20]

In contrast, Ağaoğlu's writings showed close parallels with those of Jamal
ad-Din al-Afghani and the Egyptian writer Qasım Amin (1863–1908), who had
published a book entitled *The Liberation of Woman* only two years before the

---

18   Ibid.
19   Ahmet Aghayef, "Polozhenie musul'manskih narodov. Retrospektivnyj vzgljad na istoriju,"
      Kaspii, November 14, 1903.
20   Mehrdad Kia, "Women, Islam and Modernity in Akhundzade's Plays and Unpublished
      Writings," *Middle Eastern Studies*, vol. 34, No. 3 (Jul., 1998), pp. 22–23.

publication of Ağaoğlu's *Women in Islam*.[21] Like al-Afghani and Amin, he argued that Islam was not to be blamed for the situation of Muslim women, as the religion itself was inherently compatible with reason and freedom of thought. The essentialist idea that Islam led to the lagging behind of its believers was but a false belief of people, mostly from the West, who had been under the influence of the fanatical and biased views of European bards and playwrights since the Medieval Ages.

In *Women in Islam*, he asserted that the weakness, moral poverty and social disorganisation of Muslim countries could not be ascribed solely to the influence of Islam. In so thinking, one would overlook the human, the vigorous factor in life, and attribute to human a totally passive role.

> [T]here is a persistent, vigorous and reciprocal interaction between humans and religions, even if it cannot be felt easily... Religions, which, in the beginning...galvanise humans, are influenced by new life conditions over time and are adjusted to new conditions. In short, they submit to laws of development. In accordance with the construction of new living conditions they either deform or improve.[22]

Taking a scientific approach and grasping the dynamics of the relationship between man and religion was therefore the best way to understand the function of religion in society and to comprehend the role of man in giving religion its direction. Elsewhere he wrote:

> Religion, like science and art, is a force; this force can be used for good or evil. In the Middle Ages, Catholic Christianity surely was an obstacle to initiatives; it opposed science, art and the development of free thought! Jan Huss, Galileo, Giardano Bruno and others underwent torture in the name of Christianity! But it's not the Gospel that is guilty in all this; it's its interpreters, the moral torpor, the mental ignorance of their medieval contemporaries... The holy fathers at one time sold indulgences and religious offices and propounded the theory of the Divine Right [of monarchs] as an unshakable foundation. Now they consecrate republics, work out the bases of Christian socialism, and reconcile religion to social sciences![23]

---

21 For a comparison of the views of Amin and Ağaoğlu, see Shissler, *Between Two Empires*, pp. 141–143.

22 Aghayef, *İslamlıkta Kadın*, p. 23.

23 Ahmed Aghayef, "Islam i Demokratiya," *Kaspii*, (Sept., 1909), in *Modernist Islam*, ed. Charles Kurzman, N.Y.: Oxford University Press, 2002, 229–232.

For Ağaoğlu, with the developments in the field of Orientalism in the second half of the nineteenth century, Western thinkers gained the ability to study the beliefs and customs of Eastern peoples. It became possible to understand their lives in the light of original materials and documents and to explore the development of religions by juxtaposing different time periods.[24] Any rational and objective study of the situation of women in Islam, relying on scientific research rather than drawing ideas from an unconditional fanaticism, would demonstrate that Islam essentially paved the way for the emancipation of women and their development.[25]

Ağaoğlu appealed here to historicism and posited that the best and only way to approach the subject was to look first at the historical conditions of the pre-Islamic Arab society and the situation of the surrounding peoples. Only then could a better comprehension of the causes of progress and decline in the Islamic world, that is, an in-depth understanding of the situation of women in particular and the lagging behind of Muslim societies in general, be achieved.[26]

According to this account, when one compared pre-Islamic and Islamic Arab societies, it would be seen that Islam introduced the rule of law in place of the rule of force. This was best illustrated in the case of polygamy. Islam essentially restricted in the Arab world the formerly unrestricted practice of polygamy so that a man could have no more than four wives. Moreover, it insisted that equality of treatment was both a necessity and a practical impossibility, which meant that its ultimate aim was the abolition of polygamy.[27]

In Ağaoğlu's view, Islamic culture imparted great importance to women, as illustrated by the important social positions that they held in its history. He postulated that Mohammad's attitude towards women also underpinned by its nature the place of women in society.[28] A careful reading of the Qur'an and reflection on the *hadith* of Mohammad, he asserted, would reveal how in the true Islamic view women were in fact equal to men.[29] He furthered his argument with illustrations of elite female figures in early Islamic history, contending that the deterioration of the situation of women in Islam after the death of Mohammad was the result of, first, the disappearance of such elite women;

24   Ahmed Aghayef, *İslamlıkta Kadın*, p. 21.

25   Ibid., p. 22.

26   Ağaoğlu later wrote an essay on the situation of Arabs before Islam and published it in the organ of the Society of Knowledge in Istanbul. Ahmet Aghayef, "İslamlıktan Evvel Arablar," *Bilgi Mecmuası*, No. 1 (1915), pp. 53–62.

27   Aghayef, *İslamlıkta Kadın*, p. 32.

28   Ibid., pp. 33–34.

29   Ibid., pp. 28–31.

second, the negative influences of increasing wealth; and third, moral degeneration under the degrading cultural and moral influences of the Syrians and Iranians, especially the appearance and debasement of harems, which were, for Ağaoğlu, originally Iranian institutions.[30]

In strike contrast to his French writings, he argued that of all the peoples professing Islam today, only women among the Persians had anciently been handmaids and slaves. According to Ağaoğlu, the ancient religion of Persia, Zoroastrianism, had reacted to the women so cruelly and contemptuously that at certain periods she had been considered demon. With the penetration of Islam into Persia, Zoroastrianism had initially held back with its awful concepts and regulations of the woman. However, after the degeneration of Islam in three or four centuries, the handiwork of mostly Persians acquired an enormous, almost exclusive influence on the Muslim societies of the time.[31]

> Curtains [between men and women] became thicker... The period of the ultimate predominance of disgusting eunuchs, desires and intrigues came. The personality of the woman was completely destroyed. The woman...submitted herself to the lazy and light-hearted life of the *harem* with all its morally degenerating consequences.[32]

In Ağaoğlu's view, the decay of high culture also marked the beginning of the intervention of the harem in politics, the mysterious murders and intra-palace uprisings in the history of Islam. This spirit of degeneration blighted philosophy and literature, through which a suffocating atmosphere was created in social life.

> Theosophism, a weepy scepticism and an ambiguous mysticism which disclosed the unsteadiness of the soul replaced the old traditions of rationalism, knowledge and virtues; literature became a continual outcry; miserable weak minds found consolation in cursing holy things, in meaningless symbolism...and weird descriptions. In short, everything pointed to the perishing of society. This perishing was, above all, due to the change in the situation of women.[33]

---

30 Ibid., p. 47; also see A. Agaev, "Zhenskoe obrazovanie sredi musul'man," *Kaspii*, October 5, 1901.
31 Agaev, "Zhenskoe obrazovanie sredi musul'man."
32 *İslamlıkta Kadın*, p. 47.
33 Ibid., p. 48.

But for Ağaoğlu, in those societies that had not yet been exposed to Iranian influence, namely the Tatars, Turks and the Muslims of Western Spain, the tradition of the liberty of women continued. After the Muslims lost Spain and the Turks and Tatars fell under the moral influences of the Syrians and Iranians, the liberty of women in the Islamic world faded away completely shipwrecked, "a Muslim woman has since become vegetate," infected by ignorance, corruption, stagnation and decay.

Ağaoğlu was optimistic that the past, when 'true religious and racial instincts' prevailed over 'prejudice and superstition' could expand before the eyes of Muslims again. In his account, the women had long lost their identity. They had been deprived of the opportunity to make an impact on society, family and individuals by raising awareness among them. But this picture could be reversed by returning the women the stolen laws and traditions of religion and their human rights; by bringing back 'the heyday of women's education and freedom'.[34]

As a Caucasian, he believed that the developments in Ottoman Turkey were promising in this regard. Since the Ottoman Turks came in contact with the European civilization before anyone else in the East, even before anyone thought about the women's issue in Muslim nations, they began to to take action to uplift women mentally and morally. The question of women in Turkey was already experiencing its 'second stage'.[35]

He exaggeratedly argued that among almost all Turks, the importance of the status and condition of women had already been recognized in principle and so had been the need to educate women. According to his account, the Turkish press was now focusing its attention to efforts to achieve broader women rights, such as in the administration of the liberal professions. Turkish authorities read debates on women's rights every now and then and in most cases, of controversial female writers who were vigorously advocating the interests of their own sex.[36] New girls' schools were opening throughout Turkey where students were educated in their native languages, religion, history, geography and other sciences as well as foreign languages.

Apart from children's magazines published by women in collaboration with men, there were women's weekly illustrated magazines such as *Kadınlar Gazetesi* (Women's Newspaper) whose issues were exclusively devoted to women, to the biographies and activities of famous European women, education of children and housekeeping. They were receiving contributions from

---

34   Agaev, "Zhenskoe obrazovanie sredi musul'man."
35   Ibid.
36   Ibid.

such big names as Fatma Aliye, Nigar Hanım the daughter of Osman Paşa, the famous hero of Plevne, and others, who formed a vast popularity in the East for their historical research on women's issues and literary works. As result, he added, the intellectual and spiritual elevation of women in Turkey affected all sectors of life; Turkish life observed an unusual elevation of mood, faith in itself and to its future brought progress as in Egypt and India.

According to Ağaoğlu, Russian Muslims so long lagged behind in relation to women's issues. The opening of a new all female school for Muslims in Baku with Taghiev's initiative was the first step in this direction. These Muslim girls would form future mothers giving life to new generations and educating them spiritually.[37] Notably, Ağaoğlu conceived of this school as a 'school for mothers'. As this passage in *Women in Islam* shows us, the importance he attached to women's education was mainly from a men's perspective, focusing on the social function of women rather than their individual autonomy and rights:

> The contemporary Muslim woman can fulfil her social duties beneficially only if she becomes a free and conscious mother [and] wife. Only under these conditions can she imbue her children with a profound character and will, which is very important in social life. She can inculcate in them high sentiments, noble ideas. A woman who lives a persistently lazy life of vegetation in the stuffy ambiance of the harem, which does not allow her physical development, plays the primary role in the degeneration of the race.[38]

In insisting upon the emancipation of women for the empowerment of the Eastern individual, his main concern was their *work*. Otherwise put, his advocacy of the amelioration of the situation of women in Islam was for women's successful undertaking of their 'social duties' as free and conscious mothers and wives. This communitarian idea stayed with him always.

In the eyes of the Ağaoğlu of 1901, improving the existing situation of women in the East would require a more comprehensive solution than sending girls (as the *jadidists* had suggested) to school:

> There is need for a severe tremor (*sarsıntı*) to awaken the Muslim world, to make it a member of the society of nations (*milletler cemiyeti*). Muslims must also go through their own stages of evolution, and an iron-willed, brave and self-sacrificing man must appear among them. Such a

---

37   Ibid.
38   *İslamlıkta Kadın*, p. 53.

reformer…will find a fertile soil at first hand in Islam and in its history and customs.[39]

He did not, however, elaborate in 1901 how this could happen, but instead discussed the causes of the absence of such individuals.

In his view, Qur'an or Sharia were by no means obstacles to innovation, but the *ulema* (Islamic scholars) and sheikhs were giving Islam a character that was not compatible with civilisation (he appears here to use the term civilisation synonymous with modernism). In *Islam and Teacher*, he argued that the Mullahs' fanaticism, superstitious beliefs and ignorance were among the causes of the moral poverty and inertia of the Muslims.[40] The first aim had to be to give an end to the absence of clergy that would spiritually elevate the people.

For him, anyone who was respected enough to be granted the title could become an imam, or even a *kadı* (Muslim judge) if necessary.[41] He therefore firmly wanted an institutional framework to be given to the upbringing and selection of those who would determine the moral character of people and called for "the direct election of individuals to the positions of müfti and Sheikh ul-Islam."[42] This suggestion was not unprecedented in Russia at the time, but Meyer argues that "Ağaoğlu's attacks on the spiritual assembly leadership were made in a far sharper tone than that being used by community reformers elsewhere in Russia."[43]

Charging the spiritual leadership with incompetence and writing that they were "ready to sell out Muslims for the next thousand years,"[44] Ağaoğlu argued that Muslim intellectuals must reach the people by using the holy book effectively.[45] It was not unseen, in rest of his intellectual career, that Ağaoğlu, in a Renanian manner, called intellectuals to play their parts as selfless public moralists.[46] They would interpret the holy book in a way to make it more accessible to ordinary people and, through their writings, infuse in society true religion as opposed to its abused and degenerated version.

---

39   Ibid., pp. 52–53.
40   Akçura, *Türk Yılı*, p. 429.
41   James Meyer, "Division and Alliance: Mass Politics within Muslim Communities after 1905," The National Council for Eurasian and East European Research Working Paper, (Oct., 2009), p. 12.
42   A. Agaev, "Kadij," *Kaspii*, January 19, 1902.
43   Meyer, "Division and Alliance," p. 13.
44   Ahmet Aghayef, "Sebep Gene özümüzün," *İrşad*, May 25, 1907; cf Meyer, p. 13.
45   Hajiyeva, "Ahmadbey Aghayev'in Publisistikası," p. 11.
46   A. Agaev, "Rol" intelligentnyh musul"man," *Kaspii*, April 15, 1904.

This would owe as much to increasing literacy rate. Ağaoğlu shared the belief that a simpler script was needed, because it was difficult to use the Arabic script to write Turkish-Tatar languages. The alphabets that the Turks and Tatars had used before their adoption of Islam were completely suitable for the phonetic characteristics of the language spoken by the Turkish-Tatar race.[47] The script problem was hampering literacy among Russian Muslims and obstructing "the roads that lead to the enlightenment of Muslim minds and hearts."[48]

When the winds of hope blown by the 1906 Iranian and 1908 Young Turk revolutions began to peter out in the early 1910s, Ağaoğlu turned back to the question of the reasons for the lagging behind of the Muslim nations. In his writings in *Sebilürreşad*, which were addressed to a relatively conservative and religious readership, his main concern was again the moral poverty of society. Just before the outbreak of the First Balkan War, he wrote how a society falls as follows:

> The country and motherland are first torn from the hearts of the individuals comprising a nation. No moral firmness or spiritual resistance remain in the members of a nation to sacrifice their desires and ambitions, their own emotions and personal opinions for the sake of the country's common interests. Few individuals are found to sacrifice themselves materially and spiritually to save the country and the dynasty.[49]

While Gökalp was setting out in the early 1910s to develop his anti-individualist ideas derived from Durkheim's sociology, Ağaoğlu sought to improve, if not to perfect, the relationship of man with man, in a Renanian style. He argued that moral poverty slackened and further weakened the wills of all individual members of the nation, who in turn became obstinate when they were asked to do something that was not in their own private interests.

The result, he maintained, was spiritual slavery. In such a situation, individuals lacked the ability to reason. They could not comprehend what was really happening on the broader scale of social life. Unwittingly and unintentionally, they all regarded their own opinions and emotions as infallible and

---

47   A. Aghayev, "Obzor zhurnalistiki na Vostoke," *Kaspii*, November 26, 1899; also see "Imeet li Turko-Gagarskaja rasa svoju Sobstveniuju Azbuku," *Kaspii*, 1901, cf. Hajiyeva, "Ahmadbey Aghayev'in Publisistikası," p. 12.

48   Aghaeff, *İslamlikta Kadın*, p. 53.

49   Ahmet Aghayef, "Bir Memleket Nasıl Mahv Olur?" *Sebilürreşad*, No. 22 (Sep.–Oct. 1912), pp. 421–422.

flawless. Consequently, there was a decaying of relationships among individuals, who were the real guardians of the country. "The spirit of individuality prevails over the spirit of community."[50] In his account, the once unified national body was divided into groups and parties, causing it to disintegrate. This spirit of individuality then spread into these groups and continued to divide them into smaller elements. Social order decayed, social bonds became extremely weak, and under such a state of fragmentation, any pressure from outside, mostly in the form of war, threatened society's existence and weakened it to extinction.[51] Hence was the vulnerable condition of Islamic nations at the hands of Western encroachments.

4.3   The Origins of Turkish Nationalism

The development of Turkish nationalism in the Caucasus needed a long gestation period. At the end of the nineteenth century, two thirds of the Northern Azerbaijani population was consisting of Shi'ites, while a greater majority was speaking Azerbaijani Turkish. In Russians eyes, they were Transcaucasian Tatars. In their own, they were members of the Islamic *umma*.[52] In fact, their Islamic identity drew the territories of the 'imagined community' of all Russian Muslims as a useful base for the generation of solidarity against the Tsarist authorities. Their cultural defensiveness and struggles for equality for Muslims against other ethno-religious groups of the empire show significant parallels with the Afghanian version of liberal Pan-Islamism that laid the foundations of future local nationalisms.[53] As noted before, they gave great importance to unity among the Muslims to gain their collective rights, overtly condemning the denominational clashes between the Shi'ites and the Sunnis.

As Yavuz rightly argues, the historical development of the idea of nationalism in the Near East has been deeply linked to its symbiotic relationship with Islam.[54] In the eyes of most nationalist Muslim thinkers, Islam and nationalism were not conflicting, but rather, "overlapping and interacting facets of

---

50   Ibid.
51   Ibid.
52   *Revendications de la Délégation de Paix de la République de l'Azerbaijan du Caucause présentées à la Conférence de la Paix, à Paris*, 1918, p. 7.
53   Nikki R. Keddie, "Pan-Islam as Proto-Nationalism," *The Journal of Modern History*, vol. 41, No. 1 (Mar. 1969), p. 24.
54   Hakan Yavuz, "Yusuf Akçura," pp. 175–207.

political identity."[55] In the Balkans, the Caucasus and the Near East, it was Islam that marked the boundaries of a community (or imagined community) as against others identified in terms of different religions.[56] The creation and diffusion of nationalism and its being made part of daily discourse occurred in many cases through religious symbols and institutions.[57]

While this was true for the Caucasus, there were other factors that led to the rise of nationalism in the region. Bayat tells us that in this period the high culture of Azerbaijan was affected by Russian culture and the lower strata were influenced by Persia through religion.[58] With the opening of the Baku-Batum railway to facilitate oil exportation, the increasing contact of the Caucasus with Istanbul led to increasing influences of also the post-Tanzimat Ottoman-European culture.[59] The liberal-minded intelligentsia in the 1900s, mostly Russian or Western educated outstanding figures of Azerbaijan and influenced in their early youth by the Russian *narodnik* movement and enlightenment ideas, steadily became Turkish nationalists with varying degrees in this period.

The change in Ağaoğlu from a Persian (as in his French writings) to a Turkish nationalist needs to be considered in this context. The broader policies of the Russian government was also a factor leading to the rise of Turkish nationalism. In the nineteenth century, Tsarist Russian authorities had followed a temporary policy of distancing the Azerbaijanis from Persian literary influences, because they had seen the Qajar Dynasty as their rivals in the region. To this end, they had sponsored researches into Azerbaijani Turkish language, folklore and literature and allowed Azerbaijanis to stage plays about their non-Persian past and publish journals in their native language.[60]

However, these journals had been kept under strict censorship, and starting with Hasan Zardabi's *Ekinci* (Ploughman), the first journal published in Azerbaijani Turkish, late nineteenth century Azerbaijani journals had all been

---

55   Ibid., 175.
56   Ibid., p. 179. Yavuz writes: "Religion and ethnicity are inextricably linked because religious symbols—dress codes, dietary customs, etc.—provide a reliable social marker of a community. Sacred geography—mosque, *vaktf*, or other religious institution—provides a link between past and present and between private and public zones. This sacred geography was preserved, transmitted, and expressed by means of local languages, scripts, and a soil for the construction of a particular identity."
57   Ibid., p. 179.
58   Ali Haydar Bayat, *Hüseyinzade Ali Bey*, Ankara: Atatürk Kültür Merkezi Yayınları, 1990, p. 5.
59   Ibid., p. 5.
60   Swietochowski, "The Politics of a Literary Langauge," p. 56.

short-lived.[61] Of these *Keşkül* was particularly important because it was for the first time in this journal that literary issues were discussed at length in Ottoman Turkish and the concept of 'nation' as an entity separate from religion openly debated.[62] Since these journals were mostly owned by the Sunni minority, these journals propagated a cultural orientation toward the Ottoman Empire.[63]

In 1883 Gasprinsky's review Tercüman (The Interpreter) was published with the slogan of "Unity of language, mind, and action."[64] and exerted a huge influence over a generation of Turkish thinkers.[65] His three inspirations were the Young Ottomans' advocacy of cultural and literary Westernisation, the reform suggestions of al-Afghani and Pan-Slavism.[66]

Gasprinski wanted to develop a common and simple Turkish dialect (the Ottoman Turkish spoken in Istanbul) to establish bonds with all Turks from the Balkans to China at another corner of the empire. Since the majority of Russian Muslims were of Turkic stock, Gasprinsky's appeal for their religious unification "amounted to an appeal for the national rallying of Russian Turks, with very noticeable Pan-Turkic nuances and Pan-Islamic overtones."[67] In *Tercüman*, Gasprinsky consistently defended a union of all Turkic groups in Russia, with the Ottoman Empire offering its spiritual guidance. He believed that Russian Muslims should still be involved in the life of their fatherland by sweeping away their ignorance and encouraging their education (in new methods) in their own culture as well as Russian. The only feasible way for the amelioration of inter-communal relations was the accommodation of Muslims by this means; otherwise they had the necessary force to resist any imposed assimilation.[68]

Gasprinsky wanted the Muslims to preserve their own identity and to acquire enough foreign (Russian) knowledge to provide better conditions for a

---

61   *Ekinci* was published between 1875 and 1878. Other journals included *Ziya* (Light, 1879–81), *Ziya-i Kafkasya* (The Light of the Caucasus, 1881–84) and *Keşkül* (Dervish's Satchel, 1890–91).

62   Mitat Durmuş, "Azerbaycan Sahası Türk Edebiyatında İlk Süreli Yayin Faaliyetleri ve "Molla Nasreddin" Dergisi," *Turkish Studies International Periodical for the Languages, Literature and History of Turkish or Turkic*, 3/7 (Fall 2008), p. 358.

63   Alexandre Benningsen and Chantal Lemercier-Quelquejay, *La Presse et le Mouvement National Musulman de Russie avant 1920*, Paris: Mouton, 1964, p. 29; Swietochowski, "The Politics of a Literary Language," p. 57.

64   Zenkovsky, *Pan-Turkism*, pp. 30–31; Landau, *The Politics of Pan-Islam*, p. 148.

65   Landau, *The Politics of Pan-Islam*, p. 149; Zenkovsky, *Pan-Turkism*, pp. 31–32.

66   Ahmed Aghayef, "İsmail Bey Gasprinsky," *Türk Yurdu*, No. 1 (1914).

67   Zenkovsky, *Pan-Turkism*, p. 32; Landau, *The Politics of Pan-Islam*, p. 149.

68   Ibid., p. 147.

subsequent campaign to arouse them.[69] This tells us that what Gasprinsky desired was not for the Tatars to gain their independence. Although he advocated an ethno-national awareness and unity of action among the Turks, that is their maintenance as a community (but not as a separate political entity),[70] he was a loyal subject of the Tsar and saw the Russians as a good and progressive people from whom the Turks could learn. For this reason, he supported an opening towards Russification, "emphasizing the particular need of Muslims in Russia to acquire the language of the government."[71] However, he was attacked by his fellow Tatars and co-religionists such as Zerdabi, who opposed his views by arguing that Russian Muslims must absorb the positive aspects of western culture not through Russification, but by Turkifying what was borrowed from the West.[72]

One generation later, ethno-cultural and linguistic nationalisms began to be voiced in the writings of Hüseyinzade Ali and Ahmet Ağaoğlu, and in the journals *Şarki Rus* (Eastern Russian) and *Molla Nasreddin*. Azerbaijani/Turkish nationalism was inclusive of Islamist tendencies, yet it introduced ethnic elements into the works of the former two reservedly. One of its main architects Hüseyinzade Ali is believed to have embraced Turkish nationalist ideas as early as his studentship years in St. Petersburg under the influence of his Turcophile Georgian friends in the late 1880s.[73] Imbued with growing interest and curiosity in Turkishness, he went to Istanbul after St. Petersburg to study at the Military Medicine School and became one of the founders of the Young Turk movement there. In 1904, while the Kazan Tatar Yusuf Akçura was preaching for Pan-Turkist ideas in the journal *Türk* in Cairo, Hüseyinzade Ali was writing in Baku that those people of Kazan, Orenburg and Crimea who were regarded as a separate Tatar race were originally Turks and that Turks did not need such pseudo-ideologies as Pan-Islamism and Pan-Turkism to love each other under the same Islamic beliefs and racial bonds.[74] The writers of the *Türk* would criticise Hüseyinzade Ali claiming, in reference to Namık Kemal, that a Tatar race did exist.

Hüseyinzade Ali further pressed the Turkist case in his writings in the *Hayat* (*Life*).[75] Gasprinski would celebrate the publication of *Hayat* as a consolation

69   Ibid., p. 148.
70   Shissler, *Between Two Empires*, p. 156.
71   Landau, *The Politics of Pan-Islam*, p. 148.
72   Mirza Bala, "Hasan Zerdabi Bey," *Türk Yurdu*, No. 12–14 (Dec.-Jan.-Feb., 1929).
73   Bayat, p. 31.
74   Bayat, p. 31.
75   Quliyev, *Ağaoğlu Ahmed Bey*, p. 10.

for his long-wait for a company in his nationalist struggle.[76] In fact, on its first issue, Hüseyinzade would identify the authors as 'subjects of the Russian [Empire]', and Muslims. The founders of the journal, he wrote, wanted "to achieve progress within the economic and political conditions of the Russian state!"[77] One year later, in June 1906, as the Tatar-Armenian fighting saw its height and liberties granted by Russian authorities were partially put on hold, the tone of his writings appeared to have changed not so slightly:

> We are Caucasians. [We] demand autonomy required for controlling the public administration of the Caucasian region. We are Muslims. Therefore, [we] demand whatever is required for our...religion and freedom of conscience. We are Turks. [We] struggle for the destruction of all types of walls and obstacles preventing the progress of our language.[78]

Hüseyinzade would suggest for the first time a new identity fusing Turkishness, the Islamic morality and Europeanness for the salvation of Azerbaijan. New Caucasians, he suggested, would be "moved with Turkish sentiments, devoted to the religion of Islam and civilised through the civilisation of Europe,"[79] a formula that would inspire Ziya Gökalp in the 1910s. He would at times argue for the union of Ottomans and Azerbaijanis under Islamic and Turkish bonds.

Hüseyinzade's ideas saw criticisms from within and outside the nationalist circles in the Caucasus. While such journals as *Füyuzat* (Abundance), *Yeni Füyuzat* (New Abundance) and *Şelale* (Fountain) insisted on using Ottoman Turkish to bring the Azerbaijani and Ottoman societies closer, since İsmail Shataktinski's *Şark-i Rus* (Eastern Russian) brought out in 1903, a trend of publishing in Azerbaijani Turkish re-emerged. *Molla Nasreddin* and *İkbal* (Luck) continued this trend with the belief that the way to reach people and enlighten them was to use the very language they use in their everyday lives. Jalal Mehmed Quluzade, for example, defended in *Molla Nasreddin* an independent Azerbaijani culture and nation. As such by the end of the 1900s, Azerbaijan saw the emergence two versions of linguistic nationalisms: Pan-Turkist/Ottomanist and particularistic/Azerbaijani. The latter developed sentiments of regional

76   X. Memmedov, "İ. Gasprinski'nin A. Hüseyizâde'ye 'Açık Mektubu'", *Edebiyat Gazetesi*, June 17, 1992.
77   Hüseyinzade Ali, "Gazetemizin Mesleki," *Hayat*, No. 1, 1905; cf. Cengiz Çağla, *Azerbaycan'da Milliyetçilik ve Politika*, Istanbul: Bağlam Yayınları, 2002, p. 52; Seyid-zade, p. 49.
78   Erdoğan Uygur, "Füyuzat ve Molla Nasreddin Dergilerinde Edebi Dil Tartışmaları," *Modern Türklük Araştırmaları Dergisi*, 4 (Dec., 2007), p. 55.
79   Hüseyinzade Ali, "İntikad Ediyoruz, İntikad Olunuz," *Füyuzat*, 23 (1907); cf. Bayat, p. 32.

affiliation and like the Anatolian nationalism of the late 1910s, it placed priority to the empowerment of local Azerbaijanis.

When Ağaoğlu went to Istanbul, he was already imbued with a version of nationalism, yet in his and other Russian Muslims' writings one would not find a clear-cut departure from Pan-Islamism. In *Sebilürreşad*, he repeatedly called on the Muslim nations to rally around the Caliph in a similar vein to al-Afghani's later writings. His essays on the Tripolitanian war, Italy's aggressive foreign policy in North Africa,[80] the French invasion of Morocco,[81] Russia's demands in Iran[82] and the growing tension in South East Europe before the First World War[83] all had strong Pan-Islamist elements. In these essays, he went to such lengths as to argue, as did al-Afghani in his late work, that it was possible to form an Islamic political union under the leadership of the Ottomans and their caliph sultan.[84] He often reminded Ottoman statesmen of their role as the bulwark of the world of Islam, but never elaborated on how a united Islamic government under their leadership could be established.[85]

Notably, in his thirty-two articles in *Sebilürreşad*, addressed to a more conservative audience, Ağaoğlu did not use the word 'Turk' even once, although he was elaborating on the historical origins of Turkish nationalism in *Türk Yurdu* at the same time. The differentiation between Islamism and nationalism would in fact never be complete in his writings until the end of World War I. Like most other nationalists, he regarded religion as a major component of nationhood. Only in the republican context, when he turned to scientific sources of morality, would the role of religion be degraded in his work.

Together with Gasprinski and Hüseyinzade Ali, Ağaoğlu certainly made an influence on the rise of Turkish nationalism in Istanbul also. As noted before, he was finding the idea of Ottomanism too romantic and inapplicable in the Ottoman context. Yet in the Ottoman Empire too, an ethno-nationalist consciousness among a limited number of Turkish writers had been created at least in the realm of ideas. This was due to (1) the historical influence of Pan-Islamism, (2) the scholarly products of European Orientalism in Turkish linguistics and history in the nineteenth and early twentieth centuries, (3) the

---

80   Ahmet Aghayef, "Tavassut," *Sebilürreşad*, No. 7 (Jun.–Jul., 1912), pp. 123–125; "Muharebenin Yeni Devresi," *Sebilürreşad*, No. 8 (Jun.–Jul., 1912), pp. 141–143.

81   Ahmet Aghayef, "Fas ve Trablus," *Sebilürreşad*, No. 14 (Jul.–Aug., 1912), pp. 267–268.

82   Ahmet Aghayef, "Alem-i İslam'a Umumi Bir Nazar," *Sebilürreşad*, No. 3 (May–June 1912), pp. 41–42.

83   Ahmet Aghayef, "İcmal-i Siyasi," *Sebilürreşad*, No. 251 (Aug.-Sep., 1913), pp. 283–284.

84   Ahmet Aghayef, "Siyasiyat: Vaz'iyyet-i Haziremiz," *Sebilürreşad*, No. 186 (May–Jun., 1912), pp. 66–67.

85   Ibid., p. 284.

birth of nationalist movements in the West and their reception by Turkish thinkers, either during their education in European schools or during their visits to or exile in Europe, and (4) the nationalist ideas carried to the Ottoman Empire by Russian Muslims.[86]

Until the late nineteenth century, the word 'Turk' had usually carried a derogatory connotation in the empire. It had been used occasionally but only to designate the ignorant nomads or peasants of Anatolia, or else to distinguish between a Turkish-speaking Ottoman and those who spoke other languages.[87] According to Kushner, in overturning the pejorative meaning of the term, the Europeans were the chief inspiration:

> For the Turks to apply the new nationalist or racialist theories to themselves, their self-consciousness as Turks had to be revived and the term "Turk" given respectability...the Europeans had long used the terms "Turks" or "Turkey" with reference to the Ottomans and the Ottoman Empire—in fact the term was used to include not only Turkish-speaking people, but other Muslims living within the boundaries of the Empire— while the Turks themselves allowed the term to be almost forgotten. With the growing contact between Turks and the outside world, Turkish statesmen and intellectuals became familiar with these terms. Also influential were European accounts of the Turks, which reflected two basic attitudes. On the one hand, criticism of Turkish "misdeeds" and Turks in general was prevalent, influenced by earlier centuries when Europe was facing the threat of the "terrible Turk", and expressed in many travel accounts, memoirs, articles and historical works. This gave rise to an apologetic

---

86   The works of Arthur Vambéry, A.I. de Sacy, W. Radloff, E.J.W. Gibb, the deciphering of old Turkish inscriptions by D.V. Thomsen in 1893 and most notably the French Orientalist Léon Cahun's *Introduction à l'histoire de l'Asie* of 1896 exerted huge influences in the creation of national consciousness; David Kushner, *The Rise of Turkish Nationalism, 1876–1908*, London: Frank Cass., 1977, p. 10. In one of his articles Gökalp says when he first came to Istanbul for higher education, the first book he got hold of was *Introduction à l'historie de l'Asie*, and recalls, "it was written as if to encourage the ideal of Pan-Turkism"; cf. Uriel Heyd, *Foundations of Turkish Nationalism: The Life and Teachings of Ziya Gökalp*, London: Luzac, 1950, p. 28. Cahun was influential on even such thinkers as Sabahaddin Bey. Sabahaddin also wrote an article about Turks' contribution to civilisation in history under the inspiration of Cahun. Prens Sabahaddin, "Türklerin Medeniyet Aleminde Kaydettikleri Terakkiler," cf. Nezahat N. Ege, *Prens Sabahattin Hayatı ve İlmi Müdafaaları*, Istanbul: Fakülteler Matbaası, 1977, pp. 58–64.
87   Kushner, *The Rise of Turkish Nationalism*, p. 2.

trend and Turkish publications devoted considerable space to defence of the Ottoman record.[88]

Hence, in the late nineteenth century, the current of literary Turkism came to existence with the nationalist literary products of Mehmet Emin (Yurdakul) and Mehmet Necip (Türkçü), while Necip Asım (Yazıksız) penned a book on the history of the Turks adopting Léon Cahun's *Introduction à l'histoire de l'Asie.*

In the early twentieth century, Gökalp, Akçura and Ağaoğlu, leading nationalist figures of the Second Constitutional era, brought an ideological framework to Turkism by making new formulations of nationalism, following in the footsteps of Gasprinksy in particular.[89] Although they agreed that the 1908 political revolution must be complemented by a 'social revolution' based on nationalist values, their approaches to nationalism were slightly different in terms of the methods they employed.

Akçura's famous essay "Üç Tarz-ı Siyaset" ("Three Ways of Politics"), dated March 1904, was indisputably one of the most important texts in the history of Turkish nationalism. This essay discussed the practicability of the three possible grand policies—Ottomanism, Pan-Islamism and Pan-Turkism—that the Ottoman Empire might follow in the early twentieth century as the bulwark of the Muslim world. Ottomanism was a policy, which suggested strengthening the bonds of all Ottoman subjects regardless of their religion, language or race by promoting the idea of an Ottoman nation under the umbrella of the rule of the sultan. It aimed at maintaining the unity of the empire by promoting all citizens' allegiance to the sultan, and by endowing them with further political and social rights. For Akçura, Ottomanism was, however desirable, the least feasible of all the policies the Ottomans could implement.[90] He argued that the ties between different components of the Ottoman Empire were so weak that the attempt to create an Ottoman nation would be nothing but an empty exercise. The unification of Islamic nations and Pan-Turkism, on the other hand, despite various obstacles, were more feasible to implement than the policy of Ottomanism, given the existing organic bonds between Muslims and the Turks.[91] Georgeon argues that Akçura's defence of Pan-Turkism as a state policy in the Ottoman Empire since 1904 had socio-economic motivations. According to this account, Akçura had a dual programme: on the one hand, he

---

88   Ibid., p. 9.

89   Aghayef, "İsmail Bey Gasprisnky".

90   Yusuf Akçura, *Üç Tarz-ı Siyaset*, Ankara: Türk Tarih Kurumu Basımevi, 1976, pp. 27–31.

91   Ibid., pp. 33–34.

wanted to provide a new market (the Ottoman Empire) for the Tatar bourgeoisie to complement their competition with Russian capitalism in Central Asia; and on the other, he sought to endow the Ottoman Empire with the necessary apparatus to resist disintegration by means of a new principle of solidarity, a new ethnic organisation and a new territorial structure.[92]

The distinguishing aspect of Akçura's notion of nationalism was the fact that it was purged of any form of romanticism.[93] He approached the social and political problems affecting the Turkish populations of the Russian and Ottoman Empires from a 'historicist' perspective. He believed that history, as a global phenomenon, had a logic; it was moving in a certain direction and everyone must become a part of this evolution or be left behind.[94] For him, the emergence of Turkish nationalist thought was a reflection of a fundamental socio-economic change that had already taken place among the Tatars since the second half of the nineteenth century.[95] Under the pressure of Pan-Slavism, they had strengthened their own national characteristics by studying their histories and improving their languages; they had reformed Islam by means of the modernisation of education in *medrese*; and they had elevated themselves socially and especially economically, with the growth of a Tatar bourgeoisie.[96] A similar socio-economic transformation should take place in the Ottoman Empire. The 1908 Revolution was important for creating a liberal political and economic atmosphere. What was required now was a transformation of the habits, ideas and sentiments of the people; that is, social revolution.[97]

Gökalp's 1911 article "Yeni Hayat ve Yeni Kıymetler" (New Life and New Values) shows that his notion of social revolution was remarkably similar to that of Akçura. For Gökalp, 'social revolution' meant a new life; a new form of economy, a new form of family life, new aesthetic standards, a new morality, a new conception of law and a new political system.[98] For him, the political revolution was not difficult to realize, because it meant changing the machinery of the government (into a constitutional regime). The social revolution, on the other hand, could not be attained by a simple mechanical action: "It must be the product of a long process of organic evolution."[99] Echoing Fouillée,

---

92   François Georgeon, *Osmanlı-Türk Modernleşmesi*, p. 97.

93   Ibid., p. 98.

94   François Georgeon, *Aux origines du nationalisme turc: Yusuf Akçura*, pp. 46–53.

95   Georgeon, *Osmanlı-Türk Moderleşmesi*, p. 97.

96   Ibid., p. 100.

97   Georgeon, *Aux Origines*, p. 53.

98   Ziya Gökalp, "Yeni Hayat ve Yeni Kıymetler," *Genç Kalemler*, No. 8, 1911.

99   Gökalp, "New Life and New Values," cf. Berkes, *Turkish Nationalism and Western Civilisation*, p. 56.

he wrote that the dissemination of certain *idées-forces*, such as liberty, equality and fraternity, was enough to put the political revolution into practice.

> The social revolution…is dependent upon the consummation of certain *sentiments-forces*. Acceptance or rejection of the ideas is within the power of reason. The sentiments, on the other hand, cannot evolve easily because they are the products of social habits developed in the course of several centuries.[100]

Gökalp's theory of nationality was based on Durkheim's idea of collective representations. He replaced Durkheim's 'society' with 'nation' and gave special importance to culture in his notion of nationalism. "His brand of nationalism was unequivocally based on a linguistic and cultural nationalism that was to co-exist with other nationalisms in peace and reciprocal respect."[101] Although his wartime poems manifested Pan-Turkist tendencies, as Parla argues, in none of his theoretical or political articles and essays did he systematically defend Pan-Turkism.[102] Instead, he was preoccupied with formulating a synthesis between Turkism, Islamism and Westernism drawing upon the work of Hüseyinzade Ali.

Gökalp's 'new life' denounced cosmopolitanism and instead suggested a national life. It sought to learn from the experiences and sciences of European civilisation, but the Muslims could not imitate the ready-made norms of Europe and its ways of living, because some of them were unsuited to the living conditions of the Ottoman Empire. "For us, it is necessary to have them made to order, like tailored suits, to fit our own body."[103] Since the Muslims belonged to a different *ümmet* (religion) they should create a new mode of civilisation from their understanding. "We shall create a genuine civilisation, a Turkish civilisation, which will follow the growth of a New Life."[104]

Gökalp's notion of nationalism which thus aimed at creating a Turkish civilisation was based on the concept of 'ideal'. After the Balkan wars, by utilising Durkheimian theories, he argued that "when a society experiences a great disaster or when it is confronted with grave danger, individual personality disappears and becomes immersed in society."[105] At such times national

---

100 Ibid., p. 56.
101 Parla, *The Social and Political Thought of Ziya Gökalp*, p. 34.
102 Ibid., pp. 34–35.
103 Ibid., pp. 58–59.
104 Ibid., p. 60.
105 Ziya Gökalp, "Mefkûre," *Türk Yurdu*, no. 32, 1913; cf. Berkes, *Turkish Nationalism*, pp. 66–67.

personality, which resides in the soul of the individual, becomes a living organism. Individuals do not worry about their own liberties, but consider only the survival of national independence. According to Gökalp, "this sacred thought, fused with cherished sentiments," was ideal. When the crisis comes to an end, the ideal is not extinguished in the hearts of individuals, but "continues to motivate the people constantly, as if it were a spring inside them... The lore and the civilisation peculiar to a nation come into existence only in this manner."[106] The non-existence of the ideal of nationalism among the Turks excluded the possibility of a national economy. Moreover, by the same token, the Turkish soul remained a stranger to the sort of life and to the intensive moral feelings that should form the bases of sacrifice and altruism. Hence Gökalp's notion of Turkish nationalism represented a cultural ideal and a philosophy of life which laid the basis for social solidarity, using Islam as a moral norm.[107]

Like Akçura and Gökalp, Ağaoğlu also needed to underline the importance of a complementary social revolution that would bring about a bottom-up social change after the political revolution. He wrote that although the political revolutions that took place in Iran and the Ottoman Empire were inspirational, they were insufficient for the ultimate awakening of Muslims, because the spirit of liberty had not yet grown roots among the Muslim nations.

> The truth of the slogan "Liberty is not given, it is fought for" has been proven in Iran in all its aspects. If a nation did not obtain liberty after a long period of evolution, as result of struggles and sacrifices, it is hard to control that liberty. Because no men of wisdom and intelligence who could thoroughly comprehend liberty have been brought up in such societies, because no skill and merit have appeared for the honouring and codification of liberty and especially because none of the institutions required for securing and maintaining liberty has existed, the fatal disease of anarchy prevails over liberty.[108]

His political proximity to the Young Turks, combined with the insecure environment in a foreign land, would lead him to argue that the Ottoman Empire was in a sense in safe hands, thanks to the existence of the Committee of Union

---

106 Ibid., p. 68.
107 Parla, *The Social and Political Thought of Ziya Gökalp*, p. 25.
108 Ahmed Aghayev, "Alem-i İslam, Makalât: İran"ın Mazi Haline Bir Nazar," *Sırat-ı Müstakim*, (Nov.–Dec., 1910), pp. 79–80.

and Progress as an institution safeguarding liberty and liberal institutions.[109] But he would also need to warn that the people of different social classes were still living and thinking in traditional ways, the revolution was confined to the educated classes only.[110]

Unlike Akçura, Ağaoğlu did not pay much attention to the socio-economic requirements for a social revolution in late Ottoman context. He appeared to be concerned more with the cultural elevation of the Turks, beside his above-mentioned Pan-Islamist propensities. But rather than using sociological tools, he put emphasis, in a similar vein to Akçura, on 'historical evolution'. In his view, nationalism was a stage that all nations go through in the natural course of history. As early as 1906, in discussing whether the Muslim Turks should pursue socialist or nationalist ideals, he had written:

> Socialism is such a lofty and magnificent ideal that it is impossible to despise its followers. However, we have to consider this ideal as still belonging to the realm of dreams and visions; we believe that several centuries may pass before it becomes a reality. In the meantime, nations grow and all of them have to go through the stage called nationalism. That's why we have become its adherents, following the footprints of the English, the French, the Italians and the Germans.[111]

In 1911–12, his first series of *Türk Yurdu* instalments entitled "Türk Alemi" (The Turkish World) were devoted to the subject of why the Turks had so far failed to reach the stage of nationalism. Ağaoğlu postulated that the three main causes were the centuries-long animosities and sectarian differences among various different Turkic people, the influences of the culturally more advanced peoples that they conquered, and the absence of national consciousness among them.[112] According to him, the Turks were assimilated by the people they had conquered, such as the Persians. Under their influence, they disregarded their own Turkishness and were taught to hate themselves. This was how the term 'Turk' began to carry a pejorative connotation, which was one of the chief factors impeding national consciousness among the Turks.

---

109 Ibid.

110 Ahmed Aghayev, "Darü'l-Hilâfede Maarif-i İbtidâ'iyenin Hali ve Suret-i Islahı," *Sırat-ı Mıstakim,* (Dec., 1910), pp. 151–153.

111 Ahmet Aghayef, "Sosyalizm mi, Milliyetçilik mi?" *Terakki,* vol. 37, 1906, cf. Swietochowky, *Russian Azerbaijan,* p. 58.

112 Ahmet Aghayef, "Türk Alemi 1," *Türk Yurdu,* No. 1 (1911), pp. 12–17.

For Ağaoğlu, the fact that the Turks were static and failed to make any kind of progress for centuries also hampered the appearance of Turkish nationalism. They did not understand the principle that time and humanity were constantly changing. Instead they were concerned only with preserving what they possessed, thus depriving themselves of the right to life.[113] Their failure to progress their religion, language, education, literature and to develop their economy resulted in the emergence of numerous problems that they were now unable to cope with.

Yet in another instalment which he wrote as a response to Joseph Nehama (who was writing with the pseudonym Paul Risal), who had asserted in an essay that the Turks were nomads and not inclined to the elements of civilisation, Ağaoğlu rather paradoxically argued that in different times and places the Turks always adopted the features of advanced civilisations and adapted themselves to them, which was a proof of the fact that they were more civilised than any other Asian people, except the Japanese.[114] He thus identified the Turks as open to civilisational progress on the one hand, and denounced their stationary character on the other.

Ağaoğlu's account of the birth of Turkish nationalism was Eurocentric. A product of ideas generated during the French Revolution and buttressed by the current of romanticism, nationalism, he wrote, gave birth to modern European states, institutions and pan-movements.[115] Nationalist ideas and ideals were transferred into the Islamic and Turkish world through the agency of Muslims intellectuals and as a consequence of the general expansion in trade and increasing communications with Europe. However, the reception of nationalist ideas was limited only to a small group, namely the intellectual elite, who had extensive contact with Western ideas and ways of life. For this reason, Turkish nationalists had to reach down to the roots of society and galvanize the Turks to work for their own salvation, because nationalism was a people's movement.

Whilst writing in *Sebilürreşad* that the Union of Islam was in fact possible, in his *Türk Yurdu* essays he employed a remarkably different position. For Ağaoğlu, the Islamist idea that the rise of nationalism had a destructive effect on Muslim brotherhood and the *ümmet* (Islamic religious community) was but a mistaken view, because the *ümmet* was already disunited in reality. The 'Islamic world' was an ideal in the realm of imagination, not a reality.

---

113   Ahmet Aghayef, "Türk Alemi 7," *Türk Yurdu*, vol. 2, No. 13 (1912), pp. 424–428.
114   Ahmed Aghayef, "Türk Alemi 2," *Türk Yurdu*, No. 2 (1911), pp. 36–42.
115   Ahmet Aghayef, "Türk Alemi 4," *Türk Yurdu*, 5, (1912), pp. 135–139.

There had always been ethnic tensions and feelings of superiority among the Muslim nations.[116]

The empowerment of the Islamic world could be attained, Ağaoğlu thought, only by strengthening individual Muslim nations; and this could be done by means of efficiently exploiting their local language, institutions and customs. The only way to strengthen the local people was to approach them in a way they could understand and respond to.[117] Thus, he declared that the key role in remedying social ills should be played by the men of letters, poets and men of ideas whom he blamed for a centuries-old failure to raise religious and cultural aspirations, goals and ideals:

> This recipe consists of the eradication of alienation, antagonisms, hostility and enmity that have been injected in us through discords between denominations and among the Turks. In particular, three classes of people can do this: first, religious scholars; second, teachers; and third, writers...we must admit that these three classes of people...have not completely fulfilled [their] duties in recent centuries.[118]

He believed that the Turks had continued to overlook the essential principles of life and elements of nationality during the Tanzimat era, which was a century-long waste of energy with its superficial methods of transformation. He pointed to this prodigality as a major reason for the loss of lands in the Balkan Wars.

> While imitating Europe by borrowing its codified laws and established institutions, we believed that we could use those laws and institutions as efficiently [in our country] ... We have taken into account neither the history, the traditions nor the special foundations of [our] country, nor indeed the spiritual situation of our nation. Because of this central flaw, which is the source of all other flaws, the materialisation of Tanzimat reforms was deemed to failure.[119]

He also argued that the flaws leading to the Turks' lagging behind must be sought in their self-perception and self-awareness. They knew little of their

---

116   Ahmet Aghayef, "Türk Alemi 5," *Türk Yurdu*, No. 7, (1912), pp. 195–200.

117   Ibid.

118   Ahmed Aghayef, "Türk Alemi 8," *Türk Yurdu* 2, No. 6 (1912/13), p. 547.

119   Ahmet Aghayef, "Tanzimat," *Jeune Turc*, March 14, 1913.

history, culture, traditions, religion, science and state. They had to discover who they were, the origins of their self-identity.[120]

Ağaoğlu's nationalist arguments received strong criticisms. In an open letter to Ağaoğlu, Süleyman Nazif, a well-known writer and a former governor of Trabzon and Baghdad, criticized the Turkish nationalist campaign arguing that nationalism was a dangerous ideology threatening the unity of the Ottoman Empire. He denounced the attempts of the Turkists to reduce Ottoman identity to an ethnic element within the Ottoman Empire. Underscoring the importance and existence of religious bonds between the Ottomans, he wrote that, unlike that of the Turkists, his view of history did not hark back to the time of Genghis Khan and Central Asia. Instead, he accepted "a history of religion starting with *Hicret* and a national history beginning with the time of Sultan Osman."[121] If someone were to ask him to identify himself, he would say that he was first a Muslim, secondly an Ottoman and last a Turk.[122] "Today, if I had a daughter, I wouldn't allow her to marry a pagan Turk, or even a Shi'ite. But an Arab, a Kurd, a Circassian, a Laz, a Tatar, an Indian...could be an acceptable groom for [my family]."[123]

In his response, Ağaoğlu argued that the founding element of the Ottoman Empire was the Turks.[124] "You separate the Turks into two: One...starts with the history of Ottomans; the other...who lived before or outside the Ottomans. You completely ignore the latter, you hate mentioning them. Nowhere in the world can you find a Persian, an Arab, a Frenchman, Englishman or a German who separates his nationality into two and accepts one part while rejecting the other." For Ağaoğlu, Nazif was simply omitting the bonds between the pre-Ottoman and Ottoman Turks.[125]

In his second article, Nazif rejected Ağaoğlu's claims, stressing that the Ottoman state had been founded not only by the Turks; there had also been non-Turkish groups which had played a role in the foundation of the Ottoman state and that had fought for its protection:

> With gratitude and respect, we encounter various names such as Mihail and Evranos, which are foreign to our language, but companion to our consciousness, among those...who endeavoured to constitute the high

120 Ahmet Aghayef, "Türk Medeniyeti Tarihi," *Türk Yurdu,* No. 40 (May 1913), pp. 292–293.
121 Süleyman Nazif, "A. Agayef Beyefendiye," *İçtihad,* vol. 3, No. 71 (1913), p. 1549.
122 Ibid.
123 Ibid.
124 Ahmet Ahgayef, "Sabık Trabzon Valisi Süleyman Nazif Bey Efendi'ye," *Türk Yurdu,* vol. 4, No. 9 (1913), pp. 702–704.
125 Ibid., 703.

principles of [the Ottoman] state. What will you say to those Serbians who zealously fought for [the Ottoman army], when Timurleng, whom the Turkists [highly] ...regarded, attacked the Ottomans in the plains of Ankara with his army [...] of Tatars and Turks? ...in our veins, there is only Ottoman blood. Like our language, our blood has deviated from its origins through contact and mixture. And in particular, our affinity with the Tatars and Mongols is nothing but myth.[126]

For Nazif, by attaching importance to only one of the ethnic groups in the Ottoman Empire, the Turkists were doing greater harm to unity and peace in the empire than the Balkan Wars.

Besides Nazif, Babanzade Ahmet Naim, an Islamist professor of philosophy at the University of Istanbul, called on the Islamists to wage a holy war against the Turkists, with a number of articles which targeted mainly Ağaoğlu's writings.[127] For Naim, nationalism (*kavmiyet*) was one of those evils taken over from Europe, a foreign innovation as deadly to the body of Islam as cancer is to man. He argued—with the aid of score of *hadith*—that nationalism (*kavmiyet*) was condemned and prohibited by the Shari'a and that it was the severest threat yet directed against the unity of Islam. "At a time when the enemy has set foot on our breasts," he wrote, "it is madness to divide Islam into nationalities."[128] Bringing forth a new cause next to the cause of Islamism was but to render Muslims weaker. "For the sake of Islam, for the sake of humanity, for the sake of Turkishness, for whose future I fear, I beg you, I request you not to inculcate in people 'double ideals'."[129]

Ağaoğlu replied to Naim writing that nowhere in those *hadith* to which Naim had referred was the term *kavm* (nation) used.[130] Instead, those materials used the term *asabbiya*, which had a meaning other than 'nation'. When one referred to "the latest teachings of social sciences", Ağaoğlu wrote, it would be seen that "a nation is a group of individuals who are brought together by the common sentiments they carry."[131] On the other hand, *asabbiya* refers to

---

126   Süleyman Nazif, "Cengiz Hastalığı," *İçtihad*, vol. 3, No. 72 (1913), pp. 1573–1574.

127   He later gathered the articles he penned against Ağaoğlu into a book entitled *İslamda Dava-yı Kavmiyet* (Nationalism in Islam). Babanzade Ahmet Naim, *İslamda Dava-yı Kavmiyet*, Istanbul: Tevsii Tıbaat Matbaası, 1913, p. 16.

128   Ibid., p. 27; see also Berkes, *Development of Secularism*, p. 367–377.

129   Naim, *İslamda*, p. 15.

130   Ahmet Aghayef, "İslam'da Dava-yı Milliyet," *Türk Yurdu*, vol. 6, No. 10 (1914), pp. 2320–2329; "İslam'da Dava-yı Milliyet," *Türk Yurdu*, vol. 6, No. 11 (1914), pp. 2381–2390.

131   Ağaoğlu gives this explanation in reference to Jacues Novikow's *Les lutes entre les sociétés humaines et leurs phases successives*.

societies which live as tribes, which have no national unity, self-awareness or self-consciousness. Most of those fights, rivalries and bloodshed in the history of Islam, between what Naim calls Muslim nations, were for Ağaoğlu in fact *asabbiya* wars: they were between tribes. Islam essentially tried to form a national union by putting forward a national ideal. The reason for Muslims' lagging behind was their failure to devote themselves to this ideal.

In his response, Ağaoğlu also drew a correlation between religion and civilisation which seems to form the nucleus of his later writings about civilisation as they appeared in *Three Civilisations* of 1919–20. He wrote:

> People can be categorised into three groups in terms of their lifestyles, that is their civilisations: Islamic [civilisation], Christian [civilisation] and Buddhist-Confucian [civilisation]. The factor that separates these three worlds from each other, that endows them with a special character despite all the racial, philological and cultural differences between people that form them is certainly religion… Therefore, nationalists must take into account such a factor that exercises maximum influence on the manner of the building and emergence of any nationality that has determined its path. It is apparent that nationality progresses, elevates and expands to the degree that this factor becomes influential, active, abundant and fertile. That is, for those who have [decided to follow] the path of nationality, it is one of the inevitable duties…to render this factor active, influential, rich and fertile. Islam is the religion of the Turks; it is their national religion…[132]

Together with Gökalp and Akçura, the Ağaoğlu of the 1910s asserted that nationalism and religion complemented each other by providing society with cultural and moral norms. Moreover, he rejected the argument that nationalism would be a malady and a divisive element in Ottoman society. For him, it was instead a unifying factor, because the Turkish nationalists were struggling to contribute to the peace and harmony between different components of the Ottoman Empire:

> The Turkish nationalist movement is a moral and social [movement] and is therefore imbued with humanitarian desires for other nationalities like the Turks. It desires the Arabs, Turks, Kurds, Armenians and others to progress and develop equally, without irritating or doing any harm to each other. In the eyes of a Turkish nationalist, languages and nationalities

---

132   Aghayef, "İslam'da Davayı Kavmiyet," p. 2388.

of the Arabs and other [peoples] deserve a respect close to their own language and nationality. Turkish nationalists feel special gratitude to Arabs who gave them their religion and who have formed a very important element of the Ottoman state.[133]

Turkish nationalism, he hastened to add, was not chauvinist, so was no threat to any other national group.[134] "What the Turkists demand is only the recognition of the Turks' rights to possess what all other Ottoman Muslim nationalities regard as natural to themselves." Reviving Turkish identity did not mean undermining the importance of other nationalities. For him, the peaceful coexistence of different nationalities on the same territory, when they follow the same ideal of nationalism and thus empathize with each other, was certainly possible.

That being said, he was of the belief that the Turks had yet a way to go for them to form a Turkish nationality. In 1915, he wrote:

> Today there is a Turkish nationality, but a Turkish nation has not yet been formed. Although the factors required for the creation of nationality exist among the Turks, these factors have not taken shape in a way that would form a nation. The principal [elements] of nationality consist of first, language and all types of products of the language – literature, art, music, etc.-, second, religion and all types of products of religion, and third, the marks of race. Nationality comes into existence by the combination of these three primary factors.[135]

For Ağaoğlu, the people of a nationality could build a nation by the harmonious and conscious fusion of these elements. Since, in his view, in the case of

---

133   Aghayef, "Türkler İçinde Milli Hareket," *Türk Yurdu*, p. 4326.

134   Ibid. Ağaoğlu wrote: "Today Turkish and Arabic youth get along with each other and form brotherhood better than two three years earlier. This has a simple explanation: The more national consciousness progresses in Turkish and Arab youth, the more similar goals, similar ideals are followed, they understand each other better and for the preservation and development of the same ideal they feel obliged to get closer and get along with each other well. To the degree that the Turks, Arabs and others embrace national ideals, they will not act imprudently or will not follow their personal interests, but proceed [with and] for the belief of nationality and consequently they will [want to] ...assemble and live together. As they will easily see, the day of their split and disintegration is the day of their death."

135   Ahmet Agayef, "Milli Cereyan," *Türk Yurdu*, 1915; cf. Yusuf H. Bayur, *Türk İnkılabı Tarihi*, vol. 3, Ankara: Türk Tarih Kurumu Basımevi, 1983, p. 385.

the Turks, there was still no common literary language, and they did not even know the meaning of their prayers, the emergence of a national consciousness was dependent upon their grasping Islam fully and adjusting their lives accordingly. They had to form a linguistic consciousness in order to influence "Turkish hearts, life and sentiments" by Turkish cultural products, especially in literature and music.[136]

Ağaoğlu's nationalism of the time was a hybrid nationalism involving both civic and ethno-cultural elements and combining rationalism and emotionalism. It was, however, more akin to ethno-culturalism with its accentuation of cultural, linguistic, religious and historical nationhood rather than the political. Moreover, it was primordialist in that it portrayed national identity as historically embedded.[137] Ağaoğlu sought the roots of the Turkish nation in a common cultural heritage and language, i.e. in its ethnicity, pre-dating statehood. He applied this teaching to the Ottoman context by highlighting the importance of identifying the lifestyles of pre-Ottoman Turks from which the Ottoman Turks could derive lessons. But all in all, what he wanted was no more than to form a peaceful community of communities. Given these characteristics, his nationalism of the time appeared to involve elements of liberal nationalism such as equality of nations, their peaceful existence and reciprocal respect. At the same time it conflicted with characteristics of some brands of liberalism in that it rejected voluntarism and was inimical to individualism.

Of the central themes of conventional liberalism, individuality, as in the way he understood it, was deeply denounced in Ağaoğlu's Russian and Ottoman writings. He referred to egoism and moral decay when he talked about it and stressed the need for collective action in its place. In the Russian context, he called for equality and rights along with other liberal-minded Russian Muslim intelligentsia. Where the self-strengthening of the politically, economically and morally weak Muslims were concerned, he suggested turning to rationality; studying Islam through a scientific lens and providing Muslim students, both male and female, with an education comparable to their Russian and Armenian counterparts in order to wither away bigotry and superstition in society.

There were recognisable ideological shifts in his writings of the time and often inconsistencies, stemming from his ideas' being informed by his more immediate political aims. Yet in the main one can find an endeavour where he sought the empowerment of Muslim Turks against the Tsarist imperial policies,

---

136   Ibid., p. 385.
137   Anthony Smith, *The Ethnic Origins of Nations*, Oxford: Blackwell, 1986.

and the Great Powers, drawing from the works of fellow Russian Muslims and Turkish nationalists as well as Jemal'addin al-Afghani.

In the late 1920s and '30s, Ağaoğlu's understanding of nationalism, which was born out of the ashes of Pan-Islamism, would go through an evolution toward secularism. He would turn away from Islam as a moral norm and seek secular sources for morality. As will be demonstrated in the following chapters, in the thoughts of the most prominent nationalist intellectuals of the early Republican era, the status of Islam as a state religion was contested. According to Heyd and Bozarslan, in his later work, Gökalp replaced religion with nationalism[138] and played an important role in the promotion of positivism as the new national religion,[139] while for the Ahmet Ağaoğlu of the 1930s, the new religion would be the Republic itself.

Ağaoğlu carried to the Republican context his communitarian idea of liberty, which he developed during the fermentation of his earlier ideas in the imperial contexts. His idea of liberty rested on the belief that communal and individual rights proceed from the creation of collective awareness. His understanding of history as an evolution in a certain direction, his abhorrence of individuality and continuing praise of solidarity and collectivity would form the central tenets of his thought in the 1920s and '30s. As such, his ideas of the imperial period, though less liberal, or at times even illiberal in character, in a sense formed the intellectual background to his later nationalist and communitarian liberal thought.

---

138   Heyd, *The Foundations of Turkish Nationalism*, p. 56.

139   Hamit Bozarslan, "Ziya Gökalp," in *Modern Türkiye'de Düşünce Tarihi, Tanzimat ve Meşrutiyet'in Birikimi*, Istanbul: İletişim Yayınları, 2002, p. 315.

CHAPTER 5

Founding the Republic

Ağaoğlu was arrested in Istanbul by the Ottoman police on January 15, 1919, and handed over to the British forces, being accused of crimes against the Armenians and other non-Muslims and his pro-German activities during the war.[1] These he refuted repeatedly with the petitions he sent to the British High Commissioner.[2] His wife Sitare Hanim, who was once described by a diplomat as a bluestocking, also wrote to the British, arguing that her husband was arrested purely as a consequence of intrigues worked out by personal hatred against him. "He had been given by General Thomson the permission to travel as Chief Delegate for the Azerbaijan Republic to the Paris Conference. On his return journey, he caught the Spanish fever and was lying down for two months in Constantinople. Before recovering from his illness he was imprisoned."[3]

British authorities disregarded these petitions and considered Ağaoğlu to be "an extremely dangerous man" due to his pro-German and Pan-Islamist tendencies.[4] According to British intelligence, he was of Jewish origin; he had been a member of Okhrana as agent provocateur at an early age and had studied in Moscow. He was also being accused of collaborating with Gökalp in arranging massacres in the Caucasus.[5] No evidence I could find about any of these information on Ağaoğlu's origins as put forward by the British intelligence, except, as shown previously, his pro-German and Pan-Islamist writings.

After being kept in detention in Istanbul, Ağaoğlu was taken to Moudros and then to Malta where he spent about one and a half year in prison. After his arrival in Istanbul and during his detention, he kept a diary in which he took notes on day-to-day politics of the empire, often expressing his anger to the Istanbul government, the anti-Unionists and Greeks and Armenians who were collaborating with the Allies.[6] Meanwhile, he studied English, but

---

1 Aghayef to Chancellor, April 16, 1919, TNA F0371/4174/296; Samet Ağaoğlu, *Babamdan Hatıralar,* p. 11. According to Ağaoğlu's Malta diaries, he was arrested in March 1919; see, Ahmet Ağaoğlu, "Mütareke ve Malta Hatıraları," *Akın,* May 29–August 19, 1933.
2 For more detailed account of his petitions see, TNA Fo 371/4174.
3 Sitare Agaef to High Commissioner, July 7, 1919, Fo 371/4174/307.
4 Memo on A. Aghayeff, August 26, 1919, Fo 371/4174/292.
5 Memo on A. Aghayeff, no date, Fo 371/4174/308.
6 Ahmet Ağaoğlu, "Mütareke ve Malta Hatıraları," *Akın,* May 29–August 19, 1933.

never mastered the language, and taught Russian to Hüseyin Rauf (Orbay) (1881–1964).[7]

Ağaoğlu tells us that he wrote his *Three Civilisations* while he was imprisoned in Malta.[8] He also exchanged ideas, in the abundance of free time, with other leading Unionists and Ottoman statesmen and writers such as Said Halim Paşa (1863–1921), Ali Fethi (Okyar) (1880–1943), another military officer, a close friend of Mustafa Kemal Paşa and Prime Minister of the republic in 1923 and in 1924–5; and Ziya Gökalp, who were also imprisoned in Malta.[9] From his diaries we understand that Ağaoğlu was finding Gökalp's sociologist thought which the latter was sharing with him and other prisoners interesting and important at the time, but not to the extent to employ and exploit theories of Durkheim, which would loom large in his writings in the republican period.[10] This itself makes us question if he genuinely wrote *Three Civilisations* while in Malta, as he indeed draws upon Durkheim's work in this book.

While he was away, Ağaoğlu lost his position as professor at the *Darülfünun* at Ali Kemal's command. This put the family in financial difficulty, which was why the National Assembly in Ankara would arrange a salary for them.[11] Ağaoğlu was released from Malta again thanks to the Ankara government. He left Malta in May 1921 in an exchange of war captives with the British.

Feeling indebted to Mustafa Kemal for these, he joined the National Liberation Movement led by the latter. Subsequently he found a place among the inner circle of the top echelon leaders of the Kemalists. In the 1920s, as the RPP government turned into an authoritarian one, there would be a gradual shift from his position as an enthusiastic liberal advocate of what has been called the Kemalist Revolution to a critical revolutionary, however.

As Zürcher periodises, the Kemalist Revolution, like the preceding Young Turk Revolution (1908), consisted of three phases[12]: the first phase began with the National Liberation Movement (c. 1919–1922), during which "the 'Kemalist' movement sprang up as an illegal armed resistance movement, which fought

---

7   Süreyya to Ahmet Agaef, October 8, 1919, KEKBMV 28/25; Clerk to Henderson, January 31, 1931, FO 424/274/13; Ahmet Ağaoğlu, "Ne İdik, Ne Olduk? I," *Hayat Mecmuası*, No. 6 (1978), p. 12.

8   Ahmet Ağaoğlu, *Mütareke ve Sürgün Hatıraları*, Istanbul: Doğu Kitabevi, 2013.

9   Osman Okyar, *Atatürk and Turkey of republican era*, Ankara: Union of Chambers of Commerce, Industry, Maritime Commerce and Commodity Exchanges of Turkey, 1981.

10   Ahmet Ağaoğlu, *Mütareke ve Sürgün Hatıraları*, Istanbul: Doğu Kitabevi, 2013, pp. 95–96, p. 118.

11   Ibid., p. 30.

12   Erik J. Zürcher, "The Ottoman Legacy of the Turkish Republic: An Attempt at a New Periodization," *Die Wet des Islams*, New Series, Bd. 32, No. 2 (1992), p. 239.

the occupying Entente powers, and eventually, the official government in Istanbul, which cooperated with the Entente."[13] The second phase encompassed the period between 1922 and 1925, beginning with victory in the War of Independence, followed by the transformation of the resistance movement into a political party, the People's Party, which took control of the whole country with the proclamation of the Republic, the abolition of the sultanate (1922) and the caliphate (1924) and the creation of an opposition party by prominent figures in the resistance movement who left the RPP.[14] The third phase started with the breakdown of multi-party system in 1925, "when the [RPP], confronted by a large-scale Kurdish insurrection in the East of the country and perceiving the state to be in danger, gave dictatorial powers to the government through the adoption of the *Takrir-i Sükun Kanunu* (The Law on the Maintenance of Order)." With this law the opposition party and all opposition newspapers were closed down, and the period of an authoritarian single-party rule began.

By authoritarianism, I refer here to the Linzian description where the characteristics of an authoritarian political system are argued to be (1) exercise of power by political leadership (a leader or a small group) with ill-defined limits, (2) limited, and not responsible, political pluralism, (3) absence of intensive or extensive political mobilisation, and (4) absence of an elaborate and guiding ideology, and instead, existence of distinctive mentalities.[15] This approach, much criticized for its static character, has been more dynamically interpreted by recent scholarship which invoke theories of analytic authoritarianism.[16] Their new approaches have drawn attention, besides structural elements, also to level of dependency of rulers on others to carry out their decision and how their discourses and behaviours are often socially constituted.[17] This, one may argue, refers to the fact that leaders of authoritarian regimes are not necessarily innately authoritarian, but they adopt tools of authoritarianism in response to immediate circumstances that often take shape beyond their control. Then again the quality of leadership comes into play as courses of action taken by different political leaders in similar situations differ. This constitutes the demarcation lines between authoritarian, totalitarian and liberal democratic forms of governance.

My aim here is not to engage in a detailed discussion of the meaning of authoritarianism. But, if one drew upon these approaches, it would be fair to say that

13   Ibid., p. 249.
14   Ibid., pp. 249–250.
15   Thomas J. Miley, "Franquism as Authoritarianism: Juan Linz and His Critics," *Politics, Religion and Ideology*, 12:1 (May, 2011), pp. 27–50.
16   A. Carl LeVan, "Analytic Authoritarianism and Nigeria," *Commonwealth&Comparative Politics*, 52:2 (Mar., 2014), pp. 212–231.
17   Ibid., p. 213.

early republican Turkey showed many of the characteristics of an authoritarian regime, with militarist and illiberal elements. These characteristics were dependent upon changes of circumstances that the Kemalist leadership confronted, their own motivations and goals, and the interplay between them. Ağaoğlu's liberal thought in early republican era took shape within this political milieu.

5.1   The Establishment of an Authoritarian Regime

In the first and second phases of the revolution, i.e. between 1919 and 1925, politics in Turkey was in many ways a plural one. It was perhaps more than it should have been because, since the National Assembly was established in April 1920, there were two governments in Turkey, one in Istanbul represented by the Sultan and the Sublime Porte, and the other in Ankara represented by the National Assembly. The latter was predominated by the personality of Mustafa Kemal Paşa to the extent that the main line of cleavage in the assembly was between his supporters and opponents.

His supporters consisted of those deputies who were following him almost blindly in everything and the extremists whose support was "conditional on his beating the National Pact down at all costs and flouting the wicked Powers of the West."[18] These together constituted the First Group. The personal adherents were the more numerous. Their organ was the *Hâkimiyet-i Milliye*, which had been established in 1920 at the wish of Mustafa Kemal. Kemal had often controlled the articles appearing in the journal, and edited some of them himself. The rabid extremists were a small but noisy minority, far more under Russian influence than Mustafa Kemal himself. Their organ was the *Yeni Gün* (New Day), and its editor Yunus Nadi.

The opponents of Mustafa Kemal appeared to consist of the followers of the old Union and Progress leaders also, who were organized well, of monarchist and otherwise conservative factions, and of miscellaneous personal or political adversaries of the Paşa. His conciliatory policies towards Russians caused anxieties among conservative deputies from the East, who had therefore formed the *Muhafaza-i Mukaddesat Cemiyeti* (Association for the Preservation of Sacred Institutions) to stress the importance of religion, the sultanate and the caliphate.[19] Following this, in May 1921, Mustafa Kemal organized his more unconditional followers into the *Müdafaa-i Hukuk Grubu* (Defence of Rights

---

18   H. Rumbold to Curzon, March 7, 1923, TNA FO 424/256/640.

19   Osman Okyar, Osman Okyar, *Milli Mücadele Dönemi Türk-Sovyet İlişkilerinde Mustafa Kemal (1920–1921)*, Ankara: Türkiye İş Bankası Kültür Yayınları, 1998, pp. 73–74; Eric J. Zürcher, *Turkey: A Modern History,* New York: I.B. Tauris & Co Ltd, 2001, pp. 158–159.

Group) in order to strengthen his hold on the assembly. This was followed in early 1922 by the foundation of the *İkinci Grup* (Second Group), whose members were bound together against what they perceived as Mustafa Kemal's growing autocracy and radicalism.[20] Its organ was the *Tan* newspaper, which was established on January 19, 1923.[21] By the end of the summer of 1926, all of these groups but the loyal followers of Gazi Paşa and his RPP were eliminated from the political scene.

In late 1922, when the Greek forces began to withdraw from Western Anatolia, the attention of the First Group, whose position was immensely strengthened by the victories on the battleground, turned to domestic political questions, specifically to that of the rival authorities of the Sultan and the Sublime Porte. When the Istanbul government was invited to the peace negotiations in Lausanne instead of the Ankara government (because the British had refused to recognize the latter), the National Assembly in Ankara reacted furiously and in October 1922, "revolted against the Sultan's pretensions to represent the country at the council of peace toward the establishment of which he had contributed nothing but harm."[22] Less than a month later, Mustafa Kemal Paşa proposed in a long speech the abolition of the sultanate for its treason during the War of Independence. The bill for it (the Law of Fundamental Organisation) was prepared in a few hours and was passed on the same day on November 1, 1922.

In December 1922, Mustafa Kemal Paşa declared that he was going to establish a new political party. One month later, a campaign for the creation of the organisation, to be initially called, the People's Party was launched. This coincided with the fact that the monarchist Conservative group gained prominence in January 1923 owing to the publication of a pamphlet by one Şükrü Hoca, openly condemning the policy of separating the sultanate from the Caliphate and destroying the former. This was a red rag to Mustafa Kemal, who sought unsuccessfully to deprive Şükrü Hoca of his parliamentary immunity in order that he should be prosecuted. The opposition not only had this proposal thrown out but secured after a struggle the adoption of the law on personal liberty.[23]

This was also a sign of the fact that Mustafa Kemal, despite his prestige, was not always able to get his decisions accepted by the opposition within the Assembly. He would at times receive fierce opposition at the parliamentary meeting as in early 1923 when the Lausanne talks were put on hold and when Ali Şükrü Bey, the deputy for Trabzon and the editor of *Tan*, severely criticised

20   Ibid., p. 159.
21   H. Rumbold to Curzon, March 7, 1923, TNA FO 424/256/640.
22   Berkes, *Development of Secularism,* pp. 449–450.
23   H. Rumbold to Curzon, March 7, 1923, TNA FO 424/256/640.

the Lausanne delegates for failing to protect Turkish interests in Mosul and Karaağaç.[24] One of the hampers of the pluralist environment shown at the time was the murder of Şükrü Bey by Topal Osman, a devotee of Mustafa Kemal, in March 1923.

The underlying idea of the establishment of a new political party was to combine under Mustafa Kemal Paşa's leadership his personal adherents and those of the old Union and Progress leaders.[25] In April, his Defence of Rights Group was transformed to become the People's Party (its name was changed as Republican People's Party (RPP) in 1924).[26] Yusuf Akçura, Ziya Gökalp and Ahmet Ağaoğlu, the three leading nationalist figures of the 1910s, wrote the programme of the party, which set its first aims as "guiding the exercise of national sovereignty (for the people, by the people), raising Turkey to the level of a modern state and maintaining the rule of law over all other powers in Turkey."[27] According to the programme, the RPP was a populist party, rejecting all individual, familial, class or occupational privileges; any superstitious beliefs or traditions opposed to reason were a threat to the liberty and independence of the government in enacting and exercising the people's rights. Moreover, "any individual from Turkey [*Türkiyeli*] who accepted the Turkish culture [*hars*] could participate in the [RPP]."[28]

In July 1923, when the Lausanne Treaty finally signed, Turkey emerged as a completely sovereign state. The following months saw two-stage elections, in which Mustafa Kemal himself chose all candidates, and almost all members of the new assembly became RPP deputies. On October 29, 1923, the republic was proclaimed without the consent of the opposition, which was a recipe for further fraught between the First and Second groups.

Throughout 1923, the critical press in Istanbul such as Ahmet Emin (Yalman)'s *Vatan*, Velid Ebuzziya's *Tevhid-i Efkar* and Hüseyin Cahit (Yalçın)'s *Tanin* were reporting widespread discontent among population. This would increase the next year due to, among others, grinding taxation, the scourge of brigandage in Anatolia, economic hardships suffered by the Muslim refugees exchanged from Greece and corruption of officials.[29] The closure of religious schools, the abolition

24   To this date only one book has been published about the life and activities of Şükrü Bey; Kadir Mısıroğlu, *Trabzon Meb'usu Sehid-i Muazzez Ali Şükrü Bey*, Istanbul: Sebil Yayınevi, 1978, pp. 135–36.

25   Ibid.

26   Faruk Alpkaya, *Türkiye Cumhuriyeti'nin Kuruluşu*, 1923–1924, Istanbul: İletişim Yayınevi, 1998, p. 38.

27   Ibid., p. 39.

28   Ibid., p. 39.

29   Neville Henderson to the Marquess Curzon of Kedleston, January 9, 1924, TNA FO 424/260/7.

of the Caliphate in March 1924 and the emancipation of women were sparking religious protests. Moreover, the Turkish-Islamist character of the 1924 constitution had discomforted non-Muslims and non-ethnic Turks, as in the constitution the religion of the Turkish state was declared to be Islam and all citizens of Turkey were to be called Turks regardless of their ethnic origins.

On November 17, 1924, the Second Group, now marginalised due to Mustafa Kemal Paşa's increasing control of power, established a new party, *Terakkiperver Cumhuriyet Fırkası* (Progressive Republican Party - PRP).[30] Its leading members included such prominent figures as Kazım Karabekir, the commander of the Eastern Army, Hüseyin Rauf (Orbay) and Doctor Adnan (Adıvar). During its seven-month life, the new party "never won an election or formed a government or even succeeded in having any legislation of its own passed by the National Assembly."[31] However, its foundation as a formation to challenge the power structure dominated by the RPP. According to Zürcher, the PRP was "a movement of prominent nationalist leaders who felt that the heritage of the movement of which they had been such leading figures was being monopolized illegitimately by one wing of the original movement and who saw themselves as guardians of the true traditions of the movement."

Mustafa Kemal and the party caucus were discontent with the appearance of a formal opposition. A month before the PRP was established, during his North Eastern Anatolia trip, Mustafa Kemal Paşa would make this clear: "[T]he real salvation of the country lay in the realisation of the ideals of the People's Party, and that the formation of other groups could only damage the nation's highest interests."[32] To strengthen its hold of power, a set of changes in the RPP's internal organization were also made in a way to tighten the party discipline against the now more organized opposition. In the new RPP, interpellations of the government would first be discussed within the party itself, that no interpellation could be put in the Grand Assembly, and no parliamentary question converted into an interpellation without the approval of the party; and that the declarations and writings of members had to conform to the policy of the party.[33] Moreover, one week before the PRP was established, the word "Republican" had been added to the name of People's Party with the motion of Recep Peker.

When the PRP was established, İsmet Paşa's attempts to suppress the new party was vetoed in the parliament. He was also suffering from malaria, and

---

30   Eric J. Zürcher, *Political Opposition in the Early Turkish Republic: The Progressive Republican Party*, Leiden, New York: E.J. Brill, 1991, pp. 110–111.

31   Ibid., 112.

32   Lindsay to MacDonald, October 1, 1924, TNA FO 424/261/50.

33   Lindsay to Austen Chamberlain, November 11, 1924, TNA FO 424/261/77.

shortly after, he was replaced by the moderate Fethi Bey (Okyar) as Prime Minister. The idea was that, while İsmet was recovering both physically and prestige-wise, Fethi Bey's appointment could take the winds out of the sails of the PRP and stop the disintegration of the party whose members had been leaving for the new party. As a matter of fact, the Istanbul press, which had been full of criticism of İsmet Paşa, gave Fethi its blessing on his advent to power, and remarkably toned down its criticisms to his administration.[34] Yet Fethi Bey was to face in three months' time the first serious uprising in early Republican era.

In February 1925, an insurrection led by Sheikh Said started in southeast Anatolia whose mainsprings were religious and Kurdish nationalist.[35] The new but fault system of administration was also regarded a cause of the events. *Tanin* and *Tevhid-i Efkar* reported that Sheikh Said distributed proclamations by means of British airplanes, stating that the Turkish government encouraged atheism, expelled the Caliph, led women to prostitution, that Sheikh Said was acting on behalf of religion and moral, that an independent Kurdistan would be formed and that the ex-Caliph restored.[36]

The first action of PM Fethi Bey was to proclaim martial law and introduce new laws of treason. But these were not enough for the extremists of the RPP led by Recep Peker. Fethi Bey found himself under criticism for not taking drastic action against the rebels and not suppressing the opposition party. He resisted these until the end of the month. On March 2, under strong opposition within the RPP, however, he resigned and was replaced by İsmet Paşa.

One day after İsmet Paşa returned to office, the Law on the Maintenance of Order was passed immediately. Independence Tribunals were set up and sent to the southeast following the suppression of the uprising at the end of April. The leaders of the uprisings were executed and many were imprisoned. In the second half of the 1920s, many villages were evacuated and thousands of Kurds, mostly families of the rebels, were deported to Western *vilayets* to prevent further rebellions in the region.[37]

Although the Progressives uncompromisingly denounced the rebellion, the events in the southeast served as a pretext for the closing down of their opposition party. Between March and August 1925, fifteen newspapers, including *Tanin* and *Tevhid-i Efkar* were banned.[38] Even though Ahmet Emin (Yalman)'s

---

34   Lindsay to Chamberlain, December 22, 1924, TNA FO 424/261/113.
35   Lindsay to Chamberlain, February 24, 1925, TNA FO 424/262/91.
36   Press Summary, February 24, 1925, TNA FO 424/262/92.
37   Clerk to Chamberlian, June 22, 1927, TNA FO 424/266/85.
38   Hıfzı Topuz, *II. Mahmut'tan Holdinglere: Türk Basın Tarihi*, Istanbul: Remzi Kitabevi, 2003, p. 148.

Vatan was initially spared, when he refused to write an editorial justifying the closure of the PRP, it was also closed. Ahmet Emin was trialled by the Independence Tribunals. He was eventually acquitted, but suspended from journalistic activity indefinitely.[39] Other leading writers of the time such as Zekeriya Sertel, Hüseyin Cahit (Yalçın), Velid Ebuzziya and Cevat Şakir (Kabaağaçlı) were either sent to exile or imprisoned.[40]

In a later speech delivered in 1927 during the dissolution of the Independence Tribunals, İsmet Paşa would accuse the intellectuals of provoking the rebellions in 1925:

> ...the most important event that we encountered two years ago was not the practical event that began with the Sheikh Said rebellion. The real danger was disorder...that took root in public life. [This] was created by degenerated intellectuals who were used to exploit small desires.[41]

Moreover, toward the end of 1925, smaller scale uprisings against the hat law in Sivas, Samsun, Rize, Marash and Trabzon were suppressed and rebels were executed.

In summer 1926, when an assassination attempt known as the İzmir Conspiracy, a plot by former Unionists to kill Mustafa Kemal during a visit to İzmir, was uncovered, a number of Unionists, including leaders of the Second Group such as Kazım Karabekir (1882–1948), found themselves on trial. Many former Unionists were imprisoned and some sentenced to death. Among these was Mehmed Cavid Bey, the famous Minister of Finance of the 1910s, though his direct involvement in the assassination attempt was never hard evidenced. Cavid was executed the same day a court decision was made.[42]

By the end of 1926 all groups potentially threatening the power of the Kemalists were thus eliminated. The Kemalist regime, now beginning to consolidate its power, almost perfectly fit into the Linzian description of authoritarianism. No political mobilisation other than that of the RPP was permitted. The leading figures of the revolution did take extreme courses of action against their rivals and opponents. The regime was not totalitarian yet, as there was no

---

39   Ahmet Emin Yalman, *Turkey In My Time,* Norman: University of Oklahoma Press, 1956, pp. 152–157.

40   Topuz, *Türk Basın Tarihi,* p. 151.

41   Mete Tunçay, *T.C.'de Tek Parti Yönetimi'nin Kurulması,* p. 138.

42   Nazmi Eroglu, *İttihatçıların Ünlü Maliye Nazırı Cavid Bey,* Istanbul: Ötüken Yayınları, 2008, pp. 235–253. This came as a big shock to many leading statesmen and their families who were residing in Ankara; interview with Nilüfer Gürsoy, November 24, 2004.

clear cut guiding ideology. Instead, as I shall explain in the next chapter, there was a set of mentalities that sometimes clashed with each other. And political pluralism would be limited to the party caucus and the close entourage of President Mustafa Kemal Paşa thereafter.

In the second half of the 1920s, it was the party committee that dealt with all major projects of policy. This real debating body, led by İsmet Paşa, proceeded in secret. Policies, only after being elaborated there, were scrutinized by the cabinet and the parliamentary commissions. The final acceptance of these policies at the assembly would often be unanimous. Beside this, there was another body, perhaps more powerful than the party committee, which initiated major projects. The private cabinet of Çankaya consisted of President Mustafa Kemal and his own immediate circle. It met on two or three nights a week at the President's house. The most regular members were Şükrü Kaya Bey, a former Minister of Foreign Affairs and President of the Foreign Affairs commission, Safvet Bey, secretary-general of the People's Party, Mahmud Bey and Falih Rıfkı, editors and directors of *Agence d'Anatolie* and the Government organ the *Hâkimiyet-i Milliye* (the former incidentally the president's business-man), Nuri Bey, Edib Bey and Ruşen Eşref Bey, old companion of the Gazi's days of obscurity. Kılıç Ali Bey, ex-president and member of the defunct Independence Tribunal, and Ali Cenani Bey, a former Minister of Commerce.[43]

That is, the decision making body had a dual nature, and this often became a recipe for fraught between the ruling elites. It was one of the reasons for the occasionally strained relations between İsmet Paşa and Mustafa Kemal Paşa. By the end of 1920s, İsmet developed his insistence on the constitutional nature of the Turkish state. This he did as opposed to Gazi Paşa's oft-interventions in governmental decisions. Matters almost came to a head in mid-1930, when the Turkish economy was in great vulnerability and just before the Free Party was established.[44]

Amidst this political struggle Ağaoğlu stood by Gazi Mustafa Kemal Paşa since the beginning. He was a near-regular participant of the President's dinner gatherings and his family had close relations with his wife Latife Hanım. As a matter of fact, after he had been released from Malta in May 1921 along with forty other detainees, his first destination was Istanbul. There he had received an invitation from his old friend Neriman Nerimanov, President of the Soviet Republic of Azerbaijan, to take an active role in Azerbaijani politics.[45] However, Ağaoğlu had refused this invitation, as he tells us, for three reasons: first, he did not share

---

43   Clerk to Chamberlain, June 9, 1927, TNA FO 424/266/70.

44   Clerk to Henderson, September 10, 1930, TNA FO 424/271/67.

45   Ahmet Ağaoğlu, "Ne İdik, Ne olduk 1," *Hayat Mecmuası*, No. 6, p. 12.

the official ideology of the Soviet Republic of Azerbaijan; secondly, he was still convinced that it was only the Ottoman Turks who could ensure the survival of all Turks in the world; and third, he felt indebted to the leaders of the National Liberation Movement, who had helped to obtain his release from Malta and who had provided material assistance to his family when he was in prison.[46]

Having turned down Nerimanov's invitation and learnt that he was on an Armenian blacklist,[47] Ağaoğlu went to Ankara on May 28, 1921.[48] Shortly after his arrival, he was introduced to Mustafa Kemal Paşa through Hamdullah Suphi (Tanrıöver), an active leading figure of the Turkish Hearths, and joined the former's movement.

Soon after his arrival in Ankara, Ağaoğlu, as an experienced publicist, was assigned to go to the Northern Anatolian provinces to agitate for the ideas and ideals of the Ankara government, against the Istanbul government. In early September 1921, he went to Trabzon, Erzurum and Kars, where he delivered public lectures to a large number of people.[49] In these lectures, he spoke about "the evil plans of the wicked Western Powers in Anatolia," the Armenian propaganda in the Northeast and about the heroic and sacrificing work of the Anatolian women.[50] At the same time, he wrote articles introducing the 'new centre', disseminating their aims and goals,[51] and calling intellectuals to come to Anatolia to work together on raising 'high sentiments' in society and to fight against the Entente forces.[52]

During his travels, Ağaoğlu frequently telegraphed his achievements to Mustafa Kemal. For his successful undertakings, in November 1921, he was appointed head of the Directorate of Press and Information and called back to Ankara. In his new position, he made a great effort to support the press. He lifted censorship on various journals, including *Sırat-ı Müstakim* and *Himmet*,

---

46   Ibid., p. 12. This being said, he wanted to leave the doors open to his homeland in case he would not be able to get hold of a position within the Kemalist movement. His letter sent to Nerimanov was published in the journal of *Kommunist* in June 1921. In this letter, Ağaoğlu claimed that the only government type that would save Eastern nations was that of Russia. Mevsim Aliyev, "Ahmedbey Agayev, Archivler Aciliyor," June 10, 1988; KEKBMV 44/21.

47   Veysel Usta, "Ağaoğlu Ahmet Bey'in Ermeni Propagandalarının Mahiyeti Üzerine Bir Konferansı," *Türk Dünyası Araştırmaları*, No. 131 (Apr., 2001), p. 77.

48   Ağaoğlu, "Ne İdik Ne Olduk 1," p. 12.

49   Veysel Usta, "Ağaoğlu Ahmet Bey'in Milli Mücadele'de Trabzon'da Verdiği Konferans," *Türk Kültürü*, No. 399 (1996), pp. 400–415.

50   Veysel Usta, "Ağaoğlu Ahmet Bey'in Ermeni Propagandalarının Mahiyeti Üzerine Konferansı," *Türk Dünyası Araştırmaları*, No. 131 (Apr., 2001), pp. 75–87.

51   Ağaoğlu, "Ne İdik Ne Olduk 1," p. 19.

52   Ahmet Ağaoğlu, "Münevverler Cepheye," *Vakit*, August 19, 1921.

and provided financial aid to many publications. His growing success procured his appointment, in February 1922, as editor-in-chief of *Hâkimiyet-i Milliye*. He kept this position until 1929, a clear sign of his loyalty to Mustafa Kemal Paşa throughout the 1920s.

On August 11, 1923, Ağaoğlu was elected as deputy for Kars in the second term of the National Assembly and enjoyed the benefits of holding such position until March 26, 1931. The same day he became a deputy, Zekeriya Sertel (1890–1980) took over Ağaoğlu's position as Head of the Directorate of Press and Information at İsmet Paşa's will. This event is regarded as an early indicator of the hostility between İsmet Paşa and Ağaoğlu.[53]

Next year, Ağaoğlu became a member of the special committee that drafted the 1924 Constitution. It is almost impossible to trace his influence on the articles drafted, although we know that he contributed to the heated debates during their preparation.[54] Still notable is that he always saw the 1924 Constitution as a guarantee of Republican Turkey's 'free' (*serbest*) political and economic institutions, convinced that it could meet all the needs of Turkish citizens. It indeed liberally defined individual rights and liberties. However, the fact that all three government powers were concentrated in the National Assembly had made it difficult to enforce them. The rights and liberties of the individuals could therefore be "granted or restricted as the government saw fit," and it had happened many times with political and economic restrictions imposed in the first years of the Republic.[55] Also problematic with the 1924 Constitution was that all citizens of the Republic were defined as Turks regardless of their ethnic backgrounds and the religion of the state was declared as Islam, which was to say that the constitution of the Republic was inclined to offending the non-Turkish and non-Muslims elements.

As a party man, Ağaoğlu's writings of the early 1920s seem to aim at explaining the rationale of the actions of the RPP. Against the increasing criticisms of the Second Group who were discontent with the fact that decisions such as the proclamation of the Republic and the abolition of the caliphate were being taken without the consent of all bodies in the parliament and in a rather short time, he would write:

> As long as a dynasty in Istanbul receiving support from the national budget and a republican government in Ankara coexist, neither can the

---

53   Shissler, *Between Two Empires,* p. 87.

54   A. Şeref Gözübüyük, Zekai Sezgin, *1924 Anayasası Hakkındaki Meclis Görüşmeleri,* Ankara: Balkanoğlu Matbaacılık, 1957; for Ağaoğlu's speeches, see pp. 367–370.

55   Kemal Karpat, *Turkey's Politics: The Transition to a Multi-party System,* Princeton, N.J.: Princeton University Press, 1959, pp. 137–140.

country find its balance nor can the nation find peace and tranquillity! Because as long as religion and the military are actively involved in politics, nobody will have confidence for the future, therefore these aspects of the revolution will be replenished in order to end the revolutionary phase, to establish security, peace and tranquillity in minds and mentalities and to give everyone the opportunity to be involved with their occupations with confidence and trust... The faster [these are] accomplished, the more auspicious they will be for the country.[56]

He showed firm support to the policies of the RPP in his writings and claimed that the harsh measures and the newly introduced criminal code, borrowed from Mussolini's Italy, were necessary.[57] But as much a party man was Ağaoğlu a member of the private cabinet of Mustafa Kemal. Perhaps at the suggestion of the latter, when Turkey saw circles of political crisis in the mid-1920s he prepared a private report for the president in 1926, which would later be published in national press. As shall be discussed in the next chapter, in this report, he condemned the government's policies, demanded the restructuring of the Republican People's Party for the protection of the revolution. Read very carefully by Mustafa Kemal, it also exacerbated the animosity between İsmet Paşa and Ağaoğlu.[58]

Moreover, the support of Ağaoğlu and his family to the families of the former Unionists such as Mehmed Cavid Bey during their turbulent times in 1926 was unwelcome by the İsmet Paşa leadership. In her memoirs, Süreyya Ağaoğlu mentions İsmet Paşa as a man who had never shown any sympathy neither to Ağaoğlu nor to his family.[59] The reasons for this are difficult to evidence. Ağaoğlu was no friendly in his memoirs to İsmet Paşa either, and did not explain why so.

Safa tells us that he was critical of the actions of PM İsmet in his private talks to Mustafa Kemal Paşa and suggesting his replacement.[60] Mustafa Kemal's response to Ağaoğlu was that there was nobody else to replace İsmet with. This was probably in late 1929, when, as he once told the British ambassador, Ağaoğlu encouraged Mustafa Kemal Paşa to take the affairs of the state more directly into his hands.[61] The latter indeed played with the idea of becoming PM, and

56   Ahmet Ağaoğlu, "Yeni Sayfalar," *Hâkimiyet-i Milliye,* February 29, 1924.
57   Ahmet Ağaoğlu, "İnkılâp Kıskançtır," *Milliyet,* March 10, 1926.
58   Ağaoğlu, *Serbest Fırka Hatıraları,* p. 152; Samet Ağaoğlu, *Demokrat Parti'nin Doğuş ve Yükseliş Sebepleri: Bir Soru,* Istanbul: n.p., 1972, p. 98; Sakal, *Ağaoğlu Ahmed Bey,* p. 44.
59   Süreyya Ağaoğlu, *Bir Ömür Böyle Geçti,* p. 39.
60   Peyami Safa, "Ahmet Ağaoğlu'nun İki Hikayesi," *Milliyet,* February 14, 1958.
61   Mr. Morgan (Ankara) to Henderson, March 9, 1931, TNA FO 424/274/50; Clerk to Henderson, November 3, 1929, TNA FO 424/270/85.

ceding the Presidency of the Republic to Fevzi Paşa, or alternatively re-modeling the Constitution on American lines so as to enable the head of the State to be his own PM. But, in the end, he himself decided against it because it would not be understood by the peasant, who would simply see that the President has ceased to be the first man in the State, and his prestige would suffer consequently.

Ağaoğlu, while maintaining that the Gazi's prestige and influence would not be damaged in political circles even if he were to accept the position of a simple deputy, admitted that with the peasantry it might be otherwise, but contended that the attitude of the peasantry on a matter of this kind presented very little importance. In his view, "the peasantry were...the mainstay of a country like Turkey, but all they cared for was to be able to sell their produce at a reasonable price, not to be overburdened with taxation and to be free from unduly vexatious interference by officialdom."[62]

Ağaoğlu was re-elected Deputy for Kars in September 1927, and in November became a member of the RPP's Executive and of the Constitutional Commission. In 1925, he had started to work as professor of law at Ankara Law School. His lectures were later published in book form under the title of *Hukuk-u Esasiye* (Constitutional Law).[63] Temporarily leaving these positions and his work at the Ankara Law School, he went to Vienna in 1928 for the treatment at a sanatorium of his wife Sitare Hanım who had long been struggling with tuberculosis.[64] He would return to Turkey only at the end of 1929, when the Wall Street Crash would have devastating effects on the economy. Ağaoğlu found himself at the centre stage of Turkish politics then.

5.2   The Economy and a Temporary Democracy

Throughout the 1920s, the Turkish economy dealt with the problems of an agrarian country in the process of industrialisation with the help of heavy indirect taxes, a large proportion of receipts being spent on defence and on strategic investments such as railways.[65] The revolutionary elites initially employed relatively liberal economic policies, which were exemplary in their

---

62   Ibid.
63   Ahmet Ağaoğlu, *Hukuk-i Esasiye*, Ankara: n.p, 1926.
64   Nusret Serter to Ağaoğlu Ahmet, March 7, 1928, KEKBMV 53/8.
65   Zvi Y. Hershlag, *Turkey: An Economy in Transition,* The Hague: Van Kuelen, 1959, p. 62; Osman Okyar, "Development Background of the Turkish Economy, 1923–1973," *International Journal of Middle Eastern Studies,* vol. 10, No. 3 (Aug., 1979), pp. 325–344, p. 326.

non-interventionist stance.[66] The prevailing idea was that the great predominance of foreign capital in trade, finance and communications had harmful effects on the Turkish economy.[67] Under the Treaty of Lausanne of 1923, capitulations were abolished, which led to large-scale withdrawals of foreign capital and enterprise.[68] Most of the pre-existing foreign concessions were replaced by government monopolies, such as in the arena of cabotage and the administration of ports.[69] Moreover, Turkey was prohibited from imposing any tariffs on foreign goods higher than those existing under the Ottoman Tariff of September 1, 1916, except in certain cases relating to health and security, for a period of five years, and the issue of the settlement of Ottoman debts remained unresolved until 1929.[70]

The economic difficulties were multiplied by the government's unwillingness to contract foreign loans and its simultaneous eagerness to invest in communications, transportation and other public projects at a pace. This resulted in overtaxation. The republican government took a variety of steps to spur indigenous industrialisation; the two key measures taken were the Law for the Encouragement of Industry and the abolition of the tithe.[71] The Business Bank and the Industrial and Mining Bank were founded in 1924 and 1925 respectively, to provide credit to private industrialists and enterprises. These measures were accompanied by railway construction and efforts at stabilising the currency.[72] However, any improvements in the Turkish economy were modest and inadequate to counter the effects of the worsening global economic conditions in 1929.

The Wall Street Crash led to an agrarian crisis in Turkey, exposing its lack of industrial development and its dependence on more developed countries and on their demand for raw materials.[73] Consequently, social discontent based on economic burdens emerged, especially in those regions where market relations were most developed. This meant increasing pressure on the Kemalist

---

66   Michael M. Finefrock, "Laissez-faire, the 1923 Izmir Economic Congress and early Turkish Developmental Policy in Political Perspective," *Middle Eastern Studies*, vol. 17, No. 3 (Jul., 1981), pp. 375–392; Çağlar Keyder, *The Definition of a Peripheral Economy: Turkey, 1923–29*, Cambridge: Cambridge University Press, 1981, p. 128.

67   Osman Okyar, "The Concept of Etatism," *The Economic Journal*, vol. 75, No. 297 (Mar., 1965), p. 99.

68   Ibid., pp. 20–21.

69   Walter Weiker, *Political Tutelage and Democracy in Turkey: The Free Party and Its Aftermath*, Leiden: Brill, 1973, p. 61.

70   Ibid., p. 59; Hershlag, *Turkey*, p. 62.

71   Keyder, *The Definition of a Peripheral Economy*, p. 128.

72   Ibid., p. 26.

73   Hershlag, *Turkey*, p. 61.

leadership especially in more commercialised regions such as Izmir. In the same year, the Republic started Ottoman debt payments, which exacerbated the economic situation.[74]

The effects of the Great Depression on the Turkish economy forced the government to re-examine its policies and to search for a new economic orientation with the expiry of the provisions of the Treaty of Lausanne disallowing Turkey from imposing tariffs on most products. The immediate responses of the government to the Depression were to cut its expenditure and to curtail foreign trade by abandoning convertibility, with the aim of balancing imports and exports.[75] As a result of a lack of foreign loans, Turkey decided to execute a protectionist trade policy and increase government activity in the economic field.[76] In a speech in Sivas on August 30, 1930, during celebrations on the anniversary of the decisive War of Independence battle of Dumlupınar, Prime Minister İsmet Paşa declared the new economic policy of the Republic to be *devletçilik* (étatism).[77]

This was a period of liberalisation in press as new papers were allowed to be published again after 1929. More importantly, eighteen days before İnönü's Sivas speech, the republic had begun a political venture with the establishment of the Free Republican Party (*Serbest Cumhuriyet Fırkası*) on August 12, 1930. Little is known of the real political reasons for the establishment of this new party. It is still unknown whether it was "a ruse by Mustafa Kemal to smoke out opposition which he could then easily suppress," or whether the whole idea of the Free Party was to get rid of Prime Minister İsmet Paşa, even though he backed İnönü strongly and publicly during the multi-party experience.[78]

The founding members of the new party were from the close circle of Mustafa Kemal, marking the character of the party as a 'loyal opposition'. Its leader was Ali Fethi (Okyar), lifelong friend of Mustafa Kemal,[79] former Unionist, twice Prime Minister in the Republican era and a liberal who detested militant measures against various opposition elements and who considered laissez-faire economics to be the only policy for developing Turkey's economy.

---

74 All during the 1930s the debt payments accounted for 13–18 per cent of total budget expenditures.
75 Hershlag, *Turkey*, pp. 61–62.
76 Okyar, "The Concept of Etatism,"p. 99.
77 Weiker, *Political Tutelage*, p. 84.
78 Cemil Koçak, "Belgelerle Serbest Cumhuriyet Fırkası," *Osmanlı Bankası Müzesi: Çağdaş Türkiye Seminerleri*, Istanbul, (Feb., 2005); Weiker, *Political* Tutelage, p. 55.
79 Osman Okyar; Mehmet Seyitdanlıoğlu, *Fethi Okyar'ın Anıları: Atatürk, Okyar ve Çok Partili Türkiye*, Ankara: Türkiye İş Bankası Kültür Yayınları, 1997.

Fethi had arrived in Turkey in July 1930, and at once joined Gazi at Yalova. Gazi had been unaware of the true state of affairs and of the general discontent with the administration. A trial of strength had arisen over the Government's Kurdish policy, but Fethi Bey had concentrated his attack on the Ministers of Finance and Justice and on their policies. İsmet Paşa had vigorously defended his two colleagues. In support of his case Fethi had produced the Schacht and Muller financial reports, which Gazi had never properly studied, and the decision had then been taken to publish them. As İsmet Paşa had remained obdurate, the Gazi had apparently become convinced that a change of Government was necessary, and with the double object of sparing İsmet Paşa's feeling and of leaving Fethi Bey free from the majority of the present ministers, for whom he had little use, the very complicated scheme of founding a new party had taken shape.[80]

Ağaoğlu was the second person to become a member of the new party. As we learn from his memoirs, Recep Peker, a member of parliament and later General Secretary of the Republican People's Party, had asked Mustafa Kemal to invite Ağaoğlu to join the new party, telling the President that "Ahmet Bey is the oldest and the most ardent liberal among us."[81] When Mustafa Kemal himself requested that Ağaoğlu should become a member of the party in a gathering in Yalova, Ağaoğlu's immediate reaction was hesitant and reluctant, but he was unable to reject this offer in face of Kemal's exuberance and staunch desire. Hence he left the Republican People's Party and in August 1930 he became a member of the new 'free (serbest) and liberal' party.

The first task of Ağaoğlu in the Free Party was to pen the first draft of its programme together with Fethi. This document, which he later elaborated on his own, called for republicanism, secularism and nationalism, the abolition of monopolies, the lowering of taxes, the importation of foreign capital into Turkey, the provision of incentives for entrepreneurs, the improvement of the Agricultural Bank and the Industry and Mining Bank, improvements to the legal system, better relations with neighbouring states, closer ties with the League of Nations, single-stage elections and further political rights for women.[82] Fethi presented the party's position as that of liberalism, according to which the state would help "individuals [to] act for themselves economically, unhampered by obstacles."[83] For him, the liberal system was the key to advancement, while, in a speech in Sivas, İnönü was describing liberalism

80   Helm to A. Henderson, August 12, 1930, TNA FO 424/273/35.
81   Ağaoğlu, Serbest Fırka Hatıraları, p. 16.
82   Vakit, August 13, 1930.
83   Emrence, "Politics of Discontent," p. 36.

as an ideology that "Turkey can hardly understand. We are lukewarm étatists in economy."

During the three-month-long adventure of the Free Party, Ağaoğlu was in a dispute with one or another pro-RPP editor or columnist every other day.[84] His criticisms of the RPP government, which appeared mostly in pro-Free Party newspapers such as *Yarın* (Tomorrow) and *Son Posta* (Last Mail), were wide-ranging and received broad coverage. He insisted that the new party was leftist and democratic, whereas the RPP was devoid of democratic principles.[85]

Only a month after the establishment of the Free Party, in September 1930, municipal elections took place. During the election campaign, pro-RPP writers attacked the Free Party by informing the public that reactionary forces filled its ranks. Focusing its election campaign on 'non-Republican elements' among grassroots supporters of the Free Party, the RPP alleged that the Free Party was working hand in hand with communists, non-Muslims and low-class people, whose common aim was "to do away with the republic, to return property to the Greeks, to demand the use of the Arabic alphabet and the wearing of the fez."[86] When a picture of a green flag (a symbol of Islam) was published in a newspaper supporting the Free Party, and when the same flag was seen at an election rally, the allegations reached a peak.[87] Various journals and newspapers also attacked the Free Party for being pro-communist, backing non-Muslims (or being the party of the Greeks, Armenians and Jews, because it had nominated some non-Muslim figures as mayoral candidates) and therefore being the party of the infidels (*gâvur*). Thus the Free Party was accused at one and the same time of being the voice of the Islamists and of the infidels. Furthermore, when the new party began to gain great popular support, President Mustafa Kemal Paşa, who had promised his impartiality when proposing the venture to Ali Fethi, published a letter in *Cumhuriyet* to remind the public that he was still the head of the Republican Party and that if necessary he would side with his party.

The results of the elections, at least the official ones, were not as expected on the part of the Free Party. Although they won the majority of the votes in Western Anatolia, they were able overall to win only forty-two municipalities out of 502.[88] After the elections, Ağaoğlu took an extremely angry tone in an article denouncing the atmosphere created by the Republican Party before

---

84   Weiker, *Political Tutelage,* p. 83.
85   Ahmet Ağaoğlu, "Devlet Hazinesi Çıkmaza Girmiştir: Sağ Kim? Sol Kim?," *Yarın,* August 18, 1930.
86   Ibid., p. 43.
87   Ibid., p. 43.
88   Ibid., pp. 164–170.

and during the elections.[89] According to him, there were irregularities that prevented the Free Party from holding rallies in various cities. Even after the elections, the pressure on the Free Party remained strong. Fethi made a final attempt to salvage his party by introducing a motion in parliament to censure the government for its conduct of the local elections.[90] When it was defeated, he decided to dissolve the party and on November 17, 1930, despite Mustafa Kemal's attempts to dissuade him, it was closed down.

In a private conversation with the British Ambassador Morgan, Ağaoğlu said that "[t]he disfavour into which the Liberal party soon fell was primarily due to the success of its enemies in scaring the Gazi by depicting a victory for the party at the forthcoming elections, leading perhaps even to the choice of Fethi as President of the Republic."[91] In his account, the President was in fact not unhappy with the last of the party.

On December 23, 1930, a month after the Free Party disbanded itself, a very grave incident, of religious (messianic) and anti-governmental character, took place in Menemen where a military officer called Kubilay who attempted to appease the crowd was brutally killed. Ağaoğlu and other Free Party leaders were accused of having provoked this uprising by accommodating various Islamist groups in their party. Antagonized by these criticisms, unlike all other members of the Free Party, Fethi and Ağaoğlu never returned to the ranks of the Republican People's Party after the short multiparty episode, remaining independent deputies for less than a year. Subsequently, at Mustafa Kemal's request, Fethi went to London as ambassador. And Ağaoğlu returned to Istanbul in late 1931, devoted himself to teaching law at the *Darülfünun*. He stopped contributing to journals in this period.

With the new Press Law in 1931, the opposition press such as *Yarın* (Tomorrow) and *Son Posta*, as well as the publication organs of the Greeks, Armenians and Jews were closed. That said, Fethi Bey and Ağaoğlu had one consolation for the brief existence of their party. It had justified itself by bringing about a radical change in the Government party, which was now actively employed in putting its house in order, searching for doubtful elements in it, and trying to bring itself more into harmony with popular opinion. In pursuit of this goal, while the top echelon of leaders tightened their control over its central organs, the Party was decentralised at the provincial and local levels.[92]

---

89   Ahmet Ağaoğlu, "Milli İrade Bu mudur?," *Son Posta,* October 31, 1930.
90   Weiker, *Political Tutelage,* p. 128.
91   Morgan to Henderson, March 9, 1931, TNA FO 424/274/50.
92   Weiker, *Political Tutelage,* p. 184.

In March 1932, Ağaoğlu sent Mustafa Kemal Paşa a letter to apologize to him for having been rude and speaking too strong at one of Kemal's dinners during the Free Party era. After this letter, Ağaoğlu was invited again to Mustafa Kemal's dinner parties.[93] The following year, Ağaoğlu began to launch his own journal, named *Akın* (*Torrent*) in Istanbul.

This was only four days after he was, due to his age, retired as professor of law at the University of Istanbul with the 1933 reform. Now an independent writer freed from the servitude of political parties, he attacked in *Akın* the RPP, targeting a wide range of issues from its lack of transparency to the failure to inform people fully of the activities and proceedings of parliament; from the inadequacy of economic policies in increasing agricultural produce prices[94] to the avoidable accidental deaths of mine workers[95]; and from nepotism[96] to sugar[97] and beer monopolies.[98]

On September 24, when he severely criticised the RPP for manipulating public opinion through biased publications, particularly of *Hâkimiyet-i Milliye*,[99] he found himself at Çankaya, as he tells in his memoirs, at one of the dinner parties of Gazi Mustafa Kemal, where Gazi asked Ağaoğlu to read out and explain the content of his last column with a copy of *Akın* on the table. When Ağaoğlu remained silent, Gazi got angry and reminded Ağaoğlu that he was a 'sığıntı' which refers to the fact that he was a refugee from Azerbaijan which was under Soviet rule at the time. After that day *Akın* published no more.[100]

Hence by late 1933, Ağaoğlu was deprived of two of his main incomes. His wife's death later in the same year was the third blow for Ağaoğlu. He accused the Republican leadership rather equivocally of depriving his life of meaning:

> [Living] alone in this miserable world, I can't be occupied with trade after the age of sixty. They *forced* me to choose a new occupation. Too late. Writing and expressing. These are the meanings [of my life]. Now, my life has no meaning.[101]

---

93 Özel Şahingiray, *Atatürk'ün Nöbet Defteri*, Ankara: Türk Tarih Kurumu Basımevi, 1955.
94 Ahmet Ağaoğlu, "Fazla Ucuzluk İyi Bir Alamet midir?," *Akın*, June 12, 1933.
95 Ahmet Ağaoğlu, "İktisat Vekili Celal Beyefendiye, Gene Kömür Şirketi İçin", *Akın*, September 24, 1933.
96 Ahmet Ağaoğlu, "Nepotizm," *Akın*, June 17, 1933.
97 Ahmet Ağaoğlu, "Şeker İhtikarını Kim Yapıyor?," *Akın*, July 13, 1933.
98 Ahmet Ağaoğlu, "Hükümetten İcraat Bekleniyor: Bomonthi Feshedilmelidir," *Akın*, July 31, 1933.
99 "Açık Görüşler: Hâkimiyet-i Milliye," *Akın*, September 24, 1933.
100 Samet Ağaoğlu, *Babamın Arkadaşları*, pp. 210–212.
101 Samet Ağaoğlu, *Babamdan Hatıralar*, p. 42; emphasis mine.

He sought consolation in writing. In early 1934, he wrote his Free Party memoirs and occupied himself with the publication of the works that he had written in France in the early 1890s. His *İran İnkılabı* (The Iranian Revolution) and *1500 ile 1900 Arasında İran* (Iran Between 1500 and 1900) were both published in 1934.[102] The following year his translation of Kropotkin's *Ethics: Origins and Development* came out.[103]

In mid-1934, at the invitation of his old friend Yunus Nadi, editor-in-chief of *Cumhuriyet*, Ağaoğlu began to write again for the pro-Republican People's Party newspaper. This opportunity provided him with a new source of income. Moreover, he started to organise regular meetings in the big oval living room of his house in Teşvikiye, to which he invited various Turkish intellectuals from different ideological backgrounds in order to debate contemporary issues in Turkey (See Illustrations 1, 2 and 3).

ILLUSTRATION 1 *Oval 1: The Oval Room at Ahmet Ağaoğlu's house in Teşvikiye.*
WITH PERMISSION FROM THE RAHMI M. KOÇ ARŞİVİ IN ISTANBUL,
COPYRIGHT OWNER OF THE IMAGES.

---

102 Ahmet Ağaoğlu, *İran İnkılabı*, Istanbul: Akşam Matbaası, 1934; Ağaoğlu, *1500 ile 1900 arasında İran*, Ankara: Başvekalet Basımevi, 1934; for an account of Ağaoğlu's views on Iran, see François Georgeon, "20. Yüzyıl başinda Bir Türk Aydınının Gözünde İran," in *Türk Modernleşmesi*, pp. 131–140.

103 Petr Kropotkin, *Etika: ahlâkın kaynağı ve açılması*, trans. Ahmet Ağaoğlu, Istanbul: Vakit Kütüphanesi, 1935.

ILLUSTRATION 2   *Oval 2: The Oval Room at Ahmet Ağaoğlu's house in Teşvikiye.*
WITH PERMISSION FROM THE RAHMI M. KOÇ ARŞİVİ IN ISTANBUL,
COPYRIGHT OWNER OF THE IMAGES.

ILLUSTRATION 3   *Ağaoğlu's house in Istanbul.*
WITH PERMISSION FROM THE RAHMI M. KOÇ ARŞİVİ IN ISTANBUL,
COPYRIGHT OWNER OF THE IMAGE.

At these meetings, which took place every Monday evening until Ağaoğlu's death, prominent figures holding different views, such as the famous leftist poet Nazım Hikmet (1902–1963) and the nationalist Nurullah Ataç (1898–1957), were occasionally present, while the core attendees were Ahmet Hamdi Başar (1897–1971), economic nationalist advocate of étatism, Peyami Safa (1899–1961), rightist man of letters, İsmail Hakkı Baltacıoğlu (1886–1978), prominent pedagogue and Republican politician, Hilmi Ziya Ülken (1901–1974), sociologist and moral philosopher renowned for his culturalist orientations, Mustafa Şekib Tunç (1886–1958), a philosopher known as a disciple of Henri Bergson (1859–1941) in Turkish academe, and İbrahim Fazıl Pelin (1884–1944), liberal professor of finance.[104]

The subjects discussed at the meetings formed the themes of Ağaoğlu's contemporary *Cumhuriyet* articles. The core participants of the gatherings later published their own journal, *Kültür Haftası* (The Culture Week) in 1936. The similarities and differences between Eastern and Western civilisations and Turkey's Westernisation project, the moral problems of Turkish society and the question of the reform of the self were the common themes they discussed and wrote about at the time.

Ağaoğlu also wrote for Ülken's monthly humanist journal of philosophy *İnsan* (The Human). In his *İnsan* articles he elucidated the development of modern societies, invoking Durkheim's theories. Moreover, with his instalments in *Cumhuriyet* in 1936 and later in 1939, his swansong *Ben Neyim?* (*What am I?*) came to light. His children brought together these instalments and published them in book form posthumously, a couple of months after he passed away on May 19, 1939.

---

104   Samet Ağaoğlu, *Babamdan Hatıralar,* p. 45.

CHAPTER 6

Revolution and Ideology

The Ağaoğlu of the 1920s and the 30s was an overt republican who advocated a version of republicanism which pitted liberalism and republicanism, not against one another, but against what he regarded as oppressive monarchical rule. This was not unprecedented in Western political thought.[1] Like many other liberal republicans, he persuaded himself that only a republic could bring about a social and political system that could accommodate his full faith in limited power through social control, publicity, freedom of thought and freedom of movement, his commitment to meritocracy over inherited privileges, his emphases on the natural rights of the individual and the equality of genders, and his advocacy of the pursuit of a balanced and transparent government.[2] That being said, there had been little to no mention of republicanism and national sovereignty in his earlier work, and it was only as of the 1920s, perhaps informed by his surroundings in Ankara, that he would write about republicanism and link it with his liberal ideas.

As a matter of fact, in the early days of the republic, the terms 'liberal', 'reformist/revolutionary' and 'republican' were virtual synonyms. In a 1923 article titled 'Fırkaların İçtimai Tasnifi' (The Social Classification of Political Parties) Gökalp had classified the RPP as a liberal party, arguing that conservative and liberal parties, being moderate and revolutionary (*inkılâpçı*), were normal and necessary, in contrast to extremist reactionary (*mürteci*) and radical (*radikal*) political parties.[3] The revolutionary Kemalist elites were widely referred as 'liberals' in this period. For example, just before the caliphate was abolished on March 3, 1924,[4] the popular daily newspaper *Tevhid-i Efkâr* reported this with the headline, "The Liberal Party has decided upon the complete abolition of the Caliphate."[5] In their reports to London, the British diplomats would use the word liberal to denote the Kemalist leadership.[6] In his

---

1 Bill Bruger, *Republican Theory in Political Thought: Virtuous or Virtual?* London: Macmillan Press, 1999, p. 2.
2 Ahmet Ağaoğlu, "Demokrasi ve Devletçilik".
3 Ziya Gökalp, "Fırkaların Siyasi Tasnifi," *Hâkimiyet-i Milliye*, April 19, 1923.
4 Berkes, *Development of Secularism in Turkey*, p. 458.
5 "Liberal Partisi Hilâfet'in külliyen ilgâsına karar verdi," *Tevhid-i Efkâr*, February 29, 1924.
6 Neville Henderson to the Marquess Curzon of Kedleston, January 9, 1924, TNA FO 424/260/7.

© KONINKLIJKE BRILL NV, LEIDEN, 2015 | DOI 10.1163/9789004297364_007

various journalistic articles, Ağaoğlu would also call the People's Party a 'liberal' (*liberal*) party.

The liberalism of early republicans was not a guiding ideology, however.
It was more of a mentality, or an empirical stance against monarchism and
religious reactionism and for Westernisation and secularisation. As such, early
republicans elites did not embrace values of liberalism as a wholesale system
of thought. Their understanding of liberalism was shaped by a modernist
mentality, limited to opposition to the old regime and bred by a brand of
nationalism propounded mainly in the works of Gökalp and by a militarist
understanding. The latter had emanated from the Kemalist leaders' military
background and militarist thought made popular by such figures as Colmar
Freiher von der Goltz (1843–1916), who had taught at Ottoman military schools
and commanded Ottoman armies since the late nineteenth century. Both of
these channels gave little importance to individual rights and autonomy. As
I shall discuss in the next chapter, Gökalp's nationalism was vague in its conception of the individual, while the Goltzian understanding was shaped by
militarism, nationalism and a Social Darwinism, which saw world history as an
unending struggle for existence between nations.[7] That is, the Kemalist liberalism of the early 1920s co-existed with nationalism and militarism, and it could
well lack reluctance to offend oppositional groups as well as non-Muslims and
non-ethnic Turks. It was an authoritarian version of liberalism, an oxymoron.

Ağaoğlu shared many of the beliefs and ideas of political elites in the first
years of the republic. Yet towards the end of the 1920s, his understanding of
liberalism would begin to differ from them as his conception of the individual
finally took shape along Durkheimian lines. His political and social arguments
specifically between 1926 and 1933 would mark his work as a liberal opponent
to authoritarianism at the time. Before 1926, examining his writings and
actions, we find a party man. After 1933, he became a surrendered liberal and a
defender of the regime. His writings in these periods hardly went against the
grain of the government and were laden with justifications of its actions, if not
praises.

In 1924, for example, he would write as displeased as Mustafa Kemal and
İsmet Paşas were when the Progressive Party was established. He argued in an
article entitled "Nereye Gidiyoruz?" (Where are we going?) that the foundation

7   Mustafa Oral, "Çağdaşları Tarafından Ziya Gökalp Eleştrisi," *CITAD*, 12 (Spring 2006), p. 30;
    Hamit Bozarslan, "Ziya Gökalp," in *Modern Türkiye'de Düşünce Tarihi Tanzimat ve Meşrutiyet'in
    Birikimi*, Istanbul: İletişim Yayınları, 2002, pp. 314–319; Feroze A.K. Yasamee, "Colmar Freiherr
    von der Goltz and the Rebirth of the Ottoman Empire," *Diplomacy & Statecraft*, vol.9, No. 2
    (1998), p. 95.

of the Progressive Republican Party was unnecessary; a party of this character was not in the interests of the country, because, first of all, the basic principles or ideas of the new party were no different from those of the Republican People's Party; and second, the new party was established as a consequence of merely interpersonal struggles.[8] According to Ağaoğlu, it was established not to represent a new ideology or current of thought distinct from that of the Republican People's Party. The latter, he maintained, was the mirror of the entire nation and was not formed by a single idea, ideology or interest, but instead involved "two things, two real currents. One was liberalism (*liberallik*), and the other, conservatism (*muhafazakârlık*)."[9] The RPP was a liberal party, but those who left it to found the Progressive Republican Party were not conservatives. Otherwise, he says, "if the new party were to represent a new ideology other than that of the Republican People's Party," he would "regard this split and grouping as natural and applaud them" for creating a multi-vocal atmosphere in politics.

He moreover criticised the programme of the Progressive Republican Party for bringing forward nothing new. Its republicanism, its advocacy of the enactment of the Village Law and single-stage elections; and their objections against the president's right to veto and disband the parliament and their demand for the maintenance of the sovereignty of the assembly were all groundless and unnecessary objectives because, while some of these articles were in the programme of the People's Party (the Village Law and single degree elections), some were already among their enactment plans. He claimed that the new party was going to bring nothing but demagogy and further interpersonal struggles. As a self-ascribed liberal, Ağaoğlu saw no paradox in the RPP's intolerance to opposition until the closure of the Progressive Republican Party. However, in the coming months he began to criticise the leaders of the RPP himself as new events changed the course of the revolution.

While the Kemalist political elites' more pragmatic considerations would lead them to easily drop the term liberal from their discourses in the second half of the 1920s, Ağaoğlu insisted on defending what he understood as liberalism and seeking to turn the regime to a more liberal direction as it had happened, as he believed, during the French Revolution.

---

8   Ahmet Ağaoğlu, "Nereye Gidiyoruz?" *Hâkimiyet-i Millîye*, November 18, 1924.

9   Ibid. In the same period, Zekeriya Sertel, another prominent pro-People's Party man of letters of the time wrote: "The People's Party was the party of the nation. It was not an ideological party. There were traditionalists…in the party [even] when it was based on a secular and democratic government"; cf. Mete Tunçay, *T.C.'inde Tek Parti Yönetimi'nin Kurulması, 1923–1931*, Istanbul: Cem Yayınevi, 1981, pp. 122–123.

6.1 A Liberal Revolution?

Unlike most liberals who prefer gradual change, Ağaoğlu believed that a deep political, social and moral revolution could change the ill-made traditional Eastern mentality. In his view, this was what had happened in the West since the French Revolution. He had previously hoped that the rise of the mullahs in Iran against the British Tobacco Monopoly in 1892, the Iranian Revolution of 1906 and the Young Turk Revolution of 1908 were events potentially capable of galvanising the East. All had culminated in further social turmoil and political problems. When he joined the National Liberation Movement in 1921, he pinned his hopes on the events taking place in Anatolia, which, in his view, might be the turning point in the history of the East.[10]

In the early 1920s, he repeatedly wrote that the Turkish revolution was the Eastern counterpart of the French Revolution of 1789. Essentially, the historical image of the French Revolution had been used to mirror the character and future of the Turkish Revolution since the very beginning by most fellow revolutionaries. Mustafa Kemal had himself asked Hüseyin Ragıp, the first editor-in-chief of the *Hâkimiyet-i Milliye*, to publish the Declaration of Rights of Man and the Citizens (1789) in the first issue of the journal in 1920.[11] But rare were those who attempted to analyse and put the ideals of the Turkish Revolution into an ideological framework after the image of the French experience to the degree that Ağaoğlu did at the time.

In February 1923, he wrote that both revolutions resulted from the frenzy that possessed their respective nations:

> More than a century ago, the French nation, betrayed by its ruler and by the palace circle, initiated...a movement with an ardent enthusiasm. At that time, too, all its opponents began to cry that it was frenzy. But French peasants carried the spirit and ideal that was sung in *La Marseillaise* all over Europe. They inspired dead nations and offered new ideals in the service of humanity. Today, the same frenzy is being inculcated in the East by the Turkish spirit.[12]

Ağaoğlu believed that the French Revolution had led to a wave of revolutions all over the world, which finally hit Turkey. In his account, there were astonish-

---

10   Ağaoğlu, *İhtilâl mi, İnkılâp mı?* p. 7.
11   İsmet Giritli, "Fransız İhtilali ve Etkileri," in *Atatürk Araştırma Merkezi Dergisi*, vol. 15, No. 5 (Jul., 1989).
12   Ahmet Ağaoğlu, "Türk İnkılabı: İnkılabımıza Dair," *Yeni Mecmua*, No. 69, February 1, 1923.

ing similarities between the French and the Turkish revolutions. Both aimed to demolish ancient institutions, to put an end to the monarch's sovereignty and to eradicate all types of moral, religious and material restraints on social life. The leaders of both revolutions accepted the principle that the boundaries of governments should coincide with those of nationalities, that the nation was sovereign and that this sovereign body should attempt to give its citizens the opportunity of thinking and acting freely within the same legal borders. And he noted: 'The twin of the French Revolution comes into existence in Turkey after a century, and it lays the ground in the East for the appearance of the values that the French Revolution engendered in the West.'[13]

According to Ağaoğlu, the French Revolution had been the outcome of a long gestation. The humanist movements during the northern and southern Renaissance, the Reformation and the victory of Protestantism and the emergence of the principle of freedom of thought and conscience prepared the ground for the outbreak of the Revolution.[14] The temporary ascendancy of absolute monarchies had a positive effect on this process. They functioned as a body of revolt against religious authority, the formulation 'l'état c'est moi', and gave rise to national cultures and mentalities.

Ağaoğlu claimed that Molière in literature and Descartes in philosophy had influenced France's fortunes by introducing criticism and idealism, which led to the emergence of a new intellectual culture in which literature was philosophised and philosophy was rendered literary. To prove this point, he argued that Rousseau's novels *Julie: ou La nouvelle Héloïse* and *Émile: ou De l'éducation* and his *Contrat social*, as well as Montesquieu's *Lettres persanes* and *De l'esprit des lois*, treated similar issues to a certain extent and advocated parallel theses. By criticising the status quo and idealizing the future, eighteenth-century French literature and philosophy strongly contributed to preparing the Revolution:

> All changes...in the minds of intellectuals...pertaining to such things as religion, state, government, family, individual, community, property, education and so forth, which constitute the basis of human life, since they found voice in literature, began to be disseminated to lower strata and embraced to a certain extent. That is, on the eve of the French Revolution –in some groups of French society- the principles and direction of the Revolution were already partially determined.[15]

---

13   Ibid.
14   Ibid.
15   Ibid.

Ağaoğlu thus argued that the French Revolution resulted from intellectual developments. He asserted that the struggles at the outset of the Revolution were a struggle for predominance between the ideas of Montesquieu and Rousseau. The Turkish Revolution, on the other hand, was the outcome of a somewhat different story:

> In Asia Minor there has been no profound gestation period. Essentially, for a century, we have had continually increasing relations with Europe. We are not totally ignorant of the intellectual, scientific, literary, social and political currents that emerged in Europe. In fact, some aspects of our lives have been seriously affected by these currents. For example, our literature has changed by taking European literature as a model, and eliminating Eastern themes, it has begun to Westernize... European science and educational techniques steadily begin to invade our schools.[16]

All these transformations, according to Ağaoğlu, caused "not only changes in the types of government in the last fifteen years [1908–1923], but also led to viewing the Eastern mentality with critical eyes."[17]

However, Ağaoğlu lamented, these transformations remained superficial, for they were limited to Istanbul and never touched the people of Anatolia. Neither the mentality nor the practices of the people changed in public life. Aside from Gökalp's work, no original, stimulating and lasting literature or philosophy emerged in Turkey that could deeply transform and shape mentalities and ideals by engaging critically with social, moral and economic life. Hence, in Ağaoğlu's view, whereas the French Revolution resulted directly from a process and from the literature and philosophy that this process nurtured, the Turkish Revolution had remained unstimulated by such cultural and intellectual developments. He therefore wrote that, in the coming years, liberty would have to be infused into individual hearts by means of literature, art, philosophy and science. The heart of each Turkish individual must be transformed. Otherwise, revolution and reforms would continue to remain superficial and ineffective, as they had since the days of the Young Turks. The high goals of the revolution required much sacrifice, and therefore, an enormous moral strength.[18]

With the crushing of the rebellions in the Southeast in 1925, Ağaoğlu wrote an article arguing that the Turkish Revolution had come to a crossroads.[19] In

---

16   Ibid.
17   Ibid.
18   Ahmet Ağaoğlu, "Gideceğimiz Yol," *Vatan*, August 22, 1923.
19   Ahmet Ağaoğlu, "Yol Dönümünde," *Cumhuriyet*, March 12, 1925.

his view, there was apparently a gangrene in the Southeast and it was now time to heal it by eradicating its very sources, otherwise rebellions would continue to break out and severely damage the Republic. Pointing to the social turmoil in France in the aftermath of the French Revolution, he endeavoured to show the Turkish revolutionaries the possible outcomes of their faults in governing the revolution, which, he believed, had to begin in the hearts of individuals. For him, the greatest fault of the Turkish revolutionaries was to fail to learn adequately from the traumatic experiences of the French Revolution.[20] However, he did not hesitate to continue justifying the acts of the Independence Tribunals and the Law on the Maintenance of Order, which he believed had come into existence to protect the republic and the revolution.[21] At the same time, he prepared a private report for President Mustafa Kemal in 1926 to out-line his criticisms of the existing state of the RPP.[22]

6.1.1 A Critique of the Revolutionaries

In the 1926 Report, Ağaoğlu spoke of his serious concerns with regard to the future of the revolution and the RPP. He wanted to draw attention to the fact that the Party was rapidly being dragged toward a conservative direction in the sense that the revolutionaries were creating a new system of privileges and doing nothing but to maintain their own interests. As an insider, he was warn-ing that the spiritual prestige of the revolutionary elites was being jeopardised.

In his view, the elites were asking the people to make material sacrifices and had appealed for their support in attaining their goals. They could do this only with the help of their prestige and therefore it was vital to preserve it. But cor-ruption and misconduct within the RPP and among the revolutionary elites was putting this prestige under threat. He listed three main causes: (1) the fail-ure of the Party leadership and members to make personal sacrifices rather than pursuing their individual interests, (2) the stagnation of the Party and (3) the lack of a balanced and transparent government, which could be achieved by means of checking the actions of the Party from within.[23]

A society whose spiritual and material lives are virtually completely destroyed, and in addition to this, who pay more tax, can tolerate these

---

20   Ibid.

21   Ahmet Ağaoğlu, "İstiklâl Mahkemelerinin Faaliyeti," *Hâkimiyet-i Milliye*, January 4, 1926; "İnkılâp Kıskançtır".

22   Ağaoğlu, *Serbest Fırka Hatıraları*, p. 152. He later published this report in daily newspapers in 1926 and 1930.

23   Ibid.

> sacrifices for a long time only under one condition: this condition involves
> the belief that those who make such deep and substantial demands on
> them work voluntarily...and do not consider [their self-interests].
> Everywhere and every time, the factor that destroys revolutionary groups
> is [the failure] to respect this principle.[24]

He warned that people forgot all the mistakes of the Unionists, but they could
not forget their profiteering, illegitimate transactions and extravagancies. In
his view, the Turkish revolutionaries were about to forget these historical realities, to which Turkish society was reacting very sensitively.

He contended that wittingly or unwittingly, 'deep wounds' were being inflicted
on the prestige of the Party, especially with the news of corruption coming
from various districts of Istanbul. Moreover, the Party was no longer showing
the enthusiasm that a revolutionary party would normally possess. Order
within it was very weak. It did not have any essential regulatory function. But
this was understandable: "We have to admit that when the cultural, political
and social level of the nation is taken into account, it [would be] difficult yet to
have anything better than this." In Ağaoğlu's view, the inertia of the Party was a
result of the fact that its High Council had failed to undertake its responsibilities of checking and controlling the actions of party members and of paying
attention to the social and economic problems of the people. This also distanced the party from the people. He argued that the existence of a strong
central government was an imperative, especially in those countries which
experienced substantial social transformations, but, for the same reason, the
Party must create a strong internal auditing system in order not to lose the
trust and respect of the people.

After the Free Party was established, he increased the virulence of his criticisms of the RPP this time in terms of its unconstitutional actions.[25] He wrote
that, although the RPP identified itself as a populist and a republican party and
accepted the rule of the people as one of its main principles, it did not allow
the people to govern themselves[26]: "In restructuring the municipal, village and
city organisations, these principles have by no means been acknowledged, on
the contrary, their opposite was implemented. The mayors' not being elected
by the people but being appointed is a breach of this principle."[27]

---

24   Ibid.
25   Interview with Ağaoğlu, *Son Posta*, August 21, 1930.
26   Ibid.
27   Ibid.

He moreover claimed that with new legislation, that Members of Parliament were accepted as civil servants was also a breach of the constitution, which explicitly stated that civil servants could not be MP s. He further criticised the government for raising MP s' salaries, which for him merely imposed a burden on the shoulders of the people, requiring eleven billion lira of extra expenditure. Such policies were incongruent with populism.[28]

As noted in the previous chapter, he continued his criticisms of the RPP government with his journalistic writings in 1933. In these writings, he continued to point to day-to-day issues. However, with the closure of *Akın*, his wife's death and his retirement from the university in 1933, when his income was suddenly reduced (perhaps intentionally) to a minimum, perhaps feeling cornered, Ağaoğlu's criticisms of the actions of the Party came to an end. In 1935, he acclaimed the introduction of Kemalism as the party ideology, arguing that it would reconcile the interests of society with those of the individual. He never elaborated on Kemalism as an ideology. When, in its 1935 programme, the RPP took full control of the labour and employers' movements by not allowing strikes and declaring that workers' rights vis-à-vis the employers would be protected by the state, Ağaoğlu wrote that the new acts of the government showed that it was sincerely struggling to find a balance between the rights and duties of the individual.[29] He often wrote strongly in favour of the Party's actions, emphasizing that their ultimate aim was to elevate the intellectual and physical character of Turkish citizens.[30] Furthermore, in the second half of the 1930s, he refrained from criticising the party for the closure of numerous civil society organisations (intermediary structures), to which he had always attached great importance.[31]

6.2   Ideology and the Intelligentsia

At the 1931 RPP Congress, President Mustafa Kemal addressed a manifesto to the nation, wherein he laid down six principles as the main tenets of the party ideology: secularism, nationalism, republicanism, reformism, populism and étatism, which have come to be known collectively as Kemalism. These principles, dubbed the *Altı Ok* (Six Arrows), were, according to Mustafa Kemal, the

---

28   Ibid.

29   Ahmet Ağaoğlu, "Cumhuriyet Halk Partisi Programı Etrafında," *Cumhuriyet*, May 22, 1935.

30   Ahmet Ağaoğlu, "Parti Programı Etrafında," *Cumhuriyet*, May 26, 1935.

31   Ahmet Ağaoğlu, "Cumhuriyet Halk Partisi Programı Etrafında," *Cumhuriyet*, May 24, 1935.

Party's unchangeable characteristics. The set of co-existing mentalities since the first years of the republic was now replaced by an official ideology.

As a matter of fact, early republican Turkey saw a gradual crystallisation of political ideas in a modernist authoritarian and, since the 1930s, totalitarian direction. All through, there had been among the intelligentsia a violent doctrinarianism, which had found its most complete expression in the political debates in Ankara and the columns of the press in Istanbul. The ideas of the advanced members of the intelligentsia (secondary intellectuals) class had contained and clarified such expressions as 'national sovereignty' and 'republic' and a notable addition to the vocabulary of the Turkish revolution—'*laik*'. The so-called older systems had disintegrated to a large extent. To be a constitutional monarchist of the 1908 type had meant in 1924 to be a reactionary. To go further and to wish to see any real power restored to the throne had been to be a traitor.[32]

While the Soviets had seen the regime in Turkey as the dictatorship of Kemalist bourgeoisie in 1928,[33] just before the establishment of the Free Party, President Mustafa Kemal Paşa had, in Ağaoğlu's presence, said to Fethi Bey that

> the new Turkey which he had created was an amorphous structure, neither democracy nor dictatorship, neither republic nor monarchy, and that he wished before his work was done to set her on the path towards more normal conditions, by initiating the formation of a second party.[34]

During the short-lived multi-party episode in 1930, ideological discussions had been of superficial character, revolving around mainly two questions: which one of the existing parties was the leftist party and what did étatism entail?

Fethi Bey had declared that the Free Party was inclined to the left,[35] by which he had meant that it favoured not only further freedoms, such as of expression, but also solid attempts to translate these freedoms into practice.[36] He had contended that no person inclined to rightist views could join the Free

---

32   Neville Henderson to the Marquess Curzon of Kedleston, January 9, 1924, TNA FO 424/260/7.

33   USSR Projects and Theses Department, Memo on Turkey (Moscow), February 7, 1928, RGASPI f. 493, op.1, d.160, p. 40.

34   Morgan to Henderson, March 9, 1931, TNA FO 424/274/50.

35   *Cumhuriyet*, August 11, 1930.

36   Ali Fethi went on to argue that a party more left than the Free Party would be a socialist party, and added, "there are not sufficient number of people for the establishment of a socialist party in Turkey." *Hâkimiyet-i Milliye*, August 15, 1930.

Party.[37] As a response to this, an editorial in the Republican People's Party's mouthpiece *Hâkimiyet-i Milliye* had claimed that "there is no party on the left of [the Republican People's Party], which abolished the sultanate, caliphate and the Eastern [mentality], separated religion from worldly affairs, introduced the Latin script and the hat law."[38] According to this account, to place the Republican Party on the right was to oppose the revolution and ensuing reforms. Hence both political parties in Turkey in 1930 were 'leftist'. It is fair to say that the RPP had begun to identify itself as étatist and Kemalist as of 1930. It had then started to follow a path, as Mustafa Kemal put it, "other than liberalism."[39]

The Free Party experience had brought to light for the RPP that it had neglected to educate the youth of the country in its theories and ideals. The British were informed by the Italian embassy in Ankara that the latter had been providing, 'by request', full information on the bringing up of the young fascists to the Turkish authorities.[40] Hale depicts the overall ideological ambiance at the time as follows:

> In the early 1930s, Turkish writers and journalist began to make references to fascist and socialist doctrines. Kemalist stalwarts like Yakup Kadri (Karaosmanoğlu) and Falih Rıfkı (Atay) visited Italy and Russia and wrote vivid reports of their experiences and books in favour of these countries. Moreover, İsmet İnönü visited Soviet Russia and was impressed by the Soviet industrialisation, while Recep Peker, who became the Republican People Party's Secretary General in 1931, visited Italy, and on his return, prepared a report lauding the fascist system. Hale notes that Mustafa Kemal glanced at Peker's report and said: "You'll do all that after I die!," an accurate enough prediction of Peker's probable ambitions, if not his achievements.[41]

Mustafa Kemal wanted neither fascism nor communism, but he "could not prevent many Turks from being influenced by these systems of ideas, ideas which were producing impressive political results in Italy, Germany and

37 *Akşam*, August 12, 1930.
38 *Hâkimiyet-i Milliye*, August 21, 1930.
39 Utkan Kocatürk, *Atatürkçülük*, Ankara: Birinci Kitap, 1982, p. 37; cf. Hasan Yüksel, "Atatürk'ün Devletçilik Anlayışı," *Atatürk Araştırma Merkezi Dergisi*, No. 35 (Jul., 1996).
40 Clerk to Henderson, December 8, 1930, TNA FO 424/273/129
41 William Hale, "Ideology and Economic Development in Turkey, 1930–1945," *Bulletin* (British Society for Middle Eastern Studies), Vol. 7, No. 2 (1980), pp. 100–117.

Russia."[42] The birth of Kemalism was partially a response to this: he developed his own alternative and thus presented an ideology for Turkey itself.

As far as the economy was concerned, in the 1930s, Turkey went through a restructuring and turned to its Eastern neighbour to derive lessons from the large-scale drive for industrialisation in Soviet Russia carried out under the first five-year plan, starting in 1927. In 1931, Prime Minister İsmet İnönü visited Moscow to observe the economic structure in Russia, and the Soviet Union granted Turkey an interest-free loan of $8 million.[43] In 1932, Turkey adapted the Russian example to the peculiar conditions of the Turkish economy, and subsequently launched the first Five-Year Industrialisation Plan in 1933.[44] Turkey's etatist planning entered only those fields where private enterprise had failed or was indifferent. This was clearly expressed by Mustafa Kemal in 1932 in the following words:

> The principle of étatism that we have chosen to follow is not in any way the same as in collectivism or in communism which aims at removing all instruments of production and distribution from individuals, thus organising society on a completely different basis and leaving no room for private and individual enterprise and action in the economic field. The end of étatist policy, while it recognises private initiative and action as the main basis of the economy, is to bring the nation in the shortest time possible to an adequate level of prosperity and material welfare, and in order to achieve this, to ask the state to concern itself with those affairs where this is required by the high interests of the nation, especially in the economic field.[45]

The Turkish experience, in comparison to the Soviet economy, was more of an experimental shortcut to industrialisation through a compromise between the state and the individual, between centralism and private initiative.

By 1932 there were two main fractions in the Party, conventionally known as the Business Bank group, led by Celal Bayar, Minister of Economy and former Director General of the Business Bank, and the bureaucratic group, led by Prime Minister İsmet İnönü. The two groups agreed that private enterprise should continue to be a fundamental part of Turkey's economy and that the state should take an active role in industrial investment, but their emphases differed. While that of the bureaucratic group was on the need for the govern-

---

42   Weiker, *Political Tutelage*, p. 222.
43   Okyar, "The Concept of Etatism," p. 100; Hershlag, *Turkey*, p. 64.
44   Hershlag, *Turkey*, p. 62.
45   Ibid., 68.

ment to have the right to regulate private enterprise, Bayar stressed that the aim of étatism was to encourage, rather than to replace, indigenous capitalist development.[46]

The closure of the Free Party and the Republican Party's concurrent search for an economic development strategy inaugurated a new epoch in Turkish thought, an epoch in which the Turkish intelligentsia, particularly Ağaoğlu, having lost hope of multiparty politics, partially shifted their attention from political to economic and cultural questions. In the early 1930s, contemporary intellectuals, influenced by the global ideological tendency for fascism, socialism and Nazism to emerge as alternatives to democracy and liberalism, attempted to develop an ideological framework within which to interpret the Turkish revolution.

The writers of the left-leaning *Kadro* (Cadre) journal took the lead with their writings, attempting to describe the trajectory which Turkey needed to be on, with an emphasis on further state intervention in the economy. But a group of secondary intellectuals led by Ahmet Ağaoğlu objected to the doctrinaire writings of the Kadroists. This engendered a full-scale debate over the ideology of the revolution between late 1932 and early 1933, concentrating on the limits of state intervention.

Of all discussions at the time, the one between Ağaoğlu and Şevket Süreyya Aydemir (1897–1976), the ideologue of the Kadroists, dominated the Istanbul intellectual stage. Ağaoğlu published articles which he had written in response to the *Kadro* group in a book entitled *Devlet ve Fert* (*State and the Individual*) in 1933.[47] As will be demonstrated in detail in Chapter 7, his economic views showed great similarity with those of the Business Bank group led by Celal Bayar, while the étatism of *Kadro* seemed to be closer to that of the bureaucratic group in the Republican People's Party.

Despite their intellectual rivalry, the Kadroists and Ağaoğlu shared the faith of being victims of increasing censorship. The attempts of the former to play the role of ideologues of the revolution and the Party made the Republican People's Party leaders, specifically the Secretary General, Recep Peker (1889–1950), feel uneasy. Therefore, the Party issued a journal called *Ülkü* (The Ideal) in 1933 to support the ideological pillars of the Party intellectually and to com-

---

46   Bayar also underlined that "if we leave industrialisation...to [the hands of] private initiative and its capital..., we will have to wait at least two centuries. Our principle is to... encourage and support private initiative;" cf. Tekin Alp, *Le Kemalisme*, Paris: F. Alcan, 1937, p. 202.

47   Ahmet Ağaoğlu, *Devlet ve Fert*, Sanayii Nefise Matbaası, 1933.

pete with *Kadro*.[48] The following year, in 1934, *Kadro* dissolved itself when the franchise holder of the journal, Yakup Kadri, was sent to Tirana as ambassador, which, as Güngör puts it, was a polite way of asking the group to stop publishing its journal.[49]

6.2.1   *Two Liberalisms and Democracy*

In the 1930s, as a consequence of economic sufferings all over the world, when economic liberalism was under harsh attacks, Ağaoğlu needed to elucidate what he meant by liberalism. His later writings on the theme epitomised the peculiarities of liberalism in the Turkish context as far as the tensions between political and economic liberalisms were concerned.

Ağaoğlu wrote that there were in fact two liberalisms: political and economic. In his interpretation, political liberalism was the opposite of conservatism, and it had emerged first when monarchical authorities and status quo were questioned, when inherited rights in the name of aristocracy were abolished and when people began to be emancipated from any sort of political oppression. This type of liberalism required the re-organisation of the third estate into a republic.

Later in the eighteenth century, he wrote, political liberalism was accompanied by a new liberal current:

> With Adam Smith, the theory of economic liberalism emerged. Jeremy Bentham and Richard Cobden...in Britain, [and] Jean-Baptiste Say...in France became the most extreme representatives of this type of liberalism. The renowned discourse of this theory is *laissez faire et laissez passer*. According to this theory, the state should not interfere in the economy. Every citizen should be able to work as they want and all impediments caused by customs tariffs should be lifted in foreign trade.[50]

Economic liberalism's primary concern was not the type of government or national sovereignty, as illustrated by the fact that there was still a form of monarchy in Britain, which was the cradle of this type of liberalism. The reign of Napoleon III saw the rise of economic liberalism in France. "While economic liberals," Ağaoğlu wrote, "supported Napoleon III, political liberals

---

48   Ertan Aydın, "The Peculiarities of Turkish Revolutionary Ideology in the 1930s: The *Ülkü* Version of Kemalism, 1933–1936," Unpublished PhD Thesis, Bilkent University, 2003.
49   Süleyman Güngör, *Türkiye Cumhuriyeti'nin İlk Yıllarında Politikacı-Aydın İlişkisi*, Ankara: Nobel Yayın Dağıtım, 2002.
50   Ağaoğlu, "Demokrasi ve Devletçilik."

fought against him." The latter version of liberalism had resulted from a com-
merical spirit.

The common denominator of the two types of liberalism was the freedom
of individual work.

> But ever since this freedom began to increase in favour of capital and
> against labour, again the political liberals began to complain and deman-
> ded the redistribution and amelioration of liberties, now decayed, by the
> intervention of society, that is, by the state. All Utopianists who chanted
> this complaint in the first half of the nineteenth century were political
> liberals. Even today, in any country, it is political liberal parties that avow
> the gradual increase of state interference. But for the political liberals
> there is a limit for this interference, which is the imperative of committing
> to the principles of democracy.[51]

Ağaoğlu was explicitly against classical economic liberalism in this sense of
the state's non-interference in the economy. His understanding of liberalism
was more akin to social liberalism, which he called liberal étatism and which
suggested that the state should take the initiative to redress social inequalities
where the economy was concerned.

The antagonism toward classical liberalism and the importance of the polit-
ical aspects of liberalism in early Republican Turkey found voice also in the
"Notes from the Lessons of the Revolution"[52] of Recep Peker, the Secretary
General of the People's Party, who wrote:

> Even though liberalism initially carried a meaning referring to absolute
> freedom, it began to take a shape, especially in the economic sphere,
> which impaired the living conditions of other people. Its commercial and
> industrial aspects and those related to income decayed in such a way that
> those capitalists who wanted to benefit from it took an abusive position
> against the incomes and lives of consumers and owners of raw materials,
> who would enable the establishment of industry. While, on one hand, the
> masses were fighting to acquire liberty and become liberal by eliminating
> the cartel [sic] of aristocracy, on the other, that the way the idea of liberty
> was understood in commerce and that it became a deteriorating [factor]
> has become a theme of complaint for humanity. The abuse of the word

---

51   Ibid.
52   Peker, *İnkılâp Dersleri Notları*, p. 17.

'liberal' gave way to unfavourable results for citizens who want happiness in every sense within their borders. This we call economic liberalism.[53]

This, then, was a short account of the type of liberalism that could be accommodated by the Kemalist leadership: a much limited version of political liberalism. Its meaning was confined to opposing oppressive monarchical rule and upholding the rule of reason and ordered and selective individual and collective rights. To this very short list of the characteristics of political liberalism in the early Republican context, Ağaoğlu added, with reservations, limited power, freedom of thought, freedom of movement, transparency and, perhaps most importantly, the moral emancipation of the individual, though many of what he suggested were not put into practice, nor were they very welcome in the Kemalist thought.

Notably, the absence of democracy in this list was a testimony of the fact that the arguable political liberals of the 1930s did not want to share political power with whom they believed to be less capable political masses. The single party rule, two-round election system, negligence to the rights of non-(Sunni) Muslims, and lack of democratic freedoms in the 1930s, and Ağaoğlu's indifference to such issues were demonstrating the authoritarian character of the republican and revolutionary liberalism in Turkey.

In fact, as early as the early 1920s, the Kemalist elites and Ağaoğlu were conceiving democracy as the rule of the majority and the satisfaction of its needs.[54] But in so believing, they had in mind nationalist aims. The Turks were forming the major component of the Anatolian population at the time, and it had to be them, Ağaoğlu thought, that should have had greater say in politics. Yet he warned that democracy was not the type of regime that the Turks were used to.

In countries like Turkey, he wrote, the problem was that the majority had virtually never experienced democratic rule. "From its religion to its language, the Turkish majority," he claimed, "has always been the slave of a minority. Its needs, inclinations, wants and perceptions have never been taken into account."[55] The Turks were always accustomed to following their leaders as soldiers without ever objecting false exercises.

In the mid-1930s, the growing interest in fascism and communism in Turkey spurred him to position himself against dictatorial and totalitarian regimes. He wrote that it was insane to regard parliamentary rule as a cause of the Great

---

53   Ibid., p. 17.
54   *İhtilal mi İnkılap mı?* p. 42.
55   Ibid., p. 43.

Depression and of the subsequent economic sufferings.[56] To prefer Nazism or any sort of dictatorship to parliamentary government and democracy would be the death of liberty.[57] In this period, Turkey's single party rule had already employed the language of capacity in that "until the voters gained sufficient political, social and cultural knowledge enabling them to make an informed decision," or until they were given the necessary education and reached the high standards desired, they would conform with the idea of democracy to select the secondary voters, whom they knew closely and trusted.[58]

In 1935, Ağaoğlu sketched a more detailed definition of democracy than his earlier accounts, whence Turkey was far yet. He argued that democracy was based on three principles: first, free elections. Only those representing the nation in the fullest sense of the word by means of elections must take control of the government on behalf of the nation. The second principle was that of the reciprocal duties of the members of parliament, the government and the nation. The nation must check and control the acts of the government, without remaining indifferent to their work, while the representatives and the government must fulfil all their responsibilities towards the people.[59] The third principle was the equality of all citizens before the law through the abolition of all types of privileges and by safeguarding liberty. "If even one of these principles is breached, there will be no democracy."[60] Democracy, according to his account, could come into existence only through its marriage with political rights and liberties. Given the limited freedoms and liberties in the 1930s, he would see it an important step when independent candidates were allowed to stand for election to Parliament.[61] He believed optimistically that their existence would fulfil one of the requirements of democracy, that of checking and monitoring the activities of the government.[62]

In sum, in the 1930s, the prevailing political idea in Turkey with regard to democracy was that state tutelage was needed until the masses were educated into civic minded individuals. Writing in conformity with this idea, Ağaoğlu's liberalism appeared to show parallels with the bureaucratic liberal approaches

---

56   Ahmet Ağaoğlu, "Dünulbeşer—Untermenschentum," *Akın*, June 30, 1933.

57   Ahmet Ağaoğlu, "Parlemantarizm ve Şahsi Hükümet," *Akın*, July 19, 1933.

58   Cemil Koçak, "Parliament Membership During the Single-Party System in Turkey, 1925–1945," *European Journal of Turkish Studies*, No. 3 (2005).

59   This account sat well with Ağaoğlu's understanding of democracy in a 1926 article titled "Devlet ve Ferd," *Milliyet*, May 25, 1926.

60   Ağaoğlu, "Demokrasi ve Devletçilik".

61   Ahmet Ağaoğlu, "Önderin Beyannamesi," *Cumhuriyet*, February 4, 1935; "Müstakil Saylavlık Meselesi," *Cumhuriyet*, February 8, 1935.

62   Ahmet Ağaoğlu, "Demokrasi ve Devletçilik".

in Germany (*Beamtenliberalismus*) and Russia, where bureaucratic behaviour referred to one's undertaking duties to execute policies set by his government whether or not he was in full agreement with them, showing lack of principle.[63] In his account, until the masses were elevated to a level where their ascendancy in politics could be permitted, individuals had to conform to political authority. That said, employing a Durkheimian vocabulary, he also sought to protect the individuals against the state by means of deepening communitarian ties among the former. This marked the communitarian yet individualist character of his work. How then could he be a communitarian and individualist at one and the same time?

---

63   D.C.B. Lieven, "Bureaucratic Liberalism in Late Imperial Russia: The Personality, Career and Opinions of A.N. Kulomzin," *The Slavonic and East European Review*, Vol. 60, No. 3 (Jul., 1982), pp. 413–432.

CHAPTER 7

State, Society and the Individual

Ağaoğlu's later writings on the tripartite relationship between the state, society and the individual exposed the main theoretical framework of his concept of liberalism. As noted in the introduction, existing studies on Ağaoğlu have considered him to be a 'lifelong opponent of étatism' and a defender of liberal individualism.[1] By contrast, I will argue here that the Ağaoğlu of the 1920s and 30s explicitly refused to consider himself a liberal individualist in the economic sense, but indeed stressed the need for the creation of a Turkish bourgeoisie. He stood overtly against the basic presumptions of classical economic liberalism. Instead, he sympathized with the liberal welfarism of the Roosevelt government in the United States famously known as the New Deal.[2] His ideal state would provide pensions, social benefits and publicly-funded health and education services. This lets us argue that, antagonised by the atomism of classical liberalism, Ağaoğlu was a modern or social liberal who suggested a 'responsible' or 'enabling' state. He eventually began to maintain that a version of Turkish liberal étatism was the most suitable model for the economic conditions of Turkey.[3]

Due to his stress on political aspects of liberalism and his rejection of classical economic liberalism, Coşar and Kadıoğlu rightly suggest that Ağaoğlu's liberal views were closer to the French liberal tradition.[4] However, 'French liberal tradition' is a very wide and vague phrase that includes the ideas of various different figures, which are difficult to reconcile. It is fair to say that specific French influences on Ağaoğlu's thought were threefold: we already know that he was deeply influenced by the teachings (the idea of separation of powers, the rule of law and freedom of expression and opinion) of the French encyclopaedists and enlightenment thinkers as early as the 1880s. Moreover, one of the greatest symbols of republican thought in France, Ernest Renan (who was in fact a lukewarm republican), was his highly esteemed acquaintance during his French sojourn. As noted in Chapter 2, like Renan, Ağaoğlu started investigating the means of social progress with the elevation of the individual. In the

---

1 Shissler, *Between Two Empires*, p. 80.
2 Ahmet Ağaoğlu, "İctimai Musahebeler: Zeka Tröstü," *Cumhuriyet*, November 12, 1934.
3 Ahmet Ağaoğlu, "Türk Devletçiliği," *Cumhuriyet,* August 28, 1935.
4 Coşar, "Türk Liberalizminin Açmazlarına Giriş"; Kadıoğlu, "Citizenship and Individuation in Turkey".

second half of the 1920s, his references to the works of Émile Durkheim and his attempts to win a middle way between revolutionary radicalism and liberal reformism was what was new in his thought. The originality of Ağaoğlu's liberalism in comparison to the views of his contemporaries in Turkey at the time resulted from the fact that in this period he began to invoke Durkheim's 'socialised' interpretation of liberalism.[5] The underlying philosophy of this type of liberalism was the doctrine of solidarism which intended "to harmonize individualism, corporatism and morality within an essentially liberal framework."[6]

Following Durkheim's work, Ağaoğlu attempted to determine the structural traits of modern and liberal society and to examine the complex and problematic relationships between the state, society and the individual by means of sociological and historical imagination.[7] Hence, methodologically, he began to follow a middle way between Akçura and Gökalp by concurrently employing the methods of a version of historicism and of Durkheimian positivism in disentangling the reasons for the lagging behind of Eastern societies. He tried to interpret the contemporary social and political developments in Turkey in the late 1920s and '30s in the light of Durkheim's sociology, believing that the French sociologist's theories of the division of labour and the interdependence of individuals were the key to the emergence of the Western liberal social and political order. His insistent emphasis on the symbiotic development (and importance) of the state, society and the individual—more specifically, his descriptions of the expanding role of the state, the sacredness of individual and social morality, and the historical evolution of societies from simple to complex structures—appear to be drawn, explicitly or implicitly, from Durkheim's works. As such, Ağaoğlu's long misinterpreted notion of individualism is best understood through a comparative textual analysis. Such an attempt reveals that like Durkheim, he regarded individualism as the logical completion of communitarianism—an argument that I shall defend in this and the ninth chapters.

The Durkheimian influence on Ağaoğlu's thought did not make him, unlike Sabahaddin Bey, an unconditional supporter or propagator of a French school of thought, however. In the late 1930s, he came to write that Durkheim's theory of the division of labour would be insufficient to explain all social phenomena. In his view, without taking into account the psychological teachings of Gabriel Tarde, the economic thought of Karl Marx and the anthropological and

5   Bellamy, *Liberalism and Modern Society,* p. 58.
6   Ibid., p. 63.
7   Ağaoğlu, *Hukuk-i Esasiye,* p. 11.

geographical arguments of Friedrich Ratzel, the theory of the division of labour *per se* would offer only an incomplete explanation of modern social life.[8] In his later writings, where his methods were concerned, Ağaoğlu was rather eclectic, trying to fuse the methodological teachings of different schools of thought without giving up the teachings of Durkheim.[9]

Nevertheless, it would not be false to argue that besides Gökalp, another prominent intellectual who utilised the ideas of Émile Durkheim and thus carried them into the Turkish context was Ahmet Ağaoğlu. Although it is very likely that Ağaoğlu learned of the works of Durkheim through Gökalp, his interpretation of the French sociologist's work differed slightly from Gökalp's, especially in respect of the relationship between the state, society and the individual. The Dukheimianism of Gökalp has led commentators to question whether his inclination to corporatism was a sign of his proto-fascism.[10] We see that the Durkheimian influences formed an integral element of Ağaoğlu's 'liberal' thought. In my thesis, Ağaoğlu differed from Gökalp in placing more emphasis on the concept of the individual in reference to Durkheim's work, which attached a sacred role to the individual in modern society. But neither Durkheim nor Ağaoğlu went so far as to argue that the individual prevails over society or the state.

7.1   Liberal Order

Émile Durkheim was the most widely translated and read Western European sociologist in Turkey in the early twentieth century.[11] Just before the proclamation of the Republic in 1923, the National Assembly appointed Orhan Midhat (Barbaros) to translate his *De la division du travail social* into Turkish.[12] The following year, Hüseyin Cahit (Yalçın) was assigned to translate *Les Formes Élémentaires de la vie religieuse.* But it was mainly through the work of Ziya Gökalp that his works were introduced and popularised.[13] The social

---

8   Ahmet Ağaoğlu, "Tarihte Sosyal İnkişaf," *Kültür Haftası,* No. 17 (May 1937), p. 354.

9   Ahmet Ağaoğlu, *Hukuk Tarihi,* Istanbul: Kurtuluş Matbaası, 1933, p. 33.

10   Ivan Strenski, *The New Durkheim,* New Brunswick, N.J., London: Rutgers University Press, 2006, pp. 317–327.

11   Zafer Toprak, "Anayasal Monarşi ve İttihatçıların Dramı," *Osmanlı Bankası Arşivi,* 2008.

12   Orhan Midhat, *İcitmâi Taksim-i Amâl,* Istanbul, 1923. In his article Toprak mistakenly informs the reader that Ahmet Midhat (1844–1912) translated Durkheim's work in 1923.

13   Hüseyin N. Kubali, Preface in Emile Durkheim, *Professional Ethics and Civic Morals,* trans. Cornelia Brookfield, London, New York: Routledge, 1957, p. xi; Robert F. Spencer, "Culture

liberalism of Ağaoğlu would be only one of many channels through which Durkheimian ideas penetrated into Turkish thought.

Samet Ağaoğlu (Ahmet Ağaoğlu's elder son) claims that, during the proclamation of the Republic, Gökalp and Ahmet Ağaoğlu were representing two opposing views in discussions about the shape and character of the new regime. The former was strongly of the opinion that duties prevailed over the rights of the individual. Ağaoğlu, on the other hand, insisted that the individual should prevail over the state and society.[14] Ülken backed this claim and wrote that Gökalp was the best representative of communitarianism, while Ağaoğlu was one of the three most prominent individualists in Turkey at the time, the other two being Prince Sabahaddin and Mustafa Şekib (Tunç).[15] In Ülken's somewhat vague account, Gökalp owed his communitarianism to the sociology of Durkheim, whereas Ağaoğlu's individualism was a consequence of his appeal to liberalism.[16]

In his short commemorative article on Ağaoğlu, it was again Ülken who for the first time underscored that Gökalp's sociology exerted a huge influence on Ağaoğlu's thought.[17] For Ülken, despite this, Ağaoğlu always opposed Gökalp's communitarian arguments:

> Ağaoğlu used French sociology as an instrument for defending individualism (*fertçilik*). His essays about the evolutionary stages of law which he partly penned in *İnsan* show the latest version of his ideas... Relying on the analysis of the School of Durkheim..., he analysed the development of judicial personality (*hukuki şahsiyet*). He demonstrates that the hegemonic process from tribes, which are the first social shapes, to modern societies has been that of a permanent individualisation, differentiation and privatisation. All his sociological studies prove that modern democracies and evolutionism are indispensable. It seems that the only aim of these analyses was to reject the recently prevailing idea that liberalism is a nineteenth-century ideology, a passing thought.[18]

Ülken was right in that Durkheim's sociology helped Ağaoğlu to form his final views of the relationship between the state and social and individual rights.

Process and Intellectual Current: Durkheim and Atatürk," *American Anthropologist*, vol. 60, No. 4 (Aug., 1958), pp. 640–657.

14   Samet Ağaoğlu, *Babamdan Hatıralar*, p. 10.

15   Hilmi Z. Ülken, "Ferd ve Cemiyet," *İnsan*, 1940, p. 57.

16   Ibid.

17   Ülken, "Ağaoğlu Ahmet ve Fikir Hayatı ve Mücadeleleri".

18   Ibid.

Ağaoğlu did fight for the view that liberalism was still the solution to the social problems of Eastern nations in the twentieth century and it was true that he departed from Gökalp's position with his constant emphasis on the importance of the individual. However, Ülken was mistaken when he argued that Ağaoğlu defended the supremacy of the individual in the sense of endowing him with a degree of autonomy. In fact, like Durkheim, both Gökalp and Ağaoğlu regarded the state and intermediary social structures as agents to articulate and promote the moral aims and sentiments embodied in the diffuse *conscience collective*.[19] In applying Durkheim's teachings to the Turkish context, they reformulated some of the ideas to make them more compatible with the realities of the East and downplayed the autonomy of the individual.

What Durkheim regarded as the most important factor in social development, collective representations, for example, was for Gökalp the explanation of ideals as objective phenomena.[20] Gökalp absorbed and used Durkheim's theory that collective ideas, and with them ideals, were the product of a supra-individual society, which contained a special force securing society's domination over the will of the individual. Heyd tells us that, for Gökalp, this force manifested itself to the individual in two ways:

> In its direct influence the ideal evokes in the soul of the individual emotions of love, enthusiasm and worship. The individual who is not influenced by this force feels its power indirectly, i.e. through the approval or disapproval of society by his actions. If the individual believes contrary to the ideal, he will arouse a hostile reaction in society, such as blame [or] contempt, which induces him to refrain from such actions. The ideal has on the one hand a force of attraction (*icaz kuveti*) and on the other hand a force which threatens and punishes (*teyit kuvveti*).[21]

The collective consciousness was the only stable force that united all members of society and was independent of the will of the individuals.[22] Gökalp wanted to enable the creation of such a force through nationalism and religion, which gave his work a normative character.

---

19   Ağaoğlu, *Serbest İnsanlar Ülkesinde*, Ankara: Sanayii Nefise Matbaası, 1930; Anthony Giddens, Introduction to *Durkheim on Politics and the State,* Cambridge: Polity Press, 1986, p. 9; Ensar Yılmaz, "Ziya Gökalp's Political Sociology," *International Journal of Sociology and Anthropology,* vol. 2(3), (Mar., 2010), pp. 29–33.

20   Ibid., p. 50.

21   Ibid., p. 51.

22   Ibid., p. 56.

The mutation of Durkheim's ideas in the works of Gökalp shows that he not only adopted but also modified Durkheim's sociology and was either highly selective in accepting Durkheim's theories or could access only a limited account of the French thinker's work.[23] The concept of solidarism, for instance, did not carry a normative connotation for Durkheim, whereas for Gökalp (and Ağaoğlu), it meant a social and national ideal.[24] Again, Durkheim's collective consciousness was regarded by Gökalp as an ideal illuminating the future and as an unchangeable element of collective identity. Yet Gökalp's notion of the individual was not completely congruent with Durkheim's 'cult of the individual'.

In Gökalp's early thought the place of the individual was rather vague. Bozarslan asserts that Gökalp systematically rejected the discourse of individual rights that began to permeate the Ottoman Empire after 1908.[25] Gökalp's modern individual had to 'do his duty with eyes closed', as he put it in his various poems. For him, 'there are no rights but duties', and 'no individual but society'. In the 1920s and 1930s, Ağaoğlu frequently criticised these assertions.

However, in an article he wrote upon the death of Gökalp (1924), Ağaoğlu underscored that these pronouncements were a mistake made by the political Gökalp.[26] He was referring to 'the political Gökalp', because for him, there were three different Gökalps: the first was a social and political thinker, the second a political activist in a great political organisation (Ağaoğlu must have meant the RPP), and the third a fanatical Turkist.[27] According to Ağaoğlu, the political Gökalp could undermine the importance of the individual, but those who intimately followed his works would understand 'Gökalp's high theory on rights. His high spirit conceived no rights without duty and regarded rights as an equivalent of duties.'[28] That is, Ağaoğlu was well aware that Gökalp's 1917 declaration that 'there are no rights, but duties' was not a constant in his thought.

Gökalp's post-war works in fact give us an idea of how his notion of the individual evolved over time. Following Durkheim, he accepted that "the highest moral aim of man was to turn his individuality (*ferdiyet*) into personality (*şahsiyet*)."[29] He defined personality as "the totality of feelings and thoughts existing in the consciousness of society and reflected in the consciousness of

23   Ahmet Ağaoğlu, "Ziya Gökalp'e Dair Hatıratım," *Cumhuriyet,* November 27, 1934.
24   Bozarslan, "Ziya Gökalp," p. 315.
25   Ibid., p. 316.
26   Ağaoğlu, "Ziya Gökalp'e Dair Hatıratım".
27   Ibid.
28   Ağaoğu Ahmet, "Ziya Gökalp Bey," *Türk Yurdu,* No. 3 (1924), p. 165.
29   Heyd, *The Foundations of Turkish Nationalism,* p. 53.

the individual (*şuur*)' that is, ideals. By this intensive social consciousness, the individual 'rises from the level of creature (*beşer*) to that of man (*insan*)... [He] becomes a personality by throwing off the shackles of...material factors and by learning to think and act in accordance with the ideas common to members of his society."[30] In reference to Durkheim, Gökalp claimed that the human soul was the part of man not subject to material forces. Personality was little developed in a primitive society. When society became more differentiated through the division of labour, individuals acquired different consciousnesses by associating themselves with various social groups (religious, political, occupational, etc.). For him, this was the origin of the individual personality (*ferdi şahsiyet*), which formed its own opinions and tastes.[31]

In Gökalp's works, the notion of the individual never received the insistent importance accorded to it in the works of Durkheim and Ağaoğlu, although all three thinkers were in the main communitarians. Ağaoğlu accentuated the significance of the individual as the basis of society more strongly than Gökalp, whose notion of the individual was limited to the concept of personality. Yet they shared the opinion that individualism, denoting a lack of ideals and leading to scepticism, moral instability and feelings of frustration and despair, engendered the decline of society.

7.1.1   *Durkheim and Ağaoğlu*

As indicated by direct references in his various writings,[32] Durkheim's most direct influence on Ağaoğlu's thought was through his *De la division du travail social* (1893) and *Les formes élémentaires de la vie religieuse* (1912), two studies that were translated into Turkish in 1923 and 1924. Durkheim's doctoral thesis, *De la division du travail social*, originally intended as a work entitled 'Relations between Individualism and Socialism',[33] was written in a social and political context when the Third Republicans both wanted free market society and feared the degeneration of their doctrine into a crude economic individualism.[34] Like many radical republicans of his time, Durkheim hoped "to meet the triple dangers of monopoly capitalism, socialism and traditionalism."[35]

---

30   Ibid., p. 53.

31   Ibid., p. 54.

32   Ağaoğlu, "C.H.P. Programı Etrafında," *Cumhuriyet*, May 18, 22, 24, 26, 1935; "Tarihte Sosyal İnkişaf," *Kültür Haftası*, No. 17, 20 (May, 1936); "Basitten Mürekkebe, Şekilsizlikten Şekilleşmeye Doğru," *İnsan*, No. 3, June 15, 1938.

33   Charles Marske, "Durkheim's 'Cult of the Individual' and the Moral Reconstitution of Society," *Sociological Theory*, Vol. 5, No. 1 (Spring 1987), p. 1.

34   Bellamy, *Liberalism and Modern Society*, p. 59.

35   Ibid., p. 63.

His work attempted to penetrate to the underlying alterations in morality and to arrive at a typology of the forms of social solidarity.

Its analysis of how the transition from traditional (mechanical) to modern (organic) society affected 'collective consciousness' and morality appeared to be what most captured Ağaoğlu's attention. The latter attempted to determine certain structural elements of Eastern (traditional) and Western (modern) societies and to examine the primary elements of social structure (institutions, rules, beliefs, religious creeds, etc.) with reference to Durkheim's concepts of traditional mechanical and modern organic societies.[36] He also embodied the Durkheimian idea that the evolution from traditionalism to modernity increased the level of individualism in society.[37]

Durkheim endeavoured in his doctoral study to find the 'middle way' between the British tradition of utilitarian individualism and the German tradition of Marxian collectivism.[38] He wrote that in modern organic societies, the sphere of traditional religions continually diminished[39] and "the deepest most significant value consensus in society focuses on the rights and dignity of the individual."[40] That is, the idea of the worth and dignity of the individual emerged as a religious ideal. This viewpoint was remarkably akin to that of a late nineteenth-century liberal socialist, "most sympathetic to the reformist ideas of Jean Jaurès, who also saw socialism as the logical extension of individualism."[41]

---

36 John B. Harms, "Reason and Social Change in Durkheim's Thought: The Changing Relations between Individual and Society," *The Pacific Sociological Review,* Vol. 24, No. 4 (Oct., 1981), pp. 393–410.

37 Marske, "Durkheim's Cult of the Individual," p. 2; Theodore D. Kemper, "Emile Durkheim and the Division of Labour," *Sociological Quarterly,* No. 16 (Spring 1975), pp. 190–206; Mark Cladis, *A Communitarian Defense of Liberalism: Emile Durkheim and Contemporary Social Theory,* Stanford, Calif.: Stanford University Press, 1992.

38 Hans-Peter Müller, "Social Differentiation and Organic Solidarity: The Division of Labour Revisited," *Sociological Forum,* vol. 9, No. 1 (Mar. 1994), pp. 73–86; Robert G. Perrin, "Durkheim's Division of Labour and the Shadow of Herbert Spencer," *The Sociological Quarterly,* Vol. 36, No. 4 (Autumn, 1995), pp. 791–808; Robert A. Jones, "The Positive Science of Ethics in France: German Influences on 'De le division du travail social'" *Sociological Forum,* vol. 9, No. 1 (Mar., 1994), pp. 37–57.

39 Cladis informs us that within a few years of writing this, "Durkheim reversed his position. He now claimed that religion permeates modern societies. Although its beliefs and practices have changed, at least in Europe, its basic form has not."

40 Marske, "Durkheim's Cult of the Individual," p. 2.

41 Steven Lukes, "Durkheim's 'Individualism and the Intellectuals'," *Political Studies,* Vol. 17, No. 1 (1969), pp. 14–30.

Durkheim was an individualist in the special sense he understood the term. For him, it was possible, without contradiction, to be an individualist while asserting that the individual was a product of society, rather than its cause.[42] In a 1898 article entitled "L'individualisme et les intellectuels", he drew a line between two types of individualism: one being false individualism of the utilitarian school; and the other, true individualism, which was sought to be translated into a formulae by the Declaration of the Rights of Man, more or less successfully. It was what was being taught in French schools in the Third Republic and which had become the basis of their moral catechism.[43] True individualism, in contrast to false individualism, was the only system of beliefs that could ensure the moral unity of the country:

> It is a religion of which man is, at the same time, both believer and God. But this religion is individualistic, since it has man as its object, and since man is, by definition, an individual. Indeed there is no system whose individualism is more uncompromising. Nowhere are the rights of man affirmed more energetically, since the individual is here placed on the level of sacrosanct objects; nowhere is he more jealously protected from external encroachments, whatever their source.[44]

Although Durkheim shared with Kant and Rousseau the idea that the only moral ways of acting were those which were fitting for all men equally, he differed from them on one point. He argued that Kant and Rousseau wished to deduce their individualist ethics from the notion of the isolated individual, but did not understand that individual ethics were socially constituted—the very argument that Ağaoğlu would defend in his 1935 articles.[45]

Durkheim maintained that with increasing level of individualism in society, the role of the modern state was to expand. The fundamental duty that Durkheim assigned to the state was to persist in inviting the individual to a moral life through the promotion of collective ideals.[46] His state was not inherently opposed to the individual. It was designed to set the individual free by providing for the individual's self-realisation, which could be achieved only

---

42   Lukes, "Durkheim's 'Individualism and the Intellectuals'," p. 18.

43   Ibid.

44   Ibid.

45   Ahmet Ağaoğlu, "Özcülük ve Özgecilik (Egoisme ve Altruisme)," *Cumhuriyet,* January 20, 1935; "Cumhuriyet Halk Partisi Programı Etrafında,"*Cumhuriyet*, May 18, 1935.

46   Stjepan G. Mestrovic, *Emile Durkheim and the Reformation of Sociology,* Lanham, Maryland: Rowman&Littlefield, 1993, p. 138.

through membership of a society in which the state guaranteed the rights of the individual.[47] There should be an active interplay between the state and the individual, i.e. between "government consciousness' and the views and feelings of the mass.' This constituted the basis of Durkheim's ideal democratic government. In his view, a democracy had two primary characteristics: "the existence of close, and two-way, communication between government and governed; and the increasing extension of the contacts and ties of the State with other sectors of the society."[48]

As one of the most renowned defenders of corporatism of his time, Durkheim considered occupational groups (*groupes professionnels*), professional ethics and the agency of the state to form the basis of morality, reconciling the interests of society and of the individual[49] and redressing the pathologies of the division of labour.[50] For him, the intermediary groups played a significant role in the two-way government: "A nation cannot be maintained unless, between the state and individuals, a whole range of intermediary groups are interposed."[51] In his view, intermediary groups also helped to curb individual egoism: "the only power that can serve to moderate individual egoism is that of the group; the only one that can serve to moderate the egoism of the groups is that of another group that embraces them all."[52]

Durkheim's social thought was complex and open to interpretation by later commentators. This is also why there were differences, albeit slight, in the way Gökalp and Ağaoğlu interpreted his work. Durkheim's idea of social control over the life of the individual influenced the works of both thinkers. However, as noted before, his peculiar version of individualism and his emphasis on the role and sacredness of the individual in modern societies appear to capture Ağaoğlu's attention more. Furthermore, as will be demonstrated below, in his various writings, Ağaoğlu likewise stressed the importance of the reciprocal

---

47   Marske, "Durkheim's Cult of the Individual," p. 9.

48   Ibid., pp. 7–8.

49   C.P. Wolf, "The Durkheim Thesis: Occupational Groups and Moral Integration," *Journal for the Scientific Study of Religion,* Vol. 9, No. 1 (Spring 1970), pp. 17–32.

50   Edward A. Tiryakian, "Revisiting Sociology's First Critic: 'The Division of Labour in Society and Its Actuality,' Sociological Forum, Vol. 9, No. 1, Special Issue: The 100th Anniversary of Sociology's First Classic: Durkheim's "Division of Labour in Society." (Mar., 1994), pp. 3–16.

51   Durkheim, Preface to the Second Edition, *Division of Labour in Society,* London: Macmillan, 1902, xxxii.

52   Durkheim, *Division of Labour in Society,* trans. W.D. Halls, New York: Free Press, 1984, p. 337.

responsibilities of the state and the individual[53] and the central role the intermediary groups play in modern political and moral life. Most notably, he regarded the individual as a sacred being, or the centre of the universe and saw no paradox in the parallel development of the role of the state and the freedom of the individual. This explains how he came to argue in the 1930s that there was no contradiction between étatism and private initiative.

7.1.2   Elements of Modern Liberalism: Division of Labour, Occupational Groupings and Interdependence

Ağaoğlu saw the Durkheimian principle of division of labour as a central component in understanding the liberal mentality of the West.[54] Increasing division of labour, he maintained, put an end to the struggle between *cléricalisme* and *libéralisme*, which had been single most important struggle in the history of Europe.[55] As such, Ağaoğlu adopted, and to some extent, adapted Durkheim's sociology to re-interpret the historical development of modern liberalism in the West on the basis of a binary opposition with liberal secularism and the conservative ideology of the clergy at its two ends.

He argued that the conflicts between the mentalities of *cléricalisme*, which claimed to govern and regulate both material and spiritual life, and *libéralisme* (or the secular mentality), which demanded full liberty and sovereignty in the intellectual and material spheres, gave dynamism to Europe. This conflict was brought to an end, in Ağaoğlu's account, by the principle of the division of social labour brought. The liberal mentality enjoyed a victory over clericalism:

> The principle of the division of labour and functional differentiation began to form [in the West] the very essence of the social body. While each cell and each group has a certain function and competency in a society in which there was division of labour, the pressures and tyranny of [the Church], which desired to rule everything, which considered itself superior to everything and which claimed to regulate both material and spiritual components in life, could no more be tolerated... Finally, after all those quakes, exercises and their reactions, the new spirit, the modern mentality gained the victory. The borders of the competency and prerogatives of the Church and the clergy were completely drawn and they were not allowed to exceed [these borders] ...

---

53   Ahmet Ağaoğlu, "Devlet ve Fert," *Milliyet,* May 25, 1926.
54   Ağaoğlu, *Üç Medeniyet,* p. 27.
55   Ibid., p. 27.

The principle of the division of labour and functional differentiation, which forms the essence of this century, is applied also to the Church. 'Free thought and free movement', 'Live and do not impede others' lives', 'Develop your character and do not impede others in developing their characters' have become the principles the new century depends on.[56]

Attacking Gökalp's 'political' views, Ağaoğlu defended in *Three Civilisations* the taking of Western experience as a model where liberalism prevailed over aristocracy and despotism. Like Durkheim, he traced the emergence of true individualism to the French Revolution, but he turned as much to political events as to succession of ideas:

> High individuality [*yüksek ferdiyet*] means *working* freely in a free arena; it is based on the foundation of a free environment and a free market. These principles began to be applied in the Great French Revolution and ever since then in the West all of the structures of family, state, and society have taken their inspiration from these principles. For every right a duty, for every duty a right; that's the meaning of these principles. Now there are no rights without duties, and no duties without rights.[57]

The French Revolution, he wrote, saved the material and spiritual forces of the individual from imminent extinction and allowed them to reappear in a free atmosphere where they replaced the traditional and aristocratic understanding of rights and duties. Ever since, each individual had been the sole master of his or her own destiny, rather than its being in the hands of a despotic leader, as was the case in the East.[58] Hence everyone had a chance to become whatever they desired to become, because within this free atmosphere, industriousness, energy, intelligence and merit had become the virtues determining one's status in society. Free competition engendered the appearance of these virtues and became a source for such other virtues as initiative, courage and solidarity.

Most importantly, thousands of social groups were established in Europe and new occupational organisations emerged. Individuals realized that acting as a group would allow them to achieve their goals more easily. They gathered around common interests and against common threats. These groups allowed them to save time, energy and labour and developed among individuals the

---

56   Ibid., p. 29.
57   Ibid., p. 81; emphasis mine.
58   Ibid., p. 81.

sentiments of solidarity, altruism, mutual aid and interdependence.[59] In a similar vein to Durkheim, he contended that besides setting common ideals, the formation of civil society through occupational groupings and other forms of social organisation constituted social control over the acts of the individual. These groupings impeded the appearance of egoism and developed altruistic (*özgeci*) and communitarian (*cemiyetçi*) values.[60]

Ağaoğlu attempted to bring this into evidence in *Revolt or Revolution?* (1922) by underscoring the existence of tens of thousands of communities, social organisations and occupational groupings in France and even more in Germany, England and the United States. In these countries,

> each civilised person is a member of [many groups,] social, professional, religious, moral, economic, political, industrial, etc.... That is, a civilized man...lives tens of lives, builds networks. Each of these communities and organisations provides a platform for competition and ensures the development of...social skills and faculties... Furthermore, an individual partaking in such networks, relations and groups feels, so to say, compelled to give up his selfishness and egoism at least to a certain degree, and begins to think not only of his private life and family, but also of the interests, existence and progress of his community. By this means, on one hand, while the skills and faculties of individuals improve and thus provide skilled members for society, on the other hand, they are being socially educated.[61]

In the East, by contrast, there were no properly functioning social, political or occupational groups or organisations. Pointing out the failures of the Committee of Union and Progress and the Party of Liberty and Entente (Hürriyet ve İtilaf Fırkası), he maintained that the eventual failures of both parties resulted from a lack of the spirit of collectivity which could be acquired by comprehensive regulations and sanctions and which could unite all individuals, leading them to believe in a collective spirit.

> [I]ndividuality prevails over community life. We cannot get along with each other, we lack occupational and class groupings, our political and economical parties are primitive, spiritless and unenthusiastic.[62]

---

59   Ibid., p. 83.
60   Ibid., p. 98; "Yeni Nesil Arasında," *Cumhuriyet,* March 4, 1935.
61   Ağaoğlu, *İhtilâl mi İnkılâp mı?* p. 44.
62   Ibid., p. 45.

He therefore needed to underline how important each individual and their grouping was in reference to Durkheim's concept of interdependence.

In *The Constitutional Law* of 1926, a collection of notes for lectures that he had delivered at Ankara University in 1925,[63] he argued that there were two main laws securing social happiness: 'the law of interdependence and the law of harmony [*ahenk*] and order [*nizam*].' The former, he wrote, was best explained in Durkheim's *De la division*.[64] After giving a brief summary of the latter's theory of mechanical and organic solidarity, of how individuals had similar needs and productions in mechanical solidarity and how functional differentiation increased the mutual dependence of individuals and put an end to their likemindedness, Ağaoğlu argued that a social organism is

> just like a net. Each of its chains is successively tied to all other chains. The existence, maintenance, continuation and life of each are a vehicle to others' existence, maintenance and continuation.[65]

The problem was then to determine what the limits of individual action were and what individuals must or must not do. Ağaoğlu wrote:

> Here, the obligation is only social; it does not transgress the wills and freedom of choice of individuals. If they want, individuals can break the laws. However, in the event of a violation, social life suffers unrest and destabilizes due to the interdependence of individuals.[66]

All individuals were responsible for protecting social harmony and order. In turn, the responsibility of the state was to protect the rights of the individual with limited interference in individual life.[67] The state must ensure that each party complied with the terms and conditions of agreements between the state and the individual and among individuals.[68]

The same should have started to happen in the East through a withering away of the traditional mentality which, as we saw in the Chapter 4, he had associated with the corrupt mentality of the clergy and which in his view

---

63   Ahmet Ağaoğlu, *Hukuk-i Esasiye,* p. 11; in this work, he for the first time cited Durkheim
      explicitly.
64   Ibid., p. 12.
65   Ibid., p. 12.
66   Ibid., p. 12.
67   Ibid., p. 42.
68   Ibid., p. 96.

had eradicated individuality.[69] In Ağaoğlu's interpretation, this had to be reversed because the equality of all individuals in society and their emancipation were the key to progress.

> In fact, the most influential factor for social, political, aesthetic and intellectual development is the individual... [I]ndividuals are inspired by their society and extract the elements and components of their ideas and feelings from society; the history of progress and our everyday observations prove that there is a reciprocal activity and impact [between the individual and the society]. Individuals affect their society to the same degree they are inspired by it. The individual returns with interest what he extracts from the society. Moreover, if the individual has not made this impact, if he has not inspired the society..., the society which consists of the aggregate of individuals would see no innovation, no progress.[70]

He moreover argued that the emancipation of the individual would also make social ties stronger. Nationalisation, therefore, was dependent upon liberalisation. In this context, his appeal to group solidarity was not only limited to occupational groupings to defend individual rights, it was also a prerequisite of introducing a national identity, as was the case in Gökalp.

The key to becoming a conscious nation, he wrote during the War of Independence, lay in having individuals with free thought, free opinion, free feelings and free movement, who unconditionally accepted the free appearance of social consciousness, who did not tolerate any other power than this, who knew where society went within the limits of the general will. They would have formed a "nation" which found its national consciousness only when the individuals of a society enjoyed these liberties. Otherwise, no matter what the type of government, no matter whether the people were sovereign or not, that society was but a mob.[71] As the spokesman of the National Liberation Movement, he asserted that if the role of the state was to protect the individual from the mentality of the traditionalists, it would be a legitimate action for the state to discard the institutions impeding individual development and create a free atmosphere in which the individual could work. The ultimate aim of the state must be to free the individual.

The two uses of individuality quoted above, together with Ağaoğlu's arguments in his famous *State and the Individual* of 1933, led him to be known as a

---

69   Ibid., pp. 37–38.
70   Ibid., pp. 37–38.
71   Ağaoğlu, "İhtilâl mi, İnkılâp mı?" *Hâkimiyet-i Millîye,* August 1, 1922.

liberal individualist in modern Turkey. As I discussed in Chapter 6, his opposition to absolute monarchical rule and the ascribed status of the aristocracy did not distinguish him from most other contemporary revolutionaries; it was with this constant emphasis on the emancipation of the individual that Ağaoğlu achieved a distinctive place. According to Kadıoğlu, his emphasis on the yet abstract concept of the individual (or, in Kadıoğlu's words, Ağaoğlu's individualism) was limited to a republican epistemology.[72] An equally more important boundary limiting 'the individualism of Ağaoğlu' was the impact of Durkheim's sociology on his later work.

7.1.3   Civic Equality and Individual Liberty

Just like Durkheim, Ağaoğlu argued that the growth of the state and individualisation (*fertleşme*) were positively correlated and proportional.[73] While the state went on developing more and more, the rights of the individual—believed to be actively conflicting with those of the state—and his skills had a parallel development. The society went through several stages in progressing towards modernity, as he wrote in 1933:

> each period leads the state to encounter more complex and wider [social] needs and [the state's] duties become more complex, and therefore, entail a widening of its competencies. However, the essential factor [of all these] has always been the individual activity.[74]

In Eastern nations, Ağaoğlu argued, the principle of 'there is no individual, but community; no rights, but duties' which is essentially the same as the principle of 'there is no body but the king, no rights, but arbitrariness' had been dominant for centuries, however. He best explained this in *State and the Individual* (1933):

> In the East, the individual was [...] squeezed, weakened, and made into a paltry being under an increasingly ferocious despotism and put into his own narrow and constricted scabbard. In the West, on the other hand, the individual gradually took a hold of his freedoms and, by constantly opening up, felt the pleasure of living and working as a result of the weakening of despotism. As a result, the Oriental societies composed of

---

72   Kadıoğlu, "Citizenship and Individuation in Turkey," p. 209.

73   Ağaoğlu, "Cumhuriyet Halk Partisi Programı Etrafında"; "Tarihte Sosyal İnkişaf".

74   Ağaoğlu, *Devlet ve Fert*, p. 41.

constricted individuals put into their own scabbard also became constricted and weakened.[75]

In modern Western nations, the state action was limited by two principles:
civic equality and individual liberty.[76]

In his account, in the West, all individuals were equal before the law, they
had equal access to the civil service and equality in taxation. He grouped individual liberties into two: (1) material liberties of freedom of movement, freedom of life and property, freedom of labour and social rights; (2) spiritual
liberties which included freedom of expression, freedom of conscience and
freedom of education.

Ağaoğlu added that these rights could not and must not be violated by
the state, unless, he added reservedly, "they threatened the very existence of the
state and the society."[77] That said, he was not against the idea of state tutelage.
For him, the state could not be indifferent to freedom of education, social rights
and freedom of expression, all of which were related to the spirit and economic
life of the nation. To protect social life from great harms, the state must super-
vise these rights and protect them from abuses. Especially in countries like
Turkey, where citizens had not fully comprehended the responsibilities brought
about by further liberty, it was natural that individual rights would be enjoyed
under the supervision of the state. This was what laid the groundwork to limit
individual liberties whenever the government saw it fit in the early Republic.

Like Gökalp, Ağaoğlu utilised Durkheim's teachings only selectively and for
pragmatic reasons. What Durkheim regarded as social facts, for example, carried in Ağaoğlu's writings normative implications to help shape the characteristics of the Turkish society in the early republic. His ideas were only slightly to
the level of making original contributions to Durkheim's sociology, and this we
see, as I noted above, only in reference to his re-reading of historical development of liberalism in the West in reference to Durkheim's theory of division of
labour and in terms of his application of the principles of mutual interdependence and individual rights as integral elements of his understanding of
nationalism in his later work. Notably, he did not seek, nor did he need, intellectual conversation with any of his teachers, but instead hastened to address
domestic problems through some of their teachings, which he found convincing and which he adapted for his own purposes.

---

75   Ağaoğlu, *Devlet ve Fert*, p. 27, trans. Kadıoğlu, "Citizenship and Individuation in Turkey,"
      p. 205.
76   Ağaoğlu, *Hukuk-i Esasiye*, p. 45.
77   Ibid., p. 45.

7.2   Étatism and Private Initiative

Ağaoğlu returned to the question of the relationship between the state and the individual during his discussions with the *Kadro* group in 1932 and, repeating most of what he argued in the 1920s, he attempted to follow the middle way between étatism and individualism, as far as the economy was concerned. Historically considered, Ağaoğlu's most important contribution to Turkish economic thought was through this exchange of ideas.

The discussions between the *Kadro* group and Ağaoğlu over the limits of state intervention in economic life were closely followed by various intellectuals and statesmen at the time. Although Ağaoğlu's economic thoughts lacked depth and often displayed inconsistencies, his views in these discussions represented a mentality, that of the Business Bank group, with his emphasis on the concurrent importance of the state and individual activity.

> I made a lot of noise with my fourteen articles entitled "Devlet ve Fert". Now, the press and public opinion are occupied with this noise. I fight for the individual and freedom. My opponents say that there is no Individual, but the State. I say that there is both Individual and the State.[78]

Having received no formal education in economics at any point in his life, Ağaoğlu's knowledge of modern economic thought was very limited. This explains why, before and after his discussions with the *Kadroists*, with the exception of the Free Party era writings, he rarely tackled economic issues in his articles or books. Moreover, at different times and places, he portrayed a rather vague and inconsistent understanding of étatism. When it was first introduced in Turkey in August 1930, as we learn from his Free Party memoirs, he was surprised and disappointed with the new policy of the Republican People's Party.[79] "In the beginning," he wrote, "the [Republican People's Party] was more liberal than a liberal" party; thus it was hardly possible to expect the Party to implement étatist government policies.[80] "There was no word related to étatism (*devletçilik*) [in the constitution],"[81] he added, "in fact, nobody, including me, knew that the Republican People's Party, of which I was a member, was étatist before İsmet Paşa's speech in Samsun [*sic*] ...."[82] But during and after the

---

78   Samet Ağaoğlu, *Babamdan Hatıralar*, p. 38.
79   Ahmet Ağaoğlu, *Serbest Fırka Hatıraları*, pp. 16–17.
80   Ibid., p. 16.
81   Ibid., p. 16.
82   Ibid., p. 17.

Free Party era, he would appear to defend a version of étatism, which, following the fashion among fellow Turkish writers, he regarded as an original version peculiar to the Turkish economy. This requires tracing his later economic thought during the foundation of the republic.

During the second year of the Independence War, Ağaoğlu explicitly stated in *Revolt or Revolution?* what type of an economic system he wanted to be implemented in the new Turkey:

> The success of the ruling minority [in government] depends on securing an open platform for competition for all talents and merits... So far as it is legitimate and honest, competition is the most desirable thing for a country. But closing the doors to competition and controlling [the economy] by an office just [on the pretext] that there is the possibility of the surfacing of grudge and greed in competition can definitely not be justified, because those who compete are human beings. No matter how perfect that restrictive office may become in terms of morals and merit, it may nevertheless cause more harm than greedy competitors.[83]

The above passage shows that he was a defender of a free market society based on free competition and limited state intervention. In the 1930s, he continued to hold the same view by and large. In an economic context where the idea of a classless society was gaining more and more popularity, he asserted, with direct reference to the French socialist Jean Jaurès, that the existence of a bourgeoisie was, in fact, 'not a bad thing to be scared of' as it also had a very valuable historical importance.[84] With the abolition of the long-lasting despotism, it would now be possible to create such a class in Turkey.

> I completely disagree with Karl Marx. I think class conflicts are not a disaster for humanity, but for their good. In the East, one person appeared and removed all classes on behalf of God and compelled all people to obey him. Classes were removed, but it also meant the death of man. With the death of man, his high sentiments also died. It was not the same in the West. Classes survived in the West. Nobody emerged on behalf of God to take control of all classes and all people [nor] to lead them to become a single-coloured and a single-shaped mob.[85]

83   Ahmet Ağaoğlu, *İhtilal mi İnkılâp mı?* p. 43.
84   Ahmet Ağaoğlu, "İş Kanunu Hazırlanırken Çok Düşünmek Lazım," *Cumhuriyet,* May 8, 1935.
85   Ahmet Ağaoğlu, "Hayır ve Yardım İşleri," *Cumhuriyet,* February 14, 1935.

Like French republicans, Ağaoğlu was not against capitalism, but he was against the atomism and egoism that it might possibly bring with it, destroying social ties. Yet, as noted previously, the idea of creating a strong bourgeoisie was not new in Turkey and had already been propounded most famously by President Kemal Atatürk in the 1920s, when he had said that Turkey must create million-aires.[86] In the Turkish context, the appeal to capitalism went in parallel with the idea of creating a strong enabling state, which formed the corporatist background of the Kemalist government.[87]

Despite being one of those writers who suggested both capitalism and a strong enabling state, Ağaoğlu never used the word 'corporatism'. In his view, the type of economic ideology that Turkey must follow was liberal étatism. In an interview during the Free Party era, he claimed that one of the points on which the views of the Republican People's Party and the Free Party differed was the definition of the concept of étatism. For the Free Party, it was the state's entrepreneurship in matters related to the public good.[88] In other words, the goal of the state in its undertakings was "to secure the best interests of the people" and to use its revenues for their benefit. He argued that the İsmet Paşa government took étatism completely differently. The existing state undertakings in Turkey were not beneficial for the people, because they imposed on them the yoke of heavy taxes. In the eyes of Ağaoğlu, this was best illustrated by the sugar monopoly. He claimed that despite the fact that the total production cost of sugar was 18 kuruş per oke,[89] thanks to commissioners, sugar had been sold for the price of 66 kuruş per oke. Yet a new office was established just to charge 8 kuruş of tax per oke of sugar. "In this office, eighty people have worked and annually one million liras have been spent... A lot of taxes have been imposed. All these were inflicted on the people. Is this étatism?"[90]

After the Free Party experience, while the Republican People's Party was in search of new economic policies to ameliorate the economic conditions of the early 1930s, Turkish intellectuals put forward new models for the development of the economy. One of the most assertive arguments expounded at the time was that of the *Kadro* group. *Kadro* was a monthly journal of political, economic

---

86   *Atatürk'ün Söylev ve Demeçleri,* vol. II, p. 97; cf. Artun Ünsal, "Atatürk's Reforms: Realisation
      of Utopia by a Realist," Paper presented to the seminar *Nehru and Atatürk,* New Delhi,
      1981.

87   For more information see, Taha Parla, *The Social and Political Thought of Ziya Gökalp* or
      Taha Parla&Andrew Davison, *Corporatist Ideology in Kemalist Turkey,* New York: Syracuse
      University Press, 2004.

88   *Son Posta,* August 19, 1930.

89   Oke is a unit of weight equal to about 2 and 3/4 lbs.

90   Ibid.

and social ideas published in Turkey between 1932 and 1934 by a group of 'patriotic leftist' intellectuals.[91] The ideologue of the group was Şevket Süreyya (Aydemir), a former Marxist who had studied in the Soviet Union,[92] while Yakup Kadri (Karaosmanoğlu), the famous novelist and a close friend of Mustafa Kemal, was the franchise holder of the journal. The group, as Türkeş informs us, "appointed itself to undertake the task of developing a theoretical framework to interpret the Turkish revolution and to propose a development strategy."[93] The name of the journal, *Kadro,* is derived from the French word 'cadre', reflecting the group's idea that an avant-garde revolutionary cadre (*rehber kadrosu*) should "assume the responsibility of forming the ideology of the Turkish revolution."[94] Although the Republican Party leadership did not completely employ the ideas of the group,[95] the fact that Prime Minister İsmet İnönü published an article in defence of étatism in this journal demonstrated that he sympathised with it and that there were parallels between the review's political position and that of the 'bureaucratic group' in the Republican Party.[96]

In 1932, Şevket Süreyya outlined the initial propositions formulated by the review in book form under the title of *İnkılâp ve Kadro* (*The Revolution and the Cadre*).[97] The objective of the *Kadro* group was to determine the ideology of the Turkish Revolution, which, Süreyya argued, had come into existence as a reaction to the flaws of the capitalist system.[98] In comprehending the reasons for economic backwardness, Süreyya attributed a significant role to the nature of international relations in a capitalist world system. He wrote:

> Today's world is divided into three camps—the capitalist countries, the socialist countries, and the colonies or semi-colonies of the capitalist states. Within this system, two conflicts are developing, which differ from one another—the class struggle between the proletariat and the bourgeoisie in the capitalist countries, and the national liberation struggle in the colonies or semi-colonies of imperialism... The social classes in the

91   Mustafa Türkeş, "A Patriotic Leftist Development-Strategy Proposal in Turkey in the 1930s: The Case of the Kadro (Cadre) Movement," *International Journal of Middle East Studies,* vol. 33, No. 1 (Feb., 2001), pp. 91–114.

92   Ayşe Trak, "Development Literature and Writers from Underdeveloped Countries: The Case of Turkey," *Current Anthropology,* vol. 26, No. 1 (Feb., 1985), pp. 89–102.

93   Türkeş, "A Patriotic Leftist," p. 94.

94   Trak, "Development Literature," p. 93.

95   Osman Okyar, "The Concept of Étatism," p. 100.

96   Trak, "Development Literature," p. 93.

97   Şevket Süreyya, *İnkılap ve Kadro*, Istanbul: Muallim Halit Kütüphanesi, 1932.

98   Ibid., p. 14.

countries of the 'national liberation front' and those in the industrialized countries do not have a similar formation. In the former, the existence of a capitalist class hinders industrialisation [presumably because its interests are linked to those of capitalism in the industrialized countries]. Therefore, this function devolves on the state. The establishment of industry, transport networks and major credit institutions by the state, under the state's control and within the framework of a planned economy, will bring about not just economic welfare, but also social harmony, since the state's directory role will prevent the emergence of opposing classes in the country, and thus of class conflict. The result will be the creation of a united society, without privilege or classes.[99]

In Süreyya's view, underdevelopment was based on the exploitation of colonies by the imperialist states. He insisted on the necessity of taking a road between capitalism and socialism, arguing against the application of either in Turkey.[100] As far as the institutional framework was concerned, he strongly rejected taking industrialised capitalist countries as models, constantly referring to the Great Depression as a reflection of the problems faced by Western capitalism. Because capitalism gave rise to inequalities, injustices and class conflicts and thus to the disintegration of the social fabric, he believed that the capitalist development strategy had to be substituted with a new system in which the state had to be the permanent motor of the development strategy, preventing the appearance of conflicts in society and creating a classless society.[101] It had to be entitled to regulate resource allocation and decide income distribution as well as to prevent the private sector from gaining an influential position in decision-making. Public enterprises had to be permanent measures to compensate for the lack of indigenous industrial capitalists.[102] As the state had to 'check the appearance of markets as an independent force dominating the society, and keep economic activity subordinate to the social system,' the upsurge of individual initiatives had to be rejected along with the Western emphasis on democracy and individual freedom.[103] Süreyya maintained that individuals should still be given the opportunity to participate in the building of a prosperous and just society, but this would entail sacrifices by them. The decisions taken by the cadre must be implemented, even when faced by mass opposition, because "the elite is responsible for taking the course of action

99   Ibid., p. 15, cf. William Hale, "Ideology and Economic Development in Turkey," p. 106.
100   Trak, "Development Literature," p. 94.
101   Süreyya, İnkılâp ve Kadro, p. 25.
102   Trak, "Development Literature," p. 94.
103   Süreyya, İnkılâp ve Kadro, p. 78.

which will best serve the interests of the people even if this has to be done in spite of the people."[104]

An answer to the *Kadro* group's propositions, with an expected message, came from Ahmet Ağaoğlu on November 13, 1932. Ağaoğlu was incensed by the vanguardist and anti-democratic messages of the *Kadroists*. According to him, their propositions, as revealed in *The Revolution and the Cadre*, abounded with serious mistakes, which he attempted to highlight in fourteen instalments under the title of 'Devlet ve Ferd' ('State and the Individual'), which appeared in *Cumhuriyet* until December 4, 1932.[105]

Ağaoğlu began by arguing that the age-old problem of the relations between the state and the individual was the key to understanding different ideological viewpoints in the complex social, political and economic environment of the post-war era. In his view, there were ruthless attacks all over the world: in the economic field, on capitalism and freedom of labour; and in the political field, on parliamentary rule and individual freedom.[106] The *Kadroists*, Ağaoğlu asserted, were the conveyers of this current in Turkey. He staunchly rejected Şevket Süreyya's arguments, which he found unscientifically subjective and prophetic in style.[107] According to Ağaoğlu, Süreyya was unrealistic in his interpretation of the Turkish Revolution as beginning as a reaction to the Great Depression. While Ağaoğlu agreed that one aspect of the Turkish Revolution was to confront the economic domination and oppression by foreign countries, it must be underlined that many of the important characteristics of the revolution had already been established before the Great Depression.[108] It was also important that the Turkish Revolution had domestic political aspects in the shape of the abolition of the sultanate and caliphate, the promulgation of the Republic and those reforms securing religious, familial and legal equality, which, Ağaoğlu asserted, the *Kadroists* had overlooked. It was inevitable that they would neglect these characteristics of the Revolution, because they were historical materialists and, in their view, one should first look at the infrastructure of social activity, i.e. the economy, on which would arise a superstructure of political and legal institutions.[109]

---

104 Ibid., p. 89.

105 Two days before Ağaoğlu's first article criticising the propositions of the *Kadroists* appeared in *Cumhuriyet*, the newspaper's editor-in-chief Yunus Nadi needed to note that Ağaoğlu's ideas did not reflect the views of the newspaper; Yunus Nadi, "Devletçilik ve Şahsi Teşebbüs," *Cumhuriyet*, November 11, 1932.

106 Ağaoğlu, *Devlet ve Fert*, pp. 2–4.

107 Ibid., pp. 10–11.

108 Ibid., p. 14.

109 Ibid., pp. 14–15.

The next target of Ağaoğlu's criticisms was the argument of the *Kadroists*
that by controlling the means of production, the state would drive out class
conflicts before they appeared in Turkey. The *Kadro* group suggested that social
conflicts took place only in capitalist societies. Ağaoğlu disagreed. In his
account, social conflicts had always existed in history. Adducing the examples
of social conflicts in the history of mankind in different political and historical
settings in support of this claim, he repeated that each conflict in history
between various political, economic or social groups, namely, between individuals, generated the progress of humanity—a line of argument revealing
Ağaoğlu's theory of history once again. The dynamo of this evolution was conflict and the source of conflict was individual activity.

> It is the individual [which leads] the development of the state...the indi-
> vidual accumulates capital, establishes technology, ...leads to new needs
> and new conflicts and prepares the ground for the appearance of new
> social institutions and new state functions which will meet these needs
> and eliminate conflicts.[110]

Ağaoğlu dismissed Şevket Süreyya's explanation that underdevelopment was
merely based on the exploitation of the colonies by the imperialists countries.
In his view, without construing the origins of the differences between the two
groups of countries, i.e. without looking at the nature of the relationship
between state, society and the individual, any theory would provide an incomplete picture of the phenomenon of underdevelopment.

Ağaoğlu believed that the strength of a society in the long run consisted of the
strength of the individuals composing it.[111] This was why Britain, having individuals of strong character, had been able to colonise India, which was ten times bigger
than itself, but would not dare to try colonising such smaller countries as Holland
and Denmark which were situated right beside it. As he argued elsewhere,

> The natural environment that the English have to cope with has always
> prepared them for action and struggle... [The] heavy climate, lack of land
> and infertility have always led Englishmen to seek sources abroad...
> Private initiative, perseverance, will and ambition have all been features
> that this climate has imbued in them. Free institutions that the English
> have established have laid an appropriate ground for the maximum
> development of these characteristics.[112]

---

110   Ibid., p. 41.
111   Ibid., p. 74.
112   Ağaoğlu, *İngiltere ve Hindistan*, p. 12.

The secret of the Western superiority over Eastern nations could be found in the internal strength of Western societies.

For Ağaoğlu, the pioneering role of the Turkish Revolution in the East laid in its attempt to reject Western encroachments and for the first time to protect individuals from any type of oppression. Had the *Kadro* group tried to formulate an ideology for the Turkish Revolution from the course of the revolution itself rather than from an external doctrine, they would have "come to the conclusion that our revolution aimed at saving the individual and the society which is the aggregate of individuals; that is, it attempted to establish a complete and all-inclusive system of democracy."[113] Just as the fundamental cause of the development of the Western nations was a gradual increase in individual liberty, the goal of the Turkish Revolution was the opening up of the individual.

The *Kadroist* argument that "the ideal is not to endow the individual with liberty in society which separates him from society, but to endow the nation with rights in the world, and to give the individual work and duties within this free nation" was for Ağaoğlu a testimony of the group's abhorrence of individual freedom.[114] "As the science of society demonstrated," Ağaoğlu argued with reference to Durkheim, "liberty does not separate the individual from the nation, but in contrast, it constitutes an unbreakable network of solidarity in the community which consists of the aggregate of its individuals."[115]

Ağaoğlu firmly believed that because the motor of the development of society was the individual, the state's involvement in economic activity must begin where individual activity ended. It was what the Kemalist state aimed to do: protect, encourage and ensure the progress and development of the individual. "I accept," Ağaoğlu wrote, "that the state should undertake the task of establishing infrastructure and some industries, which individual entrepreneurs are unable to do, as far as *Kadro* accepts."[116] However, he insisted that in backward countries like Turkey, a characteristic of the state was the inability of bureaucrats to deal with economic matters and the poor availability of government funds for economic projects. Therefore, to assign an important role to the state in the development process would be to perpetuate the circumstances obstructing progress.[117]

Ağaoğlu in fact assigned to the state the role of eliminating economic conflicts of interest. He argued that for the development of the individual, the state's interference in economic life should be kept, not to a minimum, but

---

113   Ağaoğlu, *Devlet ve Fert*, p. 30.
114   Ibid., pp. 21–22.
115   Ibid., p. 22.
116   Ibid., pp. 75–76.
117   Trak, "Development Literature," p. 95.

within certain limits. To put it differently, for Ağaoğlu, in backward countries such as Turkey, individuals must be left to their own devices until such time as social conflicts emerged:

> The state is responsible for maintaining order...and for eliminating the conflicts which emerge in this order. Therefore, the limit and character of interference depend on these principles...everywhere and all the time... state intervention has stemmed from the need to eliminate the conflicts which appeared in domestic life. Therefore, before the emergence of [the need for state interference], that is, before conflicts emerge within society as a result of individual activity, pre-emptive state intervention is both unnecessary and harmful...and of no use. It is harmful because it impedes individual activity which will engender conflict...as Engels says; "state intervention which does not improve the economy deeply damages it."[118]

The exchange of ideas between Süreyya and Ağaoğlu carried on after Ağaoğlu's fourteen articles. On December 10, 1932, *Cumhuriyet* informed its readers that Şevket Süreyya's responses to Ağaoğlu's arguments were to appear in the newspaper.[119] In his first article, Süreyya attempted to place the positions of Ağaoğlu and the *Kadro* within the Republican intellectual landscape, arguing that Ağaoğlu was a representative of the pre-revolutionary Turkish intellectuals and that the ideological differences between him and the *Kadro* were equivalent to those between the pre-revolutionary and revolutionary intellectuals.[120] Süreyya criticised Ağaoğlu and other intellectuals at the *Darülfünun* for taking European system as the only true and ideal system for all humanity, and for viewing European progress as a natural model of progress for all nations.

> According to them, a new national order outside the characteristics of classical democracy cannot be instituted. And [for them] what we call national revolution is nothing other than an internal reformation and... adaptation to European classical democracy.[121]

---

118   Ağaoğlu, *Devlet ve Fert*, pp. 31–32.

119   Şevket Süreyya, "Ağaoğlu Ahmet Bey'e Cevap," *Cumhuriyet*, December 10, 1932.

120   Şevket Süreyya, "Milli Kurtuluş Hareketleri Hakkında Bizim Tezimiz," *Kadro*, vol. 12, (Dec., 1932); cf. Selim İlkin, İlhan Tekeli, *Bir Cumhuriyet Öyküsü: Kadrocuları ve Kadro'yu Anlamak*, İstanbul: Tarih Vakfı Yurt Yayınları, 2003, pp. 245–246.

121   Süreyya, "Milli Kurtuluş Hareketleri Hakkında".

For Süreyya, European system was dependent upon the abuse and exploitation of both colonized nations and their individuals. In this system, exploitation was natural and tolerable, because the capitalist economy relied on the income extracted from colonies and backward countries.

> In this sense, the really important factors in the case of a complete reordering of the world are the national liberation movements, which mean the uprising of colonies. It is the duty of the intellectuals of those countries to explain these conflicts. Today, the course of the world can be explained neither by class conflicts alone nor by the conflicts with colonies alone; both should be taken into consideration. Such an explanation could not be put forth before the First World War, because in the colonies the antithesis of the current order had not yet been developed. The Turkish example had not yet appeared. It has begun to be understood that the principles and institutions of the European regime belonged only to Europe.[122]

This was why various national liberation movements began to search for principles and institutions suitable for their own structures and to question capitalism. It was the beginning of the intellectual renaissance in non-Western countries. However, Süreyya claimed, Ağaoğlu insisted on taking the national struggle of Turkey simply as an attempt at Europeanisation, which consisted of adopting legal and political principles that were now being rejected by the Europeans.[123] Moreover, he somewhat contemptuously dismissed Ağaoğlu and other lecturers at the *Darülfünun* such as İbrahim Fazıl (Pelin) as supporters of 'Cavid Bey Liberalism' who championed a classical liberal economy based on free trade and an international division of labour.[124] Ağaoğlu unequivocally rejected this, because, like the *Kadro,* he argued, his main endeavour was for the implementation of protectionist foreign trade policies; he also denounced the existence of colonisation and the unethical acts of the imperialist states.[125]

The discussion at one point concentrated on the question of whether or not the *Kadro* and Ağaoğlu really embraced the pillars of the official ideology of Kemalism: revolutionism and étatism. While Ağaoğlu argued that the proposi-

---

122   Ibid.
123   Şevket Süreyya, "Ağaoğlu Ahmet Bey'e Cevap 3," *Cumhuriyet,* December 13, 1932.
124   Şevket Süreyya, "Darülfinun İnkılap Hassasiyeti ve Cavid Bey İktisatçılığı," *Kadro,* vol. I, No. 12 (1932), pp. 38–43.
125   Ağaoğlu, *Devlet ve Fert*, pp. 110–112.

tions of the *Kadro* were not congruent with the ideals of the Turkish Revolution, Süreyya claimed that if Ağaoğlu had really been a Kemalist, a revolutionary and an étatist, he would not have joined the Free Party. Ağaoğlu replied[126]:

> I joined the Free Party as a revolutionary, democrat, liberal étatist and Kemalist. Because as a man...who has served the revolutionary elites since the very first day of the revolution, who controlled the revolutionary press for years, who headed its official organ, who penned and defended the programme of the revolutionary party, who participated in the preparation of the constitution, who was a deputy of the revolutionary party for eight years, who sat on the board of directors of the revolutionary party, I say this: Until the Free Party was established, I was of the opinion that the Republican People's Party was entirely liberal, democratic and étatist to the degree that I am étatist. Therefore, nothing has changed in my views... I am still of the opinion that the Republican People Party's étatism is many times closer to and more congruent with my understanding of étatism than that of the *Kadro*.[127]

It is rather difficult to determine to whose ideas the Republican Party's étatism was in fact closer, particularly because, as argued in Chapter 5, there were two different views of the meaning of étatism within the Party and because the Party itself seemed to maintain a substantial degree of flexibility by avoiding clear-cut definitions of étatism.[128]

The debate between Ağaoğlu and Süreyya ended in February 1933,[129] then in his writings later in the 1930s, Ağaoğlu went back to the subject of what he meant by liberal or democratic étatism. In his 1935 article "Demokrasi ve Devletçilik" (Democracy and Étatism), he wrote that there were two main types of étatism in terms of their influence over politics: one was dictatorial or oligarchic étatism, which eliminated democracy, as the Russian, German and

126   Ibid., p. 73.
127   Ibid., pp. 101–102.
128   Trak., p. 92.
129   Şevket Süreyya, "Ağaoğlu Ahmet Bey'e Cevap 4," *Cumhuriyet,* December 17, 1932; "Ağaoğlu Ahmet Bey'e Cevap 5," *Cumhuriyet,* December 18, 1932; "Ağaoğlu Ahmet Bey'e Cevap 6," *Cumhuriyet,* December 20, 1932; "Ağaoğlu Ahmet Bey'e Cevap 7," *Cumhuriyet,* December 22, 1932; "Ağaoğlu Ahmet Bey'e Cevap 8," *Cumhuriyet,* December 24, 1932; "Ağaoğlu Ahmet Bey'e Cevap 9," *Cumhuriyet,* December 27, 1932; "Kafir ve Bolşevik," *Cumhuriyet,* January 21, 1933; "Bir Münakaşanın Bilançosu," *Cumhuriyet,* January 22, 1933; "Bir Görüş Tarzı Nasıl İptizale Uğrar," *Cumhuriyet,* January 23, 1933; "Ciddi Olmayan Bir Yarenlik," *Cumhuriyet,* January 27, 1933; Ahmet Ağaoğlu, "Son Söz," *Cumhuriyet,* February 5, 1933.

Italian examples showed, and the other was liberal étatism, which preserved democracy, as observed in the American experience.[130] At a time when various Kemalist writers were speaking highly of the Russian and Italian models of government,[131] Ağaoğlu argued that in these countries democracy had turned into dictatorship or oligarchy. Representative government and parliamentary rule were undermined and no room was left for checks and balances or for individual liberty. In the case of the United States, by contrast, étatism and democracy co-existed successfully. Even though the state had the right to interfere in economic life, sovereignty still belonged to the people. The parliament continued to represent the nation and individual liberty was conserved. The checks and controls over the government continued to exist. For Ağaoğlu, Roosevelt's New Deal policy, based on the suggestions of the Brains Trust, was a perfect example of liberal étatism.[132] He claimed that the étatism implemented in Turkey was more akin to the American model.[133]

In so arguing, Ağaoğlu cited the leading figure of the Business Bank group of the Republican People's Party, Celal Bayar, then Minister of Economy. Bayar had stated that Turkish étatism was based on two principles: the first was the prime importance of the private initiatives and activities of Turkish citizens and the second was the state's taking of the initiative in areas where individuals could not act themselves.[134] According to Ağaoğlu, this étatist approach to the economy was completely in tune with his understanding of liberalism. He wrote:

> [Turkish étatism] protected and encouraged individuals and their work. Unfortunately, however, having mixed [the meaning of] political liberalism with [that of] economic liberalism for a long time, an intellectual obscurity had come into existence in our [country]. People thought that political liberalism was opposed to...economic étatism. No, it is not like that. Political liberalism opposes economic étatism only in so far as it exceeds the boundaries of democracy. Up to that point, it accepts étatism for the sake of liberty, for the sake of the freedom of labour and its protection from the oppression of the capital or for the sake of the more rapid development of the country.[135]

---

130 Ahmet Ağaoğlu, "Demokrasi ve Devletçilik," *Cumhuriyet,* June 6, 1935.

131 Falih R. Atay, *Moskova Roma,* Istanbul: Muallim Ahmet Halit Kütüphanesi, 1932.

132 Ağaoğlu, "İctimai Musahebeler: Zeka Tröstü"; "Amerika'da Buhran Savaşını Altüst eden Karar," *Cumhuriyet,* June 20, 1935; "Roosevelt'in Mücadelesi," *Cumhuriyet,* July 15, 1935.

133 Ağaoğlu, "Türk Devletçiliği"; for a very similar account see Ahmet Hamdi Başar, "Bizim Devletçiliğimiz," *Cumhuriyet,* August 26, 1935.

134 Ibid.

135 Ağaoğlu, "Demokrasi ve Devletçilik".

It is significant to note that that when it came to the relationship between bourgeoisie and workers, Ağaoğlu seemed to side with the former where there is a conflict.[136] He argued that although it was desirable to limit working hours in the interests of the workers, in countries like Turkey which were economically backward and whose labour was less skilled and less productive than those of more advanced countries, it was reasonable to have longer working hours, as was the case in Japan.[137] The role of the state was to arbitrate between the employer and the workers. If the latter had to work more for lower wages, the state should play its role by taxing the rich more and providing social services for all individuals. What guaranteed the social and political development of society were the material sacrifices of individuals, both bourgeois and the working class, because only then could strong social ties be formed between individuals.

Ağaoğlu's economic views, albeit assigning a central role to individual action, sat better with the modern liberal view, which suggested an enabling state. Ağaoğlu wanted an 'individualist society' as observed in France,[138] where there were thousands of social organisations and a huge state budget to aid people. His ideal state was thus an enabling state which was invested with an increasingly wide range of social and economic responsibilities for its citizens. That is to say that Ağaoğlu's notion of individualism in its political sense was based on the state's responsibilities towards the health, education and welfare of all individuals. It referred to the vertical relationship between the state and the individual.[139] Yet he needed to stress that if the happiness of the individual conflicted with the general wellbeing of society or the regime, individual freedom could be subject to restrictions for the good of the society. Legal measures that ensured the security of the republic and society could prevail over laws securing individual rights.[140] This was, for Ağaoğlu, a natural component of political life in countries where individual morality had not attained the desired moral maturity and where, therefore, freedom must at least initially be an ordered freedom.[141]

---

136   Ağaoğlu, "İş Kanunu".
137   Ibid.
138   Ahmet Ağaoğlu, "Özcülük ve Özgecilik," *Cumhuriyet,* January 20, 1935.
139   Ağaoğlu, *Serbest İnsanlar Ülkesinde,* p. 118.
140   Ahmet Ağaoğlu, "Ara Kanunlar ve Nazım Kanunlar," *Akın,* June 27, 1933.
141   Ahmet Ağaoğlu, "Nizamlı Hürriyet," *Akın,* June 5, 1933.

CHAPTER 8

Westernisation and Nationalism

Ağaoğlu's understanding of both the Kemalist Revolution and the tripartite relationship between the state, society and the individual in the late 1920s and the 30s were based on the models provided by the French Revolution and the Durkheimian sociology. He wanted the Turkish society to 'westernise'. This begs the question of what it would mean for a pioneer of Turkish nationalism to make Turkey a 'Western' country. Was this not a contradiction?

Ağaoğlu's conception of Westernisation did not rely on an essentialist distinction between what he called the East and the West. It was formulated more in the framework of his positivistic and dialectical theory of history, which he drew from Renan and which showed striking similarities with that of Akçura. As noted earlier, Renan's understanding of history was based on the belief that there was a spontaneous tendency and a vital force in history. Akçura, on the other hand, thought that history had a logic; it moved in a certain direction and everyone was one way or another becoming part of this evolution.

Ağaoğlu likewise believed that all nations were going through similar stages in history. The West had taken the lead in going through the stages of nationalism and liberalisation in the nineteenth century. This had resulted from the opening up of the individuals in the Western world, and their challenging existing social norms and traditions. There had been numerous social, political and economic conflicts, and each of these, once settled, had brought about progress. Both nationalism and liberalism were fruits of such conflicts and eastern nations had to become the adherents of these ideological currents now, trailing the footprints of Western nations in the early twentieth century.[1]

As such, to westernise meant for Ağaoğlu to nationalise and to liberalise the society. We find that he did not tie the Western identity with any sort of ethnic or religious marker or an ascribed culture. But instead, together with most of his pro-Westernisation contemporaries, he found in the West a civic-identity, a set of universal values borrowed from the ancient past and placed under a process of perfectionisation throughout modern history with human experience. As noted in the sixth chapter, the French Revolution, in his view, was a turning point in the history of the West. The Kemalist Revolution could play a similar

---

1 Ahmet Aghayef, "Sosyalizm mi, Milliyetçilik mi?" *Terakki*, vol. 37, 1906; cf. Swietochowky, *Russian Azerbaijan*, p. 58.

role for the realisation of the values of high individualism and the development of modern states and modern liberalism. Commitment to these values was what laid behind the Western success and it was what had united Western nations. Did Westernisation entail commitment to high individualism then? If not, what did it mean?

8.1   Turkey's Westernisation

Garpçılık or *Batıcılık* (Westernism) was an intellectual trend in the late Ottoman Empire and early Republican Turkey, which suggested borrowing certain features of Western civilisation.[2] Since Tunaya's work, it has been widely accepted that those who wanted Turkey's Westernisation wanted it either to be limited only to sciences and technology as did the 'partial Westernists' or to borrow and internalise all Western values, which entailed that the entire life style of the Ottomans or Turks had to be refashioned.[3] It would perhaps be wrong, or of little use, to divide the intelligentsia of the time into groups in a way that would reduce their viewpoints into binary oppositions, mainly because there were huge variations in their opinions not to mention the intellectual transformations that each went through.

Ağaoğlu's views about the borrowing of Western institutions, for example, had been remarkably different until the late 1920s. In his Russian writings, he had suggested finding a middle way between the old school among Muslim societies who saw sciences and technology as the only merits to be borrowed from the West and the new school who had wanted the imitation of the West as a whole. As a reformist Pan-Islamist, he had suggested at the time re-interpreting religious teachings in a way to make them more responsive to the needs of the modern world.[4]

During the National Liberation War, he argued in a similar vein that Westernisation in Turkey should be limited to science and technology, accentuating the importance of the Turkish and Islamic identity of its society.[5]

---

2 Ş. Tufan Buzpınar, "Celal Nuri's Concepts of Westernization and Religion," *Middle Eastern Studies*, Vol. 43, No. 2 (2007), pp. 247–258.

3 Tarık Z. Tunaya, *Türkiye'nin Siyasi Hayatında Batılılaşma Hareketleri*, Istanbul: Yedigün Matbaası, 1960, p. 27.

4 A. Agaev, "Panislamizm, ego harakter i napravlenie," *Kaspii*, April 14, 1901; "Polozhenie musul'manskih narodov. Jeklektizm ili panislamistskoe dvizhenie," *Kaspii*, December 24, 1903.

5 Ağaoğlu, *İhtilâl mi, İnkılâp mı?* p. 65.

Here is the kind of mentality that we desire: Being Eastern in heart and feeling; being Western in mind and thought! This is the highest ideal for our country, and the only solution we can think of. In other words, I want to stay Turkish-Islamic in terms of culture (*hars*), and become European in terms of civilisation.[6]

If he truly wrote *Three Civilisations* during his internship in Malta in 1919–20, then he significantly stepped back from his idea of total Westernisation only one year after writing that work.

In the early republican era, he asserted that, for its survival, Turkey had to adopt all of the features of the West and become a part of that civilisation.[7] Although most Westernist thinkers face the dilemma of lacking a strong ideology to include a new morality into their conception of Westernisaton,[8] the Ağaoğlu of the 1920s associated his idea of Westernisation with two ideologies, liberalism and nationalism, which he found complementary. He wanted the 'Eastern mentality' to be discarded and replaced by the Western mentality, which, he believed, resulted from the victory of liberalism. As of the late 1920s, as I shall discuss in Chapter 9, he even sought to introduce secular sources of religion.

Particularly in the 1920s, when the concept of Westernisation, together with the concepts of nationalism and revolution, was perceived as a power instrument used by the Kemalist elite to 'discipline' and elevate the level of people to that of advanced civilisations, he wrote prolifically about the meaning and functions of civilisation.[9] He saw no contradiction between Westernisation and nationalism, and, unlike mid-twentieth century liberals, between nationalism and liberalism.

As of late 1922, he would announce the new Turkish state as one to carry the nation 'from one civilisation to another.'[10] He would defend the Kemalist project against the criticisms raised by the Istanbul press. When, for example, Velid Efendi, the editor-in-chief of *Tevhid-i Efkâr,* suggested that 'there was no need for Westernisation, Eastern civilisation was sufficient for Turkey,' Ağaoğlu

---

6   Ahmet Ağaoğlu, *İhtilal mi*, p. 65.

7   Ahmet Ağaoğlu, *Üç Medeniyet*, p. 4.

8   M. Şükrü Hanioğlu, "Garpçılık: Their Attitude toward Religion and Their Impact on the Official Ideology of the Turkish Republic," *Studia Islamica*, No. 86 (1997), p. 143.

9   Hamit Bozarslan, "Kemalism, westernization and anti-liberalism", in *Turkey Beyond Nationalism: Towards Post-Nationalist Identities*, ed. Hans-Lukas Kieser (London; New York: I.B. Tauris, 2006), p. 31.

10   Ahmet Ağaoğlu, "Meclis Açılırken," *Vatan*, August 15, 1923.

would write that Velid's views could under no circumstances be those of a progressive revolutionary.[11] In his view, the establishment of a popular government by Mustafa Kemal in Ankara had started a new era. The emerging state in
Anatolia would endow the Turkish nation with the blessings of humanity
which they had long been deprived of, and thus it would open the path of happiness by means of elevating people to the level of the civilisation of the
Western world and harmonising the thoughts of Turkish nationalism with contemporary methods and mentalities.[12]

8.2   The Hidden Dialogue between Gökalp and Ağaoğlu

While attempting to resolve the tensions between Westernism and the idea of
preserving Turkish culture, Ağaoğlu was in a hidden dialogue with Gökalp,
who concurrently dealt with these questions in his writings. This dialogue is of
great importance to us and has significant implications for Ağaoğlu's notion of
liberalism and its relationship with the idea of Westernisation, because
throughout their writings of the time both Gökalp and Ağaoğlu outlined what
they understood by civilisation, specifically Western civilisation. While Gökalp
argued that Western civilisation did not consist of 'the liberal model of society
and its economic and political organisation,'[13] what Ağaoğlu referred to as the
West was diametrically opposite.

According to Ülken, Ağaoğlu's *Three Civilisations* was a fierce attack on
Gökalp's arguments about culture and civilisation.[14] The views of Ağaoğlu and
Gökalp about these concepts indeed differed on three points: firstly the
Ağaoğlu of the late 1920s was totalist, whereas Gökalp wanted partial
Westernisation. Secondly, Ağaoğlu insisted on seeing various elements of the
West as a model liberal system he wanted Turkish society to embrace, whereas
Gökalp did not regard Western civilisation as a necessarily liberal model of
society. And thirdly, for Ağaoğlu both culture and civilisation were changing
concepts, while Gökalp believed that, in contrast to civilisation, culture did not
change.

Gökalp had coined the term *hars* to refer to Turkish culture and become the
first Ottoman writer to preach the creation of a 'Turkish civilisation' that would

11   Cemal Kutay, "Garplılaşma Şarklılaşma I," *Yeni İstanbul*, December 3, 1972; Ahmet Ağaoğlu,
      "Garp ve Şark," *Vatan*, September 5, 1923.
12   *Hâkimiyet-i Milliye*, August 21, 1923.
13   Parla, *The Social and Political Thought of Ziya Gökalp*, p. 26.
14   Hilmi Z. Ülken, "Tanzimata Karşı," *İnsan*, 1937, p. 12.

combine the essentials of Western sciences and techniques, Turkish culture (*hars*) and the religion of Islam. As early as 1912, he had written that "Turkism, Islam, and Modernism were not contradictory ideals, since each answered a different need."[15] In Gökalp's account, modernism referred to the pursuit of the scientific, technological and industrial civilisation of the West, whilst "[i]t did not demand the adoption of the European 'way of life' and 'moral values'."[16]

Even though in the early 1910s Gökalp had seen no inherent contradiction between civilisation and culture, in 1918, the last year of World War I, he claimed that national culture strengthened solidarity, while civilisation was a threat to it.[17] For the Gökalp of 1918, national society was "the sum of institutions that create solidarity and interconnect individuals of a society," whereas civilisational institutions linked "the upper strata of one society to the upper strata of other societies."[18] Therefore, Gökalp suggested,

> [o]nly those elements of civilisation which are accepted, beyond the elite
> [preferences], by our people may be included in our culture. Institutions
> which are not tolerated by the people are excluded from national culture,
> even if these are accepted by the elite... There is in our country a class, the
> so-called Levantines or Cosmopolitans, who try to adopt the aesthetic,
> moral, philosophical tastes, and entire customs, ceremonies and behav-
> iour of the West rather than its scientific methods and industrial tech-
> niques. That is, they try erroneously to imitate the cultures of other
> nations under the name of civilisation.[19]

In Gökalp's view, culture was "non-utilitarian (*hasbî*), altruistic (*bimenfaaî*), public-spirited (*umumcu*), and idealistic (*mefkurevî*)," while civilisation was "utilitarian (*intifaî*), egoistic (*hodgâm*), individualistic (*fertçi*), and self-interested (*menfaatperest*)."[20] He deduced that those nations which, in contact with others, "failed to preserve their culture and subordinated it to civilisation," inevitably declined,[21] because culture was a cohesive element between the people and the elite of society, whereas civilisation, if not collectively shared,

---

15   Ziya Gökalp, "Üç Cereyan," in *Türkleşmek, İslamlaşmak, Muasırlaşmak*, p. 9; cf. Parla, *The Social and Political Thought of Ziya Gökalp*, p. 27.

16   Ibid., p. 27.

17   Ibid., p. 29.

18   Ibid., p. 29.

19   Ziya Gökalp, "Hars ve Medeniyet," *Yeni Mecmua*, No. 60 (1918); cf. Parla, p. 30.

20   Ziya Gökalp, "Hars ve Medeniyet Münasebetleri," *Yeni Mecmua*, No. 61 (1918); cf. Parla, p. 31.

21   Ibid., p. 31.

was divisive.[22] According to Parla, in so arguing Gökalp had in mind "as concrete cases a liberal (and Western) versus a solidaristic (Turkish, Islamic and a particular Western) model of society."[23]

Ağaoğlu had also been highly critical in his work of the European way of life pursued by upper-middle class Ottoman families who, in his view, were cosmetic Westerners and a by-product of the Tanzimat. This attitude which we may call superficial Westernisation[24] was collectively shared by a large number of Turkish writers, and found echoes in Turkish novel from the works of Recaizade Ekrem in the late nineteenth century to those of Orhan Pamuk today.[25]

The correlation Ağaoğu saw was not between liberalism and superficial Westernisation.[26] Nor did he make a distinction between civilisation and culture on the basis of ideals and solidarity. He sought foundations of solidarity in universal and scientific sources of morality applicable to all cultures and civilisations. This leaves us with the question of what he understood by civilisation and culture.

Unlike Gökalp, he described civilisation as an indivisible 'way of life' in *Three Civilisations*.[27] "It consists of all aspects of life," he wrote, "all its events, both spiritual and material,"[28] from the way of thinking to styles of dress. In this respect, there existed worldwide three main ways to live, three civilisations: Islamic civilisation (the East), Buddha-Brahman civilisation (the Far East) and European or Western civilisation. For him, although it was not easy to speak of sharp boundaries between these civilisations, their particular characteristics, which formed their very essence or spirit, made each different from the others. These characteristics were both material and spiritual. Material characteristics ranged from building structures to means of practising religion, while spiritual characteristics, which were related to a civilisation's mentality and sentiments, covered deeper qualities such as mores and manners.[29]

According to Ağaoğlu, by the early twentieth century the Islamic and the Buddha-Brahman civilisations had far lagged behind the Western civilization.

---

22   Ibid., p. 29.
23   Ibid., p. 31.
24   Şerif Mardin, *Türk Modernleşmesi: Makaleler*, Istanbul: İletişim Yayınları, 1991, pp. 23–81.
25   Orhan Pamuk, *Sessiz Ev*, Istanbul: İletişim Yayınları, 2012.
26   A. Aghayef, "Tanzimat", *Jeune Turc*, March 14, 1913.
27   Ağaoğlu, *Üç Medeniyet*, p. 3.
28   Ibid., p. 3.
29   Ibid., p. 5.

The latter's influence over the other two was the clearest sign.[30] They were borrowing and imitating Western institutions and practices.[31] Almost all non-Western nations were undergoing a westward transformation in "social, political and technological matters, in education and training."[32]

According to Ağaoğlu, this transformation eventually gave rise to the emergence of a struggle between two currents in all local societies: the first was the current of the proponents of the old local civilisation, which relied on customs and traditions; and the second was that of the proponents of European civilisation. The former, namely traditionalists, tried to preserve the old customs and local ways of life, while the latter, namely Westernists, regarded the ultimate aims of this conservatism as the death of society and believed that borrowing European institutions was the only way to survive.[33] In his view, historical realities demonstrated that Westernisation led to greater advancement for society.

Ağaoğlu pointed to Japan as the epitome of those societies that had made a timely and enthusiastic adoption of elements of Western civilisation, consequently managing to survive and to become more powerful, whereas those who rejected Western civilisation, especially the Islamic societies, were gradually being wiped out. Therefore, the only expedient for survival was to move closer to Western civilisation and to adopt it. The question central to Ağaoğlu's concerns at this point was how to do this. How could a civilisation be adopted? His point of view was totalist, in the fullest sense of the word:

> [Western civilisation] gained its superiority by all its features, not by some of its particular components. If science and technology have advanced more in Europe than in other parts [of the world], its causes should be sought in all features of European civilisation. European science and technology are a direct product of its own conditions and common features.[34]

Therefore, Western civilisation must be adopted with all the features which have given rise to its superiority. The alternative, adopting only some of its features, such as its science and technology, or borrowing only certain components of a whole, would prove futile. "Not only our clothes and some of our institutions, we must adjust also our minds, hearts and mentalities to [the

---

30   Ibid., p. 9.
31   Ibid., p. 27.
32   Ibid., pp. 9–10.
33   Ibid., p. 10.
34   Ibid., p. 11.

West]."[35] Would that then mean that the Turks would give up their national character for the sake of Westernisation?

Ağaoğlu was convinced that a nation would not lose its character by borrowing institutions and features from a civilisation it did not yet belong to. Human nature, he wrote, was inclined towards borrowing from others, acquiring everything that might benefit them from anywhere. In so doing, they would not lose their character; quite the contrary, they would make their character stronger. Because character was not limited to any condition, it was *sui generis* by nature; each nation, wittingly or unwittingly, would give its natural character to what it acquired afterwards.

What could destroy national character was, however, the stagnation of a nation. If the individuals and the society lost their depth and failed to express their sentiment of enthusiasm or to endow humanity with their intellectual and spiritual products, the nation would lose its character and its essence, condemning itself to death.[36] The question then was that of maintaining a vigorous culture.

In his later work, Ağaoğlu associated national character with culture.[37] In so doing, he was espousing Gökalp's 1918 conception of culture (*hars*). The latter had written:

> Culture (*hars*) is composed of an integral system of religious, moral, legal, intellectual, aesthetic, linguistic, economic and technological spheres of life of a certain nation. Civilisation, on the other hand, is the sum total of social institutions shared in common by several nations that have attained the same level of development.[38]

But the views of the two differed with regards to dynamism of the relationship between culture and civilisation. According to the Gökalp of 1918, culture was a constant, unchanging, mythical entity belonging both to past and present. Ağaoğlu was not as essentialist arguing that culture was as dynamic as civilisation and it could develop and mutate without losing its character. There was a two-way relationship between culture and civilisation: each could enrich the other, and so could they destroy one another.

Gökalp, in turn, reviewed his conception of culture in 1923, and invented another term, *tehzib,* which meant 'refined culture'. He used this term to bridge

---

35   Ibid., p. 13.
36   Ibid., *Üç* Medeniyet, p. 17.
37   Ağaoğlu, "Medeniyet ve Kültür".
38   Berkes, *Turkish Nationalism*, p. 104.

the gap between national culture and international civilisation. *Tehzib* could be acquired only through education, which instilled in individuals an intellectual culture.[39] Through *tehzib*, culture could change itself and the civilisation it belonged to. Gökalp moreover extended the communal solidarity he prescribed for national cultural groups to the civilisation group.[40] He thus gave up in his later work the idea that civilisation was divisive. Through contact with the values produced by intellectual culture, each nation and its culture could be enriched.

8.3   Nationalism Revisited

In 1926, President Mustafa Kemal Paşa would tell the British Ambassador Lindsay that the breach between the new Turkey and the old Turkey was now complete. The real change that had taken place had been "a change inside and not outside the skulls, for from the envelope it was general possible to judge of the character of the letter inside it." According to Gazi Paşa, Turkey was now completely modern and completely Europeanised.

> In the past the religious element had in every village arrogated to itself the leadership of the community; he had himself, as a young man, noticed this and its ill effects. Similarly, the holy men had exercised their influence on the Central Government, and had this constituted themselves into the intermediary between the people and the Government with a benumbing effect on the whole policy of the State. All this organisation of the past was now shattered, and under the republic there was direct contact between governors and governed. The ideas of the past had been essentially illogical and were now discarded.[41]

İsmet Paşa directly linked the suppression of the Kurds in the southeast in the 1920s with this project, taking it as a step to end the old mentality of tribalism:

> [T]he tithe in Kurdish districts had always been farmed out to the tribal chiefs, and they had used it to establish authority over the peasants and

---

39   Yücel Karadaş, "Orientalism and Invention of Tradition in Cultural Concept of Ziya Gökalp," *Euroasian Journal of Anthropology*, No. 2 (2010), pp. 44–58.
40   Parla, *The Social and Political Thought of Ziya Gökalp*, p. 32.
41   Lindsay to Chamberlain, July 21, 1926, TNA FO 424/265/8.

to perpetuate the clan system. With its abolition, which was now an accomplished fact, the authority of the chiefs, from whom all the trouble came, would be shattered, while the peasant, when he next reaped a harvest, would find that he was no longer exposed to the extortions and vexations of the past. Economic reform would provide the needed remedy, and no political change would be required.[42]

As many tribal chiefs and their families and retainers were moved to the West, the work of making the remaining Kurds good citizens would be undertaken by the Turkish Hearths and young qualified teachers sent to the south east.

Since its re-establishment in 1923, the Turkish Hearths, marrying the preaching of Gökalp and Ağaoğlu, had taken up the role of guide to Turkey's transformation westward.[43] It had accepted civilisationism (*medeniyetçilik*) as one of its main principles.[44] Its branches throughout the breadth of Turkey aimed at spreading knowledge of Western culture and of modern social and scientific ideas. To this end great stress was laid on the necessity for popular education. Evening classes were held for foreign languages, especially French, and for book-keeping, history and geography. Lectures, cinema and art exhibition shows of an educational nature were held. Foreign lecturers were sometimes enrolled. And interest in sports was taken.[45]

The approach of the Hearths to nationalism placed an element of voluntarism in the definition of a Turk in the fifth article of its charter.[46] In the view of its leaders, those who felt themselves to belong to the Turkish culture, even if they were not of Turkic origin, could be counted as Turkish. As Georgeon points out, they saw neither language nor religion as criteria for Turkishness in this period.[47] That being said, on the one hand, following the footsteps of Gökalp, its members sought the preservation and elevation of Turkish culture when Turkish society became a part of Western civilisation.[48] On the other, they suggested the Turkification of non-Turkic groups living in Turkey through their propaganda against non-Turkic and non-Muslim citizens of the republic.[49] The idea of banning the speaking of all languages other than Turkish gained

42   Lindsay to Chamberlain, March 23, 1925, TNA FO 424/262/125.
43   Hamdullah Suphi, "Hitabe," *Türk Yurdu*, June 6, 1925.
44   Their other principles were nationalism, populism and secular republicanism.
45   Clerk to Chamberlain, July 7, 1927, TNA FO 424/267/34.
46   Georgeon, "Kemalist Dönemde Türk Ocakları, 1923–1931," in *Türk Modernleşmesi*, p. 46.
47   Ibid., p. 47.
48   Karaer, *Türk Ocakları*, pp. 54–55.
49   Üstel, *İmparatorluktan Ulus-Devlete Türk Milliyetçiliği,* pp. 194–200.

popularity among the members of the Hearths over time and they took even exigent and coercive measures to realise this idea.[50] In Bulanik, Bitlis, for example, the use of Kurdish language at any rate in public was proscribed by the Turkish Hearths even though Turkish was scarcely spoken and little understood.[51]

The Hearths thus became an instrument of the policy of repression for 'modernist' aims since İsmet Paşa's speech in its 1925 Congress, where he was reported to say:

> We are frankly Nationalist... and nationalism is our only factor of cohesion. Before the Turkish majority other elements have no kind of influence. At any price, we must Turkify the inhabitants of our land, and we will annihilate those who oppose Turks or "le turquisme". What we seek in those who would serve the country is that, above all, they be Turks and turquisites. They say we lack solicitude for religious currents; we will crush all who rise before us to use religion as an instrument.[52]

Until his break with the Kemalist leadership in the late 1920s, Ağaoğlu employed similar exclusionary views. As he joined the Turkish Hearths in 1924 and became a member of its culture committee, his notion of nationalism likewise suffered from vacillating between gaining an increasingly liberal character and firmly supporting the nation-building process, based on Turkishness as the main ethnic identity, in the late 1920s. On the one hand, he denounced the use of force against those who chose to speak their own languages.[53] On the other, he found it more preferable that everyone in Turkey would speak Turkish, and in his works, he spoke of only the Turks as the citizens of the new Republic along the line of the constitution. His writings embodied assimilationist discourses such as his defence of the unity of language, and, pointing to the harms caused by foreign capital in the late Ottoman Empire, he blamed cosmopolitans (*kosmopolitçiler*) and internationalists for being the greatest enemies of Turkish nationalism.[54] Ağaoğlu the liberal showed little tolerance to diversity.

In the following decade, with the changing economic and ideological environment in Turkey, however, Ağaoğlu softened his position in a vague way.

---

50   Karaer, *Türk Ocakları*, p. 49.
51   Consul Knight to Clerk, May 25, 1927, TNA FO 424/267/36.
52   Lindsay to Chamberlain, April 28, 1925, TNA FO 424/262/156.
53   *Hâkimiyet-i Milliye*, April 9, 1928.
54   "Türk Ocakları Kongresi," *Hâkimiyet-i Milliye*, April 30, 1924.

After the closure of the Turkish Hearths in 1931 and due to his increasing contacts with the humanists and the Durkheimian influence on his thought, he came to argue that nationalism and humanism were synonymous. He contended that nationalism was a bridge between the individual and humanity.[55] "In appearance," he wrote, "the ideology of nationalism seems to separate people and raise walls between them. But in essence, it is the contrary. It has led to the assembly, rapprochement and agreement of the people."[56] It initially gave way to a process of integration among different social groupings that had been either in isolation from each other or fighting against others. Even though nationalism seemed to create differences between people, when considered in depth it was seen that it allowed the people of different nations to empathise with each other, as all were struggling for the development of their own nations, that is, for the same ideals.[57]

Arguing that, like individuals, all nations were equal, the supreme ideal of the later Ağaoğlu's notion of nationalism seemed to be the construction of a world of independent states. "Just as interdependency arises between the individuals of the same nation out of the necessity for survival, the nations of the world realize that they are mutually dependent (interdependent)." They needed other nations' labour and intellectual and material products, which engendered in the contemporary world an international solidarity. Therefore, there was no conflict between nationalism and humanism and the importance of neither must be denied.

Ağaoğlu claimed that neither Nazism and fascism were true nationalisms. For him, the type of nationalism defended in Italy and Germany had an artificial position in face of the natural historical development of nationalism, which had served as social (and international) glue. But fascism and Nazism denied the ideals of other nations and humanism.[58] He believed that Turkish nationalism, in contrast, was true nationalism in that it was synthesising cultural products with that of civilisation. Turkey, he maintained, was bridging the East and the West. In 1935, he wrote:

> The Turkish nation is...leading the East today. Its deep and comprehensive reforms–as an example for other Eastern nations—is becoming the most important...factor in eliminating the conflicts between the East and

---

55   Ahmet Ağaoğlu, "Ulusçuluk İnsancılıktır," *Cumhuriyet*, July 9, 1935.
56   Ibid.
57   Ibid.
58   Ibid.

the West and finally in the formation of a single-fronted [*tek cepheli*] humanity.[59]

He was of the opinion that the Republic was "gradually making Turkey a member of the European family."[60] But he warned that Turkey must enter that family not only wearing Western-looking clothes and with institutions borrowed from the West, but also by making Western what was inside those clothes and by fully embracing the liberal spirit of those institutions.

8.4   Monday Evening Talks

In the second half of the 1930s, as debates over the economic policies of the Republic settled with the implementation of a five-year plan in 1933 and with the introduction of Kemalism as the new official ideology, the question of how Turkey should Westernise became a topic of the discussions of the Monday Evening group.[61] Ağaoğlu's writings of the time disclosed the thinker's latest views on the subject, to which young humanist scholars brought new perspectives.[62]

The humanists of the 1930s in Turkey, who were influenced by the works of such German émigrés as Erich Auerbach, believed that the reason for Turkey's not being Westernised after all westward reforms was their "not having gotten to the ancient Latin and Greek sources which form the basis of [Western] civilisation and kept up a continuing contact with them."[63] Their perception of the universal identity of the West rested upon the idea of humanism, which had allowed the Westerns to visit the humanity's ancient heritage.

According to this account, the Turkish society, had not been able to break free from the closed mentality of the Medieval Ages.[64] Hilmi Z. Ülken, a leading figure among the young humanists, was remarkably critical of Ağaoğlu and Gökalp. He argued in 1938 that to make a clear-cut distinction between civilisation and culture (as did Gökalp and Ağaoğlu), and to treat these concepts as two distinct entities was artificial. In his view, culture was the particular efforts

---

59   Ahmet Ağaoğlu, "Doğu ve Batı," *Cumhuriyet*, August 26, 1935.

60   Ahmet Ağaoğlu, "Cemiyet Hayatımızda Noksan Prensipler," *Cumhuriyet*, March 15, 1935.

61   Ahmet Ağaoğlu, "Doğu Batı," *Milliyet*, August 16, 1935.

62   See for example, Ahmet Ağaoğlu, "Üç Kültür," *Kültür Haftası*, No. 1 (Jan., 1936), p. 5; "Bir Kültürden Ötekine," *Kültür Haftası*, No. 2 (Jan., 1936), p. 22; "Milli Kültür Nasıl Kurtulur?" *Cumhuriyet*, August 3, 1934.

63   Mümtaz Turhan, *Where are we in Westernization?* Istanbul: Türkiye Basımevi, 1959, p. 14.

64   Ibid., p. 14.

of each nation to realise the products of world civilisation. "Beethoven does not belong to the Germans only but to the entire West; Descartes is [a philosopher] of the world as much as of the French."[65] Each nation's efforts became greater with its increasing interactions with other nations. The civilised culture (*medenî kültür*) of a society which was introverted and all of whose relations with other societies were cut would weaken. Therefore, the only way for the Turks to find themselves was to look at themselves from a global perspective. He argued that the question of Turkey's Westernisation was not one of abandoning one civilisation for the other, but of renaissance, of breaking free from the boundaries of a closed civilisation, going to the deepest roots of humanity and, by means of increasing international contacts, mixing with the course of civil humanity from its very roots. True nationalism necessitated a widespread humanist movement and an in-depth reading and teaching of Greco-Roman culture in Turkey.[66]

Ülken asserted that in comparing and contrasting civilisations, Ağaoğlu did not take into account how Islamic civilisation had gradually become introverted within the imperial system and lost its creativity by cutting its ties with world civilisation. He did not consider that the Renaissance led to the opening of Western civilisation by breaking free from the boundaries of the closed Christian civilisation.[67] He instead invited the Turkish nation to accept either the East or the West. Nonetheless, Ülken argued, Ağaoğlu's was one of the most important attempts since the beginning of Tanzimat to turn the pseudo-problem of the East and the West into a question of a closed mystic civilisation versus an open world civilisation.[68] Ülken wrote:

> In our view, there is…no drama [in the shape] of the East and the West. There is a Turkish nation which tries to move towards nationalisation and intense production by casting off the loose production of the empire and the arrears of feudality. This Turkish nation will get to know its own body better while undergoing its renaissance with its historical move, which prepares it for participation in the great world evolution, and only then will it find itself. The Easternist's allegation of 'You are losing yourself!' and the Westernist's 'You are becoming introvert!' will then be rendered pointless.[69]

---

65   Ülken, "Tanzimat'a Karşı," p. 12.
66   Ibid., pp. 12–13.
67   Ibid., pp. 12.
68   Ibid., p. 13.
69   Ibid., pp. 13–14.

Although the Ağaoğlu of the late 1930s flirted with Ülken's ideas, he was of the opinion that given the existing mentality and socio-economic conditions which did not allow the opening up of individuals who would lead to social conflicts and progress in the East, 'the opening of Eastern mentality' on its own was hardly possible. He believed that the essential function of civilisation was "progress, to open up and to constantly create."[70] Western civilisation based on reason and rationale had permanently progressed, opened up, created and consequently prevailed over others after the Medieval Ages.

The other two civilisations, the Islamic and the Buddha-Brahman, must now imitate them. Inspired by Gabriel Tarde's theory of imitation, he claimed that the upbringing of a new generation was a matter of providing them with precursors.[71] In his view, the same applied to nations: the first task of each nation was to borrow successfully from other cultures. Imitating the habits of a civilisation and using its cultural products, a nation could make them habitual. By this means, he rather paradoxically argued, it could preserve its character, contribute to humanity and secure itself a place in international civilisation.

Ağaoğlu moreover maintained that in history there have been three different ways of adopting another culture: first, the invasion of a society low in culture by a high-cultured society and the latter's having the former accept its culture (as exemplified by European imperialism); second, the invasion of a society high in culture, but morally degenerate, by barbarians and the rebirth of the old high culture by means of the interactions between the dynamism of barbarians and the high culture of the conquered society (e.g. the Anglo-Saxon invasion of Roman societies); and third, the conscious attempt of a sovereign and independent society to change its culture (e.g. Russia, Japan and Turkey).[72]

None of these means of cultural change stemmed from preference, but from unwelcome necessity. If the Russians had not been subject to permanent attacks by the Swedes and Lithuanians, if the Japanese coast had not been beleaguered by the Dutch, French, Spanish, British and Portuguese, they perhaps would not even have thought of changing their culture. The Russian, Japanese and Turkish societies decided to change their cultures with one simple aim: to survive in the struggle for life. "But it is worth repeating that it was impossible to do so with their traditional outlook on life."[73] The Buddha-Brahman culture denies life and considers it an evil; the Islamic culture takes

70   Ağaoğlu, "Üç Kültür".
71   Ahmet Ağaoğlu, "Rakamlar Ne Diyor?" *Cumhuriyet*, April 4, 1935; "Genç Nesli Yetiştirmek," *Cumhuriyet*, April 8, 1935; "Tarihte Sosyal İnkişâf," *Kültür Haftası*, No. 17 (May 1937), p. 354.
72   Ağaoğlu, "Bir Kültürden Ötekine," p. 22.
73   Ibid.

it as a means to reach the afterlife and preaches reliance on it only to that degree; but Western culture accepts life as the essence of everything, preaching that everything revolves around life, which is the most valuable and important good.[74] That is why the Western way of life progresses, prevails over the other two and forces them to imitate it. Hence the 'need' to Westernise.

In its historical context, Ağaoğlu's Westernist programme, propounded initially in *Three Civilisations* and elaborated in his later articles, was among the most radical defences of Westernisation.[75] His formula was simple. Turkey must rapidly go through a nation-building process and the same liberal transformation that the West had gone through, during which people's religious, moral, individual, family and social lives and mentality had changed entirely. As such, Ağaoğlu conceived a two-fold Westernisation programme: on the one hand, as discussed in Chapters 6 and 7, it entailed the construction of a new liberal social and political order; on the other, it required the moral reconstitution of society.

---

74   Ibid., p. 22.
75   Ahmet Ağaoğlu, *Üç Medeniyet*, p. 3; "Medeniyet ve Ahlak," *Cumhuriyet*, October 25, 1925; "Doğu Batı," *Cumhuriyet*, January 24, 1936; "Medeniyet ve Kültür," *Cumhuriyet*, February 7, 1936.

CHAPTER 9

The Moral Ideology of the Republic

The Enlightenment idea that "a stable political order is built not simply on laws and institutions but on the character and mores of its citizens" undergirded Ağaoğlu's liberal thought.[1] He took the fullest elevation of the individuals' intellectual and spiritual faculties as the capital problem of his time. His later writings revealed that in his view, even the most perfect forms of government and economic systems would fail at the hands of morally degenerate individuals.[2] He therefore started a quasi-religious project seeking the inculcation of civic virtues and bringing up civic minded individuals. He at times went to such lengths to suggest the moral perfection of the individual.

The year 1928 is important for our concerns here as it was in this year, when the fourth article of the constitution was amended to read "the Republic of Turkey is a secular state", Ağaoğlu began to seek new 'scientific' moral sources. In 1929, by penning an allegorical utopian novella under the title of *Serbest İnsanlar Ülkesinde* (*In the Land of Free Men*) he attempted "to constitute the moral ideology of the Republic,"[3] just like Say who had sought to do the same in *Olbie, ou Essai sur les moyens de reformer les moeurs d'une nation.*[4] Referring to Montesquieu's argument that the republic was a form of government based on virtues, in his attempt to constitute the moral ideology of the republic, he sought not only to identify these virtues but also to introduce the republic as a new religion in this work.

Three months after the publication of his novella, following an Islamist uprising in Menemen in 1930,[5] when criticisms were directed towards Ağaoğlu for provoking this event by his statements during the Free Party era, he came to write:

> The Republic is a religion itself; it is a belief. But the [holy] book of this religion has not been written yet. No apostles to selflessly devote all their existence to the Republic, no geniuses to enlighten...the people by

---

1 Dana Villa, *Socratic Citizenship,* N.J.: Princeton University Press, 2001, p. ix.
2 Ahmet Ağaoğlu, "Ticaret ve Ahlâk," *Milliyet,* January 29, 1928.
3 Ağaoğlu, *Serbest İnsanlar Ülkesinde,* p. 1.
4 Jean-Baptiste Say, *Olbie, ou Essai sur les moyens de reformer les moeurs d'une nation,* Paris, 1800.
5 For information about the Menemen uprising, see Chapter 5.

© KONINKLIJKE BRILL NV, LEIDEN, 2015 | DOI 10.1163/9789004297364_010

penetrating into the dark layers of the mass of people have appeared! We left the Republic on its own and we were preoccupied with our...private works and interests! Here is the result![6]

This passage was the clearest account of Ağaoğlu's battle against the 'old moral system' and the role he imparted to the intellectuals in winning this fight. In his thought, republican values should have surpassed all moral systems, preparing them for a modern and democratic country which would leave behind the problems of bigotry, religious dogmatism and conformity, egoism and many other moral illnesses which he associated with the old regime.

Believing that the fundamental tenets of the long-lasting moral philosophy in the East in the main contradicted with these values, Ağaoğlu suggested a new understanding of secular morality (*yeni ahlâk*) based on altruism, self-sacrifice and communitarianism (*cemiyetçilik*) to take the place of the prevailing ill-made sentiments of egoism, self-interestedness and individualism (*ferdiyetçilik*).[7] In retrospect, it appears that Ağaoğlu's perception of the civic identity of the West in general, and Europe in particular, rested on these communitarian values, which he associated with civility.

In his interpretation, liberty could take root in social and individual life only with the inculcation of this set of communitarian values into the hearts of all individuals in the East. This could be done through the agency of the intellectuals and the state, through profound familial education and by means of the guided self-overcoming of the individual. Although he gave central importance to individual liberty in pursuit of social progress, unlike most modern liberals, he sought social control over the acts of the individual and placed no emphasis on individual autonomy in his later work either.

Notably, he did not seek to derive his new theory of ethics from Islamic teachings. His 1934 translation of Petr Kropotkin's uncompleted *Ethics: Origin and Development* was a sign of the value he attached to the teaching of the anarchist philosopher, which was, together with the work of Durkheim, a major source to which he often referred in his search for scientific sources of morality. Although we do not know when Ağaoğlu first read the works of Kropotkin, it is in his later writings that we find Kropotkinian motifs. To construe Ağaoğlu's interpretation of morality in more depth, some attention will first be devoted in this chapter to the aspects of Kropotkin's moral philosophy that influenced Ağaoğlu. Following this, Ağaoğlu's views on the differences in

---

6   Ahmet Ağaoğlu, "Vicdan Azabı Duymayanlara," *Son Posta,* January 12, 1931.
7   Ahmet Ağâoğlu, "Eski ve Yeni Ahlâk," *Hâkimiyet-i Milliye,* No. 2352, January 23, 1928.

moral life between East and West, and his attempts to establish the moral ideology of the Republic will be scrutinised, with a close reading of his later writings on morality. How, in Ağaoğlu's view, could the old moral system be
discarded and replaced by a new civic morality? What were the components of
the new moral system that Ağaoğlu wanted to see in the East? And how could
those components be inculcated into the hearts of individuals?

9.1   Petr Kropotkin and the Sources of Morality

Kropotkin's concentration on questions of morality was initially a reaction to
the increasing attention to amoralist doctrines in the last decades of the nineteenth century. The concurrent appeal of many representatives of science and
philosophy, under the influence of Darwin's theories, to the assertion that
there reigns in the world but one general law, that of the struggle for existence,
had lent support to philosophical amoralism.[8] Kropotkin endeavoured to
prove from a scientific point of view that nature is not amoral and does not
teach man a lesson of evil. His discussions with T.H. Huxley in the 1890s of the
theories of Darwin, together with his other articles in the journal *Nineteenth
Century*, formed the introduction to Kropotkin's moral philosophy,[9] while the
core of his thought can be found in *Mutual Aid: a Factor of Evolution*[10] and its
continuation *Ethics: Origin and Development*.[11]
    The questions central to Kropotkin's moral concerns in these studies were
those of whence man's moral conceptions originate and what the nature of
morality must be. In his search for answers to these questions he studied the
nature of humans as animals of a certain kind, buttressing his arguments with
examples from the history of mankind and nature. Given the development of
science in the nineteenth century, for Kropotkin it was now not only possible
but essential to pursue a scientific investigation of ethics. For him,

> [t]he investigation of society, using the methods of the natural sciences,
> the accumulation of observed material facts together with their assortment

---

8   N. Lebedev, Introduction to *Ethics: Origin and Development,* trans. Louis S. Friedland and
      Joseph H. Piroshnikoff, New York: Tudor Publishing, 1947, p. 4.
9   John Slatter, "P.A. Kropotkin On Legality and Ethics," *Studies in East European Thought,*
      Vol. 48, No. 2/4, Conceptions of Legality and Ethics in Nineteenth Century and Twentieth
      Century Russian Thought, (Sep., 1996), pp. 255–276.
10   Petr Kropotkin, *Mutual Aid: a Factor of Evolution*, London: Penguin, 1939.
11   Andrew Harrison, "Introduction," to *Ethics: Origin and Development,* p. viii.

and investigation using inductive reasoning, was urgent and would include the investigation of ethics and legality. Ethics already lagged far behind the development of the natural sciences and was in great need of a new, scientific, materialist basis.[12]

Instead of the presumption of a supernatural principle immanent in human life or the idea of superhumans ruling over lesser mortals, the basis of the new morality was to be the scientific investigation of the ethical principles of the past and present, leading to the elaboration of the basis of a future ethical regime. But, as demonstrated below, unlike Ağaoğlu's, the type of new morality Kropotkin desired was anarchistic in nature, one flourishing within "a society where legality and morality would assume a voluntary and freely chosen character without obligation or imposition from above." Kropotkin's emphasis on scientific facts led him, as Harrison puts it, to a type of naturalism, namely "the view that we may find the basis of morality in certain facts, specifically facts which, for Kropotkin, may be located in what, properly understood, we may learn from evolutionary theory, from how he understood Darwin himself, and from his own theories of animal and human instinctive behaviour."[13] Yet the science of morality which he propounded did not imply absolute rules of conduct that were all the result of nature; they were also learned, particularly by men.

Kropotkin fought against the growth of amoralist philosophy in the late nineteenth century, mostly utilising Darwinian terms, while disputes often centred on how to interpret Darwin's concepts. According to him, the utilitarian message along the lines of liberal Social Darwinism, voiced prominently by T.H. Huxley (popularly known as 'Darwin's bulldog'), was one-sided, providing rationalisation for merciless free market capitalism.[14] Huxley had interpreted Darwin's concept of the struggle for existence as meaning competition both between different species and between members of the same species for the same scarce resources. Kropotkin asserted that Darwin had not meant intraspecies struggle when he spoke of the struggle for existence, but instead the struggle against scarcity in nature, "the struggle by all species against nature itself for the means of existence. Very often this struggle involved not attacks by stronger on the weaker members of the same species, but a communal struggle by combined forces, e.g. a pack of members of the same species, to

---

12   Slatter, "P.A. Kropotkin On Legality and Ethics," p. 268.

13   Harrison, "Introduction," p. x.

14   Slatter, "P.A. Kropotkin On Legality and Ethics," p. 257.

survive and flourish jointly."[15] Warfare in nature was chiefly "limited to *struggle between different species*, [whereas] *within each species* and within groups of different species which we find living together, the practice of *mutual aid is the rule*, and therefore, the last aspects of animal life play a far greater part than does warfare in the economy of nature."[16]

In his various studies, Kropotkin attempted to bring into evidence the immense importance of mutual aid for the preservation of both animal species and the human race, and still more so for their progressive evolution; he went on to argue that 'mutual aid', as a permanent instinct, "is the predominant fact of nature."[17] It is 'always at work' in all social animals, and especially in man. This idea, as will be demonstrated, appears to have impressed Ağaoğlu the most.[18]

Kropotkin believed mankind to be the most cooperative of species, prone to helping one another and calling on other species for help. The identification of the individual with the interests of his group and these elements grew in proportion. He argued that "the lesson which man derives both from the study of Nature and his own history is the permanent presence of a *double tendency*— towards a greater development, on the one side, of *sociality*, and, on the other side, of a consequent increase of the intensity of life, which results in an increase of happiness for the *individuals*, and in progress—physical, intellectual and moral."[19] For him, the problem of the moral philosopher was to investigate the origin and development of the core elements of morality and to prove their innate character in human nature alongside other innate feelings.

A close reading of Ağaoğlu's work reveals that he turned to Darwinian teachings and pointed to nature as a source of morality, specifically, of mutual aid and altruism completely in Kropotkinian terms.[20] Moreover, Kropotkin's idea of correlation between increasing sociality and individual happiness sat well with his communitarian account of liberalism. That being said, it is hard to claim that he offered anything novel to Kropotkin's philosophy, but only utilised them in explaining the significance of altruism for social progress.

---

15   "In this struggle," Kropotkin further claimed, "no successful species in nature was competitive in the sense of being prone to attack, vanquish and kill members of its own kind." Ibid., p. 257.

16   Kropotkin, *Ethics*, p. 14.

17   Ibid., p. 14.

18   Ağaoğlu, "Tarihte Sosyal İnkişaf," p. 354; *Ben Neyim?* p. 12.

19   Ibid., pp. 19–20.

20   Ağaoğlu, "Cumhuriyet Halk Partisi Programı Etrafında"; "Özcülük ve Özgecilik"; "Terbiye Amaçlarından Birisi," *Cumhuriyet*, July 29, 1935.

9.2   The Origins of Moral Decadence Revisited

In Ağaoğlu's interpretation, moral corruption on an individual level was the source of all other moral deficiencies in society in the East. In 1919–20, he was still of the opinion that this was because the moral teachings of Islam were overlooked and that Islam was pursued for its ritualistic value alone, not as a source of moral values. He asserted that the absence of high common sentiments and collectivity in the East resulted in a shallow moral mentality, lacking both depth and openness in seeing, evaluating and exercising moral values. Individual morality could not exceed the boundaries of the issues of virginity and chastity, and even these were regarded as related only to the life of women.

Although there was a consensus in society on what was good and what was bad regarding such moral points as uprightness, hypocrisy, honesty and so forth, none of these was considered as important as the issue of the virginity and honour of women. He lamented that whereas moral lapses other than of honour in this sense could be tolerated, the issue of the honour of women was somewhat unfairly exaggerated and could not even be questioned.

Ağaoğlu traced the ill-made nature of moral relations back to the Eastern family structure:

> [O]ur family structure is not in a condition to positively influence the spirit of the child sociologically. Inequality of man and wife before the law, the veiling and the closed life it leads to…prevent the development of…the most important virtues in the child. And this situation prepares an appropriate ground for egoism to flourish.[21]

He argued that egoism was the vital factor hampering 'sociality' in the East. In *Three Civilisations*, he used the term 'individuality' as a synonym of 'egoism':

> Will the most interest-oriented aspects of individuality not excessively arise in the spirit of a child who grows up around an ignorant woman who knows that she is a slave [of her husband] and submits herself to him by her consent; who persistently observes that his/her father…is superior and dominant at home in everything; who is isolated from the world by the walls of their house…, by his/her mother's *hijab* and his/her father's *selamlık*? The source of our psychological problems should be sought in our childhood and in family influences of that period.[22]

---

21   Ibid., p. 76.

22   Ibid., p. 78.

According to Ağaoğlu, such childhood experiences naturally resulted in closed social lives:

> The [feelings] of distrust [and] strangeness rather than friendliness; solitude and selfishness and [the state of] hiding away from people rather than approaching them begins in a spirit that grows up in a persistent state of gloominess. When, in the face of this, religion and literature do not react, these manners grow roots and become the main characteristics of the spirit.[23]

Individuals who were oppressed in their private lives and deprived of the educative influences of religion and literature naturally reacted negatively to the brutal and overwhelming pressure and control of the government once they entered social life.

> How could high values with the name of 'social' be developed in individuals who live under these conditions? Everyone struggles for self-survival. Everyone acts selfishly. It is impossible to expect the appearance of private initiatives and individual bravery in such an environment, because the source of private initiative and bravery is self-confidence. And self-confidence springs from high individual aspirations and in a suitable social environment.[24]

In social life, weak individuals preferred to obey despotism and became more egoistic.

> [W]e must fight to save the individuals of the nation from the threat of egoism. To this end, the first thing to do is to respect the individual. From family organisations to the institutions in villages and municipalities, everywhere the individual must be respected, and we must open to them a platform on which to work and ensure the development of their material and spiritual powers in the field of free competition.[25]

When the Republic was promulgated, Ağaoğlu was certain that it could not coexist with the detrimental tenets of the old system of morality such as

---

23   Ibid., p. 79.
24   Ibid., p. 80.
25   Ibid., p. 81.

egoism, selfishness and the alienation of individuals from each other.[26] The first task of the Turkish citizens must be to struggle against it, to destroy the roots of egoism (*hodendişlik*) and to replace them with altruism (*gayrendişlik*),[27] inculcating in hearts the values of solidarity, dignity, mutual trust and mutual aid. The methods for these he outlined in his *In the Land of Free Men* and *What am I?*.

9.3   The Land of Free Men

In the Land of Free Men was first published as a series of instalment in *Cumhuriyet* and was later reproduced in book form at the demands and encouragement of Ağaoğlu's readers.[28] It was an allegorical novella in which he gave a practical example of the moral principles he desired society and its members to possess, applying them to an imaginary state called the Land of Free Men. He described the country from the viewpoint of a Turkish prisoner who escapes from prison in response to the call of a Turkish leader who has liberated his country from foreign invaders and the yoke of the sultan. After a long journey across the desert, the prisoner, on the way to his country, finds himself at the gates of the Land of Free Men, which seems partially to represent the ideal future of the Republic of Turkey envisaged by Ağaoğlu.[29] As Ağaoğlu puts it, the Free Men "lived and materialised the ideals of the Turkish leader". Without giving any names, by the leader of the Republic, Ağaoğlu implies, and describes, Mustafa Kemal, and introduces him as the 'prophet' of the country's citizens, the Free Men.[30]

The Free Men found their country in the aftermath of long years of wars and internecine social and political struggles.[31] They have thrown off the yoke of despotism through the experience of two hundreds years of good laws. The country is a democratic republic with three political parties positioned on the left, centre and right of the political spectrum. The citizens enjoy freedom of thought and expression, and freely criticise the government's policies.[32]

---

26   Ahmet Ağaoğlu, "Hodendişlik ve Gayrendişlik," *Hâkimiyet-i Milliye*, February 26, 1928.

27   Ağaoğlu, "Eski ve Yeni Ahlâk".

28   Ağaoğlu, *Serbest İnsanlar Ülkesinde,* p. 2.

29   In this study, Ağaoğlu perhaps speaks of himself as the prisoner, who decides to go to Turkey rather than Azerbaijan after his imprisonment in Malta for two years.

30   Ibid., p. 6.

31   Ibid., p. 12.

32   Ibid., p. 25.

Women are in the main equal to men before the law. Although they have the right to vote, they are not yet eligible to be elected as city mayors—a fact that gives rise to heated public debates.[33] It is essential for the Free Men to conduct modest lives—a sign of spiritual beauty and hygiene and the underlying factor of all the material beauties of the country, as represented by the abundance of green spaces and unostentatious but impressive buildings in urban areas.

The Free Men have recognized that the only way to banish corruption and the 'invisible chains of slavery' is to reinvigorate the moral sense and conduct of the people. They therefore initiate legislation for virtuous behaviour, with the ultimate aim of making such conduct habitual.[34] Self-awareness, truthfulness, self-abnegation and the ability to control one's will are determined as the ultimate criteria to become a citizen of the Land of Free Men. The constitution of the Free Men aims to foster these qualities in the spirit of each individual, along with such values as uprightness, courage, solidarity, industriousness and social awareness, throwing off such moral ills as cowardice, hypocrisy, sycophancy, intrusion and fraud. The fourteen articles of the constitution of the Land of Free Men read as follows:

1. Freedom relies on uprightness and courage.
2. In the Land of Free Men, fabrication of information is by no means acceptable. Those men who behave so shall be expelled from the country.
3. Hypocrisy and sycophancy are the most serious offences. Those who commit these offences shall be punished by the community.
4. Those who engage in spying (*jurnalcilik*) shall not continue to be the citizens of the Land of Free Men.
5. A citizen of the Land of Free Men shall not be a coward.
6. Those who assault or intrude on somebody shall be expelled from the country.
7. Fraud and sedition shall be penalized by the loss of citizenship.
8. Defending one's rights is a duty for all. Those who do not abide by this duty shall be expelled from the country.
9. To work is a duty for all. Those who attempt not to work shall become subject to working for the country without payment.
10. Solidarism is a duty. Those who do not abide by this duty shall be deported from the country.

---

33 Ağaoğlu might have needed to make this point to highlight the on-going disputes in the Republican Turkey over endowing women with further rights. Women's suffrage was proclaimed in Turkey in 1934.
34 Ibid., p. 4.

11. Public servants shall be appointed solely according to experience and merit.

12. Each citizen is responsible for making sure that public servants are accountable.

13. Each civil servant and each statesman is responsible for declaring to the citizens what they do and their incomes. Those who do not comply with this duty shall be penalised by a serious sentence and be eventually expelled from the country.

14. It is a duty for each citizen to be aware of the articles set out above.[35]

The rigid nature of these laws arises from the need to seed liberty in a culture that had long lacked it. "Liberty is a problem of culture,"[36] Ağaoğlu contended, and in transforming that culture one must look into the heart of man, and there alone. Because

> [i]t is not easy to instil freedom into places which have long been ruled and oppressed by despotism. In fact, the place wherein despotism is in charge is nowhere but the spirit and heart of the individual. Despotism settles and flourishes there...sometimes you deem it to have collapsed, and in practice its visible marks disappear. But in reality it still exists everywhere and in everybody. It is observed that those who appeal strongly for freedom cannot endure the freedom of their neighbours... because essentially despotism still rules in their spirits and hearts, it has not yet been detached... Eventually, as despotism, which was once observed in the acts of one (ruler), displays its marks in the deeds of everyone, so-called liberty turns into anarchy. In the end, since it is not possible for a society to long remain under these circumstances, the need to limit the acts of its people arises in the name of liberty. Therefore, those societies which are unable to detach themselves from the roots and marks of despotism become condemned to oscillating between anarchy and [despotism], which is the most disastrous form of uncertainty.[37]

He urged that the constitution of the Land of the Free Men is a guide for people to protect themselves from this uncertainty. Its aim is to overthrow the rule of despotism from their spirits and hearts, and replace it with liberty—a product of human consciousness.

---

35   Ibid., pp. 7–8.
36   Ibid., p. 14.
37   Ibid., p. 14.

In a similar vein to Durkheim, who spoke of the cult of the individual in modern societies, Ağaoğlu argues in the Land of the Free Men that human was a sacred being, 'the consciousness of universe'.[38] The problem was to generate the required circumstances in which individuals could practice their liberty. In his view, the means to achieve this is that, from their early youth, they ought to be socialized into high values, "they ought to be accustomed to behaving themselves, to reasoning and to thinking" through education and practice, through precedents and object lessons.[39] All of these qualities came to have implications for the formation of liberty within the self.

He wrote that protecting and perpetuating liberty was, however, as difficult as achieving it.[40] Whereas slavery was just to submit oneself to the will of another, liberty entailed the assumption of responsibility toward the wellbeing of fellow citizens as well as oneself. This was where Ağaoğlu turned to Durkheim again arguing that citizenship was "a network in which people are like intertwined circles; an illness affecting one of the circles immediately affects other [citizens], renders them...uncomfortable, and as long as that illness exists" the happiness and peace of society was threatened, so an infallible network of relations must be created in society to protect individuals from all types of oppression and to eradicate the remnants of despotism.[41] Individual action must be socially checked. The resistance of society must confront and eliminate any potential bad behaviour and habits.[42] To create such a resistance, individuals must have social awareness and altruistic characters (seciye).

As such, Ağaoğlu drew a close correlation between altruism and liberty, and between their opposites, egoism and slavery. A society could be free, he wrote, insofar as it was composed of altruistic men, because only in those societies could social control over bad habits and conduct be made possible.[43] In egoistic societies, on the other hand, wherein individuals were isolated from each other because of their self-interestedness, leading to the dissolution of social ties, there would be no permanent liberty.[44]

The free people of his imaginary country hence disliked egoism the most, and regarded instilling altruism in individuals as the foremost duty of all, for

---

38   Ibid., p. 10.
39   Ibid., p. 46.
40   Ibid., p. 53.
41   Ibid., p. 30.
42   Ibid., p. 52.
43   Ibid., p. 51.
44   Ibid., p. 52.

the happiness of both individuals and society.[45] "A newborn human is neither good nor bad. What makes him good or bad is society. Social education and the thoughts, sentiments and customs that society instils in the child [determine his character]."[46] The free people, therefore, believed that the only means of supporting altruism so that it could prevail over egoism was to teach the individual to control his will in his familial and school education, and more importantly by creating an intellectual and moral ambiance through the works of public moral educators.

Just as in *Three Civilisations,* Ağaoğlu assigned special roles to intellectuals in inculcating 'high sentiments' into individuals, because they were 'the mirror and living conscience of society' which was transformed by their works, they must not fall short of stressing altruism and common values in their works and speeches.[47] It was the intellectual and literary currents created by the intellectuals that had vitalized the static qualities of a nationality—common history, common race and common interests—and transformed it into a nation.[48] In a similar vein, the intellectuals could entice the spirit of the individual member of the nation and inculcate in it the high sentiments of mutual aid, solidarity and altruism—hence liberty.

This argument indeed ran through Ağaoğlu's writings. In his early work, he was writing of the importance of the teachings Islamic scholar would provide. In his later work, he turned to secular intellectuals and their work as an instrument for public moralisation.

In 1928, he had written that since Peter the Great was aware of this, for example, he had begun his reforms in Russia by establishing an academy. "Observing European institutions for a long time, Peter discovered that Russia, where social life was very similar to that of the [East] at the time, could not be elevated to the level of Europe unless its very roots and essence were healed and reformed."[49] He therefore attempted to reconstruct the entire society and its institutions. Peter had understood that a nation and a country were just patterns, which remained inert unless enlivened by ideas and sentiments.[50] That was why he had invited European (particularly German) professors to his new universities. He had known that "these institutions were the mind and

---

45   Ibid., p. 50.
46   Ibid., p. 60.
47   Ibid., pp. 67–68.
48   Ibid., p. 69.
49   Ağaoğlu, *Üç Medeniyet,* Ibid., p. 104.
50   Ibid., p. 105.

heart of a society."[51] His attempts had borne fruit with the emergence in a few generations in Russia of great scholars and of such men of letters as Pushkin and Lermontov. With the developments in Russian language and literature and a further flow of Western ideas to Russia, succeeding generations had seen the appearance of Turgenev, Dostoyevsky and Tolstoy.

For the same purposes, Ağaoğlu inserted in Land of Free Men a special group, known as the *pirs* (elders), who were responsible for public moral education. These people, who had deep knowledge of the history, politics and laws of the country, would journey all over the country and deliver speeches wherever they went as public moralists. It was the *pirs* who introduced the Free Men and their laws and moral rules to visitors.

The authority of law was the major weapon Ağaoğlu used to determine the boundaries of individual conduct to fight against the remnants of despotism in each individual heart. In the Land of Free Men, 'true' mores and conduct were imposed from above and everyone was obliged to abide by the laws. This is the point at which Ağaoğlu differed from Kropotkin, whose morality would assume a voluntary and freely chosen character without obligation or imposition from above. Kadıoğlu asserts that Ağaoğlu's descriptions of "duty-oriented, moral, selfless individuals led by *pirs*" indicate that the Land of the Free Men was a "dystopia where moral despotism reigns."[52] According to her, the emphasis given by Ağaoğlu to the role of intellectuals and *pirs* and to altruism shows that his "individualism carried both elitist and solidarist motifs."[53] Although there is no doubt that all along, Ağaoğlu assigned a special role and attached particular importance to intellectuals, which implies his intellectualism, a certain ambiguity arises from his concurrent emphasis on transformation, beginning with individual morality, democracy and, as demonstrated in his discussions with the *Kadro* movement, his antagonism in his later work towards an avant-garde group taking control of political and economic activity, inviting the question of whether or not he was an elitist.

Written to show what virtuous citizens would be like, *In the Land of Free Men* reveals that in the thought of the Ağaoğlu of 1930, the liberty and rule of the people required the perfection of the individual. This implies adjusting their behaviour to the republican values which require the individual to behave well, to reason, to think and to be an altruistic citizen, that is, to be a communitarian. Given this, Ağaoğlu's thoughts seem to display some parallels with Rousseau's paradox that "the voluntary acts require an initial educative authority,

---

51   Ibid., p. 105.

52   Kadıoğlu, "Citizenship and Individuation in Turkey," p. 208.

53   Ibid., p. 208.

[illustrated] when he had the pupil Emile say to his tutor, 'I have decided to be what you made me'."[54] As demonstrated above, the 'enlightened' (self-reasoning and thinking) Free Men likewise decide to be what the state and society want them to be.

9.4   The Divided Self

Like most nineteenth-century Francophone sociologists who drew on Rousseau's social thought,[55] Ağaoğlu believed that ending political, cultural and economic crises was premised on quelling the problems emanating from the depths of the individual. In his swansong *What am I?* he brought up the theme of the duplicitous self to argue in more detail how the individual's guided self-overcoming could take place in the East. Ağaoğlu's understanding of the duplicitous self led many later Turkish commentators to argue that his last work exhibited strong Bergsonian motifs, marking the impact of the French philosopher on Ağaoğlu's later thought. In a recent article on Bergsonism and conservative republicanism in Turkey, for example, Ağaoğlu is described as a republican-conservative and a follower of Bergson.[56] However, a close reading of Ağaoğlu's work shows how hard it is to claim that he drew on Bergson's work in his writings to the extent that he became a Bergsonian. Still, it was true that Ağaoğlu had close correspondence with the Bergsonians in Turkey.[57]

In the late 1930s Ağaoğlu stated that he sympathetically appreciated some of the philosophical perspectives brought by Henri Bergson.[58] He wrote this in his brief review of Mustafa Şekib Tunç's translation of Bergson's *L'évolution créatrice*.[59] But it is hardly possible to say that Ağaoğlu drew on the philosophy of Bergson in his work. Indeed, in his later writings, particularly in *İnsan* and *Kültür Haftası*, he continued to invoke Durkheimian theories of the historical development of societies from simple to complex structures, the division of

---

54   Cladis, *Communitarian Defence of Liberalism*, p. 36.

55   Caroline Armenteros, "Revolutionary Violence and the End of History: The Divided Self in Francophone Thought, 1762–1914," in *Historicising the French Revolution*, ed. C.Armenteros, T.Blanning, I.DiVanna, D.Dodds, Newcastle-upon-Tyne: Cambridge Scholars Publishing, 2008, pp. 2–39.

56   Nazmi İrem, "Turkish Conservative Modernism," p. 88.

57   İrem, "Turkish Conservative Modernism," pp. 92–95.

58   Ahmet Ağaoğlu, "Yaratıcı Tekamül," *Kültür Haftası*, No. 3, January 29, 1936.

59   Ibid.

social labour and the interdependence of individuals.[60] This means that Ağaoğlu did not depart from his positivist liberalism in his later work. But could it also mean that in the eclectic character of his intellectual work he gave place to the teachings of both Bergson and Durkheim? Otherwise put, to what degree did Ağaoğlu's sympathy for Bergson's spiritualist teachings allow Bergsonian philosophy to challenge the consistency of his thought?

We find the answer to these questions by comparing Ağaoğlu's brief review of Tunç's translation of *L'évolution créatrice* with his later writings. In the review, Ağaoğlu tells the reader that he was inspired by Tunç's introductory notes to Bergson's work. It is important to underscore here that when he wrote the review Ağaoğlu had not read *L'évolution créatrice* and we do not know if he read it later. He relied instead mostly on Tunç's introduction to Bergson's work. We learn this when Ağaoğlu states that for a better understanding of Bergson's philosophy he would have to read the entire book.[61] What then did Ağaoğlu capture from Bergson's thought?

According to Ağaoğlu, the most important two contributions of Bergson to philosophical thought were his theories on knowledge and epistemology, and those on the concept of the self. He wrote that Bergson introduced a new type of knowledge other than intellectually acquired knowledge of science. This new type of knowledge was non-conceptual and dealt with the inner world, while the intellect was concerned with the outer world. Bergson's belief in the existence of two selves, the outer and the inner, seemed to attract Ağaoğlu's interest the most. He summarized what he read in Tunç's introduction as follows: The outer self is "the self of intellect, science, knowledge, mind and logic."[62] On this side of the self, there is no freedom but cause and determinism. The inner self is composed of the will. "The will is in a perpetual state of creation under the outer self." It is a product of the memory's challenging of circumstances.[63] The unconscious element of the creative force is the will. It is

---

60   Ağaoğlu, "Tarihte Sosyal İnkişaf"; "Basitten Mürekkebe, Şekilsizlikten Şekilleşmeye Doğru".

61   Ağaoğlu, "Yaratıcı Tekâmül".

62   Ibid.

63   Bergson wrote the following with regards to the outer and inner stratums of individual behaviour: "When our most trustworthy friends agree in advising us to take some important step, the sentiments which they utter with so much insistence lodge on the surface of our ego and there get solidified.... Little by little they will form a thick crust which will cover up our own sentiments; we shall believe that we are acting freely, and it is only looking back to the past, later on, that we shall see how much we were mistaken. But then, at the moment when the act is going to be performed, *something* may revolt against it"; Henri Bergson, *Time and Free Will*, Auth. Trans. F.L. Pogson, London: George Allen and Unwin, Ltd., 1950, p. 169.

free and dependent only on itself, and only men of character can act using their will.[64]

Ağaoğlu's brief review of the Turkish translation of the book neglected various theories of Bergson that receive mention in the book, such as the problems that surround the theory of evolution and the problem of the relationship between mind and body. Although Ağaoğlu did use the terms 'free action', 'creation' and 'will' in some of his earlier and later writings, there is no evidence that he borrowed these from Bergson, as there is reason to doubt whether he read any of the French philosopher's works. Nowhere in Ağaoğlu's writings have I been able to find direct references to Bergson's works. However, to reiterate, it is apparent that the dualism or dividedness of the self captured Ağaoğlu's interest. He used this in his writings a number of times after reading Tunç's introduction, the first being when he began to write his memoirs in January 1936, a few weeks after the publication of his review of Bergson's book. As noted in Chapter 2, he presented his life as having been sandwiched between two worlds, East and West.[65] Recalling the day he left his hometown of Susha for his education in St. Petersburg, for example, he wrote in a rather spiritual tone:

> I was to lose the wholeness with which history and nature had endowed me. But I was not to acquire a new wholeness. I was to become a half-way patched up thing. This patched-up quality is an endless drama. It is an inner drama, it is a spiritual tragedy. At no time now do I feel complete and whole. And you know, it is a torment of Hell to feel half-patched. I enjoy both European and Eastern music, but at the same time I see and I feel that I do not experience the first as completely and fully as a European, nor the second like an Easterner.[66]

The second was in September 1936, when he set out to publish his series of instalments under the title "What am I?"[67] The topic of these instalments was his observations on the relationship between the inner and outer selves of an Eastern individual. It is to my contention that Bergson's influence on Ağaoğlu was limited to this. Ağaoğlu did not read Bergson's works with the care needed

---

64   Ağaoğlu, "Yaratıcı Tekâmül".
65   For further information, see Chapter 2.
66   Ağaoğlu, "Altmış Yedi Yıl Sonra," 1936, p. 89, trans. Shissler, *Between Two Empires*, p. 44.
67   Ahmet Ağaoğlu, "Ben Neyim?" *Cumhuriyet*, September 5, 1936. After six instalments Ağaoğlu ceased publishing the instalments for an unknown reason. In January 1939, he continued to publish the remaining instalments.

to pen essays that absorbed the depths of Bergsonian philosophy. *What am I?* which was published in book form posthumously in 1939, was no exception, because Ağaoğlu's portrayal of the inner and outer selves was remarkably different from that of Bergson.

His inner and outer selves did not refer to a distinction between heart and mind, as in Bergson. Instead, Ağaoğlu's inner self stood for the realm of thoughts and sentiments, while the outer self represented the realm of his action. Moreover, speaking of the divided and ill-made nature of the Eastern individual, Ağaoğlu preferred to turn to Kropotkin and Durkheim's moral teachings, rather than those of Bergson, repeating (and to a certain extent crystallising) most of his earlier arguments. He never abandoned his determinist explanation of history, whereas Bergson was a critic of determinism and its psychology.

For students of Turkish intellectual history, *What am I?* is nevertheless a work of great importance, as it is one of the first representative texts displaying the early Republican intellectuals' turning to the concept of the self. At the outset of the book, Ağaoğlu wrote:

> Recently, a bizarre and weird need has arisen in me: observing myself. Seeing myself as I am and displaying myself as I see. I have no doubt that those who read these lines will ridicule me and think: 'What kind of a man is this? He has come to the end of his life. He still does not know himself.' Yes, I admit that I do not know myself. Do you know yourself? Hence I have begun learning about myself and I assure you that it is not a very smooth or particularly pleasant thing. My method was very simple: By leaving my inner and outer selves on their own, I juxtaposed them, and all I had to do was to note down what I have seen and heard...[68]

What he saw were two contrasting and completely different beings. The inner self appeared in the realms of theory, expression and thoughts rather than deeds. When it came to action and deeds, the outer self took control. The individual was thus divided into two selves that appeared separately in the realms of contemplation and deeds. The way the individual conceived things and the way he acted, therefore, displayed great discrepancies in the East.

The source of all conflicts between the inner and outer selves, according to Ağaoğlu, was egoism. The most apparent characteristic of the outer self was his selfish desire to put his interests above everything, which, as Ağaoğlu had previously argued and now did again, was the major failing from which all other

---

68   Ağaoğlu, *Ben Neyim?*, p. 1.

conflicts sprang. The inner self was humanist and self-sacrificing, but not strong enough to overcome the outer self. In his account, the dichotomy between the outer and inner selves was but a dichotomy of egoism and altruism.[69] While the outer self was an untrustworthy, inconsistent and erratic being, the inner self was the seat of true mores and morality. It was unfortunate that the outer self, by controlling the deeds, represented the outward character of the Eastern individual.

As the outer self's control of the deeds and acts of the Eastern individual demonstrates, egoism was triumphant over altruism in the East.[70] This led Ağaoğlu to trace its reasons and to conclude that both altruism and egoism were innate in human nature. He claimed in a Kropotkinian manner that they were in fact biological phenomena: "the universe of living things has been dependent upon [the sentiments of altruism and egoism]."[71] But whereas altruism or egoism were only intrinsic in animals, men could transfer their altruistic instincts into the realm of consciousness and make them habitual.[72]

The key to overcoming the dichotomy between two sentiments was to strengthen the will and rehabilitate the outer self.[73] The weakness of the will was the main cause of the strength of the outer self. Since the individual was too weak to strengthen his will alone, Ağaoğlu paradoxically asserted that the suppression of the outer self would allow the inner self to hold sway over the outer self. This was not unprecedented. He argued that in England society succeeded in helping to strengthen the inner selves of individuals as opposed to their outer selves, thanks to people's active social life and to the strength of public opinion. These arose in turn from their political and economic liberties and the works of their writers, poets, thinkers and moralists, which nurtured English souls and minds. In the individuals of such a society, he wrote, "[the egoism] of the outer self naturally withers away, [while] the inner self is stimulated; the outer self remains silent, while the inner self makes decisions."[74]

Hence the individual will for Ağaoğlu, like the Durkheimian will, was not isolated from social influence, but instead was initially created within society, which demanded its loyalty to the public good (as we have seen in *In the Land of Free Men*) in return. His notion of will was in permanent interaction with the social milieu and this interaction was not one-way. Given that Ağaoğlu's individual was a social being, his will was automatically shaped by society.

---

69   Ibid., p. 3.
70   Ibid., p. 4.
71   Ibid., p. 4.
72   Ibid., p. 5.
73   Ibid., p. 19.
74   Ibid., p. 20.

But individuals, especially those of strong character (will), in turn challenged social circumstances and helped society to progress. As he often underlined, this was illustrated in the history of both the West and the East: the struggles of all those Western individuals from Socrates to Jeanne d'Arc and such Eastern individuals as Mustafa Kemal were all exemplars of the struggle of the individual will against the status quo, which required self-sacrifice and therefore a strong character.[75]

In parallel to this, in his series of articles in 1935 and 1936, comparing and contrasting the Western and the Eastern moral systems, Ağaoğlu contended that one of the demarcation lines between Eastern and Western civilisations was the static character of the East.[76] In his account, the backwardness of the Eastern nations resulted from their unresponsiveness to change, while the Western nations had always challenged their circumstances. The Western individual's struggle with circumstances engendered social conflicts. The development of the high sentiments of mutual aid, the respect for human dignity[77] and religion's retreat to the realm of spirituality ever since the Treaty of Westphalia[78] were all consequences of social conflicts. However, in the East the psychological imprint of religious conformity had prevented individuals from opening up.[79] That was why, he argued, in challenging the circumstances in the East, the Turkish Revolutionaries identified 'science and experience' as the only sources of reference in the conduct of social life through the programme of the Republican People's Party in 1923.[80]

In his late 1930s writings, Ağaoğlu continued to emphasize that the strength of the ideals intellectuals created, the power of these ideals in affecting society and, when necessary, the self-sacrifices of the intellectuals in defending their ideals at the expense of their personal interests could be the yardsticks of

---

75   In a similar vein, early Durkheim had believed that "communitarians were correct in
      arguing that the 'powerful personalities' who transform society do not rise above their
      social milieu, escaping history. Gathering the ideas and sentiments that remain tact and
      dormant in society, focusing these,' they are able to add something new to society." He
      also wrote: "once the will emerges, it reacts in turn on all those phenomena that come to
      it from outside and that are the common inheritance of society; it makes them its own,"
      Cladis, *Communitarian*, p. 36.
76   Ahmet Ağaoğlu, "Doğu ve Batı," *Cumhuriyet*, September 3, 1935; "Bir Kültürden Ötekine,"
      Kültür Haftası, No. 2, January 22, 1936.
77   Ahmet Ağaoğlu, "Doğu ve Batı," *Cumhuriyet*, August 16, 1935.
78   Ahmet Ağaoğlu, "Doğu ve Batı," *Cumhuriyet*, September 30, 1935.
79   Ibid.
80   Ibid.

whether or not they could fulfil their duties successfully.[81] In reference to Tarde's theory of imitation, he called for a moral mobilisation. Because each individual, particularly in youth, had the potential of imitating people around him or her, he wrote, those people who could be role models, such as political leaders, administrators, parents, teachers and most importantly intellectuals, must act cautiously, considering their potential influence over other people.[82] He believed that only by making individual life more intense could the faculties of altruism and mutual aid be developed. And following Kropotkon, he argued that a more intense life meant sociality, i.e. the individual's socialisation (*cemaatleşme*).

The ultimate objective of the Republic must therefore be to socialise individuals into values. What gave dynamism to static power was their strong character. In order to develop character, individuals should be imbued with the spirit of communitarianism.

> We have to prepare such an education system that alongside ensuring the maximum opening up of everybody's individual skills, it should instil the belief that there is no individual happiness beyond the happiness of society. The East is individualist [*ferdiyetçi*] in the pejorative sense of the word. The path…it has followed is egoism.[83]

In his view, a new Western spirit could be inculcated into Turkish hearts only by going to the very roots of the Western civilisation.[84] Therefore, like Ülken and other humanists of the time,[85] he suggested the introduction of Greco-Roman culture into school curriculums and the translation of Ancient Greek and Latin works into Turkish, because the modern Western culture was a continuation of these cultures.[86] This indeed occurred eventually, and an official humanist project was launched when Greek and Latin were made compulsory course modules and the works of Ancient Greek and Roman writers were taught at schools.[87]

---

81   Ağaoğlu, "Intellectuel ve Ödevleri," *Cumhuriyet*, January 12, 1936; "Entellektüellerin Borçları," *Cumhuriyet*, February 10, 1936.
82   Ahmet Ağaoğlu, "Genç Nesli Yetistirmek," *Cumhuriyet*, April 8, 1935.
83   Ahmet Ağaoğlu, "Terbiye Amaçlarından Bir Tanesi," *Cumhuriyet*, January 29, 1935.
84   Ahmet Ağaoğlu, "Münevver Zümre Meselesi," *Cumhuriyet*, January 15, 1935.
85   Peyami Safa, *Türk İnkılabına Bakışlar*, pp. 116–132.
86   Ibid.
87   Kader Konuk, *East West Mimesis: Auerbach in Turkey*, Stanford: Stanford University Press, 2010; Güneş A. Serezli, *Turkish Humanism Project in the Early Republican Period*, Unpublished Master's Dissertation, Middle East Technical University, 2006.

As noted in Chapter 7, Ağaoğlu had written that the state's attempts to ameliorate individual life, as in France, were the epitome of a praiseworthy 'individualist society' where the state assumed social services and responsibilities
with a budget of a few billion francs.[88] This earlier usage of individualism in its
positive sense was deeply related to his communitarian understanding of
morality. Ağaoğlu wrote:

> One of the features that distinguish East from West is that the East is
> individualist and anarchic, and in contrast, the West is communitarian
> and ordered. At first sight...this fact could be interpreted the other way
> around, because essentially the long-lasting despotism in the East, as
> we say over and over again, destroyed and eradicated the individual.
> However, in the West...freedom led to the opening up and empowerment
> of the individual. On the other hand...the East carries a mentality obedi-
> ent to the past and seeking [its] ideals in...traditions. The West, by con-
> trast, enjoys criticism; does not overvalue...traditions and constitutes its
> ideals for the future. All these may seem to explain the opposite of what
> we have propounded today. It may seem that the East is communitarian
> and ordered and that the West is individualist and anarchic. But it is not
> so... When a conflict arises between the interests of the individual and
> those of the community, the individual [in the East] gives priority to his
> [own] interests and does not refrain from sacrificing traditions... Here,
> the individual is...egoist, alien to the feeling of self-sacrifice for society.
> He is inclined to sacrifice a big long-term interest for a small short-term
> interest... That's why individuals in the East pursue day-to-day lives and
> chase after minute, daily interests. They fear and abstain from works that
> require patience, tolerance, industriousness and digging in.[89]

Ağaoğlu asserted that individuals in the West, by contrast, had found the
means to reconcile and fuse their private interests with those of society. Unlike
Eastern individuals, they preferred to sacrifice their small short-term interests
for the greater long-term interests of society. Thanks to their social, political
and economic freedoms, social order and regulation became habitual for
them. The more they opened up, the more communitarian [cemiyetçi] they
became; and the more communitarian they became, the more they embraced
the state in the belief that it was what held society together.[90]

88   Ağaoğlu, "Özcülük ve Özgecilik (Egoisme ve Altruisme)".
89   Ahmet Ağaoğlu, "Doğu ve Batı," *Cumhuriyet,* September 10, 1935.
90   Ibid.

Although there were numerous self-contradictions in Ağaoğlu's thought, that Ağaoğlu used the word 'individualism' with diametrically opposite meanings in his writings was no contradiction. The problem of how Ağaoğlu was simultaneously for and against individualism is resolved when we realize that he regarded individualism as synonymous with egoism so far as morality was concerned, yet synonymous with the state's protection of the basic rights of the individual in the political and economic spheres. Even when Ağaoğlu argued for the protection of individual rights, he had in mind that their basic function, that of protecting and maintaining the collectivity, was ensured. Given that his ultimate aim in defending individual rights and the reform of the self was not the happiness of the individual itself, but the perpetuation and happiness of society and social order, we can safely conclude that Ağaoğlu's individualism, in its positive usage, was the logical completion of his communitarian defence of liberalism.

CHAPTER 10

Conclusion: The Road to Liberty?

The liberalism of Ağaoğlu diverged from that of many liberals, in keeping with the long intellectual and political journey he went through in Western Europe and the Near East. His early education in secular Russian schools and his contact with Russian *Narodniks* led to his abrupt alienation from his roots (religious and familial) and to a growing admiration for Western civilisation in his youth. It was perhaps his personal experiences and his reading of Western history which led him to argue later that the Near East required a revolution (rather than gradual reform) led by heroic individuals to bring about a clean break with the past.

When he went to France for his education and embarked upon his writing career, Ağaoğlu's views of the West were mixed. He thought that the Europeans were too prejudiced against the East, in particular against the Muslim world and Islam. His early writings indicate that his main motivations in writing were to break the barriers of Western prejudice against the Muslims and to denounce the negative effects of European imperialism in the Near East. Also, he sought the means for the self-empowerment of Islamic nations. For the first time in the early 1890s, he propounded that the most pressing problem of the East was the fullest elevation of the intellectual and spiritual faculties of the individual, an idea that had previously been propounded by his teacher Ernest Renan in the context of nineteenth-century France. The Ağaoğlu of the 1890s believed that the question of the individual in the East could be resolved by improving the abased role of women in society.

Ağaoğlu felt sandwiched between his perceptions of two different aspects of the West, that which he admired because of its achievements and that which he detested because of its aggressive and ignorant attitude toward the East. The latter led to his further embracing the religious and nationalist identities as vehicles of the collective struggle for rights to match the power of the Russian Empire and the Western powers. In the late Tsarist Russian and late Ottoman imperial contexts, he wrote in favour of the social awareness and collective rights of Russian Muslims and Ottoman Turks, seeing Pan-Islamism and nationalism as liberating components. It was in this period that he began to advocate communitarian values against egoistic individualism.

In the early Turkish Republican context, Ağaoğlu propounded his communitarian defence of liberalism most clearly. His writings of the time explicitly revealed his idea that Turkish society must absorb all material and moral features

© KONINKLIJKE BRILL NV, LEIDEN, 2015 | DOI 10.1163/9789004297364_011

of the West, which he identified as a civilisation of liberal and communitarian societies. In his view, the division of labour and functional differentiation, which Durkheim later put into a theoretical framework, were the key to the triumph of the liberal mentality in the West. He appeared to capture the special type of individualism accentuated in Durkheim's work. But he did not accord the individual the autonomy accorded in the French writer's works. He was aware that the division of labour and functional differentiation granted the individual a sacred role in society, which gave rise to further respect for each individual and collectivity. But his bureaucratic liberal interpretation suggested enforced liberalism, using laws as a moral weapon.

As such, he identified the state as an ethical idea embodying the collective aspirations of society. He drew the conclusion that the state and patriotic and altruistic intellectuals must guide individuals towards moral development and the satisfaction of higher needs without fearing, as did many liberals, the spread of conformism in society. Like other contemporary Kemalists, he therefore believed that Turkish society needed a set of moral and political guiding principles, which he laid out in *In the Land of Free Men*.

The liberalism of Ağaoğlu assigned responsibilities to the individual, and not merely individual responsibilities, thus linking each individual to others by ties of caring, empathy and altruism. For him, freedom ultimately consisted in individuals acting morally. However, he took this idea to an extreme when his utopian state forced 'the free men' to act so and when he practically demanded the perfection of the individual. He wanted the citizens of the Republic to obey all the moral requirements for social happiness (or the republican principles guiding those citizens) to become good and obedient (Turkish) followers of 'the religion of republic'. He wanted a perfect system that was based on the assumption of the existence of equal and perfect citizens, yet he believed that this system would concurrently enable the elevation of individuals and their perfection.

He saw no contradiction in suggesting at one and the same time further liberty, the fullest perfection of individual manners and an aversion to tolerance, as seen in the rigid laws forming the constitution of his utopian country. Perhaps he gave too much credit to the sentiment of altruism for selfless individuals to give rise to social conflicts and a version of bureaucratic liberalism to settle them. Yet, he appeared not to think that social instability could stem from the lack of a culture of tolerance (and in certain cases respect) for imperfection. This is the underlying idea of this book which argues that his liberalism was inherently an authoritarian defense of liberalism wherein legality and morality assumed not a voluntary and freely chosen character but there were apparent elements of obligation or imposition from above, as we see in *In the Land of Free Men*.

Moreover, Ağaoğlu's conception of true individualism was fundamentally communitarian; it was the logical completion of his communitarian views. At this point one may well ask why his individualism is said to be the completion of his communitarianism, but not the other way round. The answer to this question lies in his assertion that "there is no happiness of the individual beyond the happiness of society." He saw the individual as the essential component of the apparatus of social progress, which was why the state must be responsible for paving the way for the individual to act. For example, he wanted the emancipation of women and their equality with men not for their happiness and elevation *per se*, but primarily for their work as conscious mothers and wives. In this respect, we can argue that his liberalism was a perfectionist account that suggested the collective salvation of society by means of the acts of 'free individuals'. Moreover, to call Ağaoğlu one of the early representatives of feminism would be to exaggerate somewhat.

If we need to position Ağaoğlu in the intellectual tradition of liberalism, his name will perhaps sit best with those of anti-imperialist non-European liberals on the one hand and of many French and other Continental writers on the other: the Encyclopaedists, Rousseau, the Doctrinaires and undoubtedly Durkheim. Although it has previously been mentioned that Ağaoğlu's liberal thought was more akin to 'Continental European liberalism', we have attempted in this study to demonstrate the impact of Durkheim on his writings. That being said, Ağaoğlu's liberalism was more than Durkheim's teachings, despite the central influences of the latter. It would not be false to see the individualist and communitarian work of Durkheim as opposed to various individualist ideas of Anglophone writers. When Hayek wrote in the mid-1940s that there were two individualisms, one true and the other false,[1] what he argued was diametrically opposite to what Durkheim had perceived as true and false individualisms.[2] According to Durkheim, true individualism was "the individualism of Kant and Rousseau, that of the *spiritualistes*, that which the Declaration of the Rights of Man sought, more or less successfully, to translate into a formulae, that which is currently taught in our schools and which has become the basis of our moral catechism." By contrast, Hayek claimed that the individualism of this tradition was pseudo-individualism, a product of Cartesian rationalism which regarded the individual as a highly rational and intelligent being. For Hayek, it regarded the individual man as the starting point and supposed him to form societies by the union of his particular will with another in a formal

---

1 F.A. Hayek, *Individualism and Economic Order,* Chicago: The University of Chicago Press, 1948, p. 2.
2 Émile Durkheim, "L'individualisme et les intellectuels".

contract. It was a design theory which drew the conclusion that "social processes can be made to serve human ends only if they are subjected to the control of individual human reason."[3]

Indeed, Ağaoğlu's liberal project was a design theory attributing a strong role to human reason, but at the same time expecting it to succumb to the principles of the collective good. For example, the protagonist of *In the Land of Free Men* decides, after much reasoning, that he should comply unconditionally with the rules, laws and principles set and taught by the intellectuals of the country and that he should develop a strong will to do so. In other words, he rather paradoxically decides to become what the intellectuals and statesmen of the country want him to be.

On his way back to his country, when the protagonist finds himself at a crossroads, he follows the arrow to the left, which leads him to 'the road to liberty' and eventually to the Land of Free Men. Ağaoğlu's road to liberty embodied strong elements of positive liberty, but also faith in liberty through compulsion and in the idea of following a leader wholeheartedly. In these specific terms, he did not diverge much from most bureaucratic liberals showing similarities with the ideas of German and Russian liberals, though, as far as I could trace, not by means of direct intellectual exchanges.

It would require a new and meticulous study to uncover the full legacy of Ağaoğlu's thought in contemporary Turkey. Nonetheless, it must be mentioned here that his children Süreyya and Samet and his friends from the Monday Evening Group took part in, or supported, the liberal organisation *Hür Fikirleri Yayma Cemiyeti* (The Society for the Dissemination of Free Ideas, 1947), which was established in 1947 in the same oval room where Ağaoğlu had held the Monday Evening meetings in the 1930s. This organisation was the Turkish branch of the Liberal International and firmly supported the Democratic Party. The latter was established in 1946 by making use of a great deal of the organisation of the Free Party, especially in Western Anatolia. Samet became one of the leading figures of the Democratic Party, while Celal Bayar, whose economic views Ağaoğlu shared in the 1930s, was one of its founding leaders.

I shall conclude by underlining that Ağaoğlu's liberal thought wanted to instigate, nurture and complete a revolution. According to him, the Kemalist Revolution was the Eastern counterpart of the French Revolution, which was a milestone in the emergence of the modern liberal societies of the West. Yet he hardly mentioned in his writings the social instability and the cycle of revolutions that had taken place in nineteenth-century France, the politics of which he admired. Neither did he seem to be aware of the fact that the science of

---

3 Hayek, *Individualism and Economic Order*, p. 6.

society in France, which he utilised in his later work, was invented, if I may simplify a little, to end the French Revolution of 1789.

The Republic of Turkey has likewise seen a cycle of coups d'état and military interventions in politics in virtually every decade of the second half of the twentieth century. For the Kemalists, political instability stemmed from the fact that Kemal Atatürk's sudden death left the Revolution incomplete, whereas most contemporary liberal-minded writers and thinkers in Turkey, the majority of whom are now the conveyers of Hayekian or Popperist ideas, put the blame on the Kemalists' attempts at social engineering and the design theories of their doctrinaires, including Ahmet Ağaoğlu. The recent attempts of the Justice and Development Party (JDP) to direct the nation toward a more conservation direction can be seen as a proof of how design theories have well been instilled into the mind-sets of Islamist political groups in Turkey as well. This turn in the JDP has been a testament to the predicament of democracy in Turkey in the absence of loyalty and respect for basic liberal rights. Future political, social and economic developments, along with further studies of liberalisms in Turkey, will perhaps show us whether revolutionary and anti-revolutionary Turkish liberalisms, which follow different roads to liberty, can indeed end the revolution and the cycle of military interventions and introduce a full-fledged democracy imbued with liberal values in the twenty-first century.

Bibliography

A. Archives
Başbakanlık Osmanlı Arşivi, Istanbul (BOA)
Başbakanlık Cumhuriyet Arşivi, Ankara (CA)
Kadın Eserleri Kütüphanesi ve Bilgi Merkezi, Istanbul (KEKBM)
Rossijskij Gosudarstvennyj Arkhiv Social'no-Politicheskoj Istorii, Moscow (RGASPI)
The National Archives, London (TNA)

B. Unpublished Materials
Ağaoğlu Ə. Tərcümeyi-hali-acizanəm. AMEA-nın M.Füzuli adına Əlyazmalar İnstitutu, f.21.

C. Interviews
Interview with Nilüfer Gürsoy (daughter of Celal Bayar), November 24, 2014.
Interview with Tektas Ağaoğlu (grandson of Ahmet Ağaoğlu), November 27, 2014.

D. Ahmet Ağaoğlu's Works

Books
Ağaoğlu, Ahmet, *İslam va Akhund*, Baku, 1904.
———, *Hukuk-i Esasiye*, Ankara: n.p., 1926.
———, *Üç Medeniyet*, Ankara: Türk Ocakları Merkez Heyeti Matbaası, 1928.
———, *İngiltere ve Hindistan*, Istanbul: Cumhuriyet Matbaası, 1929.
———, *Serbest İnsanlar Ülkesinde*, Istanbul: Sanayii Nefise Matbaası, 1930.
———, *Hukuk Tarihi*, Istanbul: Kurtuluş Matbaası, 1931–1932.
———, *Devlet ve Fert*, Istanbul: Sanayii Nefise Matbaası, 1933.
———, *İran İnkılabı*, Istanbul: Akşam Matbaası, 1934a.
———, *1500 ile 1900 arasında İran*, Ankara: Başvekalet Basımevi, 1934b.
———, *Etika: ahlâkın kaynağı ve açılması*, trans. Ahmet Ağaoğlu, Istanbul: Vakit Kütüphanesi, 1935.
———, *Ben Neyim?* Istanbul: Ağaoğlu Yayınevi, 1939a.
———, *Tanrı Dağında*, Istanbul: Ağaoğlu Yayınevi, 1939b.
———, *İhtilal mi, İnkılap mı?* Ankara: Alaeddin Kıral Basımevi, 1942.
———, *Gönülsüz Olmaz*, Istanbul: Güven Yayınevi, 1943.
———, *İslamlıkta Kadın*, trans. Hasan Ali Ediz, Istanbul: Nebioğlu Yayınevi, 1959.
———, *Serbest Fırka Hatıraları*, Istanbul: İletişim Yayınları, 1994.
———, *Mütareke ve Sürgün Hatıraları*, Istanbul: Doğu Kitabevi, 2013.

Articles
———, "İngiltere-Almanya," *Sebilürreşad*, No. 193, 1328a.

————, "Şark ve Garp," *Sebilürreşad*, No. 195 (1328b).

————, "Fas ve Trablus," *Sebilürreşad*, No. 197 (1328c).

————, "Taassub-u Cahilane Kimdedir?" *Sebilürreşad*, No. 197 (1328d).

————, "Tecelliyat-ı İslamiye," *Sebilürreşad*, No. 198 (1328e).

————, "Baltık Mülakatından Sonra," *Sebilürreşad*, No. 202 (1328f).

————, "Vahim Günler," *Sebilürreşad*, 12.07.1328g.

————, "Melahzat-ı Matbuat," *Sebilürreşad*, No. 203 (1328h).

————, "Ziya Gökalp Bey," *Türk Yurdu*, I/ 3, 1340.

————, "La Société Persane: la femme persane," *La Nouvelle Revue*, No. 69 (1891a), pp. 376–389.

————, "La Société Persane: le clergé," *La Nouvelle Revue*, No. 70 (1891b), pp. 792–804.

Ahmed Bey, "Le Monde Musulman," *La Revue bleue politique et littérraire*, No. 10 (3 September 1892a), pp. 318–320.

————, "La Société Persane: le clergé," *La Nouvelle Revue*, No. 70 (1892b) p. 804.

————, "La Société persane: La Religion et les Sectes religieuses," *La Nouvelle Revue*, No. 73 (1892c), pp. 539–40.

————, "La Société persane: le théâtre et ses fêtes," *La Nouvelle Revue*, No. 77 (1892d), pp. 537–538.

————, "La Société Persane: l'instruction publique et la littérature," *La Nouvelle Revue*, No. 79 (1892e), pp. 278–296.

————, "La Société Persane: les Européens en Perse," *La Nouvelle Revue*, No. 84 (1893a), pp. 792–805.

————, "Les Croyances mazdéennes dans la religion chiîte," in *Transactions of the Ninth International Congress of Orientalists*, Vol. 2, ed. Delmar Morgan, London: Kraus Reprints, 1893b, pp. 505–515.

————, "Obzor pechati," *Kaspii*, July 25, 1898.

————, "Obzor zhurnalistiki na Vostoke," *Kaspii*, November 26, 1899a.

————, "Iz zhizni Vostoka," *Kaspii*, January 28, 1899b.

————, "Panislamizm, ego harakter i napravlenie," *Kaspii*, April 14, 1901a.

————, "Zhenskoe obrazovanie sredi musul'man," *Kaspii*, October 5, 1901b.

————, "Kadij," *Kaspii*, January 19, 1902.

————, "Polozhenie musul'manskih narodov. Retrospektivnyj vzgljad na istoriju," *Kaspii*, November 14, 1903a.

————, "Polozhenie musul'manskih narodov. Jeklektizm ili panislamistskoe dvizhenie," *Kaspii*, December 24, 1903b.

————, "Vospominanija o Peterburge," *Kaspii*, March 14, 1903c.

————, "Neobhodimye raz'jasnenija k peticijam musul''man," *Kaspii*, April 1, 1905a.

————, "Peticija musul'man," *Kaspii*, April 15, 1905b.

Ahmed-bek Agaev, "Tureckij parlament i Ahmed Rza-bek," *Vestnik Baku*, December 21, 1908.

———, "Kafkasya Müslümanları," *Hikmet*, Vol. 1, No. 1, pp. 3–4, 1909.

———, "Alem-i İslam: Alem-i İslam ve Siyasiyet-i Umumiye," *Sırat-ı Müstakim*, No. 98 (Sep.–Oct., 1910a), pp. 345–347.

———, "Alem-i İslam: Alem-i İslam ve Siyasiyet-i Umumiye: Bizim Takib Edeceğimiz Meslek," *Sırat-ı Müstakim*, No. 99 (Sep.–Oct., 1910b), pp 359–360.

———, "Alem-i İslam ve Siyasiyat; Bulgarların Müdde'iyatı," *Sırat-ı Müstakim*, No. 100 (Sep.–Oct., 1910c), pp. 374–375.

———, "Alem-i İslam: Türkiya'da Muhaceret," *Sırat-ı Müstakim*, No. 102 (Oct.–Nov., 1910d), pp. 407–408.

———, "Alem-i İslam: İran'ın Mazi ve Haline Bir Nazar," *Sırat-ı Müstakim*, No. 103 (Oct.–Nov., 1910e), pp. 452–453.

———, "Alem-i İslam: İran'ın Mazi ve Haline Bir Nazar 11," *Sırat-ı Müstakim*, No. 104 (Oct.–Nov., 1910f), pp. 45–46.

———, "Alem-i İslam; İran'ın Mazi ve Haline Bir Nazar," *Sırat-ı Müstakim*, No. 105 (Oct.–Nov., 1910g), pp. 9–11.

———, "Alem-i İslam: İran'ın Hal ve Mazisine Bir Nazar," *Sırat-ı Müstakim*, No. 107 (Oct.–Nov., 1910h), pp. 426–427.

———, "Alem-i İslam: İran'ın Mazi ve Haline Bir Nazar," *Sırat-ı Müstakim*, No. 108 (Nov.–Dec., 1910i), pp. 62–63.

———, "Alem-i İslam: İran'ın Mazi ve Haline Bir Nazar," *Sırat-ı Müstakim*, No. 109 (Nov.–Dec., 1910j), pp. 79–80.

———, "Alem-i İslam: İran'ın Mazi ve Haline Bir Nazar," *Sırat-ı Müstakim*, No. 110 (Nov.–Dec., 1910k), pp. 97–98.

———, "Alem-i İslam: Türkiye'de Muhacerat Meselesi," *Sırat-ı Mütakim*, No. 111 (Nov.–Dec., 1910l), pp. 386–388.

———, "Darü'l-Hilâfede Maarif-i İbtidâ'iyenin Hali ve Suret-i Islahı," *Sırat-ı Mıstakim* (Dec., 1910m), pp. 151–153.

———, "Terbiye-i Milliye," *İctihad*, No. 27, 15.07.1911a.

———, "Türk Alemi 1," *Türk Yurdu*, No. 1 (Nov., 1911b), pp. 12–17.

———, "Türk Alemi 2," *Türk Yurdu*, No. 2 (Dec., 1911c), pp. 36–42.

———, "Türk Alemi 3," *Türk Yurdu*, No. 3 (Dec., 1911d), pp. 70–74.

———, "Türk Alemi 4," *Türk Yurdu*, No. 5 (Jan., 1912a), pp. 135–139.

———, "Türk Alemi 5," *Türk Yurdu*, No. 7 (1912b), pp. 195–200.

———, "İngiltere ve Biz," *Sebilürreşad*, No. 187 (1912c).

———, "Muharebenin Yeni Devresi," *Sebilürreşad*, No. 190 (1912d).

———, "İtalya'nın Teşebbüsat-ı Mezbuhanesi," *Sebilürreşad*, No. 192 (1912e).

———, "Türk Alemi 6," *Türk Yurdu*, No. 10 (May, 1912f), pp. 292–297.

———, "Türk Alemi 7," *Türk Yurdu*, Vol. 2, No. 13 (May, 1912g), pp. 424–428.

———, "Alem-i İslam'a Umumi Bir Nazar," *Sebilürreşad*, No. 3 (May–Jun., 1912h).

———, "Siyasiyat: Vaz'iyyet-i Haziremiz," *Sebilürreşad*, No. 186 (May–Jun., 1912i).

————, "Tavassut," *Sebilürreşad*, No. 7 (Jun.–Jul., 1912j).

————, "Muharebenin Yeni Devresi," *Sebilürreşad*, No. 8 (Jun.–Jul., 1912k).

————, "Fas ve Trablus," *Sebilürreşad*, No. 14 (Jul.–Aug., 1912l).

————, "Adem-i Merkeziyet I, II, III," *Tercümân-ı Hakikât*, Nos. 11283, 11284, 11285 (Sep., 1912m).

————, "Bir Memleket Nasıl Mahv Olur?" *Sebilürreşad*, No. 204 (Sept.–Oct., 1912n).

————, "Türk Alemi 8," *Türk Yurdu*, Vol. 2, No. 6 (1912/13), pp. 545–551.

————, "Siyasiyat: Sulh İctimami," *Tercümân-ı Hakikât*, December 28, 1912o.

————, "Siyasiyat: Akde-i Meşgulat," *Tercümân-ı Hakikât*, December 29, 1912p.

————, "Siyasiyat: Yine İntizar," *Tercümân-ı Hakikât*, December 30, 1912q.

————, "Siyasiyat: Müzakerat-ı Sulhiye," *Tercümân-ı Hakikât*, December 31, 1912r.

————, "Siyasiyat: Arab ve Türk," *Tercümân-ı Hakikât*, January 1, 1913a.

————, "Siyasiyat: Sulha Doğru," *Tercümân-ı Hakikât*, January 2, 1913b.

————, "Siyasiyat: Edirne ve Sulh," *Tercümân-ı Hakikât*, January 3, 1913c.

————, "Siyasiyat: Harb mi, Sulh mu?" *Tercümân-ı Hakikât*, January 5, 1913d.

————, "Siyasiyat: Muharebe Başlarsa," *Tercümân-ı Hakikât*, January 7, 1913e.

————, "Mechuliyet Devam Ediyor," *Tercümân-ı Hakikât*, January 8, 1913f.

————, "Romanya ve Biz," *Tercümân-ı Hakikât*, January 12, 1913g.

————, "Vilayet-i Şarkiye Meselesi," *Tercümân-ı Hakikât*, January 15, 1913h.

————, "Meçhuliyet Berdevamdır," *Tercümân-ı Hakikât*, January 16, 1913i.

————, "Müşterek Nota ve Sulh," *Tercümân-ı Hakikât*, January 17, 1913j.

————, "Müşterek Nota Etrafında," *Tercümân-ı Hakikât*, January 18, 1913k.

————, "Müşterek Nota Tahlikatı," *Tercümân-ı Hakikât*, January 19, 1913l.

————, "Cemiyetimizden Millete," *Tercümân-ı Hakikât*, January 21, 1913m.

————, "Meclis-i İstişare," *Tercümân-ı Hakikât*, January 22, 1913n.

————, "Vaziyet-i Hazıra," *Tercümân-ı Hakikât*, January 25, 1913o.

————, "Avrupa'da Tesirat," *Tercümân-ı Hakikât*, January 26, 1913p.

————, "Necatımız Kendi Elimizdedir," *Tercümân-ı Hakikât*, January 27, 1913q.

————, "Necat Kendi Elimizdedir," *Tercümân-ı Hakikât*, January 28, 1913r.

————, "Müdafaa-i Milliye," *Tercümân-ı Hakikât*, January 29, 1913s.

————, "Vazife Başına," *Tercümân-ı Hakikât*, February 1, 1913t.

————, "İbret-i Elalem," *Tercümân-ı Hakikât*, February 3, 1913u.

————, "Mahdurat-ı İslamiyet," *Tercümân-ı Hakikât*, February 11, 1913v.

————, "Sadrazam Paşa'nın Beyanatı," *Tercümân-ı Hakikât*, February 17, 1913w.

————, "Azm ve İttihad," *Tercümân-ı Hakikât*, February 20, 1913x.

————, "İngiltere Efkarı," *Tercümân-ı Hakikât*, February 22, 1913y.

————, "Hakkı Paşa'nın Beyanatı," *Tercümân-ı Hakikât*, February 23, 1913z.

————, "Yeni Esaslar," *Tercümân-ı Hakikât*, February 26, 1913aa.

————, "Anadolu'nun Tamamiyet-i Mülkiyesi," *Tercümân-ı Hakikât*, February 27, 1913ab.

———, "Osmanlılıkta Arablık I," *Tercümân-ı Hakikât*, March 3, 1913ac.

———, "Osmanlılıkta Arablık II," *Tercümân-ı Hakikât*, March 4, 1913ad.

———, "Alem-i İslamın Nidaları," *Tercümân-ı Hakikât*, March 10, 1913ae.

———, "Bir Ders-i İbret," *Tercümân-ı Hakikât*, March 11, 1913af.

———, "Tanzimat," *Jeune Turc,* March 14, 1913ag.

———, "Bir Cemile," *Tercümân-ı Hakikât*, March 19, 1913ah.

———, "Avrupa'ya Teslim-i Nefs Edemeyiz," *Tercümân-ı Hakikât*, March 20, 1913ai.

———, "İşkodra Meselesi Dolayısıyla," *Tercümân-ı Hakikât*, March 23, 1913aj.

———, "Hükümet-i Osmaniye Taahüd Altına Girmiş midir?" *Tercümân-ı Hakikât*, March 25, 1913ak.

———, "Hanımlarımızın Faaliyeti," *Tercümân-ı Hakikât*, March 27, 1913al.

———, "İngiltere ve Devlet-i Osmaniye," *Tercümân-ı Hakikât*, March 29, 1913am.

———, "İhtiyat Elzemdir," *Tercümân-ı Hakikât*, April 3., 1913an.

———, "Rusya ve İngiltere," *Tercümân-ı Hakikât*, April 8, 1913ao.

———, "Hanımların Faaliyeti II," *Tercümân-ı Hakikât*, April 9, 1913ap.

———, "Kapalı Kalan Meseleler," *Tercümân-ı Hakikât*, April 16, 1913aq.

———, "Islahata Doğru," *Tercümân-ı Hakikât*, April 19, 1913ar.

———, "Türk Medeniyeti Tarihi," *Türk Yurdu,* Vol. 4, No. 5 (May, 1913as), pp. 555–556.

———, "Sabık Trabzon Valisi Süleyman Nazif Bey Efendi'ye," *Türk Yurdu,* Vol. 4, No. 9 (1913at), pp. 702–704.

———, "İsmail Bey Gasprinski," *Türk Yurdu,* No. 1 (1913au).

———, "İcmal-i Siyasi," *Sebilürreşad*, No. 251 (Aug.–Sep., 1913av).

———, "İslam'da Dava-yı Milliyet I," *Türk Yurdu,* No. 10 (1914a), pp. 2320–2328.

———, "İslam'da Dava-yı Milliyet I," *Türk Yurdu,* No. 11 (1914b), pp. 2381–2389.

———, "Cevaba Cevap," *Türk Yurdu,* No. 12 (1914c), pp. 825–843.

———, "İslam Aleminde Görülen İnhitatın Sebepleri," *İslam Mecmuası,* No. 2 (1914d).

———, "Türkiye'nin ve İslam Aleminin Kurtuluşu," *Harb Mecmuası,* No. 1 (1915a).

———, "Almanya Seyahati İntibaatımdan: Alman Kadınlığı," *Türk Yurdu,* No. 84 (1915b).

———, "Türklüğün Nazarında Kadın," *Türk Yurdu,* No. 13 (1915c).

———, "İslamlıktan Evvel Arablar," *Bilgi Mecmuası,* No. 1 (1915d), pp. 53–62.

———, "Arşidük Maksimilyan'ın Muvaseleti Münasebetiyle," *Tercümân-ı Hakikât*, February 20, 1917.

———, "Türkçülük-Türkiyecilik," *Tercümân-ı Hakikât*, No. 13457, August 19, 1918a.

———, "Matbuatın Vazifesi," *Şule*, September 5, 1918b.

———, "Berlin Müzakereleri," *Şule*, September 9, 1918c.

———, "Harciye Nezaretimiz var mıdır, yok mudur?" *Şule*, September 11, 1918d.

———, "Şark Konfederasyonu," *Şule*, September 17, 1918e.

———, "Almanya ve Alem-i İslam," *Şule*, September 21, 1918f.

———, "Münevverler Cepheye," *Vakit*, No. 1325, September 19, 1921.

————, "Türk İnkılabı: İnkılabımıza Dair," *Yeni Mecmua*, Nos. 69, 72, February 1–March 10, 1923a.

————, "Türk İnkılabı: Teşkilat-ı Esasiye," *Yeni Mecmua,* No. 80, July 10, 1923b.

————, "Meclis Açılırken," *Vatan,* No. 137, August 15, 1923c.

————, "Yeni Sayfalar," *Hâkimiyet-i Milliye,* February 29, 1924a.

————, "Türk Ocakları Kongresi'nin Beyannamesi: On İki Sene Evvel ve On İki Sene Sonra," *Hâkimiyet-i Milliye,* No. 1109, April 29, 1924b.

————, "Ukala ile İttihatçılığa Ait Bir Muhasebe," *Cumhuriyet,* July 10, 1924c.

————, "Milli Şuur," *Hâkimiyet-i Milliye*, No. 1189, August 8, 1924d.

————, "Nereye Gidiyoruz?" *Hâkimiyet-i Milliye*, November 18, 1924e.

————, "Yol Dönümünde," *Cumhuriyet*, March 12, 1925a.

————, "Medeniyet ve Ahlak," *Cumhuriyet,* October 25, 1925b.

————, "Türk Ocakları Kongresi Münasebetiyle," *Hâkimiyet-i Milliye,* No. 1411, April 24, 1925c.

————, "Matbuat Müdürlüğünün Eser Menine Salahiyeti var mıdır?" *Cumhuriyet*, March 20–21, 1925d.

————, "İstiklal Mahkemelerinin Faaliyeti," *Hâkimiyet-i Milliye,* No. 1618, January 4, 1926a.

————, "Kanun-u Medeniyeye Dair," *Milliyet,* February 18, 1926b.

————, "Almanya ve Cemiyet-i Akvam," *Hâkimiyet-i Milliye,* No. 1664, February 21, 1926c.

————, "İnkılap Kıskançtır," *Milliyet,* No. 28, March 10, 1926d.

————, "Fesat Ocağı," *Milliyet,* No. 36, March 18, 1926e.

————, "Taşra Münevverlerimize," *Hâkimiyet-i Milliye,* No. 1701, March 30, 1926f.

————, "Etrafımızda Neler Oluyor?" *Hâkimiyet-i Milliye,* April 2, 1926g.

————, "İngiltere'de Sanayi Buhranı," *Hâkimiyet-i Milliye,* No. 1719, April 20, 1926h.

————, "İngiltere Buhranı," *Milliyet,* No. 87, May 10, 1926i.

————, "İki Cereyan," *Milliyet,* No. 88, May 11, 1926j.

————, "Grevin Nihayeti," *Milliyet,* No. 91, May 14, 1926k.

————, "Lehistan Hadiseleri," *Milliyet,* No. 93, May 16, 1926l.

————, "Bir İzah," *Milliyet,* No. 97, May 20, 1926m.

————, "Cemiyet-i Akvam'da," *Milliyet,* No. 98, May 21, 1926n.

————, "Devlet ve Fert," *Milliyet,* No. 102, May 25, 1926o.

————, "Fena Bir Yol," *Hâkimiyet-i Milliye,* No. 1765, June 5, 1926p.

————, "Fransız Buhranı," *Milliyet,* June 18, 1926q.

————, "Milli Terbiye," *Hâkimiyet-i Milliye,* No. 1808, July 21, 1926r.

————, "Çin Hareketi," *Hâkimiyet-i Milliye*, January 13, 1927a.

————, " Almanya'da," *Hâkimiyet-i Milliye*, January 15, 1927b.

————, " Avrupa'da," *Hâkimiyet-i Milliye*, January 25, 1927c.

————, "Türkiye ve Amerika," *Hâkimiyet-i Milliye*, January 27, 1927d.

————, "Yine Çin Etrafında," *Hâkimiyet-i Milliye*, January 30, 1927e.

————, "Çalışmak," *Hâkimiyet-i Milliye*, February 2, 1927f.

————, "Alman Cihanı," *Hâkimiyet-i Milliye*, February 3, 1927g.

————, "İki Beyanat Karşısında," *Hâkimiyet-i Milliye*, February 9, 1927h.

————, "Rusya-İngiltere Münasebatı," *Hâkimiyet-i Milliye*, February 23, 1927i.

————, "Güzel Bir Misal," *Hâkimiyet-i Milliye*, March 7, 1927j.

————, " İtalya-Romanya Münasebatı," *Hâkimiyet-i Milliye*, March 13, 1927k.

————, "Ali İktisat Meclisi," *Hâkimiyet-i Milliye*, March 17, 1927l.

————, "İnkişafa Doğru," *Hâkimiyet-i Milliye*, March 21, 1927m.

————, "Şanghay'da," *Hâkimiyet-i Milliye*, April 2, 1927n.

————, "Türkiye'nin Rolü," *Hâkimiyet-i Milliye*, April 12, 1927o.

————, "Adliyemiz ve Maarifimiz," *Hâkimiyet-i Milliye*, April 20, 1927p.

————, "Kurultayda," *Hâkimiyet-i Milliye*, April 28, 1927q.

————, "Bir Şeref Borcu," *Hâkimiyet-i Milliye*, September 19, 1927r.

————, "Cemiyet-i Akvamda," *Hâkimiyet-i Milliye*, September 21, 1927s.

————, "Tahrir-i Nüfus," *Hâkimiyet-i Milliye*, September 22, 1927t.

————, "Balkanlarda," *Hâkimiyet-i Milliye*, October 17, 1927u.

————, "Mücahede," *Hâkimiyet-i Milliye,* No. 2333, January 4, 1928a.

————, "Hindistan'da," *Hâkimiyet-i Milliye,* No. 2336, January 7, 1928b.

————, "Komisyonculuk," *Hâkimiyet-i Milliye,* No. 2350, January 21, 1928c.

————, "Eski ve Yeni Ahlak," *Hâkimiyet-i Milliye,* No. 2352, January 23, 1928d.

————, "İktisad Meclis-i Alisi," *Hâkimiyet-i Milliye,* No. 2354, January 25, 1928e.

————, "Ticaret ve Ahlâk," *Hâkimiyet-i Milliye,* No. 2358, January 29, 1928f.

————, "İngiltere ve Amerika," *Hâkimiyet-i Milliye,* No. 2360, January 31, 1928g.

————, "Bir Vecize," *Hâkimiyet-i Milliye,* No. 2363, February 3, 1928h.

————, "Türk Maarif Cemiyeti," *Hâkimiyet-i Milliye,* No. 2371, February 11, 1928i.

————, "Çok Mübarek Bir Teşebbüs," *Hâkimiyet-i Milliye,* No. 2378, February 18, 1928j.

————, "Ahlaki Bir Mücadele," *Hâkimiyet-i Milliye,* No. 2381, February 21, 1928k.

————, "Mükemmel Bir Enmuzec," *Hâkimiyet-i Milliye,* No. 2383, February 23, 1928l.

————, "Hod-endişlik ve Gayr-endişlik," *Hâkimiyet-i Milliye,* No. 2386, February 26, 1928m.

————, "Mussolini'nin Nutku," *Hâkimiyet-i Milliye,* No. 2395, March 6, 1928n.

————, "Garabetler ve Tezadlar," *Hâkimiyet-i Milliye,* No. 2396, March 7, 1928o.

————, "Gazi'nin Beyanatı," *Hâkimiyet-i Milliye,* No. 2398, March 9, 1928p.

————, "Medeniyette Vahdet," *Türk Yurdu,* No. 206–208 (Feb., 1929).

————, "Ahmet Rıza Bey," *Vakit,* March 6, 1930a.

————, "Devlet Hazinesi Çıkmaza Girmiştir: Sağ Kim? Sol Kim?" *Yarın,* August 18, 1930b.

————, "İkinci Fırkaya Lüzum Var mıdır?" *Son Posta,* October 11, 1930c.

————, "Serbest Fırkaya Meş'um Diyorlar, Şeamet Neededir?" *Son Posta*, October 18, 1930d.

——, "Celal Nuri Bey Kimdir?" *Son Posta,* October 19, 1930e.

——, "Milli İrade Bu Mudur?" *Son Posta,* October 31, 1930f.

——, "Yine Prensip Meselesi," *Son Posta,* November 10, 1930g.

——, "1930 Senesinin Bilançosu," *Son Posta,* December 10, 1930h.

——, "Vicdan Azabı Duymayanlara," *Son Posta,* January 12, 1931a.

——,"İptidai Türk Aile Hukuku ve İptidai Hindo-Avrupai Aile Hukuku Arasında Mukayese," *I. Türk Tarih Kongresi, Konferanslar, Müzakere Zabıtları,* Maarif Vekaleti, Ankara: 1931b, pp. 261–269.

——, "Misak-ı Milli'nin Tarihi Kıymeti," *Ülkü,* February 1, 1933a.

——, "Kadro Münakaşası," *Cumhuriyet,* No. 3140, February 2, 1933b.

——, "Son Söz," *Cumhuriyet,* February 5, 1933c.

——, "Mütareke ve Malta Hatıraları," *Akın,* Nos. 1–67, May 29–August 19, 1933d.

——, "Özcülük ve Özgecilik (Egoizm ve Altruizm)," *Akın,* No. 2, May 30, 1933e.

——, "Vazife," *Akın,* No. 3, May 31, 1933f.

——, "Herşeyden Evvel Muallim," *Akın,* No. 4, June 1, 1933g.

——, "Ortaçağ'dan Kalma Bir Müessese," *Akın,* No. 5, June 2, 1933h.

——, "Ziraat mi, Sanayi mi?" *Akın,* No. 6, June 3, 1933i.

——, "Nizamlı Hürriyet," *Akın,* No. 8, June 5, 1933j.

——, "Türk Entellektüellerinin Zaafları," *Akın,* No. 10, June 7, 1933k.

——, "Bir Kanun Münasebetiyle," *Akın,* No. 11, June 8, 1933l.

——, "Suiistimal ile Mücadele," *Akın,* No. 14, June 11, 1933m.

——, "Fazla Ucuzluk iyi bir Alamet midir?" *Akın,* No. 15, June 12, 1933n.

——, "Büyük Millet Meclisi," *Akın,* No. 16, June 13, 1933o.

——, "Devletçi Edebiyat," *Akın,* No. 21, June 18, 1933p.

——, "Haftada 40 Saatlik Mesai," *Akın,* No. 22, June 19, 1933q.

——, "Ziraatimiz," *Akın,* No. 23, June 20, 1933r.

——, "Maarifimizin Islahı," *Akın,* No. 24, June 21, 1933s.

——, "Serbest Kadın," *Akın,* No. 28, June 25, 1933t.

——, "Üniversite ve Talebesi," *Akın,* No. 29, June 26, 1933u.

——, "Ana Kanunlar ve Nazım Kanunlar," *Akın,* No. 30, June 27, 1933v.

——, "Gazinin Sualleri," *Akın,* No. 35, July 2, 1933w.

——, "Milliyetçilik," *Akın,* No. 43, July 10, 1933x.

——, "Alman Devlet Adamlarına Ne Oluyor?" No. 47, July 14, 1933y.

——, "Kemalizm ve Hitlerizm," *Akın,* No. 51, July 18, 1933z.

——, "Parlamantarizm ve Şahsi Hükümet," *Akın,* No. 52, July 19, 1933aa.

——, "Milli Kültür Nasıl Kurtulur," *Cumhuriyet,* July 3, 1934a.

——, "Parlamentarizmin Kökleri ve Açılma Tarihçesi," July 24, 1934b.

——, "Avam Kamarasında," *Cumhuriyet,* July 25, 1934c.

——, "Louis Bartu Dantonist," *Cumhuriyet,* October 12, 1934d.

——, "Yeni Nesil Arasında," *Cumhuriyet,* October 16, 1934e.

———, "Ziya Gökalp'e Dair Bazı Hatıralarım," *Cumhuriyet*, October 27, 1934f.

———, "İctimai Musahebeler: Milli Musikiyi Yaratmada İlham ve Heyecan Kaynağımız," *Cumhuriyet*, November 8, 1934g.

———, "İctimai Musahebeler: Zeka Tröstü," *Cumhuriyet*, November 12, 1934h.

———, "Fransa'daki Demokrasi Kudreti: Kanun-u Esasi Etrafında Kopan Fırtınalar," *Cumhuriyet*, November 15, 1934i.

———, "Yeni Nesil Arasında Edebiyat Münakaşaları," *Cumhuriyet*, November 17, 1934j.

———, "Yeni Nesil Arasında Spor Meselesi," *Cumhuriyet*, November 24, 1934k.

———, "İtalya'da Yeni Bir Tecrübe," *Cumhuriyet*, November 27, 1934l.

———, "Demokrasiye Doğru," *Cumhuriyet*, December 5, 1934m.

———, "Türk Kadınına Verilen Seçme ve Seçilme Hakkı," *Cumhuriyet*, December 6, 1934n.

———, " Yeni Nesil Arasında: Aile Münakaşası," *Cumhuriyet*, December 8, 1934o.

———, "Şehir ve Köy Kavgasının Doğurduğu Tezadlar," *Cumhuriyet*, December 13, 1934p.

———, "Yeni Nesil Arasında," *Cumhuriyet*, January 1, 1935a.

———, "Münevver Zümre Meselesi," *Cumhuriyet*, January 15, 1935b.

———, "Özcülük ve Özgecilik," *Cumhuriyet*, January 20, 1935c.

———, "Dil Meselesi," *Cumhuriyet*, January 27, 1935d.

———, "Önderin Beyannamesi," *Cumhuriyet*, February 4, 1935e.

———, "Müstakil Saylavlık Meselesi," *Cumhuriyet*, February 8, 1935f.

———, "Hayır Yardım İşleri," *Cumhuriyet*, February 14, 1935g.

———, "Ocak Ülküsü," *Cumhuriyet*, February 26, 1935h.

———, "Cemiyetin Milli Hayatta Rolü," *Cumhuriyet*, March 4, 1935i.

———, "Cemiyet Hayatımızda Noksan Prensipler," *Cumhuriyet*, March 15, 1935j.

———, "Örnek Eserler," *Cumhuriyet*, March 26, 1935k.

———, "Gene o Mesele," *Cumhuriyet*, March 30, 1935l.

———, "Rakamlar Ne Diyor?" *Cumhuriyet*, April 4, 1935m.

———, "Genç Nesli Yetiştirmek," *Cumhuriyet*, April 8, 1935n.

———, "Hem Haklı Hem Haksız," *Cumhuriyet*, April 15, 1935o.

———, "Şehir Sosyalizmi," *Cumhuriyet*, May 1, 1935p.

———, "İki Bayan Arasında," *Cumhuriyet*, May 6, 1935q.

———, "İş Kanununu Hazırlarken Çok Düşünmek Lazım," *Cumhuriyet*, May 8–9, 1935r.

———, "C.H.P. Programı Etrafında," *Cumhuriyet*, May 18, 1935s.

———, "Hindistan ve İngiltere'ye Dair," *Cumhuriyet*, May 19, 1935t.

———, "C.H.P. Programı Etrafında," *Cumhuriyet*, May 22, 1935u.

———, "C.H.P. Programı Etrafında," *Cumhuriyet*, May 24, 1935v.

———, "Parti Programı Etrafında," *Cumhuriyet*, May 26, 1935w.

———, "Amerika'da Buhran Savaşını Altüst eden Karar," *Cumhuriyet*, June 2, 1935x.

———, "Demokrasi ve Devletçilik," *Cumhuriyet*, June 6, 1935y.

———, "Fikir ve Hayat," *Cumhuriyet*, June 12, 1935z.

———, "Mekteb ve İmtihan," *Cumhuriyet*, June 22, 1935aa.

———, "Linç," *Cumhuriyet*, July 3, 1935ab.

———, "Ulusçuluk, İnsancıllıktır," *Cumhuriyet*, July 9, 1935ac.

———, "Roosevelt'in Mücadelesi," *Cumhuriyet*, July 15, 1935ad.

———, "Edebiyat Meselesi," *Cumhuriyet*, July 22, 1935ae.

———, "Büyük Şahsiyetler," *Cumhuriyet*, July 24, 1935af.

———, "Terbiye Amaçlarından Birisi," *Cumhuriyet*, July 29, 1935ag.

———, "Japonya Yürüyor," *Cumhuriyet*, August 6, 1935ah.

———, "Yeni Kültür Bakanından Neler Bekliyoruz?" *Cumhuriyet*, August 11, 1935ai.

———, "Doğu ve Batı," *Cumhuriyet*, August 16, 1935aj.

———, "Batı ve Doğu," *Cumhuriyet*, August 20, 1935ak.

———, "Doğu ve Batı," *Cumhuriyet*, August 23, 1935al.

———, "Türk Devletçiliği," *Cumhuriyet*, August 28, 1935am.

———, "Doğu ve Batı," *Cumhuriyet*, September 3, 1935an.

———, "Müesseselerin Ruhu," *Cumhuriyet*, September 4, 1935ao.

———, "Doğu ve Batı," *Cumhuriyet*, September 10, 1935ap.

———, "Üstür Zehebke, mezhebke, zihabke!," *Cumhuriyet*, September 16, 1935aq.

———, "Maarifte Yeni Esaslar," *Cumhuriyet*, September 22, 1935ar.

———, "Doğu ve Batı," *Cumhuriyet*, September 30, 1935as.

———, "Nüfus Sayımının Faydaları," *Cumhuriyet*, October 2, 1935at.

———, "Muallim ve Talebe," *Cumhuriyet*, October 4, 1935au.

———, "Sulh Ülküsü," *Cumhuriyet*, October 7, 1935av.

———, "İki Zihniyet," *Cumhuriyet*, October 11, 1935aw.

———, "Önemli bir Eksik," *Cumhuriyet*, October 17, 1935ax.

———, "İki Başlı Devler," *Cumhuriyet*, October 19, 1935ay.

———, "Fikir Tereddileri," *Cumhuriyet*, October 24, 1935az.

———, "Belediyeler Kongresinde ve Kamutayın Açılışı," *Cumhuriyet*, November 7, 1935ba.

———, "Celal Sahir," *Cumhuriyet*, November 24, 1935bb.

———, "Doğu ve Batı," *Cumhuriyet*, November 26, 1935bc.

———, "İngiliz İntihapları," *Cumhuriyet*, November 29, 1935bd.

———, "Sosyalizm ve Faşizm," *Cumhuriyet*, December 15, 1935be.

———, "Japonya'da Milli İrade İmanının Galeyanı," *Cumhuriyet*, December 19, 1935bf.

———, "Kültür," *Cumhuriyet*, December 31, 1935bg.

———, "Opportunizm Nedir?" *Cumhuriyet*, January 3, 1936a.

———, "Kumar Belası," *Cumhuriyet*, January 9, 1936b.

———, "Intellectuel ve Ödevleri," *Cumhuriyet*, January 12–14, 1936c.

———, "Üç Kültür," *Kültür Haftası*, No. 1, January 15, 1936d.

———, "Makine Teknik midir?" *Cumhuriyet*, January 20, 1936e.

————, "Bir Kültürden Ötekine," *Kültür Haftası*, No. 2, January 22, 1936f.

————, "Doğu ve Batı," *Cumhuriyet*, January 24, 1936g.

————, "Kültür Meselesi," *Cumhuriyet*, January 29, 1936h.

————, "Yaratıcı Tekamül," *Kültür Haftası*, No. 3, January 29, 1936i.

————, "Altmış Yedi Yıl Sonra," *Kültür Haftası*, Nos. 3–7, January 29–February 26, 1936j.

————, "İngiliz Sülalesi," *Cumhuriyet,* February 2, 1936k.

————, "Medeniyet ve Kültür," *Cumhuriyet*, February 7, 1936l.

————, "Entellektüellerin Borçları," *Cumhuriyet*, February 10, 1936m.

————, "Nisbi Temsil," *Cumhuriyet*, February 14, 1936n.

————, "Tarihte Sosyal İnkişaf," *Kültür Haftası*, Nos. 17–20, May 6–27, 1936o.

————, "Türk Hukuk Tarihinde Usul," *İnsan,* No. 1, April 15, 1938a.

————, "Hukukta Tekamül Devirleri," *İnsan*, No. 2, May 15, 1938b.

————, "Basitten Mürekkebe, Şekilsizlikten Şekilleşmeye Doğru," *İnsan*, No. 3, June 15, 1938c.

————, "Ziya'nın Şahsiyeti," *İş*, No. 19 (1939a).

————, "Türk Kadınlarının İctimai Vazifeleri," *İkdam*, April 3, 1939b.

————, "Hediye mi Hakkın İadesi mi?" *İkdam*, May 1, 1939c.

————, "Suya Sabuna Dokunmadan," *İkdam*, May 20, 1939d.

————, "Ne İdik, Ne Olduk?" (published by Tezer Taşkıran), *Hayat,* Nos. 6–10 (Feb.–Mar., 1978).

E. Other Sources

Abbaslı, Nazile, *Azerbaycan'da Özgürlük Mücadelesi*, Istanbul: Beyaz Balina Yayınları, 2001.

Adıvar, A. Adnan, "Interaction of Islamic and Western Thought in Turkey," in *Near Eastern Culture and Society,* ed. T.C. Young, Princeton: 1951, pp. 127–129.

Adıvar, Halide Edip, "Evimize Bakalım: Türkçülüğün Faaliyet Sahası," *Vakit,* 30.06.1918.

————, "Dictatorship and Reforms in Turkey," *Yale Review,* Vol. XIX, Autumn 1929.

————, *Turkey faces West,* New Haven: Yale Univ. Press, 1930.

————, *Conflict of East and West in Turkey,* Lahore: Ashraf, 1935.

————, *The Turkish Ordeal,* London: Hyperion Pr, 1981.

Ağaoğlu, Samet, *Babamdan Hatıralar*, Ankara: Ağaoğlu Külliyatı, 1940.

————, *Demokrat Parti'nin Doğuş ve Yükseliş Sebepleri: Bir Soru,* Istanbul: n.p., 1972.

————, *Babamın Arkadaşları*, Istanbul: İletişim Yayınları, 1998.

Ağaoğlu, Süreyya, *Bir Ömür Böyle Geçti,* Istanbul: İshak Basımevi, 1975.

Ahmad, Feroz, *The Young Turks; The Committee of Union and Progress in Turkish Politics, 1908–1914*, Oxford: Calerendon Pres: 1969.

Akalın, Gülseren, *Türk Düşünce ve Siyasi Hayatında Ahmet Ağaoğlu*, Bakü: Azatam, 2004.

Akçura, Yusuf, "Türklük," *Salname-i Servet-i Fünun*, February 16, 1912.

————, *Türk Yılı,* Istanbul: Yeni Matbaa, 1928.

————, *Üç Tarz-ı Siyaset,* Ankara: Türk Tarih Kurumu Basımevi, 1976

————, *Türkçülüğün Tarihi,* Istanbul: Kaynak Yayınları, 1998.

Akın, Rıdvan, *Osmanlı İmparatorluğun Dağılma Devri ve Türkçülük Hareketi 1908–1918,* Istanbul: Der Yayınları, 2002.

Akkaya, Rukiye, *Prens Sabahaddin,* Istanbul: Liberte Yayınları, 2005.

Akşin, Sina, *Jöntürkler ve İttihat ve Terakki,* Istanbul: Remzi Kitabevi, 1987.

————, "The Place of the Young Turk Revolution in Turkish History," *Young Turks Symposium,* University of Manchester, 1988, pp. 13–29.

Akyiğitzade, Musa, *İlm-i Servet veyahut İlm-i İktisat: Azâde-gi Ticaret ve Usul-I Himâye,* Istanbul: Mekteb-i Harbiye, 1316.

Alaya, Flavia M, "Arnold and Renan on the Popular Uses of History," *Journal of the History of Ideas,* Vol. 28, No. 4 (Oct.–Dec., 1967), pp. 551–574.

Alkan, Mehmet, "Düşünce Tarihimizde Önemli Bir İsim: Baha Tevfik," *Tarih ve Toplum* (Apr., 1988), pp. 41–49.

Alp, Tekin, "Ulusal Birlik Yasası: Cemiyet yok, ferd vardır," *Cumuriyet,* 30.12.1935.

————, *Le Kemalisme,* Paris: F. Alcan, 1937.

Alpkaya, Faruk, *Türkiye Cumhuriyeti'nin Kuruluşu,* 1923–1924, Istanbul: İletişim Yayınevi, 1998.

Alstadt, Audrey, "The Azerbaijani Bourgeoisie and the Cultural Enlightenment Movement in Baku: First Steps Toward Nationalism," in *Transcaucasia: Nationalism and Social Change,* ed. R.G. Suny, Ann Arbor: University of Michigan, 1983, pp. 197–208.

————, "The Baku city duma–arena for elite conflict," *Central Asian Survey,* Vol. 5, No. 3 (1986), pp. 49–66.

————, *The Azerbaijani Turks: Power and Identity under Russian Rule,* Stanford: Hoover Institution Press, 1992.

Ankara'da 1340 senesi Nisanında Toplanan Birinci Türk Ocakları Umumi Kongresi Zabıtları, Ankara: Yenigün Matbaası, 1341.

Arai, Masimo, *Turkish Nationalism in the Young Turk Era,* Leiden; New York: E.J. Brill, 1991.

Aras, Bülent, "Ahmet Ağaoğlu ve Ekonomik Alternatifi," *Birikim,* Vol. 90 (Oct., 1996), pp. 69–76.

Armenteros, Caroline, "Revolutionary Violence and the End of History: The Divided Self in Francophone Thought, 1762–1914," in *Historicising the French Revolution,* eds. C. Armenteros, T. Blanning, I. DiVanna, and D. Dodds, Newcastle-upon-Tyne: Cambridge Scholars Publishing, 2008, pp. 2–39.

Atabaki, Touraj, "Recasting and Recording Identities in the Caucasus," *Iran & the Caucasus,* Vol. 6, No. 1/2 (2002), pp. 219–235.

Atatürk, Mustafa K., *Nutuk,* numerous editions. English translations *A Speech Delivered by Ghazi Mustafa Kemal October 1927,* Leipzig, K.F. Koehler, 1929.

————, *Atatürk'ün Söylev ve Demeçleri*, 3 vols., Istanbul and Ankara, Maarif Matbaası and T.T.K. Basımevi, 1945–54.

Atay, Falih R., *Moskova-Roma*, Istanbul: Muallim Ahmet Halit Kütüphanesi, 1932.

————, *Eski Saat,* Istanbul: Akşam Matbaası, 1933.

————, *Taymis Kıyılarında,* Istanbul: Ankara: 1934.

————, *Çankaya*, 2 vols., Istanbul: Ekicigil Matbaası, 1960.

————, *Batış Yılları*, Istanbul: Dünya Yayınları, 1963.

Avagyan Arsen, *Ermeniler ve İttihat ve Terakki: İşbirliğinden Çatışmaya,* Istanbul: Aras Yayıncılık, 2005.

Avşar, Abdülhamit, *Bir Partinin Kapatılmasında Basının Rolü: Serbest Cumhuriyet Fırkası*, Istanbul, 1998.

Aybars, Ergun, *İstiklal Mahkemeleri, 1923–1927,* İzmir: Dokuz Eylül Üniversitesi Yayınları, 1988.

Aydemir, Şevket S., *İnkılap ve Kadro*, Istanbul: Muallim Halit Kütüphanesi, 1932a.

————, "Darülfinun İnkılap Hassasiyeti ve Cavid Bey İktisatçılığı," *Kadro,* Vol. I, No. 12 (1932b), pp. 38–43.

————, "Ağaoğlu Ahmet Bey'e Cevap," *Cumhuriyet,* 10.12.1932c.

————, "Ağaoğlu Ahmet Bey'e Cevap 3," *Cumhuriyet,* 13.12.1932d.

————, "Ağaoğlu Ahmet Bey'e Cevap 4," *Cumhuriyet,* 17.12.1932e.

————, "Ağaoğlu Ahmet Bey'e Cevap 5," *Cumhuriyet,* 18.12.1932f.

————, "Ağaoğlu Ahmet Bey'e Cevap 6," *Cumhuriyet,* 20.12.1932g.

————, "Ağaoğlu Ahmet Bey'e Cevap 7," *Cumhuriyet,* 22.12.1932h.

————, "Ağaoğlu Ahmet Bey'e Cevap 8," *Cumhuriyet,* 24.12.1932i.

————, "Ağaoğlu Ahmet Bey'e Cevap 9," *Cumhuriyet,* 27.12.1932j.

————, "Kafir ve Bolşevik," *Cumhuriyet,* 21.01.1933a.

————, "Bir Münakaşanın Bilançosu," *Cumhuriyet,* 22.01.1933b.

————, "Bir Görüş Tarzı Nasıl İptizale Uğrar," *Cumhuriyet,* 23.01.1933c.

————, "Ciddi Olmayan Bir Yarenlik," *Cumhuriyet,* 27.01.1933d.

————, *Suyu Arayan Adam*, Ankara: Öz Yayınları, 1959.

————, *Makedonya'dan Orta Asya'ya Enver Paşa,* Vol. 3, Istanbu: Remzi Kitabevi, 1978.

Aydın, Ertan, "The Peculiarities of Turkish Revolutionary Ideology in the 1930s: The *Ülkü* Version of Kemalism, 1933–1936," Unpublished PhD Thesis, Bilkent University, 2003.

Azizov, Eldar, *Difai: xx. Asrin evvellerinde ermeni-azerbaycanli münakişesinin ilkin tarihi şartleri ve sebepleri,* Bakı: n.p., 2009.

Babanzade, Ahmet N., *İslamda Dava-yi Kavmiyet*, Istanbul: Tevsii Tıbaat Matbaası, 1913.

Bakırezer, Güven, "Batı Medeniyeti Hayranı Bir Liberal Aydının Çelişki ve Sınırları: Ahmet Ağaoğlu," *Toplumsal Tarih,* Vol. 41 (May, 1997), pp. 39–43.

Bala, Mirza, "Hasan Zerdabi Bey," *Türk Yurdu,* No. 12–14 (Dec.–Feb., 1929).

———, "Azerbaycanlı İlk Türk Gazetecisi Hasan Bey Zerdablı I," *Türk Yurdu*, No. 2 (Sep., 1942a), pp. 58–62.

———, "Azerbaycanlı İlk Türk Gazetecisi Hasan Bey Zerdablı II," *Türk Yurdu*, No. 3 (Dec., 1942b), pp. 93–96.

Banghorn, Frederick C., "D.I. Pisarev: A Representative of Russian Nihilism," *The Review of Politics*, Vol. 10, No. 2 (Apr., 1948), pp. 190–211.

Başar, Ahmet Hamdi, "Bizim Devletçiliğimiz," *Cumhuriyet*, 26.08.1935.

———, *Atatürk'le Üç Ay ve 1930'dan sonra Türkiye*, Istanbul: Tan Matbaası, 1945.

Bayar, Celal, *Atatürk Metodolojisi*, Istanbul: Kervan Yayınları, 1978.

Bayat, Ali Haydar, *Hüseyinzade Ali Bey*, Ankara: Atatürk Kültür Merkezi Yayınları, 1990,

Baykara, Hüseyin, *Azerbaycan'da Yenileşme Hareketleri*, Ankara: Türk Kültürünü Araştırma Enstitüsü, 1966.

Bayur, Yusuf H., *Türk İnkilabı Tarihi*, Vol. 3, Ankara: Türk Tarih Kurumu Basımevi, 1983.

Belge, Murat, "Individual in the Turkish context," in *The Predicament of the Individual in the Middle East*, ed. Hazim Saghie, London: Saqi Books, 2001, pp. 42–50.

———, "Mustafa Kemal ve Kemalizm," *Kemalizm* volume in *Modern Türkiye'de Siyasi Düşünce*, Istanbul: İletişim Yayınları, 2001, p. 34.

Bellamy, Richard, *Liberalism and Modern Society: An Historical Argument*, Cambridge: Polity Press, 1992.

Benningsen, A., and Lemercer Quelqujay, *La Presse et le Mouvement National Musulman de Russie avant 1920*, Paris: Mouton, 1964.

Bergson, Henri, *Time and Free Will*, trans. F.L. Pogson, London: George Allen and Unwin, Ltd., 1950.

———, *Yaratıcı Tekâmül*, trans. Mustafa Şekib Tunç, Istanbul: Milli Eğitim Basımevi, 1986.

Berkes, Niyazi, "Sociology in Turkey," *The American Journal of Sociology*, Vol. 42, No. 2 (Sep., 1936), pp. 238–246.

———, *Turkish Nationalism and Western Civilisation: Selected Essays of Ziya Gökalp*, New York: Columbia University Press, 1959.

———, *The Development of Secularism in Turkey*, London: C. Hurst, 1998.

Betin, Saffet Ö., *Atatürk İnkilabı ve Ziya Gökalp, Yahya Kemal, Halide Edip* (Istanbul: Güven B., 1951).

Bierer, Dana, "Renan and His Interpreters: A Study in French Intellectual Warfare," *The Journal of Modern History*, Vol. 25, No. 4 (Dec., 1953), pp. 375–389.

Birgen, Muhittin, "Türk Ordusu'nun Azerbaycan'a Yardımı," *Yakın Tarihimiz*, Vol. 2, No. 5 (1962a), pp. 44–45.

———, "Bizimkiler ve Azerbaycan," *Yakın Tarihimiz*, Vol. 2, No. 18 (1962b), pp. 157–158.

———, (Haz. Zeki Arıkan) *İttihat ve Terakki'de On Sene*, Istanbul: Kitap Yayınevi, 2006.

Birinci, Ali, *Hürriyet ve İtilaf Fırkası, II.Meşrutiyet Devrinde İttihat ve Terakki'ye Karşı Çıkanlar*, Istanbul: Dergah Yayınları, 1990.

Boratav, Korkut, "1923–1939 Yıllarının İktisat Politikası Açısından Dönemlendirilmesi," *Atatürk Döneminin Ekonimik ve Toplumsal Sorunları, 1923–1938 Sempozyumu,* Istanbul: Yüksek İktisad ve Ticaret Mektebi Mezunları Derneği Yay., 1977, pp. 39–52.

Bozarslan, Hamit, "Ziya Gökalp," in *Modern Türkiye'de Düşünce Tarihi, Tanzimat ve Meşrutiyet'in Birikimi,* Istanbul: İletişim Yayınları, 2002, pp. 314–319.

Brower, Daniel R., "Fathers, Sons and Grandfathers: Social Origins of Radical Intellectuals in the Nineteenth Century in Russia," *Journal of Social History,* Vol. 2, No. 4 (Summer 1969), pp. 333–355.

Bruger, Bill, *Republican Theory in Political Thought: Virtuous or Virtual?* London: Macmillan Press, 1999.

Brynn, Robert J., "A Note on the 'Raznochintsy'," *Journal of Social History,* Vol. 10, No. 3 (Spring 1977), pp. 354–359.

Buzpınar, Ş. Tufan, "Celal Nuri's concepts of Westernization and Religion," *Middle Eastern Studies,* Vol. 43 (2007), pp. 247–258.

Caferoğlu, Ahmet, "Ziya Gökalp'in Azerbaycan Türklüğü Üzerindeki Tesiri," *Tarih Kurumu,* Vol. 2, No. 24 (1964), pp. 10–16.

Çağaptay, Soner, *Islam, Nationalism and Secularism in Turkey: Who is a Turk?* London: Routledge, 2005.

Çağla, Cengiz, *Azerbaycan'da Milliyetçilik ve Politika,* Istanbul: Bağlam Yayınları, 2002.

Çavdar, Tevfik, *Türkiye'de Liberalizm,* Ankara, 1992.

———, *Türkiye'de Demokrasi Tarihi 1839–1950,* Ankara: İmge Kitabevi, 1995.

Cavid, Mehmed, "Ticaret Odaları," *Ulum-i Iktisadiye ve İçtimaiye Mecmuasi,* No. 2 (1908), pp. 199.

———, "1327 Senesi Esbab-i Mucibe Lahiyasi," *Ulum-i İktisadiye ve İçtimaiye Mecmuası,* No. 23 (1911), pp. 1052–1108.

Chadbourne, Richard M., *Ernest Renan as an Essayist,* Ithaca; New York: Cornell University Press, 1957.

Chartier, Roger, *The Cultural Orgins of the French Revolution,* trans. Lydra Cochnane, London; Durham: Duke Unv. Press, 1991.

Cladis, Mark S., *A Communitarian Defense of Liberalism: Emile Durkheim and Contemporary Social Theory,* Stanford, Calif.: Stanford University Press, 1992a.

———, "Durkheim's Individual in Society: A Sacred Marriage?" *Journal of the History of Ideas,* Vol. 53, No. 1 (Jan., 1992b), pp. 71–90.

Claeys, Gregory, "'Individualism', 'Socialism', and 'Social Science': Further Notes on a Process of Conceptual Formation, 1800–1850," *Journal of the History of Ideas,* Vol. 47, No. 1 (Jan., 1986), pp. 81–93.

———, "Liberalism," in *Encyclopedia of Nineteenth-Century Thought,* London: Routledge, 2005.

Collini, Stefan, *Public Moralists: Political Thought and Intellectual Life in Britain,* Oxford: Clarendon, 1991.

Coşar, Nevin, *Türkiye'de Devletçilik*, Istanbul: Bağlam Yayıncılık, 1995.

Coşar, Simten, "Ahmet Ağaoğlu: Türk Liberalizminin Açmazlarına Giriş," *Toplum ve Bilim,* 74 (Fall 1997), pp. 155–175.

————, "Liberal Thought and Democracy in Turkey," *Journal of Political Ideologies*, No. 1 (Feb., 2004), pp. 71–98.

Craiutu, Aurelian, *Liberalism under Siege: The Political Thought of the French Doctrinaires,* Oxford: Lexington Books, 2003.

Cumhur, Müjgan, *Ziya Gökalp: Yeni Hayat/Doğru Yol,* Ankara: Kültür Bakanlığı Yayınları, 1976.

Dadayan, Xachatur, *Armyani i Baku 1850–1920*, Erevan: Nof Norabank, 2007.

Darmesteter, James, *Essais Orientaux,* Paris: A. Lévy, 1883.

————, *Critique et politique*, Paris: Ancienne Maison Mchel Levy Freres, 1895.

Darmesteter, Mary R., *The Life of Ernest Renan*, London: Methuen & Co., 1898.

Deren, Seçil, "From Pan-Turkism to Turkish Nationalism: Modernisation and the German Influence in the Late Ottoman Period," in *Disrupting and Reshaping: Early Stages of Nation-Building in the Balkans*, eds. Marco Dogo and Guido Franzinetti, Europe and the Balkans International Network, 17 (Ravenna: Longo Editore, 2002), pp. 117–139.

Derin, Haldun, *Türkiye'de Devletçilik,* Istanbul, 1940.

Devlet, Nadir, *Rusya Türklerinin Milli Mücadele Tarihi, 1905–1917*, Ankara: Türk Kültürünü Araştırma Enstitüsü, 1985.

Drozd, Andrew M., *Chernishevskii's What is to be Done? A Reevaluation*, Evanston, Illinois: Northwestern University Press, 2001.

Duff, Mountstuart G., *Ernest Renan,* London; New York: Macmillan and Co., 1893.

Dumont, Paul, "La Revue *Turk Yurdu* et les musulmans de l'empire russe: 1908–1914," *Cahiers du monde russe et soviétique,* Vol. 15, Nos. 3–4 (1974), pp. 315–331.

Durkheim, Émile, "L'Individualisme et les intellectuals," *Revue bleue,* 4ᵉ série, 10 (1898), pp. 7–13.

————, *The Division of Labour in Society,* Second Edition, London: Macmillan, 1902.

————, *Professional Ethics and Civic Morals,* trans. Cornelia Brookfield, London, New York: Routledge, 1957.

————, *Selected Writings*, London: Cambridge University Press, 1972.

————, *The Division of Labour in Society*, trans. W.D. Halls, New York: Free Press, 1984.

Doğan, Avni, *Kurtuluş, Kuruluş ve Sonrası,* Istanbul: Dünya Yayınları, 1964.

Dyson, Kenneth H.F., *The State Tradition in Western Europe: A Study of an Idea and Institution,* Oxford: Martin Robertson, 1980.

Earle, Edward M., "The New Constitution of Turkey," *Political Science Quarterly*, Vol. 40, No. 1 (Mar., 1925), pp. 73–100.

Ege, Nezahat N., *Prens Sabahattin Hayatı ve İlmi Müdafaaları*, Istanbul: Fakülteler Matbaası, 1977, pp. 58–64.

Egeli, Münir H., *Atatürk'ten Bilinmeyen Hatıralar,* Istanbul, 1959.

Emrence, Cem, ""Politics of Discontent in the Midst of the Great Depression: The Free Republican Party of Turkey (1930)," *New Perspectives on Turkey* 23 (Fall 2000), pp. 31–52.

Erdoğan, Mustafa, "Liberalizm ve Türkiye'deki Serüveni," in *Liberalizm, Modern Türkiye'de Siyasal Düşünce*, ed. Murat Yılmaz, Istanbul: İletişim Yayınları, 2005, pp. 23–40.

Erkul, Ali, "Prens Sabahattin," in *Türk Toplum Bilimcileri*, ed. Emre Kongar, İstanbul: Remzi Kitabevi, 2003.

Eroğlu, Nazmi, "Mehmed Cavid Bey'in İktisadi Görüşleri", *İstanbul Üniversitesi Atatürk İlkeleri ve İnkılap Tarihi Enstitüsü Dergisi: Yakın Dönem Türkiye Araştırmaları* (2002), 163–183, p. 164.

———— *İttihatçıların Ünlü Maliye Nazırı Cavid Bey*, Istanbul: Otüken Yayınları, 2008.

Espinasse, Francis, *Life of Ernest Renan*, London: Walter Scott, Limited, 1895.

Etem, Sadri, *Türk İnkılabının Karakterleri,* Istanbul: Devlet Matbaası, 1933.

Farmer, Paul, *France Reviews Its Revolutionary Origins: Social Politics and Historical Opinions in the Third Republic,* New York: Octagon Books, 1973.

Femia, Joseph V., "A Historicist Critique of 'Revisionist' Methods for Studying the History of Ideas," *History and Theory,* Vol. 20, No. 2 (May, 1981), pp. 113–134.

Fındıkoğlu, Ziyaeddin F., *Fransız İhtilali ve Tanzimat*, Istanbul: Türkiye Felsefi, Harsi ve İctimai Araştırmalar Merkezi Kitapları, sayı: 11.

Findley, Carter V., "The Advent of the Ideology in the Islamic Middle East (Part I)," *Studia Islamica*, No. 55 (1982a), pp. 143–169.

————, "The Advent of the Ideology in the Islamic Middle East (Part II)," *Studia Islamica*, No. 56 (1982b), pp. 147–180.

Finefrock, Michael M., "Laissez-Faire, the 1923 Izmir Economic Congress and Early Turkish Developmental Policy in Political Perspective," *Middle Eastern Studies*, Vol. 17, No. 3 (Jul., 1981), pp. 375–392.

Gardaz, Michel, "The Age of Discoveries and Patriotism: James Darmesteter's Assessment of French Orientalism," *Religion*, No. 30 (2000), pp. 353–365.

Gencer, Mustafa, *Jöntürk Modenizmi ve "Alman Ruhu,"* Istanbul: İletişim Yayınları, 2003.

George, Henry W., "Montesquieu and de Tocqueville and Corporative Individualism," *The American Political Science Review*, Vol. 16, No. 1 (Feb., 1922), pp. 10–21.

Georgeon, François, *Aux origines du nationalisme turc: Yusuf Akçura,1876–1935*, Paris: Éditions ADPF, 1980.

————, "Les Debuts d'un Intellectuel Azerbaidjanais: Ahmed Ağaoğlu en France 1888–1894," in *Passe Turco Tatar Present Sovietique*, eds. Ch. Lemercier-Quelquejay, G. Veinstein and S.E. Wimbush, Etudes offertes a Alexandre Bennigsen, Louvain and Paris: Editions Peeters, 1986.

————, "Ahmet Ağaoğlu, un Intellectuel Turc Admirateur des Lumières et de la Révolution," *Revue du Monde Musulman et de la Mediterranée*, Vols. 52–53 (1989), pp. 186–197.

————, *Osmanli-Türk Modernleşmesi, 1900–1930*, trans. Ali Berktay, Istanbul: Yapı Kredi Yayınları, 2006.

Geyikdağı, V. Necla, "The Relationship between Trade and Foreign Direct Investment: Testing Ahmed Midhat Efendi's Hypothesis," *International Journal of Middle East Studies*, Vol. 40 (2008), pp. 547–549.

Giddens, Anthony, *Durkheim on Politics and the State*, Cambridge: Polity Press, 1986.

Gildea, Robert, *The Third Republic in France, 1870–1940*, London; New York: Longman, 1996.

Giritli, İsmet, "Fransız İhtilali ve Etkileri," in *Atatürk Araştırma Merkezi Dergisi*, Vol. 15, No. 5 (Jul., 1989).

Gökalp, Ziya, "Yeni Hayat ve Yeni Kıymetler," *Genç Kalemler*, No. 8 (1911).

————, "Fırkaların Siyâsi Tasnifi," *Hâkimiyet-i Milliye*, 19.04.1923.

————, *Turkish Nationalism and Western Civilization: Selected Essays*, trans. Niyazi Berkes, London: Allen & Unwin, 1959.

————, *Türkleşmek, İslamlaşmak, Muasırlaşmak*, Ankara: Yeni Matbaa, 1960.

————, *Makaleler IX*, Istanbul: Kültür Bakanlığı Yayınları, 1980.

Gökay, Bülent, *A Clash of Empires: Turkey between Russian Bolshevism and British Imperialism, 1918–1923*, London, N.Y.: I.B. Tauris, 1997.

Goldstein, Marc A., *Social and Political Thought of the French Revolution, 1788–1797: An Anthology of Original Texts*, New York: P. Lang, 1997.

Gözübüyük, A. Şeref, *1924 Anayasası Hakkındaki Meclis Görüşmeleri*, Ankara: SBF Yayınları, 1957.

————, *Açıklamalı Türk Anayasaları 1876, 1921, 1924, 1961, 1982, Anayasaların Yapılışları, özellikleri ve yapılan değişiklikler*, Ankara: Turhan Kitabevi Yayınları, 2005.

Gray, John, *Liberalism*, Buckingham: Open University Press, 1995.

Gulbenkian, Calouste S., *La Transcaucasie et la Péninsule d'Apchéron: Souvenirs de Voyage*, Paris: Libraire Hachette et Cie, 1891.

Gündoğdu, Abdullah, *Ümmetten Millete: Ahmet Ağaoğlu'nun Sırat-ı Müstakim ve Sebilürreşad Dergilerindeki Yazıları Üzerine Bir İnceleme*, Istanbul: IQ Yayıncılık, 2007.

Güneş, İhsan, *Birinci TBMM'nin Düşünce Yapısı, 1920–1923*, Istanbul: Türkiye İş Bankası Kültür Yayınları, 1997.

Güngör, Süleyman, *Türkiye Cumhuriyeti'nin İlk Yıllarında Politikacı-Aydın İlişkisi*, Ankara: Nobel Yayın Dağıtım, 2002.

Hajiyeva, Lala Osman, "Ahmadbey Aghayev'in Publisistikası: Kaspi qazetinin materiallari esasinda," Unpublished masters thesis, Baku State University, 2006.

Hale, William, "Ideology and Economic Development in Turkey, 1930–1945," *Bulletin* (British Society for Middle Eastern Studies), Vol. 7, No. 2 (1980), pp. 100–117.

Hanioğlu, M. Şükrü, "Garpçılık: Their Attitude toward Religion and Their Impact on the Official Ideology of the Turkish Republic," *Studia Islamica,* No. 86 (1997), pp. 133–158.

———, *Preparation for a Revolution, the Young Turks, 1902–1908*, New York, Oxford: Oxford University Press, 2001.

Hansen, Eric C., *Disaffection and Decadence, A Crisis in French Intellectual Thought, 1848–1898,* Washington: University Press of America, 1982.

Harms, John B., "Reason and Social Change in Durkheim's Thought: The Changing Relations between Individual and Society," *The Pacific Sociological Review*, Vol. 24, No. 4 (Oct., 1981), pp. 393–410.

Hayek, Friedrich A., *Individualism and Economic Order*, Chicago: The University of Chicago Press, 1948.

Hazareesingh, Sudhir, *Intellectual Founders of the Republic, Five Studies in Nineteenth Century French Republican Political Thought*, Oxford; New York: Oxford University Press, 2001.

Hershlag, Zvi Y., *Turkey: An Economy in Transition*, The Hague: Van Kuelen, 1959.

Heyd, Uriel, *The Foundations of Turkish Nationalism: The Life and Teachings of Ziya Gökalp*, London: Luzac, 1950.

Hilgar, Marie-France, "Juliette Adam et la 'Nouvelle Revue'," *Rocky Mountain Review of Language and Literature*, Vol. 51, No. 2 (1997), pp. 11–18.

Hirai, Atsuko, *Individualism and Socialism: The Life and Thought of Kawai Eijiro, 1891–1944*, Cambridge, London: Council on East Asian Studies, Harvard University, 1986.

Hirsch, Eva and Hirsh, Abraham, "Changes in Agricultural Output per Capita of Rural Population in Turkey, 1927–1960," *Economic Development and Cultural Change*, Vol. xi, No. 4 (Jul., 1963).

İlkin, Selim; Tekeli, İlhan, "Devletçilik Döneminin İlk Yıllarında İşçi Sorununa Yaklaşım ve 1932 İş Kanunu Tasarısı," *ODTÜ Gelişme Dergisi*, Türkiye İktisat Tarihi Üzerine Araştırmalar [I], 1978, pp. 252–348.

———, *Uygulamaya Geçerken Türkiye'de Devletçiliğin Oluşumu*, Ankara: Ortadoğu Teknik Üniversitesi Yayınları, 1982.

———, *Bir Cumhuriyet Öyküsü: Kadrocuları ve Kadro'yu Anlamak*, Istanbul: Tarih Vakfı Yurt Yayınları, 2003.

İlmen, Süreyya, *4 Ay Yaşamış Olan Zavallı Serbest Fırka*, Istanbul: Muallim Fuat Güçüyener, 1951.

Infantino, Lorenzo, *Individualism in Modern Thought: From Adam Smith to Hayek*, London: Routledge, 1998.

İnönü, İsmet, *İnönü'nün Söylev ve Demeçleri*, Istanbul: Milli Eğitim Basımevi, 1946.

İnsel, Ahmet, "Türkiye'de Liberalizm Kavramının Soyçizgisi," in *Liberalizm, Modern Türkiye'de Siyasal Düşünce*, ed. Murat Yılmaz, Istanbul: İletişim Yayınları, 2005, pp. 41–69.

İrem, Nazım, "Turkish Conservative Modernism: Birth of a Nationalist Quest for Cultural Renewal," *International Journal of Middle Eastern Studies*, Vol. 34 (2002), pp. 87–112.

Ishakhov, C.M., *A.M. Topchubashi: Dokumenty iz Lichnykh Arkhivov, 1903–1934*, Moscow: Izdatelstvo, 2012.

Janowski, Maciej, *Polish Liberal Thought,* Budapest: Central European Press, 2004.

Jaume, Lucien, *L'individu efface ou le paradoxe le libéralisme français,* Paris: Fayard, 1997.

Jones, Robert A., "The Positive Science of Ethics in France: German Influences on 'De le division du travail social'" *Sociological Forum,* Vol. 9, No. 1 (Mar., 1994), pp. 37–57.

Jones, H.S., *Intellect and Character in Victorian England: Mark Pattison and the Invention of the Don,* Cambridge: Cambridge University Press, 2007.

———, "French Liberalism and the Legacy of the Revolution," in *Historicising the French Revolution,* eds. C. Armenteros, I. DiVanna, and T. Blanning, Newcastle-upon-Tyne: Cambridge Scholars Publishing, 2008, pp. 189–206.

Kadıoğlu, Ayşe, *Cumhuriyet İradesi Demokrasi Muhakemesi*, Istanbul: Metis Yayınları, 1999.

———, "Citizenship and Individuation in Turkey: The Triumph of Will over Reason," in *Civil Society, Religion and Nation: Modernization in Intercultural Context: Russia, Japan, Turkey,* eds. Gerrit Steunebrink and Evert van der Zweerde, Amsterdam: Editions Rodopi, 2004, pp. 191–212.

Kahan, Alan S., *Liberalism in Nineteenth Century Europe*: *The Political Culture of Limited Suffrage*, Basingstoke: Palgrave Macmillan, 2003.

Kant, Immanuel, *Foundations of the Metaphysics of Morals: And What is Enlightenment?* trans. Lewis W. Beck, New York: Liberal Arts Press, 1959.

Kaplan, Mehmet, *Atatürk Devri Fikir Hayatı I–II*, 2 vols., Ankara: Kültür Bakanlığı Yayınları, 1992.

Kara, İsmail, *Türkiye'de İslamcılık Düşüncesi, Metinler/Kişiler,* I, Istanbul: Kitabevi Yayınları, 1988.

Karadaş, Yücel, "Orientalism and Invention of Tradition in Cultural Concept of Ziya Gökalp," *Euroasian Journal of Anthropology*, No. 2 (2010), pp. 44–58.

Karaer, İbrahim, *Türk Ocakları, 1912–1931*, Ankara: Türk Yurdu Neşriyatı, 1992.

Karaman, Deniz, *Cavid Bey ve Ulum-i İktisadiye ve İctimaiye Mecmuası*, Ankara: Liberte Yayınları, 2001.

———, "Ulum-i Iktisadiye Mecmuasi," *C.U. Sosyal Bilimler Dergisi* 28/1 (May, 2004), pp. 65–87, p. 73.

Karaosmanoğlu, Yakup K., *Ankara*, Istanbul: Birikim Yayınları, 1981.

Karpat, Kemah, *Turkey's Politics: The Transition to a Multi-party System*, Princeton, N.J.: Princeton University Press, 1959.

Kazamias, Andreas, *Education and the Quest for Modernity in Turkey*, Chicago: University of Chicago Press, 1966.

Keddie, Nikki R. , "Pan-Islam as Proto-Nationalism," *The Journal of Modern History*, Vol. 41, No. 1 (Mar. 1969), pp. 17–28.

Kelly, Donald, "Intellectual History in a Global Age," *Journal of the History of Ideas*, Vol. 66, No. 2 (Apr., 2005), pp. 155–167.

Kemper, Theodore D., "Emile Durkheim and the Division of Labour," *Sociological Quarterly*, No. 16 (Spring 1975), pp. 190–206.

Kerwin, Robert W., "Private Enterprise in Turkish Industrial Development," *Middle East Journal*, Vol. v, No. 1 (Winter, 1951).

Keyder, Çağlar, "Cumhuriyetin İlk Yıllarında Türk Tüccarının Milli'leşmesi," *ODTÜ Gelişme Dergisi* (1979–80 Special Edition), pp. 239–255.

————, *The Definition of a Peripheral Economy: Turkey, 1923–29,* Cambridge: Cambridge University Press, 1981.

Kia, Mehrdad, "Mirza Fath Ali Akhundzade and the Call for Modernization in the Islamic World," *Middle Eastern Studies*, Vol. 31, No. 3 (Jul., 1995), pp. 422–448.

————, "Pan-Islamism in Late Nineteenth Century Iran," *Middle Eastern Studies*, Vol. 32, No. 1 (Jan., 1996), pp. 30–52.

————, "Women, Islam and Modernity in Akhundzade's Plays and Unpublished Writings," *Middle Eastern Studies*, Vol. 34, No. 3 (Jul., 1998), pp. 1–33.

Koçak, Cemil, "Belgelerle Serbest Cumhuriyet Fırkası," Osmanlı Bankası Müzesi: Çağdaş Türkiye Seminerleri (Feb., 2005).

————, "Parliament Membership during the Single-Party System in Turkey, 1925–1945," *European Journal of Turkish Studies*, No. 3 (2005), (http://ejts.revues.org/497).

Kologlu, Orhan, *Aydınlarımızın Bunalım Yılı 1918: Zafer-i Nihaiyeden Tam Teslimiyete*, Istanbul: Boyut Yayınları, 2000.

Konuk, Kader, *East West Mimesis: Auerbach in Turkey*, Stanford: Stanford University Press, 2010.

Köroğlu, Erol, *Ottoman Propaganda and Turkish Identity, Literature in Turkey during World War I*, London&N.Y.: I.B. Tauris & Co. Ltd., 2007.

Kropotkin, Petr A., *Mutual Aid: A Factor of Evolution*, London: Penguin, 1939.

————, *Ethics: Origin and Development*, trans. Louis S. Friedland and Joseph H. Piroshnikoff, New York: Tudor Publishing, 1947.

Kümbül, Bengi, *Tercümân-ı Hakikat Gazetesine Göre Osmanlı Ermenileri, 1914–1918*, Istanbul: Yeniden Anadolu ve Müdafaa-i Hukuk Yayınları, 2006.

Kurzman, Charles, ed. *Modernist Islam*, N.Y.: Oxford University Press, 2002.

Kushner, David, *The Rise of Turkish Nationalism, 1876–1908*, London: Frank Cass., 1977.

Kutay, Cemal, "Şarklılaşma-Garplılaşma I–II," *Yeni Istanbul,* December 3–4, 1972.

Landau, Jacob M., *The Politics of Pan-Islam: Ideology and Organisation,* Oxford: Clarendon Press, 1990.

———, *Pan-Turkism: From Irredentism to Cooperation,* London: C. Hurst, 1995.

Lazarus, Josephine, "Book Review: Selected Essays of James Darmesteter," *International Journal of Ethics,* Vol. 6, No. 2 (Jan., 1896), pp. 261–264.

Leeuw, Charles van der, *Azerbaijan: A Quest for Identity, A Short History,* Surrey: Curzon Press, 2000.

Lefrançais, J.D., *Lectures Patriotique sur l'histoire de France A l'usage des écoles primaires,* Paris: Librairie Ch. Delagrave, 1882.

Lehning, James, *To be a Citizen The Political Culture of the Early French Republic,* Ithaca, London: Cornell University Press, 2001.

Lenoir, Raymond, "Renan and the Study of Humanity," *The American Journal of Sociology,* No. 3 (Nov., 1925), pp. 289–317.

LeVan, Carl, "Analytic Authoritarianism and Nigeria," *Commonwealth&Comparative Politics,* Vol. 52, No. 2 (Mar., 2014), pp. 212–231.

Lewis, Edwin, "Some Definitions of Individualism," *The American Journal of Sociology,* Vol. 17, No. 2 (Sep., 1911), pp. 223–253.

———, "Liberal Partisi Hilâfet'in külliyen ilgâsına karar Verdi," *Tevhid-i Efkâr,* February 29, 1924.

Lieven, D.C.B., "Bureaucratic Liberalism in Late Imperial Russia: The Personality, Career and Opinions of A.N. Kulomzin," *The Slavonic and East European Review,* Vol. 60, No. 3 (Jul., 1982), pp. 413–432.

Lovejoy, Arthur O., *The Great Chain of Being: A Study of the History of an Idea,* Cambridge, Mass.: Harvard University Press, 1936.

Lukes, Steven, "Durkheim's 'Individualism and the Intellectuals'," *Political Studies,* Vol. 17, No. 1 (Mar., 1969), pp. 14–30.

———, "The Meanings of Individualism," *Journal of the History of Ideas,* Vol. 32, No. 1 (Jan., 1971), pp. 45–66.

———, *Emile Durkheim, His Life and Work: A Historical and Critical Study,* London: Allen Lane, 1973a.

———, *Individualism,* Oxford: Blackwell, 1973b.

Manaf Süleymanov, *Azerbaycan Milyonçuları: Haci Zeynalabdin Tağıyev,* Baku: Gençlik, 1996

Manent, Pierre, *An intellectual history of liberalism,* Princeton, N.J.: Princeton University Press, 1995.

Manning, D.J., *Liberalism,* N.Y.: St. Martin's Press, 1976.

Mardin, Şerif, "Ideology and Religion in the Turkish Revolution," *International Journal of Middle East Studies,* Vol. 2, No. 3 (Jul., 1971), pp. 197–211, p. 198."

———, *Jöntürklerin Siyasi Fikirleri, 1895–1908,* Istanbul: İletişim Yayınları, 1983.

———, *Türk Modernleşmesi: Makaleler,* Istanbul: İletişim Yayınları, 1991, pp. 23–81.

————, *The Genesis of Young Ottoman Thought: A Study in the Modernization of Turkish Political Ideas,* Syracuse: Syracuse University Press, 2000.

Marske, Charles, "Durkheim's 'Cult of the Individual' and the Moral Reconstitution of Society," *Sociological Theory,* Vol. 5, No. 1 (Spring 1987), pp. 1–14.

McKechnie, W. S., *The State and the Individual,* Glasgow, 1896.

Mehmed Cavid Bey, *Felaket Günleri: Mütareke Günlerinin Feci Tarihi,* Istanbul: Temel, 2000a.

————, *Zindandan Mektuplar,* Ankara: Liberte Yayınları, 2000b.

————, *İlm-i İktisad,* Ankara: Liberte Yayınları, 2001.

Melzig, Herbert, *Atatürk'ün Başlıca Nutukları 1920–1938,* Istanbul: Ülkü Matbaası, 1942.

Memmedov, X, "İ. Gasprinski'nin A. Hüseyizâde'ye 'Açık Mektubu," *Edebiyat Gazetesi,* June 17, 1992.

Mert, Muhit, "Osmanlı'dan Cumhuriyete Geçiş Döneminde Ahmet Ağaoğlu'nin Dini Düşünceleri," *Hitit Üniversitesi İlahiyat Fakültesi Dergisi,* No. 10 (Feb., 2006), pp. 7–27.

Mestrovic, Stjepan G., *Emile Durkheim and the Reformation of Sociology,* Lanham, Maryland: Rowman&Littlefield, 1993.

Meyer, James, "Immigration, Return and the Politics of Citizenship: Russian Muslims in the Ottoman Empire, 1860–1914," *International Journal of Middle Eastern Studies,* 39 (2007), 15–32.

————, "Division and Alliance: Mass Politics within Muslim Communities after 1905," The National Council for Eurasian and East European Research Working Paper (Oct., 2009).

Midhat, Orhan, *İcitmâi Taksim-i Amâl,* Istanbul: n.p., 1923.

Miley, Thomas J., "Franquism as Authoritarianism: Juan Linz and His Critics," *Politics, Religion and Ideology,* Vol. 12, No. 1 (May, 2011), pp. 27–50.

Mills, Charles W., "Race and the Social Contract Tradition," in *Ethics: The Big Questions,* ed. James P. Sterba, London: Wiley-Blackwell, 1998, pp. 315–330.

Mismer, Charles, *Souvenirs du Monde Musulman,* Paris: Librairie Hachette Et C, 1892.

Mounier, Emmanuel, *Personalism,* Notre Dame; Ind.; London: University of Notre Dame Press, 1975.

Movlaeva, S.A., *Propaganda Russkoj i Azerbajdzhanskoj Kul'tury na Ctranicah Gazety Kaspij,* Baku, 1983.

Müller, Hans-Peter, "Social Differentiation and Organic Solidarity: The Division of Labour Revisited," *Sociological Forum,* Vol. 9, No. 1 (Mar., 1994), pp. 73–86.

Nadi, Yunus, "Milli İktisat," *Cumhuriyet,* August 9, 1929.

————, "Devletçilik ve Şahsi Teşebbüs," *Cumhuriyet,* November 11, 1932.

Nazif, Süleyman, "A. Agayef Beyefendiye," *İçtihad,* Vol. 3, No. 71 (1913a).

————, "Cengiz Hastalığı," *İçtihad,* Vol. 3, No. 72 (1913b).

Okyar, Fethi, *Üç Devirde Bir Adam,* Istanbul: Tercüman, 1980.

————, *Serbest Cumhuriyet Fırkası Nasıl Doğdu Nasıl Feshedildi?* Istanbul, 1987.

Okyar, Osman; Seyitdanlıoğlu; Mehmet, "The Concept of Étatism," *The Economic Journal*, Vol. 75, No. 297 (Mar., 1965), pp. 98–111.

————, "Development Background of the Turkish Economy, 1923–1973," *International Journal of Middle Eastern Studies,* Vol. 10, No. 3 (Aug., 1979), pp. 325–344.

————, *Atatürk and Turkey of Republican Era,* Ankara: Union of Chambers of Commerce, Industry, Maritime Commerce and Commodity exchanges of Turkey, 1981.

————, *Fethi Okyar'ın Anıları: Atatürk-Okyar ve Çok Partili Türkiye,* Istanbul: İş Bankası Kültür Yayınları, 1997.

————, *Milli Mücadele Dönemi Türk-Sovyet İlişkilerinde Mustafa Kemal,* 1920–1921, Ankara: Türkiye İş Bankası, 1998.

Olson, Robert, "Kurdish Rebellions of the Sheikh Said (1925), Mt Ararat (1930), and Dersim (1937–38): Their Impact on the Development of Turkish Air Force and on Kurdish and Turkish Nationalism," *Die Welt des Islams,* New Series, Vol. 40, No. 1 (Mar., 2000), pp. 67–94.

Oral, Mustafa, "Çağdaşları Tarafından Ziya Gokalp Eleştirisi *CITAD*, 12 (Spring 2006), pp. 21–34.

Oruç, Arif, *Vatandaşın Birinci Hürriyeti,* Istanbul: Tecelli M., 1932.

Özavcı, H. Ozan, "Prens Sabahaddin'in Fikri Kaynakları: Le Play ve Toplum Bilim," *Doğu Batı* (Jul., 2007), pp. 231–254.

————, "The French Revolution from a Turkish Perspective: Ahmet Ağaoğlu and High Individualism," in *Historicising the French Revolution*, eds. C. Armenteros, T. Blanning, I. DiVanna, and D. Dodds, Newcastle-upon-Tyne: Cambridge Scholars Publishing, 2008, pp. 146–168.

Özcan, Ufuk, *Ahmet Ağaoğlu ve Rol Değişikliği: Yüzyıl Dönümünde Batıcı Bir Aydın,* Istanbul: Don Kişot Yayınları, 2002.

Öztürk, Kazım, *Türk Parlemento Tarihi,* Ankara: TBMM Vakfı Yayınları, No. 9, 1993.

Paris, Gaston, *Penseurs et Poètes: James Darmesteter, Frédéric Mistral, Sully Prudhomme, Alexandre Bida, Ernest Renan, Albert Sorel,* Paris: Ancienne Maison Michel Levy Frères, 1896.

Parla, Taha, *The Social and Political Thought of Ziya Gökalp,* Leiden: E.J. Brill, 1985.

Parla Taha; Davison, Andrew, *Corporatist Ideology in Kemalist Turkey,* New York: Syracuse University Press, 2004.

Peker, Recep, *İnkılâp Dersleri Notları,* Ankara: Ulus Basımevi, 1935.

Perrin, Robert, "Durkheim's Division of Labour and the Shadow of Herbert Spencer," *The Sociological Quarterly,* Vol. 36, No. 4 (Autumn, 1995), pp. 791–808.

Petrovic, P, *Rabochie Bakinskaga Neftepromishlennago Raiona,* Tiflis, 1911.

Pickering, Mary, *Auguste Comte: An Intellectual Biography*, Vol. I, Cambridge: Cambridge University Press, 1993.

Pinson, Mark, "Turkish Revolution and Reform (1919–1928) in Soviet Historiography," *Middle East Journal,* Vol. 17, No. 4 (Fall, 1963), pp. 466–478.

Pipes, Richard, "The Historical Evolution of the Russian Intelligentsia," *Daedalus,* Vol. 89, No. 3 (Summer, 1960), pp. 487–502.

Pitt, Alan, "The Cultural Impact of Science in France: Ernest Renan and the *Vie de Jesus*," *The Historical Journal,* Vol. 43, No. 1 (Mar., 2000), pp. 79–101.

Pocock, J.G.A., "Languages and Their Implications: The Transformation of the Study of Political Thought," *Politics, Language and Time: Essays on Political Thought and History,* New York: Atheneum, 1971.

Popper, Karl R., *The Open Society and Its Enemies*, Third Edition, Vols. I–II, London: Routledge, 1945.

Quliyev, Vilayet, *Ahmed Bey Ağaoğlu: Seçme Eserleri*, Baku: Şarq-Garp, 2007.

Reinach, Salomon, *James Darmesteter*, Paris: Les cahiers d'etudes juives, 1932.

Renan, Ernest, *La réforme intellectuelle et morale*, Paris: n.p., 1875.

———, *Qu'est-que est une nation? conference faite á la Sorbonne, le 11 Mars 1882.*

———, *L'Islamisme et la science: conference faite á la Sorbonne, le 29 Mars 1883*, Paris: C. Lévy, 1883.

———, *L'Avenir de la science, pensées de 1848*, Paris: Ancienne Maison Michel Levy Freres, 1890.

Revendications de la Délégation de Paix de la République de l'Azerbaijan du Caucause présentées à la Conférence de la Paix, à Paris, 1918.

Rustow, Dankwart A., "The Army and the Founding of the Turkish Republic," *World Politics*, Vol. 11, No. 4 (Jul., 1959), pp. 513–552.

Sabahaddin, Mehmed, *Türkiye Nasıl Kurtarılabilir?* Istanbul: Ayraç Yayınları, 1999.

Safa, Peyami, *Türk İnkılabına Bakışlar,* Istanbul: İnkılap Yayınevi, 1938.

———, "Ahmet Ağaoğlu," *Cumhuriyet*, May 24, 1939.

———, "Ahmet Ağaoğlu'nun İki Hikayesi," *Milliyet*, February 14, 1958.

———, *Doğu Batı Sentezi,* Istanbul: Yağur Yayınevi, 1973.

Şahingiray, Özel, *Atatürk'ün Nöbet Defteri,* Ankara: Türk Tarih Kurumu Basımevi, 1955.

Sakal, Fahri, "Ağaoğlu Ahmed'in Harp Yıllarında Kaleme Aldığı Birlik ve Beraberlik Yazıları," *Atatürk Araştırma Merkezi Dergisi*, C.X, No. 33 (Nov., 1995), pp. 699–707.

———, "Ağaoğlu Ahmed'in Yakın Tarihimizdeki yeri," *Akademik Açı*, No. 2 (1996a), pp. 135–147.

———, "Ağaoğlu Ahmed'in Demokrasi Anlayışı," *Atatürk Araştırma Merkezi Dergisi*, C.X, No. 34 (Mar., 1996b), pp. 195–222.

——— *Ağaoğlu Ahmed Bey*, Ankara: Türk Tarih Kurumu Basımevi, 1999.

Salvadori, Massimo, *The Liberal Heresy: Origins and Historical Development,* New York: St. Martin's Press, 1977.

Sanders, Arthur, "The Meaning of Liberalism and Conservatism," *Polity*, Vol. 19, No. 1 (Aug., 1986), pp. 123–135.

Sarıahmetoğlu Karagür, Nesrin, *Petrolün Sihirli Dünyası Bakü*, Istanbul: IQ Yayıncılık, 2007.

Sayar, Ahmed G., *Osmanlı İktisad Düşüncesinin Çağdaşlaşması*, Istanbul: Dev Yayınları, 1986.

Schissler, Holly, "A Student Abroad in Late Ottoman Times: Ahmet Ağaoğlu and French Paradigms in Turkish Thought," in *Iran and Beyond: Essays in Middle Eastern History in Honor of Nikki Keddie*, eds. Rudi Mathee and Beth Baon, CA: Mazda, 2000.

———, *Between Two Empires: Ahmet Ağaoğlu and the New Turkey*, London; New York: I.B. Tauris, 2003.

Schrerrer, Jutta, "Intelligentsia, religion, révolution: Prèmier manifestation d'un socialisme chrétien en Russie, 1905–1907," *Cahiers du Monde russe et soviétique*, Vol. 17, No. 4 (Oct.–Dec., 1976), pp. 427–466.

Seregny, Scott J., "Russian Teachers and Peasant Revolution, 1895–1917," in *Modernisation and Revolution: Dilemmas of Progress in Late Imperial Russia*, eds. Edward H. Judge and James Y. Simms, New York: East European Monographs, 1992, pp. 59–67.

Serezli, Güneş A., *Turkish Humanism Project in the Early Republican Period*, Unpublished Master's Dissertation, Middle East Technical University, 2006.

Şerif, Muzaffer, "Benliğin Doyurulması," *İnsan*, No. 1, April 15, 1938.

Seyid-zade, Dilara, *Azerbaijan in the Beginning of XXth Century: Roads Leading to Independence*, trans. G. Bayramov, Baku: OKA Offset, 2010.

Shapiro, Gary, "Nietzsche contra Renan," *History and Theory*, Vol. 21, No. 2 (May, 1982), pp. 193–222.

Şimşir, Bilal, *Malta Sürgünleri*, Ankara: Bilgi Yayınevi, 1985.

Skinner, Quentin, "Meaning and Understanding in the History of Ideas," *History and Theory*, Vol. 8, No. 1 (1969), pp. 3–53.

———, *Liberty before Liberalism*, Cambridge: Cambridge University Press, 1998.

Slatter, John, "P.A. Kropotkin On Legality and Ethics," *Studies in East European Thought*, Vol. 48, No. 2/4, Conceptions of Legality and Ethics in Nineteenth Century and Twentieth Century Russian Thought (Sep., 1996), pp. 255–276.

Smith, Anthony, *The Ethnic Origins of Nations*, Oxford: Blackwell, 1986.

Sofiyev, Xaladdin, *Şarq-Qarb madaniyatları ve Ahmad Bay Ağaoğlu*, Bakü: Ocak, 2004.

Sohrabi, Nader, "Historicizing the Revolutions: Constitutional Revolutions in the Ottoman Empire, Iran and Russia, 1905–1908," *The American Journal of Sociology*, Vol. 100, No. 6 (May, 1995), p. 1407.

Soman, Mariette, *La formation philosophique d'Ernest Renan jusqu'à L'Avenir de la Science d'après des document inédits*, Paris: Émile Larose, 1914.

Soyak, Hasan R., *Atatürk'ten Hatıralar*, Vols. I–II, Ankara: Yapı Kredi Bankası, 1973.

Spencer, Robert F., "Culture Process and Intellectual Current: Durkheim and Atatürk," *American Anthropologist*, Vol. 60, No. 4 (Aug., 1958), pp. 640–657.

Strenski, Ivan, *The New Durkheim*, New Brunswick, N.J., London: Rutgers University Press, 2006.

Stoddard, Lothrop, "Pan-Turanism," *American Political Science Association*, Vol. 11, No. 1 (Feb., 1917), pp. 12–23.

Suphi, Hamdullah, "Hitabe," *Türk Yurdu*, June 9, 1925.

———, "Türk Ocağının Tarihçesi ve İftiralara Karşı Cevaplarımız," *Türk Yurdu*, No. 3, V/25, 1930.

Swart, Koneraad, "Individualism in the mid-nineteenth century (1826–1860)," *Journal of the History of Ideas*, Vol. 23, No. 1 (Jan., 1962), pp. 77–90.

Swietochowski, Tadeusz, *Russian Azerbaijan, 1905–1920: The Shaping of a National Identity in a Muslim Country*, Cambridge: Cambridge University Press, 1985.

Tachau, Frank, "The Search for National Identity among the Turks," *Die Welt des Islams*, Vol. 8, No. 3 (1963), pp. 165–176.

Tanyu, Hikmet, *Ziya Gökalp: Yeni Türkiye'nin Hedefleri*, Ankara: Hür B. Yayınları, 1956.

Temir, Ahmet, *Yusuf Akçura*, Ankara: Kültür Bakanlığı Yayınları, 1987.

Tevfik, Baha, *Felsefe-i Ferd*, Istanbul: Yumuşak G. Yayınları, 1997.

Tielrooy, Johannes, *Ernest Renan: Sa Vie et Ses Ouvres*, Paris: Mercure de France, 1958.

Tiryakian, Edward A., "Revisiting Sociology's First Critic: "The Division of Labour in Society" and Its Actuality," Sociological Forum, Vol. 9, No. 1, Special Issue: The 100th Anniversary of Sociology's First Classic: Durkheim's "Division of Labour in Society" (Mar., 1994), pp. 3–16.

Toprak, Zafer, *Türkiye'de Milli İktisat, 1908–1918*, Ankara: Yurt Yayınları, 1982.

———, "Anayasal Monarşi ve İttihatçıların Dramı," *Osmanlı Bankası Arşivi*, 2008.

Topuz, Hıfzı, *II. Mahmut'tan Holdinglere Türkiye'de Basın Tarihi*, Istanbul: Remzi Kitabevi, 2003.

Trak, Ayşe, "Devlet ve Ferd: Gecikmiş Bir Kitap Eleştrisi," *Toplum ve Bilim*, No. 14, 1981, pp. 71–77.

———, "Development Literature and Writers from Underdeveloped Countries: The Case of Turkey," *Current Anthropology*, Vol. 26, No. 1 (Feb., 1985), pp. 89–102.

Tufan, M. Naim, *Rise of the Young Turks*, N.Y., London: I.B. Tauris, 2000

Tully, James, ed., *Meaning and Context, Meaning and Context*, Princeton, N.J.: Princeton University Press, 1988.

Tunaya, Tarık Z., *Türkiye'nin Siyasi Hayatında Batılılaşma Hareketleri*, Istanbul: Yedigün Matbaası, 1960.

———, *İslamcılık Cereyanı*, Istanbul: Baha Matbaası, 1962.

———, *Türkiye'de Siyasi Partiler*, Vols. I–III, Istanbul: Hürriyet Vakfı Yayınları, 1989.

Tunçay, Mete, *T.C.'inde Tek Parti Yönetimi'nin Kurulması, 1923–1931*, Istanbul: Cem Yayınevi, 1981.

Turhan, Mümtaz, *Where are We in Westernization?* Istanbul: Türkiye Basımevi, 1959.

Türkeş, Mustafa, "A Patriotic Leftist Development Strategy Proposal in Turkey in the1930s: The Case of the Kadro (Cadre) Movement," *International Journal of Middle East Studies,* Vol. 33, No. 1 (2002), pp. 91–114.

Tütengil, Cavit O., *Prens Sabahattin,* Istanbul: İstanbul Matbaası, 1954.

Ülgener, Sabri F., *İktisadi Çözülmenin Ahlak ve Zihniyet Dünyası,* Istanbul, 1980.

Ülken, Hilmi Z., *Türkiye'de Çağdaş Düşünce Tarihi,* Istanbul: Ülken Yayınları, 1992.

———, "Hangi Garp," *İnsan,* No. 1 (1938).

———, "Ağaoğlu Ahmet ve Fikir Hayatı ve Mücadeleleri," *Ses,* May 25, 1939.

———, "Ferd ve Cemiyet," *İnsan,* No. 17 (1940).

Ünsal, Artun, "Atatürk's Reforms: Realisation of Utopia by a Realist," Paper presented to the seminar *Nehru and Atatürk,* New Delhi, 1981.

Usta, Veysel, "Ağaoğlu Ahmet Bey'in Milli Mücadele'de Trabzon'da Verdiği Konferans," *Türk Kültürü,* No. 399 (1996), pp. 400–415.

———, "Ağaoğlu Ahmet Bey'in Ermeni Propagandalarının Mahiyeti Üzerine Bir Konferansı," *Türk Dünyası Araştırmaları,* No. 131 (Apr., 2001), pp. 75–87.

Üstel, Füsun, *İmparatorluktan Ulus-Devlete Türk Milliyetçiliği: Türk Ocakları, 1912–1931,* Istanbul: İletişim Yayınları, 1997.

Uyar, Hakkı, "Ağaoğlu Ahmet'in Liberal Muhalif Gazetesi 'Akın' (1933)," *Modern Türkiye'de Siyasal Düşünce, Liberalizm,* Istanbul: İletişim Yayınları, 2005.

Uygur, Erdoğan, "Füyuzat ve Molla Nasreddin Dergilerinde Edebi Dil Tartışması," *Modern Türklük Araştırmaları Dergisi,* 4, (Dec., 2007), pp. 53–64.

Villa, Dana R., *Socratic Citizenship,* Princeton, N.J.: Oxford: Princeton University Press, 2001.

Vovelle, Michel, *Ideologies and Mentalities,* trans. Eamon O'Flaherty, Oxford: Polity Press, 1990.

Weiker, Walter F., *Political Tutelage and Democracy in Turkey: The Free Party and Its Aftermath,* Leiden: Brill, 1973.

Wolf, C.P., "The Durkheim Thesis: Occupational Groups and Moral Integration," *Journal for the Scientific Study of Religion,* Vol. 9, No. 1 (Spring 1970), pp. 17–32.

Wyatt, S.C., "Turkey: The Economic Situation and the Five Years Plan," *International Affairs (Royal Institute of International Affairs 1931–1939),* Vol. 13, No. 6. (Nov.–Dec., 1934), pp. 826–844.

Yalman, Ahmet E., *Turkey in My Time,* Oklahoma: University of Oklahoma Press, 1956.

Yasamee, Feroze A.K., "Colmar Freiherr von der Goltz and the Rebirth of the Ottoman Empire," Diplomacy & Statecraft, Vol. 9, No. 2 (1998), pp. 91–128.

Yavuz, Hakan M., "Nationalism and Islam: Yusuf Akçura and Üç Tarz-ı Siyaset," *Journal of Islamic Studies,* Vol. 4, No. 2 (1993), pp. 175–207.

Yayla, Atilla, "Liberalizme Bir Bakış," *Türkiye Günlüğü,* No. 17 (Winter 1991), pp. 32–63.

Yazıcı, Nevin, *Osmanlılık Fİkri ve Genç Osmanlılar Cemiyeti,* Ankara: T.C. Kültür Bakanlığı Yayınları, 2002.

Ybert, Edyth, "Islam, Nationalism and Socialism in the Parties and Political Organisations of Azerbaijani Muslims in the Early Twentieth Century," *Caucasus Survey*, Vol. 1, No. 1 (Oct., 2013), pp. 43–58.

Ybert-Chabrier, Édith, "La pétition des musulmans du Caucase en réponse ál'oukase du 18 février 1905," Cahiers du Monde russe, Vol. 48, No. 2/3, Les résonances de 1905 (Apr.–Sep., 2007), p. 244.

Yeşilot, Okan, *Hacı Zeynelabidin Tagiyev: Azerbaycan'da Birçok İlki Gerçekleştirmiş Efsanevi Petrol Kralının Hazin Son, Şöhreti, Serveti ve Hayırseverliği*, Istanbul: Kaktüs Yayınları, 2004

Yılmaz, Ensar, "Ziya Gökalp's Political Sociology," *International Journal of Sociology and Anthropology*, Vol. 2, No. 3 (Mar., 2010), pp. 29–33.

Yılmaz, Murat, "Ahmet Ağaoğlu ve Milliyetçilik Anlayışı," *Türkiye Günlüğü* (Winter 1993), pp. 26–36.

———, "Ahmet Ağaoğlu ve Liberalizm Anlayışı," *Türkiye Günlüğü* (Summer 1993), pp. 56–71.

Yoshino, Kosaku, *Cultural Nationalism in Contemporary Japan: A Social Enquiry*, London, N.Y.: Routledge, 1992

Yüksel, Hasan, "Atatürk'ün Devletçilik Anlayışı," *Atatürk Araştırma Merkezi Dergisi*, No. 35 (Jul., 1996).

Zenkovsky, Serge A., *Pan-Turkism and Islam in Russia*, Cambridge; Massachusets: Harvard University Press, 1960.

Zimmerman, Judith E., "The Uses and Misuses of Tsarist Educational Policy," *History of Education Quarterly*, Vol. 16, No. 4 (Winter 1976), pp. 487–494.

Zürcher, Eric J., *The Unionist Factor: The Role of the Commitee of Union and Progress in the Turkish Natinalist Movement, 1905–1926*, Leiden: E.J. Brill, 1984.

———, *Political Opposition in the Early Turkish Republic: The Progressive Republican Party, 1924–25*, Leiden, New York, Kobenhavn, Köln: E.J. Brill, 1991.

———, "The Ottoman Legacy of the Turkish Republic: An Attempt at a New Periodization," *Die Wet des Islams*, New Series, Bd. 32, No. 2 (1992), pp. 237–253.

———, *Turkey: A Modern History*, New York: I.B. Tauris & Co Ltd, 2001.

Index